Jayjit Sarkar, Auritra Munshi (eds.)

border and bordering
Politics, Poetics, Precariousness

With a Foreword by Bill Ashcroft

Jayjit Sarkar, Auritra Munshi (eds.)

BORDER AND BORDERING

Politics, Poetics, Precariousness

With a Foreword by Bill Ashcroft

Bibliografische Information der Deutschen Nationalbibliothek
Die Deutsche Nationalbibliothek verzeichnet diese Publikation in der Deutschen Nationalbibliografie; detaillierte bibliografische Daten sind im Internet über http://dnb.d-nb.de abrufbar.

Bibliographic information published by the Deutsche Nationalbibliothek
Die Deutsche Nationalbibliothek lists this publication in the Deutsche Nationalbibliografie; detailed bibliographic data are available in the Internet at http://dnb.d-nb.de.

ISBN-13: 978-3-8382-1462-7
© *ibidem*-Verlag, Stuttgart 2021
Alle Rechte vorbehalten

Das Werk einschließlich aller seiner Teile ist urheberrechtlich geschützt. Jede Verwertung außerhalb der engen Grenzen des Urheberrechtsgesetzes ist ohne Zustimmung des Verlages unzulässig und strafbar. Dies gilt insbesondere für Vervielfältigungen, Übersetzungen, Mikroverfilmungen und elektronische Speicherformen sowie die Einspeicherung und Verarbeitung in elektronischen Systemen.

All rights reserved. No part of this publication may be reproduced, stored in or introduced into a retrieval system, or transmitted, in any form, or by any means (electronic, mechanical, photocopying, recording or otherwise) without the prior written permission of the publisher. Any person who does any unauthorized act in relation to this publication may be liable to criminal prosecution and civil claims for damages.

Printed in the EU

For all their permeability, the borders snaking across the world have never been of greater importance. This is the dance of history in our age: slow, slow, quick, quick, slow, back and forth and from side to side, we step across these fixed and shifting lines.

-Salman Rushdie

Contents

Contents 7
Foreword by *Bill Ashcroft* 9
Preface by *Jayjit Sarkar and Auritra Munshi* 13
Introduction 15

Emma Musty
Contemporary Fiction as a Cultural Map of Migration 41

Nicoletta Policek
Statelessness and the Tensions between Open Borders and the Claims of Community 65

Salvatore Perri
Rejection, Reconstruction and Erosion of Borders: The Identity Path of Grisélidis Réal 91

Priya Menon
A Place Not Our Own: Gulf Emigration and Bordered Lives in Benyamin's *Jasmine Days* 121

Sharmistha Chatterjee Sriwastav
Challenges and Resistance to the Partition of Bengal: Impact of Baul and Marafati Oral Tradition 141

Amanda Rutherford and Sarah Baker
Bordering the Screen: Separation Themes in Popular Film and Television 159

Sharmistha Das
Representation of Incarcerated Women in *Orange is the New Black*: An Intersectional Feminist Approach 183

Sandip Mondal
Tracks and Borders: Railways in Ray's *Apu Trilogy* 207

Oriol J. Batalla
Oceanic Borders: Climate Refugees, Borders and Extinction in
the Necrocene 217

Ratul Nandi
Fuzzy (B)ordering: More than Human Agencies and the Ethics
of (Dis)avowal 245

Rajarshi Bagchi
'I alone ... was on both sides': The Hyphenated Self in Hélène
Cixous's *Reveries of the Wild Woman* 257

Aditya Kant Ghising
Borders in South Asia: Language, Culture and Religion from
Colonialism to Globalization 275

Debapriya Paul
Missing Links or the Diasporic Journey of a Rebel: A Study of
H P Malet's *Lost Links in Indian Mutiny* (1867) 289

Nirjhar Sarkar
Un-blinding Doctrine and Exiting 'Molar Lines' in Arnold's
The Scholar Gipsy 303

Priyanka Chatterjee
Reorganising (B)orders: Reading the Women's Writing in
Colonial Bengal 317

Goutam Buddha Sural
Erasing the Borders: Tagore's Engagement with the Subalterns
in *Sahaj Path* 359

Contributors **371**
Index **377**

Foreword

The world has never been more mobile, more connected, never more characterised by the movement of refugees and asylum seekers and as nation states move hysterically to protect their borders from this mobile precariat, borders have become the most significant and most questioned phenomenon in the globalised world. So what would the world look like without borders? How might the utopian dream of a borderless world come about? Could rich nations open their borders with no regard for the control of migration? Could some nations and not others open their borders? These questions make us realise how recalcitrant borders are in political life. The ideology of the nation and the rigidity of its borders often preclude us thinking of any alternative. In the words of a US President who wants to build a wall along the Mexican border, "if you don't have borders you don't have a nation." The apparent impossibility of a borderless world is due not only to the spectre raised by this mobility of people, but to the most destructive force of modern times, the force that keeps borders in place—nationalism. Nationalism is *always* complicated by ethnocentrism, racism and populism and as nationalism proliferates, violence increases.

Borders could only be dissolved if the distinction that holds them in place—between rich and poor nations, democratic and undemocratic, colonised and colonising, the nation and its others, us and them—was itself dissolved. In other words borders maintain the system of inequality without which modern global capitalism (and national antipathy) could not function. If rich nations opened their borders the poor would flood in putting untenable demands on resources. Like a racial melting pot "big enough to take the world and all it's got" as the song goes, a borderless world might lead to equality, increase the wealth of the poor, and reduce the wealth of the wealthy. But at what level of economic and cultural security would it settle?

Borders exist because of fear and that fear is increasing. At the end of World War II, there were seven border walls or fences in the world. By the time the Berlin Wall fell in 1989, there were 15. Today, there are at least 77 walls or fences—half of which were erected since 2001. But the interesting thing about walls throughout history, the Great Wall of China, Hadrian's Wall, the Berlin wall, is that they all eventually failed. While these contemporary boundary fences may be seen as a terrified response to the phenomenon of global mobility they may also be seen in a different way as a sign of the productive force of border crossers.

As Salman Rushdie says "The frontier is an elusive line, visible and invisible, physical and metaphorical, amoral and moral." So there are many frontiers, many boundaries that we cross every day. But there is, of course, a deeply psychological dimension to boundaries: we understand who we are by determining who we are not. Our 'others' define us. Although borders go hand in hand with the emergence of nations they go deep into the history of Western modernity and its notions of space and time. Boundaries and ocularcentrism became inextricable in Western epistemology. As works in social theory, philosophy and human geography make abundantly clear western thinking proceeds according to the metaphors of visuality. The ocularcentrism of western thought is inseparable from the notion of boundaries.

The central issue of transnational/diasporic studies as many of the following essays reveal, is the crossing of borders, a crossing that leads to various kinds of conflicts and tensions. In *Step Across This Line* (2002), Salman Rushdie says: 'Good writing assumes a frontierless nation. Writers who serve frontiers have become border guards.' The literary accounts of journeys across national boundaries belong with these stories of the journey of becoming. "In our deepest natures," says Rushdie, "we are frontier-crossing beings. We know this by the stories we tell ourselves; for we are story-telling animals, too." (76)

What is a border? We tend to think of borders as geographical, as outlining territory, particularly the territory of a nation. The wall and the fence appear to embody them completely. But boundaries are profoundly ideological. A border is not a thing but a *practice*, a practice that produces power relationships, and establishes inequalities between those who are in and those who are not. Most importantly, perhaps, borders are synonymous with global capitalism and the precarity it constructs by constituting migrants as exploitable workers and individuals with low status and limited rights. Borders are both a consequence and a production of power relationships. And the process of othering on which they are based is fundamental to the fiction of identity produced within those borders. The practice of bordering answers that perennial question "Who are we?" How else can we discover who we are than by determining who is other? As Saussure made clear, signs signify not by referring but by their difference from other signs. How else can we discover who we are than by determining who is other than by establishing borders of difference? Bordering practices, whether carried out by the hegemonic activities of the state, or the cultural bordering that sets up borders of ethnicity, sexuality, class, satisfy the myriad ways in which subjects might determine their 'others'. The scope and variety of theses bordering practices are explored in this volume.

Bill Ashcroft
Professor Emeritus
School of the Arts and Media
UNSW

Preface

The volume contains sixteen essays on various aspects of thinking border as well as border-thinking: as we find in literature, philosophy, historiography, strategic and area studies, film and TV series. Such diffusion and diversity only reinforce the idea that borders, and especially the more unfathomable bordering, are omnipresent in almost all discursive practices: be it in discourses which are considered "normative" and/or in the discourses which are now being called "precarious". Border and bordering are forms of world-making. Border and bordering are knowledge and sites of knowledge production, at the same time. The phenomena have become so pivotal to our understanding of the contemporary world that these have ceased to remain mere an episteme and become a method in itself. The volume contains essays which are about these precarious entanglements between thinking border and border-thinking. The work is also aware of the fact that there is no water tight compartment and more often than not the poetics, politics and precarity leak into each other. The poetics of border and border in poetics are not free from the politics of border and border in politics, and vice-versa in every possible way. Precariousness, on the other hand, and especially the spectral aspects of precariousness haunt the poetics and politics of border and, in general, the ontology of any being (including the concept of nation-state) in a quite Freudian/Derridean way.

    This making and unmaking of borders would not have been possible without the support of the contributors from all over the world. It is mostly with their support and cooperation that we have been able to deliver a collection like this. We are grateful to Prof. Bill Ashcroft for writing a generous foreword for the volume. We thank Jakob Horstmann, the commissioning editor and the series editors of *Beyond the Social Sciences*: Michael Kuhn, Hebe Vessuri, and Shujiro Yazawa at ibidem for helping us to shape and materialize this project. We would also like to thank the members of the Department of English, Raiganj University for their help. We are also indebted to Prof. Himadri Lahiri, Prof. Pramod K. Nayar,

Prof. Swatahsiddha Sarkar, Prof. Ranjan Ghosh, Prof. Nandana Dutta, Prof. Anindya Sekhar Purakayastha and Prof. Swargajyoti Gohain for their constant support and encouragement. A section in the Introduction was published earlier in *The Himalayan Miscellany: An Area Studies Journal in Social Sciences Vols. 28 & 29 (2017-18)*. We are especially thankful to the editor of the journal for allowing us to republish it. We are also grateful to our friend Jagannath Basu for his relentless assistance and vital suggestions. And, last but not the least, our respective friends and family members for being so considerate and for extending their support when needed.

Jayjit Sarkar
Auritra Munshi
Raiganj University
March 18, 2020

Introduction

I've been a crime reporter for many years, and I've seen a lot of bodies — and a lot of drowning.... You get numb to it, but when you see something like this it re-sensitizes you. You could see that the father had put her inside his T-shirt so the current wouldn't pull her away.
He died trying to save his daughter's life.
Will it change anything? It should. These families have nothing, and they are risking everything for a better life. If scenes like this don't make us think again — if they don't move our decision-makers — then our society is in a bad way.

Julia Le Duc to *The Guardian* (Wednesday, 28 June 2019)

One of the most incredible experiences of my and @vasfsf's career bringing to life the conceptual drawings of the Teetertotter Wall from 2009 in an event filled with joy, excitement, and togetherness at the borderwall. The wall became a literal fulcrum for U.S. — Mexico relations and children and adults were connected in meaningful ways on both sides with the recognition that the actions that take place on one side have a direct consequence on the other side. Amazing thanks to everyone who made this event possible like Omar Rios @colectivo.chopeke for collaborating with us, the guys at Taller Herrería in #CiudadJuarez for their fine craftsmanship, @anateresafernandez for encouragement and support, and everyone who showed up on both sides including the beautiful families from Colonia Anapra, and
@kerrydoyle2010, @kateggreen, @ersela_kripa, @stphn_mllr, @wakawaffles, @chris_inabox and many others (you know who you are).
#raelsanfratello #borderwallasarchitecture #teetertotterwall #seesaw #subibaja

Ronald Rael [@rrael] (2019, July 29)

The first epigraph is an excerpt from an interview given by Julia Le Duc, the Mexican photojournalist, to *The Guardian* after she took the now-famous photograph of the bodies of a father and his daughter lying upside down on the banks of the Rio Grande near Matamoros, Mexico. The father, Oscar Alberto Ramirez, 23, and the daughter, Valerie, barely 2, drowned while crossing the US-Mexico border. This haunting image of the young girl tucked inside her father's shirt as they both lie flat face down took the world by storm, created ripples around and quite naturally brought Julia Le Duc all of a sudden to the limelight. The photograph reminded us of how the borders have become 'lines of death', and of how brutal the borders are. The perils of international migration and at the same time the sheer desperation of the migrants in crossing the border into the

Promised Land in search of better economic opportunities and a better life are some of the glaring aspects of contemporary politics, which this photograph highlights. The photograph also brought back the unsettling memories of little Aylan, the three year old Syrian boy, who got drowned and whose body washed up to the shores of the Mediterranean. Contemporary politics is increasingly becoming border politics as it is being performed on a daily basis at the borders. Border penetration and border management has turned into an everyday reality nowadays. The family of three, escaped from El Salvador, undertook a long journey, crossed borders, took desperate measures, and finally succumbed to the pressures of stringent immigration laws and border surveillance technologies. Such laws and technologies are often overtly hostile and violent to the immigrants and asylum seekers: the dehumanized 'others' of any modern nation-state. The large scale performance of violence at the international border is now quite rampant these days: an unprecedented phenomenon in the history of human civilization.

The second epigraph is the Instagram post of Ronald Rael, Professor of Architecture at the University of California, Berkeley who along with Virginia San Fratello, Associate Professor of Interior Design at San Jose University, installed pink seesaws along the metal walls between the El Paso in Texas, the United States and Ciudad Juarez, Mexico. The installation of the seesaws, and that too pink seesaws (#universal love #friendship #affection), transformed for that moment the otherwise extremely serious and contentious US-Mexico border into something 'kitschy'. The same border which saw the young Salvadorian family falling prey to its violent politics just a few months before transformed in this case into an objet d'art. This act of children coming from both sides of the border and playing together suspended momentarily, through its poetics, the immanent violence and hostility amongst the citizens on both the sides. The wall, as Rael himself points out through his post, became "a literal fulcrum" for US-Mexico relations: an embodiment of connection, hospitality and altruism. This performance filled with "joy, excitement, and togetherness" was certainly not an act of undermining the realpolitik: at the cost of any one of those ground realities of the immigrants. Instead, it transcended momentarily the boundaries of conventional politics—an act where a border frees itself from the politics of bordering, an act where a border ceases to remain a boundary and becomes a bridge, and consequently subverting the idea of 'good fences make good neighbours' into 'good seesaws make good neighbours'.

We are frontier-making and frontier-crossing beings: we make, break, cross, remake, break again and cross again the borders of the land and of the mind. Borders are equivocal. Borders limit, borders connect, but more importantly borders are omnipresent. Borders exist in the way we perceive the world, and there is an inherent politics as well as poetics in the manner a border exists. Border-politics and border-poetics are immanent to the way we understand border and its various incarnations. We all are in that way connected and disconnected. This (dis)connection may be based on causality or acausality or even complicated causality but the fact of the matter remains that we are all (dis)connected; and as Professor Rael attempts to make us realize how the actions that take place on one side have a direct consequence on the other.

A border is not always a signifier of transcendental nihilism, rather, as Derrida understood, thinking and (de)creating at the threshold. It is not a *telos* or the Ultimate but a crossing over—keeping up strategically the possibility of overstepping, trespassing and transgression alive. Derrida, while referring to Seneca, writes: "... the border (*finis*)... would be more essential, more originary, and more proper than those of any other territory in the world" (1993: 3). A border is not the end but *by* the end. There is always a sense of possibility at the border. Border is death, in the Derridean sense. The French word for death, *trépas*, entails both passage and trespass at the same time.

The work, as the readers will find, postulates a different take on border and bordering: different from that of critical border studies with its rigorous methodologies. It deals with the lived experiences—both epic and banal—at the borders. It is precisely for this reason that we have incorporated the word 'bordering' in the title itself as it signifies border as a 'becoming' or simply, a process. Bordering is spacing and timing. There is a sense of 'world-making' in bordering. Border makes and unmakes itself through bordering. The volume also makes an effort in this direction by trying to understand this making and unmaking of borders with the help of phenomena like bordering, debordering and rebordering. We have tried to capture all the three aspects of border(ing) here: the creative aspect (poetics), the debilitating aspect (politics) and the more perplexing, precariousness. The perspectives in the volume are different from the perspective of traditional methodological schemes of social sciences. Though not completely denying the former's merit, the volume takes a different path altogether. For example, we have given equal importance to popular culture which for a long time traditional social sciences have ignored. Our take on border and bordering is more credible, grounded, and close to the lived realities of the time. Unlike other works which tend to overemphasize the abstract academic discourses and almost ruthless methodologies, free from the experiences at ground zero. It is indeed difficult to intellectualize through the prevalent methods of critical border studies of how the same border could entail two completely disparate experiences: the photograph of the bodies of a father and his daughter lying upside down on the banks of the Rio Grande near Matamoros, Mexico and the image of the children playing with the recently installed pink seesaws along the same metal walls.

The disparate chapters in the volume are symptomatic of the very interdisciplinarity of borders and the varied experiences of bordering as manifested in different modes of expression. This study of the multiplicity of experiences is intrinsic to our understanding of borders: so much so that the volume prescribes, that borders can *only* be read through an interdisciplinary approach. This interdisciplinarity is immanent to the concept of border and imminent ("to come") to the phenomenon of bordering. Also, the volume quite explicitly deals with the *metaphors* of border or border as metaphor: as a border may not necessarily be always visible or tangible—that these can also be cognitive and metaphysical. The volume, therefore, intends to attract not only academicians but also common readers. This is the reason that it has been designed in such a way. Please note that this is not yet-another volume on critical border studies and area studies. In thinking border, we have moved beyond the boundaries of border studies and area studies—as we believe that nowadays 'studies' of border studies and area studies are as regimented as the borders of the nation-state.

Border and Bordering focuses on the idea of border and its various geopolitical, sociocultural and cognitive incarnations. In recent times, border has emerged as a common trope in contemporary narratives with concepts such as 'bordering', 'borderless', 'building borders', 'breaking borders', 'crossing borders', 'porous borders' and 'shifting borders'. Whether concrete or shadow, borders are omnipresent. They have been frequently erected and decimated in history and will be in future depending upon the need of the hour. Such 'needs', as this series has highlighted, are always generated *from* the above, *by* the above. It seems social sciences and humanities are obsessed with borders and the latter have been invoked intermittently to prove a point and also the opposite: that is, to negate a point. Even in the daily humdrum of life, we never fail to feel the eerie presence or rather absent-presence of border. At times, it is WE who knowingly or unknowingly create these building blocks: brick after brick piled upon each other and cemented together, so that we can keep the 'other', the 'stranger', the 'foreigner' at bay. Borders are important in keeping "us" safe and feel secure from "them". Borders are in the air we breathe. Is it possible then to do away with borders altogether? But before coming to that we need to posit another question: is it possible to do away with modernity? Because, as the work suggests, the birth of modernity is also the birth of the borders.

***

Modernity creates its own exceptions: spaces within a space, which, although counter-intuitive and counter-discursive to the project of modernity, are actually an integral part of the so-called project as anything else. Such spaces are deemed as "pre-modern" so that these can be claimed, shaped and with time subsumed under the category of the modern. These spaces are addressed as "alternative modernities" so that no matter what the narrative is, which is most often singular, modernity remains the protagonist. These are called "counter-modernities" so that the vantage point remains with that of modernity. Modernity includes; modernity excludes; but more importantly, modernity includes by excluding. The status quo of inclusion through exclusion is always meant to be partial inclusion and never complete; the realpolitik here *is* actually in this suspension and deferment. It includes the other by making it the 'other' in the first instance — modernity claims the other *as* other through the process of otherization; modernity also colonizes the other *as* other through the process of colonization. "The rhetoric of modernity", as Walter Mignolo points out, "is that of salvation, whereas the logic of coloniality is a logic of imperial oppression. They go hand in hand, and you cannot have modernity without coloniality; the unfinished project of modernity carries over its shoulders the unfinished project of coloniality" (2006: 313). The other, thus, is suspended, entangled and eventually made a part of the habitat of the self: it can neither make itself completely free from the self nor is it allowed to become part of the self. Modernity is, at the same time, hospitable and hostile towards the other. Objects and beings, which in any case considered exotic and sacred implicitly, are made 'exotic' and 'sacred' — the others of modernity — so much so that these ideas cease to exist altogether once modernity is bracketed out. The idea of the exotic and the idea of the sacred are among many such ideas which now cannot exist beyond the realm of modernity; the very meaning of the exotic and the sacred can now only be tweaked out of the dough of modernity. So, what remains at the end of the day are the pre-, the post-, the alternative, the sub-, and the counter- of that one all-encompassing "grand narrative" called modernity. The others of modernity are not modernity's other, rather part of the same discursive practice.

Modernity, hence, is an end in itself. It does not lead to anywhere. It is a project, an ever unfinished project: a journey whose marked destination is also modernity. It is a project of domination and colonization, of mind and body, of physics and metaphysics, of existence and essence. Unlike the modern, which is ideationally static and sedentary, modernity is constantly on the move. Modern is being; modernity is being and becoming at the same time. While hinting at the aspect of stasis and kinesis, Dilip Gaonkar in his 'On Alternative Modernities' lists some of the unforgettable figures of modernity: Marx's "revolutionary", Baudelaire's "dandy", Nietzsche's "superman", Weber's "social scientist", Simmel's "stranger", Musil's "man without qualities" and Benjamin's "flaneur", and points out how "each is caught and carried in the intoxicating rush of an epochal change and yet finds himself and formulated by a disciplinary system of social roles and functions" (1999: 3). Modernity, as many have pointed out, was a reaction to a very specific socio-cultural, geographical and historical event; but what happened eventually is, because of colonization and later globalization, that it has turned into a phenomenon which is regarded as transcendental and universal. Therefore, what was primarily conceived as and meant to be local has, because of certain definite turns in world history and politics, turned out to be universal. This is what we call dissemination of modernity which has led to the rise of, what is often quoted now as, global modernity. Our argument is: there is nothing which we can call and point out as global modernity but rather globalization of a certain set of local modernities, a set of narratives which are overtly and covertly white, west European, masculine, and Christian. Modernity is a milieu of these modernities or narratives, which are mostly provincial, and which are more often than not considered and hailed as transcendental and disembodied. It is incorrectly believed to be atemporal and aspatial in characteristics and in function. The *here* of modernity in such scenario becomes the *everywhere* and the *now* of modernity, the *always*. This is what we describe as 'modernity-history singularity': the point at which the history of human civilization and the historical development of modernity turned into one and the same thing. Our effort here would be to look for those openings and prospects where we could disentangle the latter from the former—where history and historiography cease to remain mere discourses of modernity and affirm agencies of their own.

The dissemination of modernity across the globe started with those initial encounters and transactions between west European countries and new found lands; stratified with the imperial powers annexing those new found lands and turning them into new territories; and consolidated with the birth of modern nation-states in those new territories. Now, in the age of late capitalism, globalization and post-nationalism, it has more or less become the dominant worldview of the world—it even dictates the way the world looks upon itself. Even in several ongoing postcolonial studies across the world with its indulgence on non-hegemonic and non-Eurocentric understandings and strategies one can easily find traces of this trope and this kind of worldview.

We would disagree with those who point out the plural nature of modernity and talk about different modernities which are absolutely discreet and different from each other. We would also, at the same time, disagree with those who suggest its singular and monolithic nature. Modernity, rather, is slightly more complicated than that. It is, we think, a complex wave of several attributes or narratives—it is neither singular nor plural in nature. It is certainly a grand narrative, consisting of much petit or micro-modernities. It is a whole: a summation of all such narratives and, more correctly, much more than the summation of those narratives. It is, for instance, white, Eurocentric, anthropocentric, capital driven, patriarchal and many others and yet, it is much more than that. These phenomena are certainly not petit or micro in their nature and function and have agencies of their own; but since they blend, add on to and eventually propel that one greater narrative called modernity, we have called these petit or micro-modernities.

A modern nation-state—an embodiment of all that modernity is and stands for—can also prove for our study a laboratory where all these phenomena could be dissected and understood in a far effective and heuristic manner. A modern nation-state with its precise and well maintained geopolitical boundaries is a reification of this grand and yet, complex narrative of modernity. The edges of the nation-state are also the edges of modernity and the space between the two edges—the space where one political block ends and another begins—is what we understand as borderland. This space, which also has its own temporality, is also the space where one set of modernities ends and another begins. But we would here negate our own thesis if we consider this space to be a vacuum; we are not saying that borderlands are free of modernity, which obviously these are not in any case. We are also not naïve enough to point out here that borderlands are spaces or zones beyond modernity—pristine, untouched and untrodden—but rather have an ambiguous, often confusing and far more complicated sort of modernity. Like that of mainland, borderland modernity is also a complex; and yet a suture of several overlapping modernities whose agencies, as opposed to the former, are feebly and not so persuasively asserted. Borderland modernity is confused and convoluted kind of modernity: borderlands are where the narrative of modernity, which works quite succinctly in and around the mainland, covers the distance from the centre to the periphery, and in the process starts to lose its might and vigor. This already 'weak' modernity, when at an everyday level starts encountering with the other just on the other side of the border, becomes more, as we have already mentioned, confused and convoluted. It is at this stage/state that it starts contradicting and challenging itself in a more explicit manner: it is where it becomes a paradox of/in itself. Borderland modernity is the result of some of the inherent *aporias* in the system of modernity, understanding of which can enable us to use it as a strategic tool—a mode of deconstructing the hitherto 'natural' and transcendental aspects of modernity.

In its day to day negotiation with the other and, here in case, in the physical presence of the other, modernity finds itself in a tricky position. Mainland modernity is more comfortable with homogeneity and generally thinks in terms of binaries (that is, either/or); but as soon as it hits the borderland, the ground becomes slippery. It finds itself difficult to stand on the ground which was hitherto solid and based on certain *a priori* principles, and now, has suddenly become unstable and unreliable. As opposed to the reliable topography of the mainland, borderland poses a lot of difficulties to the praxis of modernity. There occurs a sudden rupture between the theory and praxis of modernity which is hard to reconcile. It is at this juncture that the borderland, amidst this continuous and quite congested traffic between the self and the other, invents a sort of its own cult faintly different from that of modernity—faintly and not radical because a borderland still remains a part of the grand narrative called modernity. There is no outside here, or anywhere! This is what we can call borderland modernity, which is also in a way borderland-modernity: a continuous negotiation, an extremely volatile conflict-confluence dynamic.

The relationship between border, especially geopolitical border, and borderland is peculiar and, more than anything else, arbitrary. A geopolitical border may or may not entail borderland: the latter can exist anywhere in the system other than the centre. It is not necessary to have a physical border to be/become borderland: it is 'free floating' in that sense. More than the location, the factor which affects the most in this case is the locationality. And, the locationality of a borderland is very different from the location of a border; the former is more *relational* in nature. A borderland is where and when the system challenges itself. A border is where the system physically encounters the other; a borderland is where the system starts becoming its own other. The latter is more precisely where the system starts becoming its own other but never becomes one. A borderland, then, is a tensional space between becoming other and being other. It is associated more with an 'opening' as compared to a border which has a sense of 'closing'. Borderlands are openings in the system through which the 'other' creeps in and starts haunting and, henceforth, create a lot of apprehension, uneasiness and nervousness within the system. Borderlands are where a system becomes more anxious to the imminent and immanent threat of dissolution and dissolving into the other.

A border "is a dividing line," as Gloria Anzaldúa points out in her seminal *Borderland/La Frontera*, "a narrow strip along a steep edge. A borderland is a vague and undetermined place created by the emotional residue of an unnatural boundary" (1987: 3). As opposed to the act of border-making (the act of turning the more obscure frontiers of the empires into the rigid borders of the nation-states), which is comparatively a recent phenomenon and often a voluntary act dictated by the dominant political class of the day, borderlands are involuntary; the latter may clearly predate the border but in a different form altogether or emerge afterwards involuntarily because of the incessant negotiations and transactions across two or more edges. Border cuts anything into *mita y mita* – 'half and half' – borderland is ontologically 'half and half', either-or, neither-nor, both. Like Mary Louis Pratt's "contact zone", borderlands also refer to social spaces where "cultures meet, clash, and grapple with each other, often in contexts of highly asymmetrical relations of power" (1992: 3); where all borderlands are contact zones but all contact zones may not necessarily transcend into and be-come a "borderland". A borderland has its own *ontology* and comes with an *agenda*: it is more political as compared to a contact zone which is more social. Borderlands are more in the line of Edward Soja's "thirding", a *conscious* act in which "everything comes together... subjectivity and objectivity, the abstract and the concrete, the real and the imagined, the knowable and the unimaginable, the repetitive and the differential, structure and agency, mind and body, consciousness and the unconscious, the disciplined and the transdisciplinary, everyday life and unending history" (1996: 56-7).

But unlike politics where borderlands are conceived as spaces of fear and anxiety – as xenophobic and agoraphobic spaces; in poetics and aesthetics borderlands are celebrated as creative and ingenious spaces. The incessant tension between *this* side of the border and *that* side, which is often regarded as a problem in politics, becomes an important precondition in art and literature. The "other" is an important category in both politics and poetics so much so that one cannot do either of them without it. While in the former the other is envisaged with a lot of suspiciousness and as a threat to the self, in the latter, the other is instrumental in opening up a plethora of new possibilities. It is not through politics but through art and literature that the other speaks. Doing art and literature is one of the modes of conversation with the other. They serve as an important vantage point from and through which the other can speak to the self; as opposed to politics which is generally a monologue of the self. So, in order to understand borderland modernity, and concomitantly borderland, which is often conceived of as ambiguous and perplexing, borderland poetics can serve as a better means than borderland politics. Borderland poetics, as opposed to borderland politics, refuses to see borderland as a mere flat topography. The crests and troughs of the thousand plateaus of borderland can only justifiably be observed through its poetics.

It must be understood here that we are, without doubt, not promulgating a strict binary understanding of poetics and politics. There is a certain amount of politics in poetics; and poetics on the other hand, has its own share of politics. But what is different here is the sense of alterity: compared to politics which is most of the time hostile towards the other, poetics thrives upon its hospitality towards the same. This does not mean a complete surrender, rather a tensional space of collaborations, convergences and contestations which is "neither the site of assimilation nor the making of an alien Other" (Singh and Schmidt, 2000: 6). The other is welcomed and made part of the "habitus" (see also Bourdieu, 1977) in poetics as opposed to the "will to power" in politics (see also Nietzsche, 1968). One must also note here that our understanding of borderland poetics is more in the vein of inherent poetics of the space and certainly not a perspective from the outside: the innate poetics which flows out of the lived-experience of being and becoming borderland. The poetics of and on borderland has always been dictated by these perspectives from the outside (of borderland) which are overwhelmingly and unapologetically centrist and mainland-ish. Our understanding of borderland poetics is rather more in the sense of borderland-poetics: which is less observational and more enlivened, a poetics which comes *through* and *from* borderland. This is the kind of poetics which makes possible for us for clearer ways of understanding borderland modernity which has its own share of complexities, different from that of mainland modernity. What Mary Louis Pratt proclaims in her formulation of "contact zone", especially the literary part, can also very well be appropriated here in our understanding of borderland poetics:

Auto-ethnography, transculturation, critique, collaboration, bilingualism, meditation, parody, denunciation, imaginary dialogue, vernacular expression—these are some of the literate arts of the contact zone. Miscomprehension, incomprehension, dead letters, unread masterpieces, absolute heterogeneity of meaning—these are some of the perils of writing in the contact zone. (1999: 373)

***

Maps shape our view of the world and mirror our cultures. They can chart us at the centre of the universe or make us disappear. Just as a writer may be described as a cartographer, a novel may be described as a map. Liminal spaces act as moments of interaction between the people and cultures of the world while at the same time performing an act of transition within the self. As the traveler leaves his or her place of origin he/she steps into the role of the other through both an internal and external process. Such moments are imagined and documented in literature. In the opening chapter, Emma Musty discusses the fractured lines and interspaces, the borderlands and borderlines depicted in two recent literary works, *Signs Preceding the End of the World*, by Yuri Herrera and *The Gurugu Pledge*, by Juan Tomás Ávila Laurel, two novels which are representative of a new trend in migration literature that reflects our atomised societies. The maps created by contemporary fiction are important interrogators of existing ideas of identity and culture in this time of globalization and migration. Driving the need for critical reflection on these cultural artefacts, which not only record the times we live in, but frame the questions we ask about our increasingly diverse and transient cultures.

In Chapter 2, Nicoletta Policek articulates a commitment to open borders which is compatible with a deep appreciation for the value of community and the importance of belonging as experienced by stateless children. Human beings need geographic ties to a physical dwelling, but also, and perhaps more importantly, they need spiritual ties to particular traditions, habits and practices that make up their sense of belonging. They also need legal ties which manifest in rights that come with nationality. This contribution calls for the need to deconstruct the importance of borders, to have margins without living at the margins, to claim citizenship and community for those who would be otherwise considered as redundant surplus.

In Chapter 3, Salvatore Perri has analysed the autobiographical writings of Grisélidis Réal (1929-2005), Swiss writer, painter and prostitute. The principal aim of his survey has been that of tracing the identity reappropriation path that has marked the life and, subsequently, the artistic expressions of the author. Starting with the principal instance in which Réal herself saw the matrix of the difficulties felt in recognizing her own physical and emotional individuality—namely the rigid interdiction toward sexuality imposed by her mother—he has identified and described the emergence of a complex and protean strategy of self-construction and affirmation, centred on the revindication of control over her own corporality and sexuality. In his study, Perri has largely analysed this gradual, and also violent, process of emancipation from a system of physical and psychological auscultation and sanction, that he has reconnected to the idea of ceremonial punishment theorized by Michel Foucault in *Discipline and Punish*. He has subsequently pointed out that, in order to release herself from the "cage" she felt to be trapped in, Grisélidis Réal has performed a concrete (and also textual) rejection of her social status (she was born in the cultivate and wealthy milieu of Swiss middle-class) and of all the moral values that characterized it, allocating her emotional and bodily self into the domain of abjection. Thus, Grisélidis Réal has conceived of herself—on the ashes of the renegade "native one"—a large and controversial axiological system, in which body and writing constitute a powerful device of intimate (and political) claim. The "Abject", majorly represented by a borderless and feral idea of reality and a fetishized inclination for black men, is the antagonistic tool that the author has used to subvert the "white", catholic and obscurantist narrative absorbed in the Swiss native context. The strategy of self affirmation of Grisélidis Réal, then, culminated in over thirty years of sex work, assumed as an act of self-determination that deserves social recognition and respect and, in the specific picture of Réal's life and self-narration, as the ultimate way to be the "maîtresse" of a body on which, for years, a confining system of symbols had been engraved.

Non-citizens are a significant part of the contemporary population of Gulf Cooperation Council States. For instance, over 90 percent of the population in UAE and Qatar are emigrants primarily from neighbouring South Asian countries such as India, Nepal, Bangladesh, Sri Lanka, Philippines, and Pakistan. Such mass emigration has not only allowed for the rapid economic expansion of these Gulf countries, but at the same time they have also produced a number of cultural and socio-economic consequences for the Gulf states. Every year, the number of emigrants to the Gulf continues to rise. Why do so many seek expatriation; particularly, when the host country is partially hostile? More importantly, how do the emigrants disseminate information about their lives in the Gulf? How are these experiences registered in the literary fabric of the diasporic countries? Lack of institutional support from host and home countries contribute towards what Andrew Gardner calls "Structural Violence" that reveal a lack of emigrant agency. Using a representative novel, Benyamin's *Jasmine Days*, winner of the inaugural JCB Prize in 2018, Priya Menon in Chapter 4 explores the bordered emigrant lives of different South Asian communities in the Gulf set against the backdrop of the Arab Spring.

The commoners of the Indian subcontinent, in their pristine domesticity and rural bliss had never believed in Partition which had been clamped on them in 1947 and again in 1971, in the name of religion. Lamenting over the loss of unified idyllic space, sensitive artists like Jibanananda Das in Bengal and Amrita Pritam in Punjab have often painted a nostalgic world in their poems. Emulating a tradition of seeking support as in the epics, poets such as Rabindranath Tagore, Kazi Nazrul Islam and Amrita Pritam have invoked and amalgamated the Bhakti and the Sufi saints like Lalon Shah and Waris Shah to appeal to the spirit of harmony. While these artistic productions have at best remained confined in urban, intellectual congregations, the Baul and Marafati songs and tradition still continue to be practiced among rural illiterates, in pockets of India, thus veritably challenging the rationale of 'bordering'. Lalon Shah, particularly, born at Kushtia in Bangladesh

(1772), continues to combat the divisive forces of caste, creed, gender and religion through his unnumbered songs and eclectic rituals practiced by his followers in both Bengals till today. His songs, handed down orally and practiced in 'Akhras' at Kushtia and Nadia discuss an amalgamation of beliefs derived from Islam, Vaishnavite, Tantric and Buddhist Sahajiya tradition, thus attacking the very principle of 'neatly drawn boundaries'. Hounded down as heretics, these marginalized people continue to challenge societal and religious domination by congregating yearly at 'Dolpurnima' in Kushtia, Joydev Mela at Kenduli or Poush Mela at Shantiniketan to spread the message of 'Manab Dharma' or 'the religion of humanity'. Seeking to understand Sri Ramakrishna's belief in his 'Kathaamrita' that the 'Sain' or the Baul Guru is a person of supreme perfection, Chapter 5 attempts to trace the impact of the Baul and Marafati songs and practices in Bengal—in creating a microcosmic, yet alternative 'eutopia' (the good world) which had existed and continues to exist as 'unified Bengal', utterly rejecting the state constructed borders and boundaries. Sharmistha Chatterjee Srivastav makes us aware that this Baul tradition has in contemporary times become a mode of fashion and a fusion art. Her search, however, has avoided such pitfalls and concentrate on the original philosophical objectives and the praxis of the followers at the grass root level.

In Chapter 6, Amanda Rutherford and Sarah Baker look at how contemporary film and television continue to expand on themes of borders and walls within their narratives, creating ever-growing interest in popular culture. These storylines delve into cultural anxieties surrounding ideas of the threat of war and terrorism, alienation and isolation, consumerism and loss of individualism, as well as religion and apocalyptic events. Film provides a visual platform to explore these concerns by utilizing boundaries and walls as separators between that which is deemed to be the safe and secure, from the unknown 'other' in the form of zombies, infected animals or humans, foreign species or those considered to be of lower class or social standing. This chapter investigates the trope of boundaries and walls found in film and television such as *The Colony* (2016-), *Game of Thrones* (2011-), *The*

Walking Dead (2010-2018), *The Hunger Games* (2012-2015), the *Jurassic Park films* (1993, 1997, 2001, 2018), *Zoo* (2015-2017), *Blade Runner 2049* (2017), *The Maze Runner* (2014), *Mortal Engines* (2018) and others where the threat of separation is at the forefront of human existence. These examples from popular culture are utilized as a means to explore the advantage given to those behind the wall or separation divider, as well as to showcase the alienated, viral, disadvantaged or poverty stricken who are often left behind. These fears are teased out and recreated into several genres such as horror, science fiction, post-apocalyptic, thriller and dramas with many receiving huge success and fame. The physical boundaries and barriers are examined and interrogated how they manifest into modern representation for everyday contemporary society.

Although 'prison show' genres in recent years have increased portrayals of incarcerated women, criminal narratives, both in literature and media, have neglected women and their lived experiences. And sadly, such matters have received very less scholarly attention compared to the more rigidly academic contents. Chapter 6 attempts to analyze the Netflix original series *Orange is the New Black* (OITNB) that premiered in North America in 2013 and had the longest running span and portrayed the experiences of incarcerated women convicts. It is loosely based on a memoir of the same title by Piper Kerman (2010) in which she had documented her custodial experiences in a federal prison in Danbury Connecticut. OITNB had received massive viewership and critical acclaim and awards, and is often considered as an atypical feminist classic hiding as it does unsuspected depths of societal, racial, and gender complications, authenticated by the experiences of a white middle class woman convict.

The prison space in itself is an intriguing metaphor that combines the ideas of loss of freedom and innocence, enforced obedience, an ostracized condition marked by ambivalence between hope and despair. It is an assumed correctional home that fosters empathy, apathy, and violence. Functioning as it does under a panoptical gaze and its ruthless official agents, the prisoners' life and lived experience is paradoxically both, a warrant and a travesty of the notions of border and order. This (post)structural binary of border/chaos; subject/state vis-à-vis legal order(ing) provides a suitable paradigm to read this visual text. And, this chapter does so by deploying the theoretical framework of Intersectional Feminisms to analyse its characters and contexts focusing on the cross-referentiality of the themes of race, class, gender, and sexuality. As a concomitant issue, Sharmistha Das also tries to understand how this show aligns itself with the perspectives of criminalized, incarcerated woman; and as a cultural trope how far this representation challenges and reifies the hegemonic concepts of heteronormativity, race, class, and gender.

Train, as a marker of mobility appears in innumerable cultural texts where individuals and community are also placed in the context of modernity. In the Indian context, this however becomes concurrent with colonial modernity. The selected films of *Apu Trilogy* by Satyajit Ray have been analysed by Sandip Mondal as a site for the performance of several socio-cultural narratives seen in the first half of twentieth century Bengal. The reference of train and railways apart from forming visual metaphors discernible in all three films develop larger cultural narratives than merely contributing to the concerned stories of those films. But apparently conceived of as a mode of communication, railways can also function as an agency of emulating desire, memory, alienation and estrangement, of ideas amenable to the notions of border. This metaphorical track of railways developing the binaries of past and present, country and city, memory and desire continues to inform the culture of colonial Bengal more as a border. In Chapter 8, Mondal attempts to discuss the *Apu Trilogy* from this perspective.

The contemporary world has become "one marked by the globalization of markets, the privatization of the world under the aegis of neoliberalism, and the increasing imbrication of the financial markets, the postimperial military complex and electronic and digital technologies" (Mbembe, 2017: 3) in which the Zizekian paradigm that it seems easier to imagine the end of the world than the end of the capitalist system is more present than ever. Populist nationalist-infused politics of fear are on the rise which leads to a localization of borders and tough xenophobic immigration policies, not based on race or origin solely anymore, but on the purchase level of individuals. Bearing this in mind, the Earth is currently facing the Necrocene epoch, a geological age triggered by Capital mass-accumulation which "reframes the history of capitalism's expansion through the process of becoming extinction" (McBrien, 2016), not only of species, but languages, peoples, resources and the (de)construction through pollution. The Necrocene is already affecting, amongst other entities, the peoples from islands and coastline areas. The current estimates of sea-level rise rates predict a human cataclysm by the end of the 21st Century which will change our perception of our global reality in a catastrophic event never acquainted before, devaluing the prediction of future events through previous knowledge. In Chapter 9, Oriol J. Batalla seeks to explore the conflict of the climate refugees from coastline areas and islands from a Political Ecology and Environmental Humanities perspective, related to the conceptualizations of (b)order and (b)ordering, and the dialectic it predicts between locality and globality amidst the ability to thrive amongst the different populations affected. This work also aims to produce alternative narratives towards a rethinking and reordering of the Contemporary and its politics regarding Environment, Politics, Culture and a Degrowth future.

The idea of nature has always been of central importance to the idea of what a human being is. Different images of nature have historically shaped different ideas of human society—a solid and dense background of our lives against which we have routinely defined ourselves. However, the current sense of global ecological disaster has seriously questioned our sovereign Romantic liberal-humanist concept of 'Nature' as some pristine and organic background of our lives. The threats of Global Warming, Climate Change, overpopulation and more explicitly our planet entering the Anthropocene era are issues that confound both Natural Sciences and the Humanities alike. All these factors have contributed to the birth of a new 'Re-invented Nature', a nature having its own agency as opposed to something seen solely as an object of human control and representations. The urgency of this kind of crisis is something that is without any historical precedence and as such disruptive of all our representational schematics with which the people in the Humanities feel familiar. Faced with such an unprecedented situation, we are forced to ask ourselves some uneasy and pressing questions like: Is there anything called 'Nature' exists today? Can the Humanities scholars have anything to offer to this crisis? If yes, then what will exactly be its own counter-text? Can we still talk about 'the Humanities' and 'Natural Sciences' in separate and monolithic terms, as in the past? In what follows, the chapter attempts to draw attention to new eco-logics of nature at a time of anthropogenic Climate Change that would lead to a Re-imagining of the humanities discipline in particular and human life in general. In Chapter 10, Ratul Nandi aims to build the responses towards the question of how to deal with this new 'deconstructed nature' and particularly to what possibilities are open to our arts and literature for dealing with this crisis.

The concept of a 'border' accommodates the contradictory connotations of 'nearness' and 'separation'. As Derrida argues in relation to the 'hyphen', a demarcation line not only separates but *always, already* joins the entities on either side of it. Transgression is therefore structural to any (b)order, including that of self/other, home/abroad, human/nonhuman, etc. The 'shadow lines' of any border are always in motion, re-producing it as a liminal space which keeps-erasing itself. It is this operation of *trace* which makes every border a site of intense conflict and contestation, especially for those caught in the undecided in-between. Chapter 11 explores this onto-ethical and political implications of such a hyphenated existence, caught between moving (b)orders of nationality, race, class, and gender. If we consider the self to be our most intimate *home*, the discussion then spirals out to issues of roots and routes — to cultural hybridity, transnationality and the postcolonial condition at large. Rajarshi Bagchi thus, attempts a comparative study on selfhood and agency by taking up Homi K. Bhabha's postcolonial idea of the culturally *hybrid* subject and juxtaposing it with the French feminist thinker Hélène Cixous's anti-phallogocentric conception of *feminine* 'self/s'. Finally, the chapter engages with Cixous's diasporic auto-fiction, *Reveries of the Wild Woman: Primal Scenes*, in order to explore how a hyphenated existence affects one's self-identity.

South Asia presents a peculiar yet spectacular mix of cultures, languages, religions, customs and traditions that have evolved over time to shape the distinctiveness that it possesses today. The Mauryans, the Mughals and the Cholas to name a few, along with the British East India Company and the subsequent British Raj have all contributed towards this shaping of South Asia as we know it today. Following the independence of India, new realities of 'border-ism' were born ending with the creation of Bangladesh in 1971. Furthermore, in the fast-paced and inter-connected lives of states, borders have come to be understood in many forms, one of them being the rising concept of border-lands. In the wake of the discipline of Area Studies in the United States, the term 'South Asia' was created, perhaps in an attempt to categorize the Asian sub-continent. The term however, is understood to be an anomaly due to the fact that South Asia with its ultra-wide selection of languages, cultures and customs is still categorized as one single region. The term 'Indian Sub-continent' is rarely used in academic parlance today and has largely given way to 'South Asia'. It is with this idea that this chapter seeks to explore the various cultures, subcultures, languages, socio-economic and geopolitical aspects of South Asia and whether its borders have evolved over time to play an important role in connecting forces rather than dividing-lines in the region. For a detailed analysis of the region, the historical legacy of the South Asian borders cannot be overlooked. However, in the context of the tightly-knit multipolar global order of today, these perceptions need to be changed to adapt to the demands of economic globalization. In Chapter 12, Aditya Kant Ghising looks at how this may be achieved. Inter-state relations in South Asia have largely been guided by a sense of shared culture and historical background. This can further be given a positive direction amidst economic gains in today's global order characterized by an increasing focus on connectivity. The study of borders and cultures has fascinated scholars for generations and his chapter aims to make a humble contribution to the existing literature.

Written in the wake of the Indian Rebellion of 1857, almost a decade after the events in India, *Lost Links in Indian Mutiny* by H P Malet opens up one such strange 'diaspora space'. The novel begins with Yusuff's sojourn to Mecca, for Hadj. In a weirdly episodic narrative it follows the strange tale of Hoossein ben Hassan, son of Yusuff's friend and fellow pilgrim in Hadj, Hassan, who died during the pilgrimage. Dictated by strange talismanic scroll Hoossein joins an English family as a servant, subsequently he serves in the palace of the Mughal Emperor in Delhi, then joins the thugs in their flourishing business, nearly escaping the gallows by becoming an 'approver' — a government spy and witness, against the thugs as the British administration put an end to this nefarious practice. With his scope as an approver shrinking with the sinking fortunes of the thugs, Hoossein plans to settle down in Calcutta by marrying Yusuff's daughter Ameena. But strange circumstances lead him to be abducted by unknown goons to be transported to the West Indies as plantation labour. Hoossein subsequently comes back to India in the eventful year 1857, only to be drawn into the vortex of the storm and to be hanged by the victorious British, apparently fulfilling the destiny as it was dictated by the talismanic scroll in Hoossein's possession. In Malet's narration of Hoossein's life from the point of view of a former British officer in India, the protagonist's identity always remains steeped in an intersectional cusp. On one hand, there is the inscrutability of fate as it has been dictated by the scroll, on the other hand there is the openness and readiness to choose what comes in life. In Chapter 13, Debapriya Paul intends to investigate Hoossein's sojourn to the West Indies, his journey overseas, how he fares in that strange climate, and what makes him come back. Pal treats Hoossein's journey as one of the earliest examples of a fictional representation of the South Asian diaspora, namely the phenomenon of the indentured labour system, which has received a masterly treatment in recent years in Amitav Ghosh's *Sea of Poppies* (2008). In the historiography of Indian Rebellion, it is noted that after the failure of the uprising a lot of rebels fled to the far away countries in order to escape the British wrath. But in *Lost Links in Indian Mutiny* we have a protagonist who does just the opposite. His study explores the very site of Hoossein's diasporic commitment to his native land that propels him to sacrifice himself for a 'just' cause.

Against the sterile clichés of opinion (doxa), Matthew Arnold pitted culture for its fresh possibility of "fusing horizons". Though commonly taken as an apologist for 'high culture' and Englishness as norms, Arnold found culture to be far from stabilizing and actually fissured with differences. Finding English culture 'ambivalent' and 'antagonistic' and Victorian ideologies barren, Arnold came to share actively the burgeoning interests in Gypsies in the 1850s and 1860s. Material realities of changing Victorian society had inspired in Arnold the creative process of 'becoming different' and 'active individuation' by wilful displacement to and fascination for peripheral locations. Arnold's re-telling of Glanvil's seventeenth-century story of a legendary scholar's voluntary withdrawal from Oxford evinces how 'nomadic multiplicities' can offer a leeway to the tutelage of Victorian ideology and its closed and bounded horizon. In foregrounding mutation and creative transformation in the Gypsy life and its 'wild brotherhood', Arnold's poem contravenes fixed ways of existing. Chapter 14 attempts to read how the contours of space and time are redrawn in Arnold's poem; in charting the roving of a scholar in and around Oxford and its countryside where it extols the illegitimate presence of the 'margin' and its overhaul of culture's homogenizing, nationalistic affiliation. With Deleuze and Guattari's conceptual apparatus of 'line of flight' and 'striated space', Nirjhar Sarkar tries to understand the process of overcoming or transcending spatio-temporal belonging, hindrance of fixed and identifiable points which are germane to conventional mode of existence. As individuals create lines of flight from segmented life for them to unstructure the received ideas and de-throne 'intellectual' glory, Arnoldian hero in *The Scholar Gypsy* may said to have entered a passional 'molecular' phase of life. By creating and transforming the world, his story continues to be a bold antidote against blinding doctrines of border.

As political consciousness was gaining force in late nineteenth and early twentieth century colonial India, nationalistic concerns found its way into every aspect of social, cultural and materialistic existence. It is with the rise of such concerns that the segregation between public and private domains manifested itself in numerous ways to suit the nationalistic project. The effects of such compartmentalization was ubiquitous upon women who by now had become the most contested object of reform movements triggered by both the colonizing mission of 'saving the brown woman from the brown man' and the nationalistic mission of transcreating women as goddess/mother/nation. Within these contradictory pulls of the time, women found themselves trapped for a voice and a vocabulary which could give shape to their anxieties and misgivings while also allowing them to recognize the ways of moving out and identifying their subjectivities formed for themselves. It was the drive towards education of women which created the perforation in an otherwise claustrophobic existence within concentric borders of control. Education which was supposed to prepare women according to the nationalistic need, transformed them into subjects who now set out to remake, recast women into new roles. New, not *adhunik*, or modern as we know it now, but *nabya* was how change was understood then, which also would lead us to understand the indigenous parameters of modernity. It is this 'new woman' or *nobeena*, who constantly tries to move out from her constrictions, mainly using the tool of education. What then emerged was the 'lekhika', the phenomenon of the woman writer in the late nineteenth century and early twentieth century, who blurred the borders of private and public existence by writing about her private life for the public readers. While it would be too far-fetched to state that women writers were not implicit subjects of patriarchy, it is also true that it was through these writers that the patriarchal citadel of existence was rocked from within the very *andarmahals* of the *bhadralok* household. While concentrating on the very act of writing by women, Chapter 15 tries to understand how the idea of 'new woman' gained currency in the intellectual world of late nineteenth and early twentieth century colonial Bengal where the blurring of the private and public domains of existence for women became a consistent act of striking against the world, the *bahir*, while also trying to comprehend the meanings within the home, the *ghar*. In this respect, Priyanka Chatterjee refers to similar movements in England during the same time frame, the differences it posed against the indigenous counterpart and the impact the idea of 'new woman' had in the encounters of women regarding the public-private divide which led to complicated representations of the character of women detectives in fictions by women in both England and colonial Bengal.

Children's texts or primers are not as innocent as they appear to be. They often carry the ideology of the hegemonic groups and ruling class. Tagore's *Sahaj Path* is a children's text, but we may unravel the text to pick up threads of challenging interpretations. In *Sahaj Path*, the presence of some characters who may be called subalterns is consciously highlighted by Tagore. They are accorded a place of honour and importance. These people, as portrayed by Tagore, are not merely treated as adjunct to the upper class people, used as soft targets to be wished away at will, instead they play vital roles in the society. *Sahaj Path* endorses Tagore's notion of meaningful negotiation between the rich and the poor and thereby attempts to erase the psychological margins between the economically weak working class and the members of the wealthy upper class. In a way, the two parts of *Sahaj Path* re-vision the prevalent social structure and inculcate in young learners a vision of an ideal society that honours the dignity of labour and recognises the status of all classes, castes and genders.

In the last chapter, Goutam Buddha Sural shows how the lessons, to a certain extent, oppose subalternization of 'marginal' characters, thereby challenging a hegemonic reading of the text(s). The primer opposes the disproportionate influence of the wealthy on the working class people who enjoy a space of their own in social life. Most of the members of the upper class society as represented in these texts do not believe and participate in the marginalization of people belonging to the lower social order and this mutuality helps in the establishment of a 'felt-community' by invisibilizing the psychological borders between the rich and the poor.

References

Anzaldua, Gloria (1987). *Borderlands = La Frontera: The New Mestiza*. San Francisco, US: Spinters/Aunt Lute.

Bourdieu, Pierre (1977). *Outline of a Theory of Practice*. Cambridge and New York: Cambridge University Press.

Derrida, Jacques (1993). *Aporias: Dying – awaiting (one Another At) the "limits of Truth"*. California: Stanford University Press.

Gaonkar, Dilip (2001). *Alternative Modernities*. Durham: Duke University Press.

McBrien, Justin (2016). Accumulating Extinction: Planetary Catastrophism in the Necrocene in Jason W. Moore's (Ed.) *Anthropocene or capitalocene?: Nature, history and the crisis of capitalism*. Oakland: PM Press. 116-137

Mignolo, Walter (2006). Citizenship, Knowledge, and the Limits of Humanity. *American Literary History*, 18(2), 312-321

Mbembe, Achille (2017). *Critique of Black Reason*. (translated by Lauren Dubois). Durham/London: Duke University Press.

Nietzsche, Friedrich Wilhelm (1968). *The Will to Power* (translated by Walter Kauffman, and R. J. Hollindale). New York: Vintage Books

Pratt, Mary (1991). Arts of the Contact Zone. *Profession*, 33-40. Retrieved from www.jstor.org/stable/25595469

Singh, Amritjit & Peter Schmidt. (2000). *Postcolonial Theory and the United States: Race, Ethnicity, and Literature*. Jackson: University Press of Mississippi.

Soja, Edward (1996). *Thirdspace: Journeys to Los Angeles and Other Real and Imagined Places*. Oxford: Blackwell Publishing

Contemporary Fiction as a Cultural Map of Migration

Emma Musty

We live in a world in which everyone seems to be constantly on the move. Even as I sit to write this chapter I am doing so in an airport. I would currently say that I actually travel too much, as many others also do. I travel because I am a writer, because I am an activist, because I am an academic and because my family is spread throughout the four corners of the world. But the reason I can travel so easily is because I am British, because the forces of colonialism, imperialism and capitalism have made it so. Freedom of movement in this context has become a privilege, one often abused, and which has come from a history of abuse, and not the human right it is so often purported to be. As Mimi Sheller notes in *Mobility Justice: The Politics of Movement in an Age of Extremes*:

> Freedom of mobility may be considered a universal human right, yet in practice it exists in relation to class, race, sexuality, gender and ability, exclusions from public space, from national citizenship, from access to resources, and from the means of mobility at all scales. (Sheller 2018, p. 20)

I come from one of the countries that drew many of our maps and created many of the borders contained within them. My freedom of movement exists in relation to this history and affords me a privileged access to the world not enjoyed by all.

To understand contemporary literature as a cultural map of migration one must draw upon similar areas to that of mobility justice, those of "colonial, corporeal and planetary histories and interrelations" (Sheller 2018, p. 21). To this end I will argue that not only can a writer be described as a cartographer, but that a novel may thus be described as a map which exists in relation to the cultural and political history of both the writer and that which is written; the characters, landscapes and intervals exposed through the narrative. As examples I will use two recent literary works, *Signs Preceding the end of the World,* by Mexican author and political scientist Yuri Herrera and *The Gurugu Pledge*, by Equatoguinean author and activist Juan Tomás Ávila Laurel, novels that reflect our atomised societies.

Maps created by contemporary fiction such as these are important interrogators of existing ideas of identity and culture in this time of globalization and migration. Driving the need for critical reflection on these cultural artefacts, which not only record the times we live in, but frame the questions we ask about our increasingly diverse and transient cultures. Reece Jones (2018, p. 162) in Violent Borders asks, "Are humans defined by our attachment to place or by movement?" It seems it is increasingly the latter. The literature of migration allows us to view maps and the borders etched upon them in a different light. It shows the human impact of border systems reflects our colonial past and elucidates our mobile present.

Though there has been much research into negative and harmful aspects of migratory discourse in recent years (Greussing and Boomgaarden 2017; Matar 2017; Volpicelli 2015), few possible alternatives to these dominant narratives have been brought to light. In the area of critical migration research it has been noted by Dr Kerry Moore that, "…migrants are rarely afforded a voice in the news…" (Moore 2015, p. 1), that although they are often cited as statistics, the discourse is depersonalised and emotionally removed. Contemporary fiction can, I will argue, fill this gap and by doing so re-humanise the migration debate, furthering the discourse surrounding mobility justice while highlighting the hybrid nature of our cross border cultures.

In *The Rise of Trapped Populations*, April T. Humble also raises concerns, highlighting the role of the border in creating new and informal spaces, prompting the need for further academic research into the impact of border security on migrant populations:

> There are many hotspots where concentrated groups of people become trapped due to border security—such as in northern France, north-west Turkey, northern Bangladesh and North Korea—often congregating in informal 'migrant camps', with many similar scenarios worldwide. (Humble 2014, p. 56)

Both Social and Human sciences have long histories of viewing and negotiating borders. In the Foreword to *Migration without Borders: Essays on the Free Movement of People*, Pierre Sane asks us to "Imagine a world without borders..." (Pecoud and de Guchteneire (eds.) 2007, p. ix) while laying out a legal argument utilising current human rights legislation:

> According to Article 13-2 of the Universal Declaration of Human Rights, 'Everyone has the right to leave any country, including his own, and to return to his country'. But the right to leave is not complemented by the right to enter; one may emigrate, but not immigrate. From a human rights point of view, we are faced with an incomplete situation that sees many people being deprived of their right to emigrate by an absence of possibilities to immigrate. It is therefore worth envisaging a right to mobility: in a world of flows, mobility is a resource to which everyone should have access. (Pecoud and de Guchteneire (eds.) 2007, p. ix)

There is no room here to offer a comprehensive overview of the current debate in other disciplines, but I will touch upon several as we move forward.

Writer as Cartographer

"A story or novel is a kind of map because, like a map, it is not a world, but it evokes one (or at least one, for each reader)" (Turchi 2004, p. 166). In *Maps of the Imagination: The Writer as Cartographer*, the writer and academic Peter Turchi argues that there are parallels between the practice of the writer and that of the cartographer. He sees this most clearly in the editing process. In both maps and works of fiction he suggests there are choices between what is left in and what is left out, as well as the point of view inhabited. He uses early American maps as an example: "Native American tribal areas were not included on early European maps of the Americas, giving early readers of those maps the impression no one lived there — at least no one of consequence" (Turchi 2004, p. 33).

Even as I wrote this chapter I had to create order out of disorder, I had to border the sections, I had to cut and rewrite. What would be the equivalent of this editorial decision in fiction? The voices represented, perhaps? Maps and writing assign blank space, just as the American map does, as a form of silence. In poetry this could include the physical layout of a poem but it also applies in fiction to what is shown and what is hidden; the dropped stitches which allow the reader room to draw their own conclusions. Turchi goes further to suggest that a piece of fiction can act in itself as a map: "We compel readers to look in the direction we want them to look, to see what we want them to see, in the way that we want them to see it" (Turchi 2004, p.82). When writing a novel a limited number of perspectives can be included. The writer directs the gaze of the reader just as the cartographer allows the viewer to see only what she has decided to include within the perimeters of the map. When Turchi states that, "The first lie of a map—also the first lie of fiction—is that it is the truth" (Turchi 2004, p. 73), he reveals the constructed nature of both.

Both books and maps are constructions which show us a carefully-crafted view of the world. This is not to say they are out to trick us necessarily, but that the magic they perform is to show us something that we would not have been able to see without them. When Robert Louis Stevenson wrote *Treasure Island* he drew the map of the island first while stuck inside his house on a rainy Scottish day. Before he knew it, he was writing a novel based upon his doodle, but when he sent it off to the publishers the original map was lost. He had to draw another, this time painstakingly recreating it from the novel, a far harder task. He felt that this new map never truly represented *Treasure Island* as the first one had. The original map had been unique and could never be remade in the same way that the original manuscript of a novel, if lost, would have been impossible to replicate (Turchi 2004, p. 227). Both maps and literature are thus constructed and are unique to their author and to their time of making.

In *Cartographies of Culture: New Geographies of Welsh Writing in English*, Damien Walford Davies suggests that works of literature can in themselves represent an atlas of complex cultural interrelations: "in the Anglophone literature of Wales, maps are a means of signalling and contesting cultural differences and emplacement" (Davies 2012, p. 15). In a bilingual country whose first language was subjugated by English and whose geography is squeezed between England and the Irish Sea, a preoccupation with maps is understandable. Maps, in whatever form—oral, written or drawn—allow us to place ourselves culturally as well as geographically. They allow us to consider where we belong and to whom. Katherine Harmon, who brought together a collection of artist maps and essays in *You are here: personal geographies and other maps of the imagination,* suggests that "humans have an urge to map—and that this mapping instinct, like our opposable thumbs, is part of what makes us human" (Harmon 2004, p. 10).

Our need to locate ourselves, to map our territory, is far older than the property laws and national boundaries which mark the maps of the modern world. It could even be argued that maps have been, and remain, necessary for survival: "The earliest maps are thought to have been created to help people find their way and to reduce their fear of the unknown. We want to know the location of what we deem life-sustaining (hunting grounds and sources of freshwater, then; now, utility lines and grocery stores) and life-threatening (another people's lands; the toxic runoff from a landfill)" (Turchi 2004, p. 11).

Maps offer us parameters in which to live in practical terms, as above, but potentially the idea of orientation also includes social or even spiritual connotations. As writer Stephen S. Hall suggests: "Orienting begins with geography, but it reflects the need of the conscious, self-aware organism for a kind of transcendent orientation that asks not just where am I, but where do I fit into this landscape" (Harmon 2004, p. 15). Duncan Campbell, cited by Walford Davies, defines psychogeography as "a species of border-writing, standing uneasily between so many oppositions (mind and world, city and country, myth and history), never resolving in favour of one side or another, and above all, never forgetting" (Davies, p. 23). To say that one belongs *here* is implicitly saying one does not belong *elsewhere.*

Maps and the (In)visible

Maps shape our view of the world and mirror our cultures. They can chart us at the centre of the universe or make us disappear. It is this power that can make them dangerous.

> Etymologically the map is a conception of the arrangement of something as much as it is a representation of the earth's surface. The state's cartographic violence thus helps it define who or what exists and in what order. Maps are thus a means of both physical colonization and conceptual control, involving both a cognitive paradigm as well as a practical means of political administration. (Neoclaus 2003, p. 419)

Mark Neoclaus in *Off the Map: On Violence and Cartography* discusses the relationship between the map and the state arguing that the widespread use of cartography was concurrent with the birth of the nation state (circa 1600) and that since this point maps have been utilised as a state tool to legitimise and control state territory. Such a political understanding of cartographic practice is at odds with more traditional views. The International Cartographic Association has defined the map as "a symbolized image of geographic reality, representing selected features or characteristics, resulting from the creative efforts of cartographers and designed for use when spatial relationships are of special relevance." (International Cartographic Society cited in Dorling and Fairbairn 1997, p. 3) Although this definition is broad and allows for the 'creative', the map is designated as an object containing 'geographic reality' and attributing the ability to create this reality to a specific profession: 'cartographers'. Further to this, cartography is understood to utilise scientific methods which suggests scientific certainty or at least objectivity on the part of the creator (Godlewska 1999, p. 21). The subjective choices of the cartographer must then come at the point of selecting which 'features or characteristics' to represent. It is into this gap between the objective and subjective that Dennis Wood, author of *The Power of Maps*, steps, suggesting that "... all maps, inevitably, unavoidably, necessarily embody their authors' prejudices, biases and partialities..." (Wood 1992, p. 24). Taking the map as a text which is contrived, conceived and edited it would necessarily contain the 'prejudices, biases and partialities' of the author not only through what is included, but also though what is omitted; an overtly political, and potentially violent, act.

Karen Piper, author of *Cartographic Fictions: Maps, Race and Identity*, suggests that the editing process utilised by cartographers, the decision over what is shown and what is hidden, always has a political agenda:

> The history of cartography has [...] been a history of coding the enemy, making a "them" and "us" that can be defended with a clear border. It has been, above all, a history of pushing "them" out of territory that is considered ours — denying their existence, deleting their maps, drawing lines in the sand. (Piper 2002, p. x)

Such a schism between the political reality of a country and its representation, has led J. B. Hartley to question the 'geographic reality' proposed by the International Cartographic Society: "If a map asserts that the status quo is good, and the status quo is actually evil, then the map is to that extent incorrect..." (Hartley 2002, p. 21). To what extent it is the role of a map to address concepts such as 'good' and 'evil' is questionable yet if maps can be conceived as providing us with "reality" (Wood 1992, p. 4), which Wood suggests goes beyond geography alone, then it seems unavoidable that they should contain some form of value judgement. Viewed in this moral context, a map of a country under fascist rule could, as Woods states, be described as 'incorrect' as the 'status quo' represented is generally considered unacceptable, and in the case of many countries in Europe during the Second World War was fatal for a large proportion of the population. A novel, on the other hand, has the ability to articulate the human experience of living within the geographical space in which the action takes place.

To be 'Off the map' according to the *Oxford English Dictionary* is to be "Out of existence... an insignificant position; of no account; obsolete" (OED cited in Neoclaus 2003, p. 417). This is often the case for spaces inhabited by the marginalised and bordered, the migrant 'jungles' in France for example are invisible upon the map of France and thus exit both inside and outside of French territory in the political imagination.

This is perhaps best highlighted by Michael Shapiro, author of *The New Violent Cartography*, who points to the Pentagon's new 'map of danger':

> From the point of view of the US executive branch's geography of enmity, not being an intimate in the global exchange of resources — for example being an Iran rather than a Saudi Arabia — increases your chances of becoming a 'rogue state' or part of the 'axis of evil' and thus a potential target. (Shapiro 2007, p. 304)

A point clearly reinforced by Trump's 2017 travel ban on Muslim majority countries Libya, Iran, Somalia, Syria and Yemen as well as North Korea and Venezuela. Shapiro believes the maps necessarily create this 'enmity' between 'vulnerable bodies' and that this aspect of mapmaking, which he dates back to the Westphalia Treaty of 1648, has dangerous consequences in the modern world:

> Ultimately, the biopolitical dimensions of USA's anti-terrorism initiatives (the decisions about what lives to waste and what ones require exclusion or containment) are deployed on particular bodies, both those that are targets and those that are the ones that must confront those bodies in dangerous terrain. (Shapiro, 2007, p. 299)

When Shapiro discusses Tomas Munita's photo of an American soldier in an abandoned building used as a look out post in Afghanistan he points to:

> ... a history of vulnerable bodies seeking temporary refuge and a place for safe observation in hostile landscapes that seem both benign, because they are temporarily devoid of hostile engagement, and threatening, because their encompassing scale appears to thwart human attempts to manage them securely. (Shapiro 2007, p. 293)

Here the vulnerable body is that of both the state actor (in this case an actor from a foreign state, protecting state interests far from the borders of the territory they seek to protect) and, if we consider the unseen other, their opposite, out of view because they are also vulnerable to attack. Mapping has sought to alleviate the fear of the state and thus its actors by creating a defined territory that can be easily defended against outsiders. The project of the nation state has relied upon this concept since its birth. As Neoclaus states: "the political importance of the map is obvious: it is one of the most explicit assertions of sovereignty" (Neoclaus 2003, p. 419). If an area such as the 'jungle' does not exist on the map then it does not exist in the state and can be easily defined as an area of 'otherness'. The refusal to accept the existence of a portion of society, and thus their potential claim to state resources such as health care or financial support, is a fundamentally violent act against 'vulnerable bodies', in this case the body of the migrant. Yet this perceived vulnerability must also be called into question, as Yurimar Bonilla, cited by Sheller (2018, p. 104), "Vulnerability is not simply a product of natural conditions; it is a political state and colonial condition." and as Jones argues it is the border itself which creates the violence it seeks to prevent (Jones 2017, p. 91) and the state which creates an individual's vulnerability to such violence.

The etymology of 'territory' itself gives pause for concern:

> The notion of 'territory' is derived from a complex of terms: from *terra* (of earth, and thus a domain) and *territōrium*, referring to a place from which people are warned off, but it also links to *terrére*, meaning to frighten. And the notion of region derives from the Latin *regere* (to rule) with its connotations of military power. Territory is a land occupied and maintained through terror; a region is space ruled through force. The secret to territoriality is thus violence: the force necessary for the production of space and the terror crucial to the creation of boundaries. (Neoclaus 2003, p. 412)

This clearly links back to Shapiro's argument: the state's mapped territory must be defended, it is a place from which some people will be 'warned off'. This definition suggests that the creation of a territory necessitates the maintenance of said territory through violent means and such violence is ultimately enacted on the bodies of both those who are perceived as threatening, but also those who are employed to protect the state. A juxtaposition which can only exist in relation to the border, leading Jones (2015, p. 5) to assert that: "The hardening of the border through new security practices is the source of the violence, not a response to it."

The Lines on the Map

Liminal spaces can act as moments of interaction between the people and cultures of the world while at the same time performing an act of transition within the self. As the traveler leaves his or her place of origin they step into the role of others through both an internal and external process. Such moments are imagined and documented in literature, but before pursuing this further we must look at the term 'border'.

Within this framework, borders may be understood as:

> ...arbitrary dividing lines that are simultaneously social, cultural and psychic, territories to be patrolled against those whom they construct as outsiders, aliens, the Others; forms of demarcation where the very act of prohibition inscribes transgressions; zones where fear of the Other is the fear of the self; places where claims to ownership—claims to 'mine', 'yours' and 'theirs'—are staked out, contested, defended and fought over. (Brah 2003 p. 198)

Avtar Brah's definition of borders exemplifies the complex nature of the term. He describes them as being both physical and psychological barriers combining social and geographical dimensions as we have seen above. In this understanding of the term, borders can exist beyond the lines on a map to become aspects of societal beliefs. In constructing a sense of self through such shared beliefs it is possible to construct an 'us' thus enabling the construction of an 'other'. In the texts discussed below, ideas of borders are related to both the physical and the psychological while beginning to consider the idea of the 'other' as someone who exists on the opposite side of a border.

> Many characterised interactions between the state and outsiders are a contrast between civilisation and barbarity, but we know this version because states write their histories from their perspective, while many mobile people did not record their experiences. (Jones 2015, p. 91)

Literature, especially that which deals with migration, potentially redresses this imbalance, and calls into question how civilised the bordered state truly is when the violence enacted upon the mobile migrant body is brought to light and removed from the invisible liminal area. Due to the nature of mapping, borders become normalised in the public consciousness as do the hierarchies associated with those who can and cannot cross them. This suggests that they are as much a work of the imagination as they are a geographical reality, a concept described by James Procter as "imaginative geography" (Procter 2003 p. 1).

Brah also highlights the relationship between borders and narrative: "Each border embodies a unique narrative, even while it resonates with common themes with other borders" (Brah 2003, p. 198). This narrative is not the sole preserve of the state, there are other voices present. In fact the border itself is in some way defined, can only exist, in relation to the other. As Trinh T. Minh-ha puts it, borders are:

> Constantly guarded, reinforced, destroyed, set up, and reclaimed, boundaries not only express the desire to free/to subject one practice, one culture, one national community from/to another, but also expose the extent to which cultures are products of the continuing struggle between official and unofficial narratives: those largely circulated in favour of the State and its policies of inclusion, incorporation and validation, as well as of exclusion, appropriation and dispossession. (Minh-ha 1996, p. 1)

Migration literature is arguably a form of unofficial border narrative. Yet even set in opposition to an official state narrative or map, it unavoidably reinforces the border through the very method it utilises to destroy it. Crossing the border, especially clandestinely, similarly recognises its power while also negating it.

Migration Literature

Within literary criticism there has been a shift from the literature of exile to migrant literature which is said to offer a "transnational, cosmopolitan, multilingual and hybrid map of the world that redraws boundaries" (Mardorossian 2002, p. 17). Yet this term still defines the author rather than the literature, maintaining the borders which so much of this literature seeks to cross. In *Migration and Literature: Günter Grass, Milan Kundera, Salman Rushdie, and Jan Kjærstad*, Søren Frank instead suggests that the term used should be 'migration literature' as it " not only calls for a redrawing of the map of literary history but also challenges the way literary studies is often organized in nationally separated contexts" (Frank 2008, p. 10). It is this term I will use when discussing the novels and related texts in this chapter, viewed within the wider realms of contemporary and postcolonial literatures.

Literature as a Cultural Map of Migration

While there is precedent for using literature as a cultural artefact for better understanding migration in several disciplines, it has yet to be seen or utilised as a map of contemporary migration. The editors of *Writing Across Worlds: Literature and Migration* offer us an argument for using literature as a way of gaining insights into the experience of migration:

> Literary accounts focus in a very direct and penetrating way on issues such as place perception, landscape symbolism, senses of displacement and transformation, communities lost and created anew, exploitation, nostalgia, attitudes towards return, family relationships, self-denial and self-discovery and many more. (King, Connell and White (eds.) 1995, p. x)

Amanda Lagji has moved this argument forward by writing on the inter-relationship between literature and mobility studies as literature is "embedded in and reflective of cultural imaginaries" and "helps us to see how we make meaning out of, and subscribe meaning to mobilities, foregrounding the interpretive work of making sense of movement and stillness" (Lagji 2018, p. 7). If we look specifically at mobility in terms of migration, contemporary fiction, and more specifically migration literature, can thus be argued as 'making meaning out of' both the journeys described in such works and the moments of stillness during which waiting (for a chance to cross a border, for news from a smuggler, for money to arrive, for an asylum claim etc.) is also a form of moving forward. This discussion feeds into the idea of contemporary fiction as a cultural map of migration. As the borders are crossed, so the map is drawn, but the authors of, and the visible bodies within, this map is not only the state actors who have imposed the border upon the landscape, but the border crossers and border writers themselves.

Landscapes, Vulnerable Bodies and Imagined Others

In *The Gurugu Pledge* a group of black Africans who have travelled from all over the continent wait on Mount Gurugu in Northern Morocco for their chance to cross the border into Melilla, Spain. They play football and tell stories to pass the time. When two women in the group become ill after a sexual assault and one of them experiences a miscarriage, the group tries to climb the fence on mass, leaving the women, who are too weak to climb, tied to the top to be found and taken care of. It is likely that they die there. The character with the last word, for the narration switches in and out of third person and inhabits different characters along the way, decides not to cross and remains on the mountain but facing south, towards the Zambezi river and away from Europe. At this moment, a common understanding of the journey is inverted. The route charted on maps of modern migration takes us from the south to the north, yet the final geographical gaze of the novel faces pointedly in the opposite direction.

In *Signs Preceding the End of the World,* Makina travels from Mexico to the USA in search of her brother and to deliver a package for one the men who help her cross. Surviving a clash at the border during which she is shot, she makes her way to the city where her brother should be, but she cannot find him. In the end she discovers that he has changed his identity, taking on that of a young American man who signed up to the army without his parents' permission, and thus she realises her brother will not come home. Makina, having always believed she would return, also ends up getting American papers.

The novels deal specifically with liminal areas, the Spanish/Moroccan border and US/Mexico border respectively and their characters' identities are shaped in relation to the landscape they inhabit, the cultures they bring with them, and the cultures they meet in the countries they journey to. The landscape then must also be shaped by them in some way. Both novels also include the epic themes of journey, death and the underworld and discussions on migration, immigration, nativism, profiling, transnationalism, transculturalism, language hybridity, the apocalypse/end of the world, thus lending themselves to an investigation such as this.

In both works there is a tension between the body and the border. The vulnerability exposed by the breakdown of previous collective identities and the creation of a new identity, that of the migrant. In *The Gurugu Pledge* we see this clearly when one of the protagonists states: "They told me I no longer have a country, that's what they said at the border: you've no country any more, now you're just black." (Laurel 2017, p. 75). This happens as he crosses into Morocco. The transition between one state and another is thus both physical, as in the crossing of a boundary between two territories, and internal, changing the very nature of his identity. Makina's search for her lost brother in *Signs Preceding the End of the World* can also be viewed as a search for a stable identity within a new culture. Whereas the characters portrayed as living on Mount Gurugu in Morocco, located near the Spanish territory of Melilla, speak of their stories and journeys as a way of both commemorating and shedding their pasts, a process which feels necessary for them to survive this passage into a new culture that awaits them on the other side of the fence.

In his exploration of diasporic identity Brah also expresses this link been migrant identity and the repetition of narrative:

> This means that these multiple journeys may configure into one journey via a *confluence of narratives* as it is lived and re-lived, produced, reproduced and transformed through individual as well as collective memory and re-memory. It is within this confluence of narrativity that 'diasporic community' is differently imagined under different historical circumstances. By this I mean that the identity of a diasporic imagined community is far from fixed or pre-given. It is constituted within the crucible of the materiality of everyday life; in the everyday stories we tell ourselves individually and collectively. (Brah 2003, p. 183).

Although this echoes the repetition of stories within the camp on Mount Gurugu, I would argue that a diasporic perspective does not cover the transient nature of the migrant camps we now have at the borders of Europe and within Europe itself, that this situation more generally, and specifically within *The Gurugu Pledge*, somehow creates a further displacement, as there is nowhere to settle, yet history has also been lost. This is also represented by the 'invisible' nature of these spaces within traditional maps, and the invisibility thus transferred to the occupants.

One character in *The Gurugu Pledge* states: "none of us are from anywhere" (Laurel 2017, p. 121), during the process of storytelling, and another, "...I will not mention anyone or anywhere by name" (Laurel 2017, p. 15). As Carol Phillips notes, a migrant's relationship to home can become complicated, both as a form of protection (to be identified by their true origins may endanger the traveler), and emotionally as there is often no possibility to return to the place in which you once 'belonged': "Our identities are fluid. Belonging is a contested state. Home is a place riddled with vexing questions" (Phillips 2001 p. 6). A map of this nature thus naturally draws lines between countries and interspaces which may seem geographically distant and culturally disparate.

Signs Preceding the End of the World goes as far as to use geographical markers as chapter breaks—The Earth, The Water Crossing, The Place Where The Hills Meet, The Obsidian Mound, The Place Where The Wind Cuts Like A Knife, The Place Where Flags Wave, The Place Where People's Hearts Are Eaten, The Snake That Lies in Wait, The Obsidian Place With No Windows Or Holes For The Smoke. These headings are laid out to depict Makina's journey, creating a map personal to her, 'drawn' in her own words and reflective of her culture, while also suggestive of the ancient pathway to the underworld as understood in ancient Aztec mythology and consequently referencing Spanish colonial history in Mexico. *The Gurugu Pledge* instead uses stories with geographical descriptions to map people's journeys and experiences across the continent—even though this is most often done without place names.

In fact, both works can be described as 'geographically non-explicit', and name very few specific sites as they would be recognised on a traditional map. The language used is also often 'displaced', a dynamic carried through the translation, another form of 'displacement'. As Roger Bromley notes in the concluding chapter of *Cross Addressing: Resistance Literature and Cultural Borders*, texts written in the language of the colonizer often act to violate this language, "Transformation and textual negotiation are key features of the uses of language in border writing: this is also true of its narrative practice" (Hawley (ed.) 1996, p. 276). In *Signs Preceding the End of the World* for example "jarchar", meaning to leave, which has an Arabic route and had to transition from Spanish and then to English, became "to verse", thus the novel creates a new language of movement, required for a new understating of border crossing, and a new map of contemporary migration.

Indeed languages and translations can act as journeys or border crossings in their own right, imposing their own territorial constraints.

> In a world full of travellers, borders control and regulate how we move around and who can or who cannot move from one space to another. It is precisely these movements of people (and ideas, capital and things) that contribute to the constant evolution of cultures. Translation is one way in which ideas can move across borders; intercultural communication implies that borders have already been crossed in some way. The existence of borders indicates that there is movement across them, which someone considers needs to be controlled. (Evans and Ringrow 2017, p. 3)

Makina herself is a site of this 'language journey': "You are the door, not the one who walks through it" (Herrera 2015, p. 18) says one character to Makina because she runs the switchboard in her village and speaks three languages. She is a site of transition. She embodies the US/Mexico border through translating between local languages and English before she even physically approaches the line of demarcation.

In *The Gurugu Pledge* languages are also mixed up, broken down and played with. The author takes words from French, Spanish and Latin thus spanning more than one colonial past while at the same time expressing a neo-colonial present. Much of the novel's structure is based around a poem in Latin. Written by the father of Peter, known previously in his village as Ngambo (most characters have multiple names), the poem is in the Conceptismo style (from the 17th century Spanish tradition), written in French and with a gloss (a notation on the poem) in English in an unnamed African country which used English as its primary language, "or imposed language, imposed by rich whites…"(Laurel 2017, p. 12), as one character states, re-imposing the history of these borders and the current map of Africa. Later in the work, another character states that people use, "Eat or manger, according to whichever history the whites chose for you" (Laurel 2017, p. 64).

The Story of Peter's father's poem is told in 3 parts and is about Charon, his boat and the payment made, a retelling of the ancient story from Greek mythology. Charon is the ferryman of Hades who carries souls of the newly deceased across the rivers Styx and Acheron which divided the world of the living and the dead. The poem represents the journey to come for these young people, the price they will pay and the danger it involves. These fractured journeys and selves are reflected in the very structure of these novels. As I said previously, in *The Gurugu Pledge*, narration swaps in and out of third person, with the 'voice' of the story frequently changing. The author states this is because all of their voices needed to be heard, creating, I would posit, a more accurate map of this area in Morocco.

The Final Border

In both works the final physical border crossing is in fact a culmination of all the borders that have come before, though we meet the characters at the gates of Europe or America, their very beings hold the journeys taken, borders crossed and maps traversed up until that point. And in *Signs Preceding the End of the World*, even when Makina is in the USA, echoes of the border continue and she continues to cross them. This is often embodied in language. The people Makina meets in the US are both "homegrown" and "anglo" — "Their gestures and tastes reveal both ancient memory and the wonderment of a new people" (Herrera 2015, p. 63). They speak an "intermediary" tongue described as a "hinge pivoting between two like but distant souls, and then two more, and then two more, never exactly the same ones; something that serves as a link." (Herrera 2015, p. 63) and "their tongue is a nebulous territory between what is dying out and what is not yet born" (Herrera 2015, p. 63), thus creating "the world happening anew…" (Herrera 2015, p. 66).

And what of the border itself, the site of physical transition. As soon as she crosses the sky it already looks different to Makina, "more distant or less blue." (Herrera 2015, p. 40), is has gained something, distance, and lost something, colour and familiarity, just as Makina will. She arranges for her crossing back while she is still at home because of a friend who returned and:

> ...everything was similar but not the same: his mother was no longer his mother, his brothers and sisters were no longer his brother and sisters, they were people with difficult names and improbable mannerisms, as if they'd been copied off an original that no longer existed; even the air, he said, warmed his chest in a different way. (Herrera 2015, p. 20)

The border changes the make-up of things, the transition from one to the other is visible even in sentence structure. When Makina meets her brother he has assumed an American identity and will not come home. He has become, through the process of border crossing, another person. She is not his sister. His mother is not his mother. The boy she knew is gone.

The fragility of the body, its ability to be appropriated, damaged or destroyed also takes more concrete form. In *Signs Preceding the End of the World* they find a corpse at the border. From afar it looks like a pregnant woman, but it is in fact a bloated body. And in *The Gurugu Pledge* hospitals don't treat "blacks without papers" (Laurel 2017, p. 77) reasserting the idea that vulnerability is actually an imposed state rather than a natural one. Towards the end of the novel, a journalist who visits those living on Mount Gurugu shows a video of dead Africans on a beach, and states that they have not drowned, but been shot, presumably by state actors (Laurel 2017, p. 178), thus reinforcing Jones' description of the border as creating the violence which takes place there. Border crossing in both novels is a form of death "I'm dead, Makina said to herself..." on the first page, and later in the text someone asks her, "Off to the other side?" (Herrera, 2015, p. 14), directly linking the transition between Mexico and the USA to that between life and death.

In discussing the relationship between the migrant and the society to which they move, Iain Chambers suggests an appropriation of the metropolitan by the figure of the migrant. In this way he links migrant experience and the cityscape:

> There is an emergence at the centre of the previously peripheral and marginal. For the modern metropolitan figure is the migrant: she and he are the active formulators of metropolitan aesthetics and lifestyles, reinventing the language and appropriating the streets of the master. (Chambers 1994, p. 23)

Makina's character also speaks to this relationship, though in stronger words. Having been caught without papers by a police officer she has to write poetry on behalf of another arrestee:

> We are to blame for this destruction, we who don't speak your tongue and don't know how to keep quiet either. We who didn't come by boat, who dirty up your doorsteps with our dust, who break your barbed wire. We who came to take your jobs, who dream of wiping your shit, who long to work all hours. We who fill your shiny clean streets with the smell of food, who brought you violence you'd never known, who deliver your dope, who deserve to be chained by neck and feet. We who are happy to die for you, what else could we do? We, the ones who are waiting for who knows what. We the dark, the short, the greasy, the shifty, the fat, the anemic. We the barbarians. (Herrera 2015, p.99)

Here the presence of Mexicans in the Big Chilango (the name given to the American city described in the novel) is violently drawn, but they have presence nonetheless, and the officer who has tried to arrest Makina walks away in confusion having read her response. In *The Gurugu Pledge* however, that characters are instead described as having failing eyesight from staring at the city (Laurel 2017, p. 60). They are forever trapped outside and growing old with the wait. Even though the city is physically close, for most the dream of the city will never be achieved. Such distance cannot be viewed upon a traditional map. As Sheller states (2018, p. 20), mobility exists in relation to "class, race, sexuality, gender and ability, exclusions from public space, from national citizenship, from access to resources, and from the means of mobility at all scales." Within this work we find not only proof of this statement, but as readers we experience the human impact of such relations.

In the final phase of *Signs Preceding the end of the World*, Makina walks through a labyrinth of city streets with her guide, Chucho, until they reach a small door, through which she enters alone. She walks down the steps to a place of complete silence, devoid of people. Here, in the underworld, she is given her new documents. She has left her previous self behind, the girl who left Mexico has disappeared, but a new person has been born in her stead. When she reaches the moment of transition, she realises that she is prepared:

> ...the Big Chilango, all those colors, and she saw that what was happening was not a cataclysm; she understood with all of her body and all of her memory, she truly understood, and when everything in the world fell silent finally she said to herself I'm ready. (Herrera 2015, p. 107)

Conclusion

> Each *textual* journey over multiple ethnic, linguistic, cultural, national and political-economic borders has to be articulated with the historical and contemporary journey of the exile, immigrant and refugee. They are journeys of displacement, alienation, pain loss and, perhaps even in the end for some, of opportunity. The subject of address, the object of representation, unvoiced and invisible, the border crosser met and meets that hostility reserved for the stranger who comes today *and* the discriminatory and exclusionary legislation shaped for the stranger who stays, or might stay, tomorrow. (Hawley 1996, p. 276)

It is true that for some these journeys offer opportunity, an idea played upon in *The Gurugu Pledge* "... everyone had a brilliant future that awaited them in Europe" (Laurel 2017, p. 25). However, the idea of the border crosser as 'unvoiced and invisible' can now be called into question as migration literature works to illuminate these liminal areas while elucidating the impact of such 'discriminatory and exclusionary legislation'. If border crossers are still perceived to be 'invisible' it is because the viewer has refused to look, as shown through the alternative border narratives discussed in this chapter. Thus, in a re-humanisation of the migration debate, works such as these create new maps for our time, depicting the lived experiences of those who interact with the lines that cut across our world maps, while interrogating preconceptions of borders and border crossers. The border areas discussed above are by their nature violent, but they are also spaces in which unexpected things may happen. Sites of transition; they hover in the murky zone between life and death. The peripheries, for the very reason that they are further from the centre and the ideas of conformity associated with it, can offer potential; but current motilities (the abilities of different people to move independently through and within spaces) mean that for some they are deadly and for many others damaging.

Migration literature also exists in relation to other literatures that touch upon similar subjects and discuss other histories of movement. The late American writer Toni Cade Bambara provides a powerful example:

> Stories are important. They keep us alive. In the ships, in the camps, in the quarters, field, prisons, on the road, on the run, underground, under siege, in the throes, on the verge—the storyteller snatches us back from the edge to hear the next chapter. In which we are the subjects. We, the hero of the tales. Our lives preserved. How it was, how it be. Passing it along in a relay. That is what I work to do: to produce stories that save our lives. (cited in Hawley, 1996, p. 41)

Originally published in 1985 and referring to a long history of slavery and colonisation in the USA this passage could have been written far more recently and refer to contemporary migration and migration literature. It shows the confluence of border narratives, the relationships that exist between colonial, corporeal and planetary histories and interrelations (Sheller 2018, p. 21) and the importance of understanding such texts in relation to each other, thus allowing us to better understand our current border spaces, ourselves as border crossers and the historical, cultural and political contexts which either control or privilege our mobility. The works discussed in this chapter draw maps of two contested borderscapes, they show the damage done, the lives on hold and on the move, the dance of our cultures across these liminal spaces, the choices that need to be made if mobility justice is to be achieved, and the proof that such great changes have previously be attained and are possible.

References

Anderson, B. (2006). *Imagined Communities*. London: Verso.

Brah, A. (2003). *Cartographies of Diaspora: Contesting Identities*. London: Routledge.

Carter, E., J. Donald and J. Squires (eds.) (1993). *Space and Place: theories of identity and location*. London: Lawrence and Wishart.

Castles, S. and M. Miller (eds.) (1998). *The Age of Migration: International Population Movements in the Modern World*. London: Macmillan.

Cesarani, D. and M. Fulbrook (eds.) (1996). *Citizenship, Nationality and Migration in Europe*. London: Routledge.

Chambers, I. (1994). *migrancy, culture, identity*. London: Routledge.

De León, J. (2015). *The Land of Open Graves: Living and Dying on the Migrant trail*, Oakland: University of California.

Dorling, D. and D. Fairbairn (1997). *Mapping: Ways of Representing the World*. Harlow: Pearson.

Eco, U. (2013). *Inventing the Enemy: essays on everything*. London: Vintage.

Evans, J. and H. Ringrow (2017). 'Introduction: Borders in Translation and Intercultural Communication'. *TranscUlturAl*, 9.2, 1-12. http://ejournals.library.ualberta.ca/index.php/TC

Foucault, M. (1980). *Language, Counter-memory, Practice: Selected Essays and Interviews*. New York: Cornell University Press

Frank, S. (2008). *Migration and Literature: Günter Grass, Milan Kundera, Salman Rushdie, and Jan Kjærstad*. New York: Palgrave Macmillan US.

Garfield, S. (2012). *On the Map: Why the World Looks the Way it Does*. London: Profile Books.

Godlewska, A. M. C. (1999) *Geography Unbound*. Chicago: University of Chicago Press.

Greussing, E. and H. G. Boomgaarden (2017). 'Shifting the refugee narrative? An automated frame analysis of Europe's 2015 refugee crisis'. *Journal of Ethnic and Migration Studies*, 43(11): 1749-1774. doi: https://doi.org/10.1080/1369183X.2017.1282813

Halbwachs, M. (1992). *On Collective Memory*. Chicago: The University of Chicago Press.

Harmon, K. A. (2004) *You are here: personal geographies and other maps of the imagination*. New York: Princeton Architectural Press.

Harley, J. B. (2002). *The New Nature of Maps: Essays in the History of Cartography*. London: The John Hopkins University Press.

Hawley, J. C. (ed.) (1996). *Cross Addressing: Resistance Literature and Cultural Borders*. New York: State University of New York Press.

Herrera, Y. (2015). *Signs Preceding the End of the World*. London: & Other Stories.

Hobsbawm, E. and R. Terence (eds.) (1992) *The Invention of Tradition*, Cambridge: CUP.

Humble, A. T. (2014). The rise of trapped populations. *Forced Migration Review*, (45): 56-57.

Jones, R. (2017). Violent Borders: Refugees and the Right to Move. London: Verso.

King, R., J. Connell and P. White (eds.) (1995). *Writing across Worlds: literature and migration*. London: Routledge.

Kryza, F. T. (2006). *The Race for Timbuktu: In Search of Africa's City of Gold*. New York: Harper Collins.

Lagji A. (2018). Waiting in motion: mapping postcolonial fiction, new mobilities, and migration through Mohsin Hamid's ExitWest, *Mobilities*, 14 (2): 218-232. doi: https://doi.org/10.1080/17450101.2018.1533684

Laurel, J. T. Á. (2017). *The Gurugu Pledge*. London: & Other Stories.

Law, Jane M. (2006). Introduction: Cultural Memory, the Past and the Static of the Present. *Acta Orientalia Vilnensia*, 7 (1-2) 7-12 doi: 10.15388/AOV.2006.3770

Mardorossian, C. M. (2002). 'From Literature of Exile to Migrant Literature'. *Modern Language Studies*, 32 (2) 15-33. doi: 10.2307/3252040

Matar, Di. (2017). 'Media Coverage of the Migration Crisis in Europe: a Confused and Polarized Narrative'. In VA, *IEMed Mediterranean Yearbook 2017* (Barcelona: IEMed, 2017) 292-295.

Moorhead, C. (2006). *Human Cargo: A Journey Among Refugees*. London: Vintage.

Moore, Kerry (2015). The Meaning of Migration. *JOMEC Journal*, (7): p. None. doi: http://dx.doi.org/10.18573/j.2015.10001

Moretti, F. (1999). *Atlas of the European Novel 1800-1900*. London: Verso.

Papastergiadis, N. (2000). *The Turbulence of Migration*. Cambridge: Polity Press.

Perec, G. (1997). *Species of Spaces and Other Pieces*. London: Penguin.

Pecoud, A. and P. de Guchteneire (eds.) (2007). *Migration Without Borders: Essays On The Free Movement Of People*. Paris: UNESCO Publishing/Berghahn Books.

Phillips, C. (2001). *A New World Order*. London: Random House.

Piper, K. (2002). *Cartographic Fictions: Maps, Race, and Identity*. London: Rutgers University Press.

Relano, F. (2002). *The Shaping of Africa.* Aldershot: Ashgate Publishing Ltd.

Rushdie, S. (1991). *Imaginary Homelands: Essays and Criticism 1981 – 1991.* London: Penguin.

Sheller, M. (2018). *Mobility Justice: The Politics of Movement in an Age of Extremes.* London: Verso.

Sibley, D. (1995). *Geographies of Exclusion.* London: Routledge.

Soyinka, W. (2004). *The Climate of Fear: The Reith Lectures 2004.* London: Profile Books.

Turchi, P. (2004). *Maps of the Imagination: writer as cartographer.* San Antonio: Trinity University Press.

Walford Davies, D. (2012). *Cartographies of Culture: New Geographies of Welsh Writing in English.* Cardiff: University of Wales Press.

Welchman, J. C. (ed.) (1996). *Rethinking Borders.* London: Macmillan.

Wood, D. (1992). *The Power of Maps.* London: The Guilford Press.

Woods, A. (2000). *The Map is not the Territory.* Manchester: MUP

Volpicelli, S. (2015). *Who's Afraid of ... Migration? A New European Narrative of Migration. IAI Working Papers 15/32.* Rome: Istituto Affari Internazionali. doi: 978-88-98650-56-9

Statelessness and the Tensions between Open Borders and the Claims of Community

Nicoletta Policek

Introduction

Statelessness is to have no place to call home — to be unwanted and to lose a community, it is what Arendt (1958) calls superfluousness and it is tied to isolation, loneliness and uprootedness. To be stateless is to be deprived of human freedom and from rights that come with nationality. States determine who can obtain nationality and under what circumstances this is possible in their national laws (Brown, 2010). Usually, when children are born, they receive nationality either based on the place of birth (*jus soli*) or on the nationality of the parents (*jus sanguinis*) or on a combination of the two (Bloom et al., 2017). In some circumstances, a conflict between different nationality laws may mean that a child fails to obtain any nationality, therefore ending up stateless (Cody & Plan International, 2009). An, admittedly oversimplified, example is that of a child who is born to parents with a *jus soli*-nationality, but on the territory of a *jus sanguinis* state. In that case the state of birth will presume that the child obtains the nationality of the parents, but the parents cannot pass on their nationality because their state's legal system does not foresee this (Policek, 2016).

The right to a nationality is preserved in numerous international declarations and conventions other than the 1948 Universal Declaration of Human Rights (Gibney, 2014). In particular, the 1954 Convention relating to the Status of Stateless Persons defines a stateless person as "a person who is not considered as a national by any State under the operation of its law." Furthermore, the 1961 Convention on the Reduction of Statelessness deals specifically with statelessness. There exists a list of other workable legal instruments such as the 1957 Convention on the Nationality of Married Women, the 1963 International Convention on the Elimination of All Forms of Racial Discrimination and the 1966 International Covenant on Civil and Political Rights. Statelessness is also considered in the 1979 Convention on the Elimination of All Forms of Discrimination against Women, the 1989 Convention on the Rights of the Child, the 2003 International Convention on the Protection of the Rights of All Migrant Workers and Members of Their Families and the 2006 Convention on the Rights of Persons with Disabilities (van Waas & De Chickera, 2017). Nevertheless, these international instruments are not enforceable and their implementation is far from uniform around the globe. International human rights law provides that the right of states to decide who their nationals are is not absolute and, in particular, states must comply with their human rights obligations concerning the granting and loss of nationality. While they are complemented by regional treaty standards and international human rights law, the two statelessness conventions are the only global conventions of their kind (Southwick & Lynch, 2009).

The discussion that follows pieces together the essence of longing for a border as experienced by stateless children. Expressed in the dichotomy between the possible desire and necessity of having borders and the acknowledgment that for many stateless children to have borders means to enhance opportunities to be marginalised and often criminalised (Policek, 2016), this entry provides an overview of statelessness whilst simultaneously considering individuals' needs and desires to have borders. Key hurdles associated with statelessness as experienced by children can be encapsulated in having no access to health care and in the lack of social and legal protection. Children are particularly vulnerable to negative sequelae of statelessness (van Waas & De Chickera, 2017): they cannot benefit from education (Policek, 2016), which in turn is translated into poor employment prospects, labour rights violations and ultimately poverty. Not having a national identity, makes children subjected to social stigma and discrimination. They are also vulnerable to trafficking, harassment, and violence (Policek, 2019). Stateless children, through no fault of their own, inherit circumstances that limit their potential and provide, at best, an uncertain future. They are born, live and, unless they can resolve their situation, die as almost invisible people (Policek, 2016).

Subsequently, the focus is on the ways that borders are experienced, and experienced differently, for different people (Balibar, 2002), stateless children in particular. The concluding segment of this contribution evidences the aspiration to claim citizenship and community for those who would be otherwise considered a redundant surplus (Mizruchi, 1983) and their plea to having margins without living at the margin.

Being Stateless

Under international law, a stateless person is someone who is not considered as a national by any state under the operation of its law (Weissbrodt & Collins, 2006). Nationality, in this context, refers to a particular type of legal bond between an individual and a state. It is a type of formal membership that results in rights and duties on both sides. The individual, for instance, holds the right to reside in the territory and the state bears a corresponding duty of admission: the individual holds a duty of allegiance (which may include a duty to perform military and/or national service) and the state the right to exercise diplomatic protection on behalf of its nationals abroad (Aird et al., 2002). Where a person lacks any nationality, he or she does not enjoy the attached rights or duties, resulting in a lack of protection. A stateless person is seen and treated as a foreigner everywhere, as a national nowhere. Each state sets the conditions for acquisition and loss of its nationality—an act which is an expression of self-determination and a legitimate exercise of sovereignty—within the limits set by international law (including in relation to the avoidance of statelessness) (Ball et al., 2017). Whether an individual is considered to be a national by a particular state will therefore depend on that state's domestic nationality law, including how the rules are interpreted and applied in practice (Bhabha, 2011). A person is left stateless either where he or she has failed to acquire any nationality to begin with (i.e. at birth), or where he or she has lost or been deprived of a nationality that was once held, without acquiring another. For the purposes of determining whether a person is stateless in accordance with international law, it is not relevant how or when he or she came to be without a nationality, only whether a nationality is held at the time the assessment is being made (Blitz, 2011).

Statelessness is mostly perceived as a mere technical legal issue (Doná & Veale, 2011), thus neglecting the devastating consequences to individuals, in particular children, who have no rights that naturally come with nationality. Even quantifying statelessness is a problematical task, because embedded in the definition of statelessness is the notion that a stateless person is not considered as a national under the operation of its law. This has been authoritatively interpreted as being both a question of fact and law. Consequently, there are individuals who would legally be eligible for a particular nationality, who are nonetheless not considered as nationals by the state, and whose statelessness is consequently hidden (Bhabha, 2009; 2011). Furthermore, often states may give insufficient priority to the implementation of measures to identify statelessness or accurately quantify it. Sometimes, there is even a deliberate strategy to deny the prevalence of statelessness by asserting that such persons are nationals of another country (Blitz, 2011). Even where data on statelessness can be collected, this does not always harvest comprehensive or reliable results, due to an incorrect interpretation of the definition (Bloom et al., 2017). Often, some such exercises have been limited in their scope, focusing only on one ethnic group (Chen, 2009) or geographical area of a country (Chatty & Mansour, 2011) and do not therefore produce a complete picture. To add to the complexity of collecting data on statelessness, many stateless persons do not see themselves as being stateless (Cody & Plan International, 2009). Even if they do, there is often reluctance to draw attention to this and therefore, data collection which relies on self-identification is not entirely accurate. Undocumented persons and those who are of undetermined nationality may be at risk of statelessness and indeed, some of them are likely to already be stateless (ENS, 2015). However, when such persons are in their own countries, they will almost always receive greater protection if confirmed to be nationals and consequently the stateless label can be counterproductive. Nevertheless, even in such situations, where the denial of documentation is long-lasting (even intergenerational), there would come a point when it is better to acknowledge such persons as stateless (Aird et al., 2002).

Not all countries in the world are able to report data on statelessness. Figures for different countries are compiled from different data sets—that use different methodologies—and do not always reveal the full picture. The data collated by the United Nations High Commissioner for Refugees (UNHCR) is drawn from information produced by different actors, in different places, using different approaches—not all of which deliver the same level of reliability or produce readily-comparable data (ENS, 2015). Only persons exclusively under UNHCR's statelessness protection mandate are reported in its statelessness statistics: UNHCR's statistical reporting on statelessness excludes stateless persons who also fall within the protection mandates of other UN Agencies (at present, only the UN Relief and Works Agency—UNRWA), and those who also come under other UNHCR protection mandates (such as refugees or asylum seekers).

The identification of stateless persons and the collation of statistical information on statelessness, is relevant not only to assess states' compliance with the statelessness treaties, but also with the more widely ratified human rights treaties. It is important to point out that in finding a person to be stateless, it is not relevant where in the world that person is. A child can be stateless in the country in which he or she was born, has always lived and has all family ties (Policek, 2016). Equally, a child can be stateless in a migratory context—for instance, losing nationality prior to, as a consequence of or at some point after crossing an international border (Blitz & Lynch, 2011). Statelessness rests on the fact of lacking any nationality, nothing more. Most stateless children have not moved from their homes and live in what can be described as their own country. Yet, due to the added vulnerability of stateless persons to discrimination, human rights abuse and even persecution, statelessness can also prompt forced displacement. Some stateless children, then, become internally displaced persons (IDPs), asylum seekers and refugees. Where a person who is not considered as a national by any state under the operation of its law also falls within the scope of the 1951 UN Convention relating to the Status of Refugees, he or she is a stateless refugee. That someone can simultaneously be both stateless and a refugee, asylum seeker or IDP does not lessen their experience of statelessness, which should be taken into consideration when protecting and finding durable solutions for them.

With regard to the identification of stateless children, for the purposes of statistical reporting or otherwise, it is also important to note the distinction between statelessness and the situation of being undocumented, of undetermined nationality and/or at risk of statelessness. Universal birth registration and the provision of other life documents remains a significant challenge in many parts of the world (Cai, 2013). The lack of such documentation can mean that the child is stateless (e.g. where denied documentation because the state does not consider the person to be a national), but more often, such lack of documentation does not mean a lack of nationality, despite it being a significant barrier to proving nationality (De Genova, 2013). Indeed, children without documentation are at heightened risk of statelessness when compared with those who do have adequate documents, and some may become stateless in the future (e.g. where unable to establish or prove links to the state of nationality such that this state no longer considers the person as a national) (Goris et al., 2009).

In some countries, there is no commonly held definitive proof of nationality, therefore evidence of statelessness may be built up over multiple rejections for documentation by the state (refusal to register to vote, refusal of ID card, refusal of passport, for example) (Hayter, 2000). When dealing with children, it is appropriate to question if identifying them as stateless would serve any protection purpose. The starting point must be to push for them to be recognised as nationals by the country to which they have the strongest links (High, 2013). This would often require scrutiny and assessment of nationality laws and policies, their implementation and the documentation that confirms nationality. If children of undetermined nationality and/or at risk of statelessness are ultimately recognised as nationals of a particular country, without ever being deemed to be stateless, this would be the ideal outcome (Manby, 2012). However, the question of how long their status is to remain undetermined, before concluding that they are actually stateless is a difficult one, to which international law does not seem to have a complete answer (Policek, 2016).

The grey area between statelessness and nationality highlights how it can be harmful to address the one without sensitivity to the impact on the other. There are a variety of circumstances that give rise to statelessness at birth or in later life, and there is often an element of discrimination and/or arbitrariness at play, when children or even entire groups become stateless (Milbrandt, 2011). Discrimination and arbitrariness can manifest itself in an obvious, aggressive and even persecutory manner, such as when large communities are deprived of their nationality based on ethnicity or religion (Southwick & Lynch, 2009); or it can be more subtle and latent, such as the failure of states to prioritise legal reform that would plug gaps in the law which could cause statelessness (Tucker, 2014). While states do have significant freedom to set out their own membership criteria, they also have a responsibility to protect against discrimination and arbitrariness, and to uphold international standards.

Unless safeguards are in place in the law to prevent statelessness from arising, the regular operation of these states' nationality laws can leave people stateless. While this may seem like an unlikely and marginal occurrence, the scale of international migration today is such that conflicts of nationality laws are becoming more commonplace, increasing the need for safeguards to ensure the avoidance of statelessness (ENS, 2015).

A specific context in which the risk of a conflict of nationality laws is high, and where a large number of persons may simultaneously be affected, is that of state succession (Aird et al., 2002). When part of a state secedes and becomes independent, or when a state dissolves into multiple new states, the question emerges as to what happens to the nationality of the persons affected (Ball et al., 2017). The new nationality laws of successor states may conflict and leave people without any nationality, while the re-definition of who is a national of the original state (where it continues to exist) may also render people stateless. Most often in the context of state succession, it is vulnerable minorities who are associated with either the successor or parent state who are deprived of nationality, exposing the discriminatory motivations and arbitrary nature for such exclusion. Common types of state succession which have resulted in large-scale statelessness are the dissolution of federal states into independent republics (for instance, in the countries of the former Soviet Union and Yugoslavia) (Aird et al., 2002; Shulze, 2017)) and the more recent cases of state secession (for instance, with the splitting off of Eritrea from Ethiopia and South Sudan from Sudan) (Twomey, 2012). Situations of emerging or contested statehood complicate this picture further, leading to unique challenges around nationality and statelessness, for instance, for the Palestinians and the Sahrawi (Smith, 1986).

Many of the large scale and entrenched situations of statelessness in the world were born out of the experiences of colonisation, de-colonisation and consequent nation-building (Spivak, 1999) where borders were erected for a reason: they place people on the "outside" (Torpey, 2000). In such contexts, newly independent states (many of which never had a common pre-colonial national identity) have had to deal with borders arbitrarily drawn (often dividing ethnic groups) peoples forcibly migrated (for labour) and the consequences of decades, sometimes centuries of colonial rule which successfully opposed different ethnic and religious groups against each other, privileging some and marginalising others, as part of a wider divide and rule policy (Garelli & Tazzioli, 2013). It is not surprising that many newly independent states thus struggled with nation building, national identity and the treatment of minorities. For them, borders are a reminder of their colonial past. While colonial history does not justify in any way discrimination, arbitrariness and disenfranchisement, this historical context must be understood and addressed in order to reduce statelessness.

Large-scale statelessness can also be caused by the arbitrary deprivation of nationality outside the context of state succession (Doná & Veale, 2011). Arbitrary acts can involve the collective withdrawal or denial of nationality to a whole population group, commonly singled out in a discriminatory manner on the basis of characteristics such as ethnicity, language or religion, but it can also impact individuals who are deprived of their nationality on arbitrary and discriminatory grounds. In many cases, the group concerned forms a minority in the country in which they live (Goris et al., 2009). Sometimes they are perceived as having ties to another state, where they perhaps share common characteristics or even ancestral roots with a part of the state's population, such as in the case of the Rohingya in Myanmar (van Waas and De Chickera, 2017) and persons of Haitian descent in the Dominican Republic (Walters, 2010). In other instances, the state uses the manipulation of nationality policy as a means of asserting or constructing a particular national identity to the exclusion of those who do not fit the mould, such as in the case of the Kurds in Syria in the 1960s (Bhabha, 2011) and the black population in Mauritania in the 1980s (Blitz, 2011). Nationality law may also be designed to restrict the access of certain groups to economic power, especially the right to own property, such as in Liberia or Sierra Leone, where only those who are of African descent may be citizens from birth (Bloom et al., 2017). In some instances, individuals or groups are targeted for their political beliefs, since nationality is the gateway to political rights and its withdrawal can be a means of silencing political opponents. Deprivation of nationality on security grounds can also be arbitrary if certain criteria—including due process standards—are not met. Other forms of discrimination in nationality policy can also create, perpetuate or prolong problems of statelessness (McInerney, 2014). For instance, where a woman does not enjoy the same right to transmit nationality to her child as a man, children are put at heightened risk of statelessness (Policek, 2016). A stateless, absent or unknown father, or one who cannot or does not want to take any steps that might be required to confer his nationality to the child, can spell statelessness because the mother is powerless to pass on her nationality. This form of gender discrimination is still present in more than 25 countries around the world and many more laws contain other elements of discrimination against women—or sometimes men—in the change, retention or transmission of nationality (Milbrandt, 2011).

The sole prime cause of statelessness globally in any given year—in the absence of large-scale situations stemming from one of the above problems—is the inheritance of statelessness (Bhabha, 2011). Many contemporary situations of statelessness have their roots at a particular moment in history, such as state succession, the first registration of citizens or the adoption of a discriminatory nationality decree stripping a whole group of nationality, as outlined above. Yet these situations endure and even grow over time because the states concerned have not put any measures in place to stop statelessness being passed from parent to child—or do not implement existing measures to that effect. Furthermore, these situations migrate to new countries along with the (often forced) migration of stateless persons abroad, as in migratory contexts too, statelessness is allowed to continue into the next generations (Rigo, 2005). This means that most new cases of statelessness affect children, from birth, such that they may never know the protection of nationality. It also means that stateless groups suffer from intergenerational marginalisation and exclusion, which affects the social fabric of entire communities always longing to have borders.

Longing to Have Borders

Borders are not only spatial locations, but are also social, political and economic expressions of belonging and exclusion (Vaughan-Williams, 2012). They are more than just a line, a divide, a single and static territorial location. Rather than treating the concept of the border as a territorially fixed, therefore, the border encompasses a series of practices. Such "reading" entails a more political and actor-oriented stance on how divisions between entities appear or are produced and sustained. The shift in focus also brings a sense of the dynamism of borders and bordering practices, for both are increasingly mobile—just as are the goods, services and people that they seek to control (Varsanyi, 2008). van Houtum & Strüver (2002) draw attention to the ways that borders are performed into being and describe this as a shift toward considering the human practices that constitute and represent differences in space. They add that this can be thought of as a shift toward understanding the border as a verb in the sense of "bordering". Vaughan-Williams (2012) echoes this analysis, arguing that it is crucial to consider the schisms that are produced by borders and to treat borders as active structures that rely on practices of bordering. To think of the border as a verb is to think of it as something that must be done in order to come into being, and that does not exist as a noun without this active, processual, doing of the border. Borders become not spaces marked on a map, or onto territory, but instead actions that must be performed by human beings in relation to one another (Brown, 2010).

The shift toward thinking about how human practices construct borders, and about the processes that enact borders, marks a shift in the conception of borders that also makes it necessary to pay attention to the question of where borders are, but also what they are and what they do. Subsequently, this points to the need to articulate not to take for granted the concept of the border, but instead to ask what sort of concept it is. What sort of logic does a border both follow and impose? The question of what a border is, is not assumed to have a single ontological answer, but instead one that cannot be resolved without asking what borders do. Balibar (2002) addresses this interrogation with a caution: the question is absurd as he claims that a border has no essence. He explains that a border is different in each instance and in every experience of border-crossing, that to cross one border is not the same as to cross another, and that to cross with one passport is not the same as to cross with another (Balibar, 2004). With reference to the discussion proposed in this contribution, crossing a border without a passport, is even more complex for stateless children who are seeking to have borders in order to claim protection under nationality laws. This singularity of the border, or rather its differential existence, makes it nearly impossible to define the border, since there is no definition which would be capable of holding together these differences. To this caution, Balibar (2002) adds another warning: a border is the thing that defines a territory. It marks the limit of a territory; it defines the interior and exterior of a nation-state and in doing this, it inscribes identity.

Any act of definition inevitably involves the tracing of a boundary and therefore the construction of a border. The definition of the border forms a recursive loop. To construct a border is to define, and to define is to construct a border. For this reason, any theory seeking to pin a definition to the border is at risk of going around and around in circles, identifying borders by constructing still more borders. However, to think of a border as that which defines is, of course, already to give a sort of definition, and to enter into the recursive cycle of borders. Therefore, the caution reads as at least partly disingenuous. Taking a cue from Balibar's (2002) caution, it could be claimed that to ask what a border is denotes a problem because the borders of different nation-states are different at different moments of history and in relation to different people, stateless children in particular. For such reasons, a universalizing ontology of borders *per se* is unfeasible. Furthermore, attempts to answer such questions would unavoidably construct a border. In this way, to answer the question is to reduce the complexity of the experiences of borders and would also participate in constructing borders (Balibar, 2002). Instead of working from a definition, a suggestion could be to look at what borders do and at what particular borders do at particular historical moments. To paraphrase Balibar (2002), it is possible to refer to what he calls the "equivocal character" of borders. Here the term "equivocal" gives not only the sense of a border as not being quite what it appears or claims to be, but also the sense of multiple voices and multiple meanings—of more than one possible existence of a border (see also De Genova, 2013). This equivocal character of the border is both a border's multiplicity and its duplicity. Even as a border might appear as a simple, singular phenomenon, this is an illusion. A border is not what it seems, and it is not to be trusted. The word "equivocal" also contains within it the notion of divergent voices ("equi-vocal"). If a border deceives, it does so through the presence of many voices and many experiences, all singular and all different.

A border has many identities and many realities—those who live within the confinement of a border and those who long to have a border, as stateless children often do, experience a border differently. Borders therefore can be described as polysemic, meaning that borders do not have the same meaning for everyone, and indeed this differential meaning is essential to the function of the border. Borders are, nonetheless, sites of administrative control (De Genova et al., 2014). The selective controls that filter populations and control the movement of people are the function of the border (Anzaldúa, 1999). These controls are always concentrated along a geographic line that marks the territorial limit of the nation-state. However, these sites of administrative control have been dispersed throughout social space and, therefore, some borders are no longer situated at the borders at all, in the geographical, political and administrative sense of the term. They are in fact elsewhere, wherever selective controls are to be found specifically (Policek et al. 2020) where the rhetoric of danger is too often associated with the status of being a foreigner.

In another formulation of the same idea, borders become dislocated if not ubiquitous as they are replicated by other "checkpoints" within the territories of the state (Doty, 2011). Understanding the border as the site where selective controls are enacted provides an incredibly dynamic and flexible view of the border. If borders exist where they are enacted, then they can not only be in many different spaces, mapped and unmapped, but they can also move, appear and disappear (Hayter, 2000). Inevitably, this also means that as these practices of control take place throughout national space, the border also moves from a liminal geographic space to something that is enacted and experienced throughout national space. While there are the recognizable infrastructures of control (airport border control, for example, is often explicitly labelled as the border, despite being located internally within the nation), it also allows for a consideration of the less obvious sites where the border materializes. Borders can in fact become ubiquitous when they are thought of in relation to the enactment of control (van Houtum & Strüver, 2002).An example of borders appearing through their enactment is provided by the carrier sanctions administered by the United Kingdom's government that makes carriers liable for any undocumented persons they may transport to the country, even if these people are stowaways and the carrier was unaware of their presence on the vehicle (Chacon, 2009). Due to these liability laws, carriers seeking to avoid fines for transporting undocumented passengers have introduced measures to deter and police would-be migrants. In particular, lorries arriving to the United Kingdom from Europe more and more often have been built to be securely locked, their design impenetrable to would-be stowaways. The defensive construction of the lorries is accompanied by a compulsory methodical inspection of the carriage area by the driver. It could be argued that these sanctions move the border to the very surface of the lorries crossing international boundaries and that the border moves with these lorries. Thus, the entire road transportation system becomes a kind of networked border. The border transforms into a mobile, non-contiguous zone materializing at the very surface of the lorry and every place it stops. In this manner, the border comes into being (materialises) not only when the driver stops the lorry and inspects it, but also in the very materiality of the lorry that is designed to obstruct the migrant. In other words, there is a border wherever there is a measure taken to prevent migration, and it is a border that can appear and disappear through the performance of specific practices (Diener & Hagen, 2012).

Different Borders for Different People

The border is designed to give different people (those from different social classes) different experiences of the law and of freedom. Border law enables some to pass national frontiers, while denying others the same opportunity; it upholds the freedom of circulation of some, while depriving others of this same freedom (Varsanyi, 2008). Following from these differential experiences, Balibar (2002) highlights how the function of the border is vigorously to differentiate between individuals in terms of social class. This is to say that the fundamental function of the border is to distinguish between people and to produce differential social placements and experiences. For the rich person from the rich country, the border becomes a symbolic reaffirmation of a surplus of rights, while for a poor person from a poor country the border is a solid barrier, one which is confronted as an obstacle and which repeatedly emerges as it marks the limits of life. For this latter figure, the border becomes omnipresent, indeed becomes the place where the migrant resides (Willen, 2010). Therefore, it could be argued, the role of the border is fundamentally to differentiate people from one another. That is, borders must be understood not only as enacting distinction, but as actively administering and producing difference. Their function is not only to separate the rich from the poor, the internationally mobile from the nationally confined, but to construct and enact the categories used to distinguish one person from the next, and then to grant passage and mobility and all of their attendant privileges to some, while denying them to others.

Borders therefore can become instruments of differentiation: this differentiation is always in the service of capital, and indeed the distinction is between those who circulate capital and those who are circulated by capital. Here Balibar's (2002) contribution allows the opportunity to discuss borders by acknowledging a clearly articulated rationale for a shift away from thinking in terms of stable sites, as well as a defense the beginning of an articulation of what borders do that draws attention to this doing. He locates the implementation of the border as the site of the border: it exists where it is done. As a consequence, borders as operations of power become visible as different for different people (different people are done differently by the border), as implicated in instituting and producing difference, and as not situated at stable and delimited sites. Balibar (2002) encourages a shift toward thinking of borders in terms of existing where they are done, and as most importantly about practices and encounters with these practices.

Addressing the experience of being stateless, especially with reference to children, the shift in border practices leads to more diffuse internal policing and the externalization of border controls consequently defines border(s) in terms of "deterritorialization" (Andrijasevic, 2010). The deterritorialization of borders refers to the ways that borders increasingly and in a variety of ways operate at both sites that are geographically external to the nations that are represented by them, and within the internal space marked by the border. Seeing the border as one that has been "deterritorialized" is a way to look at the dislocation of controls once enacted at national border posts and now exercised in a spatially disaggregated way and via a variety of means (Andrijasevic, 2010). These means specifically including the functions that have been externalized to host countries, as well as other policing measures that are carried out internally, such as identity controls carried out by police and carrier liability legislation that makes transportation companies accountable for the people they transport (Andrijasevic, 2010). In addition to pointing to both international and external practices of bordering, speaking in terms of a deterritorialized border instead of an externalized border has the advantage of not repeating the presumption of a neat inside/outside division between national spaces. Borders for individuals who are stateless emerge from this discussion in a new form and are captured via new metaphors. Instead of being linear structures firmly located at the edges of territory, the borders of a nation can be depicted as "mobile and dispersed" (Rumford, 2012, p.159), "discontinuous and porous" (Andrijasevic, 2010, p.155), "networked" (Walters, 2006, p.195), "ephemeral and/or palpable" (Vaughan-Williams, 2012, p.583), and biopolitical (Vaughan-Williams, 2012). What these accounts have in common is that they shift from considering the border in its most obvious space—where it is resolutely, structurally instituted at the limits of a national territory—toward thinking of the border as the site where the control function of the border is performed.

The right to a nationality implies the right of each individual to acquire change and retain a nationality. The right to a nationality remains a fundamental human right as afforded by article 15 of the 1948 Universal Declaration of Human Rights (UDHR) providing that "[e]veryone has the right to a nationality" and that "[n]o one shall be arbitrarily deprived of his nationality nor denied the right to change his nationality." In this way, article 15, enshrining citizenship and the right to be free from arbitrary deprivation of citizenship as human rights in and of themselves, establishes the bedrock legal relationship between individuals and states. While all states are bound to respect the human rights of all individuals without distinction, an individual's legal bond to a particular state through citizenship (Wastl-Walter, 2011; see also Weiss Brodt & Collins, 2006) is in practice an essential prerequisite to the enjoyment and protection of the full range of human rights. The proliferation of human rights norms in international and regional instruments has fostered substantive limitations on state sovereignty over citizenship regulation that gives meaning to that provision. In particular, the universal anti-discrimination norm and the principle that statelessness should be avoided have emerged to constrain state discretion on citizenship (Salter, 2008; 2010).

Some significant gaps in the international legal framework on nationality persist considering, for instance, that few normative principles prescribe conditions for granting citizenship (Salter, 2012). Furthermore, there is a lack of consensus on what constitutes statelessness arising from ineffective citizenship which in turn perpetuate the experience of different borders for different people. While human rights developments over the years have made great strides in giving content and meaning to article 15 of the UDHR, further normative and practical developments remain essential to fulfil the valuable promise of that provision. Because states have the sovereign right to determine the procedures and conditions for acquisition and loss of citizenship, statelessness and disputed nationality must ultimately be resolved by governments so that borders mean exactly the same of all citizens (Popescu, 2012).

The right to retain a nationality corresponds to the prohibition of arbitrary deprivation of nationality (Rigo, 2005). Arbitrary deprivation of nationality, therefore, effectively places the affected persons in a more disadvantaged situation concerning the enjoyment of their human rights because some of these rights may be subjected to lawful limitations that otherwise would not apply (Ramalo, 2011), but also because these persons are placed in a situation of increased vulnerability to human rights violations (Reed, 2006).

Having Margins without Living at the Margin

The notion of control at the border relies on a presumption of a precise separation between internal territory and the external borders of the space (Paasi, 2011). This conception reproduces an inside/outside dichotomy which reinforces the challenges faced by stateless individuals almost suspended between the need to belong to a community and the acknowledgment that belonging entails a legal and emotional shift to their status.

Longing to belong and have borders is an aspiration rather than a choice. Mizruchi (1983) argues that societies create abeyance structures to regulate the impact of surplus populations in the city by holding potentially dissident, marginal people under surveillance in control situations, until status vacancies open elsewhere. Stateless people are treated as a surplus population, despite their claim to community and entitlement to citizenship. Many stateless people are eligible for a residence permit on different grounds other than statelessness, and they are often not aware of the existing procedure for the recognition of the stateless status (Nguyen & Sperfeldt, 2012). Even though those people may have a regular permit of stay, they face difficulties due to their lack of nationality at the moment they have to enjoy some specific rights, such as the right to marry. For those people, as well as for the organizations they get in touch with (for instance, NGOs, hospitals, National Registrar), many problems could be solved through campaigns spreading information on statelessness (Gibney, 2014). Stateless people could also find themselves in need of applying for refugee status or a form of subsidiary protection (George, 2013). Even in case they are recognised as having the right to refugee status or subsidiary protection, they can however be prevented from fully enjoying the exercise of their rights because of their lack of nationality. Moreover, many of the people entitled to refugee status or a form of subsidiary protection, albeit being stateless, are not aware of the procedure for accessing the relevant legislations which could offer protection (Howard, 2017). Different routes are, in fact, set out in order to reduce and to prevent childhood statelessness. The Human Right Council has addressed the enjoyment of the right to a nationality and the avoidance of statelessness in several resolutions on "Human rights and arbitrary deprivation of nationality": in particular, Resolution 7/10 (2008), Resolution 10/13 (2009), Resolution 13/2 (2010), Resolution 20/4 on the Right to a Nationality: Women and Children (2012), Resolution 20/5 (2012) and Resolution 26/14 (2014). Mostly, statelessness may be the result of factors such as political change (McInerney, 2014), expulsion of people from a territory (Ihrda, 2011), discrimination, nationality based solely on descent, and laws regulating marriage and birth registration (Milbrandt, 2011).

Conclusion

Borders are artefacts of dominant processes (Hayes, 2012) that have led to the fencing off of portions of territory and people from one another, but they are also an aspiration for individuals who are stateless. Longing to have borders for those who are stateless means claiming community through citizenship and nationality rights. Securing rights however, is not a straightforward and linear endeavour as legal loopholes in the current available legislation make it problematic if not impossible for stateless children to claim the legal safety that comes with having borders. Having borders for children who are stateless means access to education, housing and health care and legal protection from state and interpersonal violence (Policek, 2019). Borders, nonetheless, as this contribution has contended, are not simply practical phenomena that can be taken as given. They are complex human creations that are perpetually open to question. At an extreme, perhaps, existing borders are the result of processes in the past that are either no longer operative (Manby, 2012) or are increasingly eclipsed by transnational or global pressures (Li et al., 2010). In other words, borders are increasingly redundant, and thinking constrained by them restricts thinking about alternative political, social, and economic possibilities. It is paramount to change the way in which nation states think about borders to openly acknowledge their equivocal character (De Genova et al., 2014). In other words, a border should be seen not as that which is either fixed or as such must be overcome, but as an evolving creation that has both merits and problems that must be constantly reconsidered (Anderson & O'Dowd, 1999). Consequently, the reaction to what borders do should always be related to the overriding ethical concern that they serve and not undermine human dignity and what it is commonly understood as the right to a decent life embedded in the aspiration to belong to a community (Blitz & Lynch, 2011). From this standpoint, rather than reflecting an unambiguous sovereignty that ends/begins at a border or that must be overcome as such, border thinking should open up to consider territorial spaces as dwelling rather than national spaces (Brown, 2010). In this way, statelessness and the tensions between open borders and the claims of community can be fully addressed. Furthermore, political responsibility for pursuit of a decent life as extending beyond the borders of any particular state should be unquestionably granted to all human beings, irrespectively whether they have a state to call their own or they are stateless. Borders do matter both because they have real effects on individuals and their communities and because they trap thinking about and acting in the world in territorial terms (Anzaldúa, 1999).

When claiming community and borders for stateless children, the most common pathway is that a child's birth is not registered in the country in which the child was born; that is, although the child may be entitled to citizenship, an official birth record has not yet been obtained (Allerton, 2014). Birth registration provides official evidence of a state's recognition of a child's existence within a country and as a member of a nation-state. It is the first and often the definitive step to citizenship and entitlements such as public education, health, and other state services (Ensor and Godziak, 2010). Often another scenario, pertinent to undocumented labour migration, is that a child is born in one country and travels without documentation across international borders to live in another country (ENS, 2015). Regardless of whether the child's birth was registered in the country of birth, they lack citizenship rights in the country in which they now reside: they have become functionally stateless (Bhabha, 2011). This appears to be a common scenario for children who travel independently or who are trafficked, and for children of mothers and fathers who migrate across borders without documentation, and who often remain—with or without their parents—in the host country for a number of years (van Waas& De Chickera, 2017), rendering them functionally stateless.

As highlighted in this contribution, key hurdles associated with statelessness as experienced by children can be encapsulated in having no access to health care and in the lack of social and legal protection (Aird et al., 2002). Children are particularly vulnerable to negative sequelae of statelessness (Bokhari, 2008) because they cannot benefit from education, which in turn is translated into poor employment prospects, labour rights violations and ultimately poverty (Doná & Veale, 2011). Not having a national identity, makes children subjected to social stigma and discrimination. They are also vulnerable to trafficking, harassment, and violence (Policek, 2019).

In contexts of transnational labour migration, circumstances that have an effect on birth registration are mostly muddled by parents' mobility within and between countries (Salter, 2010). Figures can only be estimated (Gibney, 2014) and, with ENS (2015) assessing that three percent of the world's population are involved in documented transnational migration, some scholars (Sharma, 2006; Stumpf, 2006; Walters, 2010) put forward an estimated comparable scale of undocumented transnational migration.

Discussing statelessness and the need to have borders requires abandoning the either/or approach to borders that currently dominates most thinking about them. This approach does not redefine borders what borders "are" and "do", on the contrary, by considering borders and bordering as instances of the same process, it not only brings to the surface their ambivalences and repositioning, but also the inexorable materiality of their linear inscription.

For those who live at the margin, for the redundant surplus (Mizruchi, 1983), borders do not only regulate movements of things, money, and people, but they also restrain the exercise of intellect, imagination, and political will (Ahmed, 2014).

References

Ahmed, I., ed. (2010). *The Plight of the Stateless Rohingyas: Responses of the State, Society & the International Community.* University Press.

Ahmed, S. (2014). *The Cultural Politics of Emotion,* 2nd ed., Edinburgh: Edinburgh University Press.

Aird, S., Harnett, H., & Shah, P. (2002). *Stateless children: Youth who are without citizenship.* Youth Advocate Program International.

Allerton, C. (2014). "Statelessness and the Lives of the Children of Migrants in Sabah, East Malaysia", *Tilburg Law Review,* Volume 19, Issue 1-2.

Anderson, J., & O'Dowd, L. (1999). Borders, border regions and territoriality: Contradictory meanings, changing significance. *Regional Studies,* 33, 593–604.

Andrijasevic, R. (2010). 'From Exception to Excess: Detention and Deportations across the Mediterranean Space' in De Genova, N. and Peutz, N., eds., *The Deportation Regime: Sovereignty, Space and the Freedom of Movement,* Duke University Press, 147-165.

Anzaldúa, G. (1999). *Borderlands: La frontera: The New Mestiza,* 2 ed., San Francisco: Aunt Lute Books.

Arendt, H. (1958). *The Origins of Totalitarianism,* New York: Harcourt Brace Jovanovich.

Balibar, E. (2002). *Politics and the Other Scene,* London: Verso.

Balibar, E. (2004). *We, the People of Europe?: Reflections on Transnational Citizenship,* Translation/Transnation., English ed., Princeton, N.J.: Princeton University Press.

Ball, J., Butt, L., & Beazley, H. (2017). Birth registration and protection for children of transnational labor migrants in Indonesia. *Journal of Immigrant & Refugee Studies,* 15(3), 305-325.

Bhabha, J. (2009). Arendt's children: Do today's migrant children have a right to have rights?. *Human Rights Quarterly,* 31.2: 410-451.

Bhabha, J. (2011). *Children without a State: A Global Human Rights Challenge,* MA: The MIT Press.

Blitz, B. K. (2011). Neither seen nor heard: compound deprivation among stateless children. In: Bhahba, J., (ed.) *Children without a state: a global human rights challenge.* Cambridge, MA: The MIT Press, 43-66.

Blitz, B. K., & Lynch, M. (Eds.). (2011). *Statelessness and citizenship: A comparative study on the benefits of nationality.* Edward Elgar Publishing.

Bloom, T., Tonkiss, K., & Cole, P. (Eds.). (2017). *Understanding Statelessness.* London: Taylor & Francis.

Bokhari, F. (2008). Falling through the gaps: Safeguarding children trafficked into the UK. *Children & Society*, 22.3: 201-211.

Brown, W. (2010). *Walled States, Waning Sovereignty*, New York: Zone Books.

Cai, Y. (2013). "China's New Demographic Reality: Learning from the 2010 Census". Population and Development Review 39 (September), pages 371-396.

Chacon, J. M. (2009). 'Managing Migration Through Crime', *Columbia Law Review*, 109, 135-148.

Chatty, D., & Mansour, N. (2011). *Bedouin in Lebanon: Statelessness and Marginality*, Refugee Studies Centre, Winter Newsletter.

Chen, T. (2009). "Palestinian Refugees in Arab Countries and their Impacts", *Journal of Middle Eastern and Islamic Studies (in Asia)*, Vol. 3, No. 3.

Cody, C., & Plan-International. (2009). *Count every child: the right to birth registration*. Plan.

De Genova, N. (2013). 'Spectacles of migrant "illegality": The scene of exclusion, the obscene of inclusion', *Ethnic and Racial Studies*, 36(7), 1180-1198.

De Genova, N., Mezzadra, S., & Pickles, J. (2014). 'New Keywords: Migration and Borders', *Cultural Studies*, 1-33.

Diener, A. C., & Hagen, J. (2012). *Borders. A very short introduction*. Oxford and New York: Oxford University Press.

Doná, G., & Veale, A. (2011). Divergent discourses, children and forced migration. *Journal of Ethnic and Migration Studies*, 37.8: 1273-1289.

Doty, R. L. (2011). 'Bare Life: border-crossing deaths and spaces of moral alibi', *Environment and Planning D: Society and Space*, 29, 599-612.

ENS (2015). Ending Childhood Statelessness: A comparative study of safeguards to ensure the right to a nationality for children born in Europe, Working Paper 09/15.

Ensor, M. O., & Gozdziak, E. M., (Eds.). (2010). *Children and migration: At the crossroads of resiliency and vulnerability*. London: Palgrave Macmillan.

Garelli, G., & Tazzioli, M. (2013). "Challenging the discipline of migration: militant research in migration studies, an introduction", *Postcolonial Studies*, 16(3), 245-249.

George, J. (2013). *Statelessness and nationality in South Africa*, Lawyers for Human Rights.

Gibney, M. (2014). "Statelessness and Citizenship in Ethical and Political Perspective", A. Edwards and L. van Waas (eds.), *Nationality and Statelessness under International Law*, Cambridge University Press.

Goris, I., Harrington, J., & Kohn, S. (2009). Statelessness: what it is and why it matters. *Forced migration review*, 32.6: 4-6.

Hayes, P., ed. (2012). *The Making of Modern Immigration: An Encyclopedia of People and Ideas*, Santa Barbara, California: ABC-CLIO.

Hayter, T. (2000). *Open Borders: The Case Against Immigration Controls*, London: Pluto Press.

High, A. (2013). "China's Orphan Welfare System: Laws, Policies And Filled Gaps" *University of Pennsylvania East Asia Law Review* vol. 8, pages 127-176.

Howard, D. M. (2017). *Analyzing the causes of statelessness in Syrian refugee children*. Tex. Int'l LJ, 52, 281.

IHRDA, (June 2011). *3 ½ years later, Mauritanian refugees still await restoration of citizenship*, reparation.

Li, S., Zhang, Y., & Feldman, M. (2010). "Birth Registration in China: Practices, Problems and Policies", *Population Research and Policy Review*, Vol. 29 (3), pages 297-317.

Manby, B. (2012). *The Right to Nationality and the Secession of South Sudan: A Commentary on the Impact of the New Laws*, Open Society Foundations.

McInerney, C. (2014). "Accessing Malagasy Citizenship: The Nationality Code and Its Impact on the Karana", *Tilburg Law Review*, Vol.19.

Milbrandt, J. (2011). Stateless. *Cardozo J. Int'l & Comp. L.*, 20: 75.

Miller, M. (2012). *Ethnic and racial minorities in Asia. Inclusion or exclusion?* London: Routledge.

Mizruchi, E. H. (1983). *Regulating society: Marginality and social control in historical perspective*. New York: Free Press.

Nguyen, L., & Sperfeldt, C. (2012). *A boat without anchors – A report on the legal status of ethnic Vietnamese minority populations in Cambodia under domestic and international laws governing nationality and statelessness*, Jesuit Refugee Service.

Paasi, A. (2011). A border theory: An unattainable dream or a realistic aim for border scholars? In D. Wastl-Walter (Ed.), *The Ashgate Research companion to border studies* (pp. 11–32). Farnham: Ashgate.

Policek, N. (2016). Turning the Invisible into the Visible: Stateless Children in Italy. In Ensor, M. O. and Gozdziak, E. M. (Eds.), *Children and Forced Migration: Durable Solutions during Transient Years Studies in Childhood and Youth Series*. pp. 79-102. London: Palgrave Macmillan.

Policek, N. (2019). Identifiable challenges as global complexities: Globalisation, gender violence and statelessness. in Boskovic, M., *Globalization and Its Impact on Violence Against Vulnerable Groups*, IGI Global.

Policek, N., Ravagnani, L. & Romano, C.A. (2020). Victimization of foreign young people in Italy. In *European Journal of Criminology*.

Popescu, G. (2012). *Bordering and ordering the twenty-first century. Understanding borders*. Plymouth: Rowman & Littlefield.

Ramalo, N. (2011). *Stateless – Undocumented Indians*, South East Asia Human Rights Watch.

Reed, A. (2006) 'Documents Unfolding' in Riles, A., ed. *Documents: Artifacts of Modern Knowledge*, USA: University of Michigan Press, 158-177.

Rigo, E. (2005). 'Citizenship at Europe's Borders: Some Reflections on the Postcolonial Condition of Europe in the Context of EU Enlargement', *Citizenship Studies* 9(1), 3-22.

Rumford, C. (2012). 'Towards a Multiperspectival Study of Borders', *Geopolitics*, 17(4), 887-902.

Salter, M. B. (2008). 'When the exception becomes the rule: borders, sovereignty, and citizenship', *Citizenship Studies*, 12(4), 365-380.

Salter, M. B. (2010). 'Borders, passports, and the global mobility' in Turner, B. S., ed. *The Routledge international handbook of globalization studies*, New York: Routledge, 514-530.

Salter, M. B. (2012). 'Theory of the /: The Suture and Critical Border Studies', *Geopolitics*, 17(4), 734-755.

Schulze, J. L. (2017). *Does Russia Matter? European Institutions, Strategic Framing, and the Case of Stateless Children in Estonia and Latvia. Problems of Post-Communism*, 64(5), 257-275.

Sharma, N. R. (2006). *Home Economics: Nationalism and the Making of 'Migrant Workers' in Canada*, Toronto: University of Toronto Press.

Smith, P. A. (1986). "The Palestinian Diaspora, 1948-1985", *Journal of Palestine Studies*, Vol. 15, No. 3.

Southwick, K., & Lynch, M. (2009). *Nationality rights for all: A progress report and global survey on statelessness*. Refugees International. UNHCR Division of International Protection, UNHCR action to address statelessness, http://www.unhcr.org/pages/49c3646c155.html

Spivak, G. C. (1999). *A Critique of Postcolonial Reason: Toward a History of the Vanishing Present*, London: Harvard University Press.

Stumpf, J. (2006). 'The Crimmigration Crisis: Immigrants, Crime and Sovereign Power', *American University Law Review*, 56(2), 367-419.

Torpey, J. (2000). *The Invention of the Passport: Surveillance, Citizenship, and the State*, Cambridge: Cambridge University Press.

Tucker, J. (2014). Exploring Statelessness and Nationality in Iran. *Available at SSRN 2441850*.

Twomey, C. (2012). 'Severed Hands: Authenticating Atrocity in the Congo, 1904-13' in Batchen, G., Gidley, M., Miller, N. K. and Prosser, J., eds., *Picturing Atrocity: Photography in Crisis*, London: Reaktion Books, 39-50.

van Houtum, H. J., & Strüver, A. (2002). Where is the border? *Journal of creative geography*, Vol. 4, No. 1, pp. 20-2.

van Waas, L., & De Chickera, A. (Eds.). (2017). *The World's Stateless: Children*. Wolf Legal Publishers (WLP).

Varsanyi, M. (2008). 'Immigration Policing Through the Backdoor: City Ordinances, The "Right to the City," and the Exclusion of Undocumented Day Laborers', *Urban Geography*, 29(1), 29-52.

Vaughan-Williams, N. (2012). *Border Politics: The Limits of Sovereign Power*, Edinburgh: Edinburgh University Press.

Walters, W. (2006). 'Border/Control', *European Journal of Social Theory*, 9(2), 187-203.

Walters, W. (2010). 'Deportation, Expulsion, and the International Police of Aliens' in De Genova, N. and Peutz, N., eds., *The Deportation Regime: Sovereignty, Space, and the Freedom of Movement*, Durham & London: Duke University Press, 69-100.

Wastl-Walter, D. (2011). *The Ashgate Research Companion to Border Studies*, Farnham: Ashgate.

Weissbrodt, D. S., & Collins, C. (2006). The human rights of stateless persons. *Human Rights Quarterly*, 28.1: 245-276.

Willen, S. S. (2010). 'Citizens, "Real" Others, and "Other" Others: The Biopolitics of Otherness and the Deportation of Unauthorized Migrant Workers from Tel Aviv, Israel' in De Genova, N. and Peutz, N., eds., *The Deportation Regime: Sovereignty, Space, and the Freedom of Movement*, Durham & London: Duke University Press, 262-294.

Rejection, Reconstruction and Erosion of Borders: The Identity Path of Grisélidis Réal

Salvatore Perri

« Je suis une prostituée. Je l'étais, je ne l'étais plus, Je le suis rede-venue.
On n'échappe ni à soi-même, ni aux autres.
Il faut s'assumer dans toutes ses dimensions, dans ses manques, dans ses évasions. »

(I am a prostitute. I have been one, I no longer was, I became one again. We cannot escape from ourselves, nor from others. It is necessary to affirm our own self in each of its dimensions, of its lacks, of its escapes.)[1]

This is how Grisélidis Réal describes herself in "Parle, nuditéviolée", evoking an affirmation of multiplicity that has been central in her all existence. Born in 1929 in a middle-class family of Lausanne, Réal has exercised prostitution for over 30 years In Geneva. This activity, started as "accidental", has become the cornerstone of the private and public life of the artist, and somehow the landing place of a restless identity research.

The large literary *corpus* produced by Réal — concerning the genres in which it is declined — is extremely heterogeneous: it is made of short compositions in prose, articles, poetries, a memoir and a great number of letters. The epistolary "portion" constitutes, in the perspective of my analysis, a first "structural sign" of the borderless nature of this written heritage. It is impossible, indeed, to treat it as ancillary, as a marginal attachment to poetry and prose, which, on the contrary, would be the theoretical "rule", according — in particular — with the structuralist theorization proposed by Gerard Genette in his seminal text *Seuils*: in the latter, correspondence is labelled as "paratext" (and, more specifically, "epitext"), namely everything which gravitates outside the text itself. Réal's letters, instead, must be interpreted as part — and a

---

[1] Réal, G., *Parle, nudité violée*, in *Mémoires de l'inachevé*, Verticales, Paris, 2011, p. 336.

preponderant one—of a peculiar written geography, in which adopting a "compartmentalized" approach would inevitably impoverish the analysis. In this specific framework, indeed, I would probably call impossible—on a content level rather than on a merely structural one—to operate a distinction between text and paratext. Here, *everything* is text, which multiple forms continuously chase and recall themselves.

All these written elements, together with her own body of woman and prostitute, as we will discover, represent the ponderous, cluttered and polymorphic tale of Réal's existence. There is no threshold (which means *seuils*, precisely, in French) in her work: while approaching the texts of Grisélidis Réal, the reader is always thrown in the middle of the "narrative room", almost forcibly subjected to a display that might be rabid, tender, obsessive, vulgar, ironic, but that is never, in any of its manifestations, liminal compared to something else.

"The letter is a representation of the self", Bernard Beugnot used to say; and it is through every written act that Grisélidis Réal represents herself, while avoiding the fear of being (again) represented by someone else. A *mise en scène* in which correspondence occupies a paramount role, in a way that coincides perfectly with the perspective expressed by Vincent Kauffman in his analysis of Antonin Artaud's letters, where he effectively describes the « incontournable continuité entre les textes proprement dits et les lettres, presque toujours destinées à se confondre avec l'œuvre, à s'y substituer [...] ». ("inevitable continuity between texts as such and the letters, nearly always meant to get confused with the literary work, and to substitute for it.").[2]

A striking manifesto-life, that of Grisélidis Réal, whose initial trigger was precisely a ban to self-expression.

---

[2] Kauffmann, V., *Lettres ouvertes, in L'épistolarité à travers les siècles — geste de communication et ou d'écriture*, Franz Steiner Verlag, Stuttgart, 1990, pp. 58–67, p. 58).

1. Living in the Abject, Abjecting the "Right"

> A Woman has only two choices: either to experience herself in sex hyperabstractly (in an "immediately universal" way, as Hegel would say) so as to make herself worthy of divine grace and assimilation to the symbolic order, or else to experience herself as different, other, fallen (or, in Hegel's terms again, "immediately particular"). But she will not be able to achieve her complexity as divided, heterogeneous being, a "fold-catastrophe" of the "to-be" (or, in Hegel's terms, the "never singular")[3]

This is how Julia Kristeva — in an evocative and complex analysis of the symbolic apparatus that lies behind the iconographic representations of the Virgin Mary, maternal trope *par excellence* — identifies the possibilities given to a woman of experiencing her own sexuality: on the one hand, the adhesion to an idea of body as unrelated to pleasure and prone towards a symbolic order that describes — and prescribes — female corporeity as an "innocent shell"; on the other hand, the choice of a damned otherness, of a "fall" that removes woman from the paradigm of rightfulness, giving her the chance of "testing" her carnal, sexualised dimension, but at the price of becoming an inconceivable "difference". It is the third possibility described by Kristeva — heterogeneity — that appears as completely forbidden and unimaginable, according to the archetype. This last apparently unobtainable multiplicity, in my view, must be considered as the core of Grisélidis Réal's identity chasing. Being the "never singular" — prostitute, activist, mother, writer, painter — has become her mission, a process of self-knowledge and affirmation that has gone through a long and complex "frequentation" of both normative dimensions described above.

The first "possibility of being a woman" recognized in *Stabat Mater* coincides with the auroral phase of Réal's identity development: the erasure of the body in its sexualised form is, indeed, central in the education received by Réal from her mother Gisèle. An education that has been passively suffered and then

---

[3] Kristeva J., Goldhammer, A., "Stabat Mater", in *Poetics Today*, Vol 6, No. ½, The Female Body in Western Culture: Semiotic Perspectives, pp. 133-152, Duke University Press, 1985, p. 142.

vehemently rejected, and that represents a true *casus belli* in the life of the author, a stain deeply etched in the perception of her childlike and then adult bodily self:

> « C'est ainsi qu'ayant subi dès l'âge de six ans jusqu'à passés vingt ans, les menaces, punitions et reproches moralisateurs de ma mère, elle a réussi, et brillamment, à me culpabiliser à mort, à m'assassiner ma sexualité, mon mariage, ma vie amoureuse et même ma vie tout-court. »
> (I have suffered, since I was six and until my late twenties, all the threats, punishments and moralizing reproaches of my mother, and she has been able — brilliantly — to guilt me to death, to kill my sexuality, my marriage, my love life and even my life at whole.)[4]

It must be accounted that Grisélidis Réal does not directly describe the educational method of her mother in its "concrete" exercise. Therefore, it is in the conversations she had with Jean-Luc Hennig — for the book "Grisélidis, Courtisane" — that is possible to find an effective illustration of it:

> She still remembers how her mother tormented them, her and her two younger sisters. Sometimes every day, and in general one time a week, she forced them to lie on the bed, legs up in the air, spread apart, and she investigated their little girls' sexes. She used to say "Ah, it is red! You will be punished.". The poor girl didn't even know why she was punished like that. The only thing she knew was that she was the only one who had that redness that betrayed her.
> « Elle se rappelle encore aujourd'hui comment sa mère les tourmentait, elle et ses deux sœurs cadettes, avec ses idées trop strictes. Quelquefois tous les jours, ou tout bonnement une fois par semaine, elle les faisait mettre en rang sur un lit, les jambes en l'air, écartées, et elle inspectait leur petit sexe de gamines. Elle disait: << Ah c'est rouge ! Tu seras punie. >>. La malheureuse ne savait pas vraiment pourquoi on la punissait ainsi, sinon qu'elle était la seule à avoir ces rougeurs qui la trahissaient. »[5]

The dawn of the physical self-discovery of Grisélidis Réal is therefore marked by a maternal presence who monitors and sanctions, carrying out an inhibitory ritual made of punctual auscultation and reproaches, and which precision suggests a familiarity with that that Foucault — in *Discipline and Punish* — identified as the "ceremony of execution". In his work, the French

---

[4] Réal, G., *Les Sphinx*, Verticales, Paris, 2006, p. 122.
[5] Hennig, J.L., *Grisélidis Courtisane*, Verticales, Paris, 2011, p. 13.

philosopher underlines the insinuating control that power exercises over bodies' docility, which is peculiar exactly for the way in which it is put in place: a coercion that is stretched out in time and that examines and contains the action of the body, which enters in a mechanism that frisks it, disarticulates it, *remakes* it. It is a capillary process to which Foucault gives the name of "discipline" and — in the case of a widely recognized legitimacy — "institution". And it is "institution" the word chosen by Adrienne Rich to talk about maternity in *Of Woman Born: Motherhood as Experience and Institution*. Here, Rich describes maternal behaviour as "readable" in two overlapping declinations: the one that is purely linked to the female experience in relation with her capacity of giving birth, and the one that is instead designed as a social structure similar to any other type of institution, therefore characterized by a dense net of collusions and links to a superior power:

> I try to distinguish between two meaning of motherhood, one superimposed on the other: the potential relationship of any woman to her powers of reproduction and to children; and the institution, which aims at ensuring that that potential — and all women — shall remain under male control.[6]

It is therefore the male power, according to this view, that moulds and imposes the guidelines of motherhood. For Rich, patriarchal control is deeply wedged in the maternal experience, and it exploits the fundamentally formative role of the latter to corroborate the construction of a symbolic universe that is radically masculine, and continuously involved in renovating a paternal language that, to quote Luce Irigaray, is "called, wrongfully, maternal"[7]. The "type" of motherhood that Grisélidis Réal's parent puts in place is akin with the one that has just been outlined, namely the one sired to an idea of femininity built over arcane masculine codes, in which woman is prevented from "frequenting" and investigating her own corporeality. The role that the mother, therefore, seems to play is

---

[6] Rich, A., *Of Woman Born: Motherhood as Experience and Institution*, W W Norton & Co Inc, 1995, p. 13.

[7] « […] appellée, à tort, maternelle ». (Irigaray, L., *Sexes et parentés*, Les édition de minuit, Paris, 1987, p. 28).

that of the vestal of a silenced and "canonized" body—the hyper-abstract one described in 'Stabat Mother'.

Thus, maternal education had transformed body and sexuality into the protagonists of an abjecting process. Réal's desire finds itself punctually frustrated, being part of a game between forces that are opposite but equally irrepressible. A game in which—for a long time—the influence of the martial parental power got the better of the carnal instinct. Here is a passage in which the author tells an episode that can be clearly linked to it:

> « En Grèce, à 8 ans, j'ai vécu ma première rencontre amoureuse physique dans les toilettes d'un hôtel, un petit garçon m'avait suivie, m'avait demandé de baisser ma culotte pour regarder et toucher, très poliment, très délicatement, en me priant de faire de même sur lui, sur sa petite queue qu'il avait mise à l'air. Hélas ! L'horrible <<éducation>> reprenant le dessus et tranchant comme un couperet le désir, m'avait fait m'enfuir, malgré ma curiosité et mon envie »
>
> (In Greece, when I was 8 years old, I had my first physical amorous encounter in the toilets of a hotel. A little boy had followed me, and he had asked me to drop my culottes, to watch and touch. He asked it very kindly, very gently, begging me to do the same with him, with his little dick that he had already pulled out. And then, sadly, the horrible "education" took over, cutting the desire like a knife, making me run away despite my curiosity and my longing. […] and voilà, that is how we are assassinated.)[8]

Réal remembers, with these words, how the horrible "education" (where "education" significantly has quotation marks around it) was able to silence her—although extremely developed—desire: the purity inherent in the will of discover her own body and that of others is transformed into the abject attack to an idea of purity that, on the contrary, demands that that body does not unveil itself nor, especially, let someone else does it. In Réal's perspective, this is the abortion of an epiphanic passage, to which she traces back all the sexual issues that, on her view, afflict her and Europe as a whole: "Such a weight of damnation crushes us from the outset, and paralyse us, poisoning all sexual joys. It is no surprise if Europe is

---

[8] « […] et voilà, c'est ainsi qu'on nous assassine. » (Réal, G., *Mémoires de l'inachevé*, op. cit, p. 36).

populated by neurosis, frigidity and impotence."⁹. In her own maternal experience (however complex and problematic), Réal has tried to exercise a complete subversion of the castrating rules she had undergone. The anatomy of the body and its sexual functioning- rather than be taboos- are shown and explained to her children, in the moment in which they manifest interest on the matter:

> « C'est arrivé un jour, ils avaient 7 ans et 9 ans (Igor e Leonore), Où poussés par une curiosité tout à fait naturelle — et pas du tout malsaine — ils sont venus vers moi un matin et ont demandé: « Montre-nous d'où nous sommes sortis, et aussi où nous avons tété ... ». Ont suivi les inévitables questions: « Ça ne t'a pas fait mal ? Il n'y a plus de lait, etc. ». Ils ont voulu voir, de tout près, et même toucher (à peine, d'ailleurs). Une fois rassurés, ayant vu et compris le mécanisme de ces organes du corps, ils n'en ont plus jamais reparlé et n'ont plus jamais demandé à le voir. »

> (One day, they had 7 and 9 years old (Igor and Leonore, the two older children of Réal A/N), driven by a completely natural and absolutely not unhealthy curiosity, my children came to me and asked: "Show us the place from where we came out, and also where we have suckled." And then the inevitable questions followed: "Didn't it hurt? Is there any milk left, etc. "They had wanted to see, from up close, and also (barely) touching. Once reassured and having seen and understood the mechanism of these organs of the body, they never talked about it again or asking of see anything.)¹⁰

Being a mother therefore represents a further instrument of redemption, the possibility — being on the other side — of putting in place an upheaval of the predicates suffered for years, that can finally be re-discussed and maybe defeated. In this perspective, parenthood becomes an extremely powerful chance of restoration, a tool that, rather than demarcate limits for instinct, complies with the latter, initiating these "new" beings to the knowledge of their body and that of the others.

As can be seen so far, the marked contrast between two poles, that of freedom and that of restriction, constantly returns. The

---

[9] « Un tel poids de damnation nous écrase d'avance, et nous paralyse, que toute joie sexuelle s'en trouve déjà empoisonnée. Il ne faut pas donc s'étonner si l'Europe est peuplée de névroses, de frigidité, d'impuissances. » (Réal, G., *Mémoires de l'inachevé*, op. cit., p. 332).

[10] Réal, G., *Mémoires de l'inachevé*, op. cit., p. 340.

"deregulated prescriptions" of Grisélidis Réal's idea of education opposed to the way in which she was raised is a good illustration of what has been, on a large scale, her response to the condition of "castrated" individuals. It will be precisely through the use of the same, but reversed, "abjecting procedure" — the one that wanted sexuality confined to the role of a repellent danger — that the author will start her identity reconstruction.

An idea of abjection provided with agency and discursiveness, one in which the unmoulded violence of the primitive and helpless sense of rebellion towards the borders imposed becomes a powerful, active voice for oppressed alterities, starting a process in which body and word walk together, representing an equivalence in which the subtraction of the right of the bodily-self to choose for its own turns into the drive to eagerly reaffirm its centrality.

In the further excerpt, Réal — in her seventies — reflects on her own choices, and on the reasons that have triggered them:

> « [...] Tout cela (l'éducation) a débouché sur la révolte sanglante que vous savez : il a fallu fuir, au péril de sa vie, se lancer à l'assaut des hommes dans la Prostitution, l'autodestruction peu à peu muée en subtile et flamboyante victoire, abondamment médiatisée et transformée en littérature, conférences, émissions radiophoniques et télévisées. Dommage, ma mère est morte trop tôt, en 1971, elle n'a pas tout vu. »
>
> ([...] All of that (the education N/A), has led to the bloody riot that you know: it has been necessary, at risk of life, to launch myself in Prostitution, with this sense of self-destruction little by little transformed into subtile but explosive victory, abundantly media-covered, and turned into literature, conferences, television and radio broadcasting. Too bad, my mother died soon, in 1971, and she hasn't been able to see it all.)[11]

Talking about the path accomplished as both a consequence and a response to her past, Grisélidis Réal uses the phrase "il a fallu", which in English means "it has been necessary", and it clearly remarks the peremptory nature she recognizes in her acting. We also encounter the expressions « bloody riot », « at risk of life", "to launch an assault", "subtle but explosive victory", which are all part of a warlike imagine. It is clear, therefore, that the "reconquer"

---

[11] Réal, G., *Les Sphinx*, op.cit., p. 122.

of the "usurped" body is symbolically equivalent to a war. And a war, being as such, incorporates the possibility of a sacrifice, the "self-destruction" of a body– which is battlefield and soldier at the same time– behaved to give it the chance of eventually being saved from coercion. To do so, Grisélidis Réal establishes for herself a refuge that might be symbolically synthetized as "The Black":

> « Le Noir, couleur du mystère, s'inscrit dans l'ombre de toutes choses et les pénètre comme un philtre, les ramenant à la grande nuit des origines. [...] La couleur noire n'existe pas. La puissance de sa négation confond toutes les existences et les absorbe en elle plus sûrement que le jour. »
>
> (Black, colour of mystery, inscribes itself in the shadow of all things, and penetrates them like a filter, leads them back to the great night of origins [...] Black colour does not exist. The power of its denial blends all existences into it and absorbs them much more than the daylight can do.)[12]

Through this passage, we see how — in her idea of black -Réal recognizes the ramifications of the entropy hidden behind an artificial reality. "All things" are thus reunited in "the great night of origins", in the crisis that precedes any kind of boundary. Furthermore, the author underlines how the denial of black does nothing but affirming it, because it is precisely in the effort of ignoring its existence that black keeps expanding — blurring contours that during the day are solidly prescribed. A view that is akin to that of Mary Douglas, who points out — in *Purity and Danger* — how it is precisely the establishment of boundaries that "produces" reality. In light of a study that goes from the Leviticus to the Indian system of castes and the tribal ritualiy, the English anthropologist concludes that humanity has always affirmed itself by refusing the inconceivability of indefiniteness. Always and everywhere, indeed, the concept of reality pivots on the identification of a sacred sphere that is opposed to a liminal one — filthy and rejected. Moreover, a fundamental condition for maintaining the integrity of reality is that the two dimensions never get mixed. Boundaries, then, are also at the centre of *Gender Trouble*, by Judith Butler, who says:

---

[12] Réal, G., *Le Noir est une couleur*, Verticales, Paris, 2007, p. 11.

> Regardless of the compelling metaphors of the spatial distinctions of inner and outer, they remain linguistic terms that facilitate and articulate a set of fantasies, feared and desired. "Inner" and "outer" make sense only with reference to a mediating boundary that strives for stability. And this stability, this coherence, is determined in large part by cultural orders that sanction the subject and compel its differentiation from the abject. Hence, "inner" and "outer" constitute a binary distinction that stabilizes and consolidates the coherent subject.[13]

In *Bodies that Matter*, Butler also suggests that subjectivities relegated on the edge of the normative *locus* — and that, precisely because "abjected", contribute to create and maintain the "regular" identities — can be capable of putting in place the same strategy that they have suffered, in order to affirm themselves:

> Clearly, the power differentials by which such subjects are instituted and sustained are quite different. And yet, there is some risk that in making the articulation of a subject-position into the political task, some of the strategies of abjection wielded through and by hegemonic subject-positions have come to structure and contain the articulatory struggles of those in subordinate or erased positionalities.[14]

I have mentioned the works of Douglas and Butler because I believe that the "identity r-evolution" of Réal, especially at its beginning, is developed precisely on the persistence and the utilization of the "filthy/clean" dyad. The first step in the reappropriation of the self consists, for the author, in moulding herself through the dichotomy that she has always been (painfully) familiar with. The physical pulsion, "killed" for decades, finally gets to demand the property of the body in which it dwells, and it does so through the abjecting process of which it was a victim. Abjection, therefore, becomes a "trigger of culture", a way out from the "unconsciousness" of the body. Black and White, as already underlined, creates a system. And, according to Douglas, nothing is filthy for itself, but become so because of the location saved for it in the "institution" of reality; and Réal's subversion is exercised precisely through this criterion: the author translates her body in the denied portion of world that

---

[13] Butler, J., *Gender Trouble, Feminism and the Subversion of Identity*, Routledge, New York and London, 1999, p. 170-171.
[14] Butler, J., *Bodies That Matter*, Routledge, New York, 2011, p. 75.

can finally give her the chance of experimenting her individuality. And, once transferred into the abject, that body—now alive and able to speak—starts to abject the "right" side.

The "abjected deliverance" of Réal also takes ethnic connotations: "Me, I am of gipsy race. I love night and it's invisible breath that gives to the universe its borderless space."[15]. Réal had been very close to the gitano world during her years in Germany. Leaving as an illegal immigrant in Munich, indeed, she found refuge for several months, together with her children, in a Roma camp. In "Le Noir est une couleur", her memoir, Réal describes Tata, the patriarch who had harboured her, with these words: "Tata, old heart slashed and warm [...], you, whose race is contained in this immense word: stateless."[16]. Again, the imperative of the unlimited returns, represented—this time—by the condition of eternal nomadism of the gipsies. It is a need of not belonging that, by contrast, is realized through a "reorganization" of social belonging: the "abjuration" of what we can call "White" (which identifies her bourgeois, European origins and all the cultural and religious beliefs that it entails) and the reallocation into the "borderless borders" of "Black", which finally brings Réal to recognize herself. Furthermore, the safeness of "Black" appears to be rooted—as the traumatic action of "White"—in childhood. Réal, indeed, lived for some years in Alexandria, where her father was the Principal of the *École Suisse*. Reading the memories of the Egyptian years, it is clear how that context has helped to build the racial implications inherent in the antagonisms that mark the adulthood of the author:

> « À six ans, on m'assit sur les genoux d'un infirmier noir, dans un hôpital d'Alexandrie. Un médecin allemand m'enleva une partie des amygdales sous une légère anesthésie. Le visage du Noir immobile scintillait au-dessus de sa blouse blanche et la grande douceur de ses mains posées sur moi m'enleva la douleur. »

---

[15] « Moi, je suis de race gitane. J'aime la nuit et son haleine invisible qui donne à l'univers son espace sans limites. » (Réal, G., *Le noir est une couleur*, op.cit., p. 11).

[16] « Tata, au vieux cœur fendu et chaleureux [...] Toi dont la race est contenue dans ce mot immense : apatride. » (Réal, G., ibid., p. 98).

> (At six years, they sat me on the knees of a black nurse, in a hospital of Alexandria. A German doctor took off a portion of my tonsils, under slight anaesthesia. The face of the black, immobile, sparkled through his white blouse, and the mighty sweetness of his hands on me took the pain away)[17]

The characters of this cultural and emotional dichotomy — the white doctor and the black nurse — are both in the act of "removing" something. The European entity, though, deprives the child of a part of her body, inflicting her pain. The same pain that the black man, instead, is going to take off. This intuition of safeness, already glimpsed during infancy, takes the form of a conscious crossing of the boundary, as we see in the passage relating to the departure in Germany, at the beginning of "Le Noir est une couleur":

> « Je partais, je rejoignais le grand troupeau des nomades en transhumance, et dans le taxi qui nous emportait, serrés parmi les valises et les animaux en peluche, je voyais le crane énorme du Noir se détacher sur l'orange du soleil couchant comme un phallus. C'était l'obscurcissement préfiguré de toute ma vie. Le Noir, le Noir sacré s'emparait du soleil et me plongeait dans les entrailles de la nuit pour toujours.»

> (I was leaving, I was catching the huge flock of nomads in transhumance and, in the cab that was taking us away, packed between luggage and stuffed animals, I saw the enormous skull of the Black (Bill, her lover A/N) falling over that orange sun that was getting down like a phallus. It was the predestined darkening of my entire life: The Black, the sacred Black was taking over the sun and plunging me into the guts of the night, forever.)[18]

This travel, physical and symbolic, is charged with initiatory value: Réal leaves behind Switzerland and all that it represents for her, and she meets a human flow that she calls "transhumance", a word that leads back to the praised dimension of animality and nature. Black is, again, the officiant of this baptism, this time in the guise of Bill, the lover she is running away with. Night can be interpreted as a new mother, that can bear her and give her birth again.

Once she created her abjected compagages — made of a life far from Switzerland, sexually free and lived among the outcasts of society — it came the time to raise her voice and abject the opposite pole, realizing what we could call her revenge. Bohm e Kaplan, in

---

[17] Réal, G., ibid., p. 11.
[18] Réal, G., ibid., p. 12.

Revenge: On the Dynamics of a Frightening Urge and Its Taming, seen in "shamelessness" one of the matrices of the vengeful instinct:

> Shamelessness is shown when one individual [...] forces their way into another individual's most private sphere. What has taken place is an assault, there is a "victim" and a "perpetrator". The victim is left with destructive wounds while the perpetrator goes free.[19]

According to this perspective, the "perpetrator" — devoid of any shame — introduces himself in the private sphere of the one who is identified as the victim (and "to-be avenger"), destroying his intimacy. In Réal's case, the perpetrator is a protean complex constituted by her mother and, by diffusion, the bourgeois and catholic society. This horde, in the strength of the lack of shame inspired by the certainty of being right, overwhelms his daughter of invalidating shame and gets away with it. And it is exactly in the field of this unpunished affliction that the seed of revenge will grow: Réal can shift from being the oppressed object to being a free subject only if she becomes bereft of shame, only if she imposes her impudence to the old oppressor, only by making feel him — in turn — ashamed:

> « Nous irons baiser, cracher, pisser et chier sur vos tombes, jouir sur vos cadavres et nos orgasmes hurleront comme des loups en en-culant vos ombres. /Nous réintégrerons nos corps après avoir rongé et dégueulé vos os !/Oui moi/Moi l'enfant/Vous m'avez donc volé ma peau/Lié mes mains/Scellé mon sexe /Vous m'avez dérobé l'amant de mes huit ans et l'amante de mes quatorze ans/Vous m'avez rendue frigide suicidaire paranoïaque/Et Putain/Je vous vomis papa mama caca gaga/Le Foutre aux tombes la Merde au cœur la Mort au Cul et l'âme aux Chiens/Qu'on m'exorcise moi je veux tous les corps contre le mien/Bites bouches couilles cul tripes con vagin langues doigts/Mimosa violettes algues prunelles grenades/Orange amère mon père ma mère ma sœur mon frère /Qu'on m'ouvre enfin le ventre/Qu'on y foute l'univers/Tant que nous n'aurons pas éjaculé nos morts/La vie n'est pas possible »

> (We will fuck, spit, piss and shit over your graves, and we will come over your corpses and our orgasms will scream as wolves while they are screwing your shadows

---

[19] Bhom, T., Kaplan, S., *Revenge: On the Dynamics of a Frightening Urge and Its Taming*, Karnak Book Ltd, London, 2011, p. 21.

> We will reintegrate our bodies after we have mauled and vomited your bones!
> Yes, me
> Me the child
> You have stolen my skin
> Tide up my hands
> Sealed my sex
> You have robbed the male lover of my eight years and the female lover of my fourteen
> You made me frigid suicidal paranoid
> And a whore
> [...]
> Exorcise me I want all bodies against mine
> Bites mouths balls ass guts cunt vagin tongues fingers
> Mimosa violets algae sloe pomegranates
> Bitter orange my father my mother my sister my brother
> Shall my womb finally be opened
> They shall throw inside it the whole universe
> Until we don't have ejaculated our dead
> Life is not possible)[20]

In this excerpt, which is the finale of "Les Dragon du Sexe" (part of the collection titled "La Passeimaginare"), the anger against the educational system dramatically emerges. In the ferocious initial image, Réal puts in place a metaphorical contempt of her parents' corpses, acted by a "We" that includes all those that, like her, grew under the poisonous influence of certain rules. The whole text revolves around the concept of a suffered violence then transformed into a "to return" violence. The textual structure, in this matter, is also evocative: "Les Dragon du sexe", indeed, starts as a series of considerations about gender constructions and the weight of sin, enriched with quotations from Nietzsche, Bataille, Khayyam and Iff. Apparently, though, a rigorous dissertation that, gradually, abandons punctuation, got "broken" and coprolalic, and ultimately explodes in the just quoted piece, in a perfect written impression of the deflagrating progress of fury. It is also evident the will of the author to affirm her body as a container finally opened. Réal talks about a sex "sealed" by parental acting, and then prays for her womb to be opened up and filled with the "whole universe". The idea of a silent, closed, impregnable body is in contrast with

---

[20] Réal, G., *Mémoires de l'inachevé*, op. cit., 2011, p. 333-334.

that of a bottomless flesh. The act of sex, here, is an "exorcism", and the bodies are the prayers to launch against the demons of shame and repression.

Also, a series of references to the male member can be appreciated in the abovementioned text; this is a common trend in the work of Réal: the opposite sex, that had always been "so forbidden, hidden, damned ... untouchable."[21] during the time spent in the shadow of maternal inflexibility, is- by contrast— praised during adulthood, translated into a plethoric hagiography which aims to enhance its power and its saving action. In "Les Dragon du Sexe", while talking about the expulsion of the childhood's ghosts, Réal writes: "Until we don't have ejaculated our dead/Life is not possible." The final liberation from the oppressor is therefore symbolically performed through the act of ejaculating, underling once more the pivotal role she refers to masculine anatomy. The largest part of what might be called a "phallic celebration" involves black men, for whom Réal harboured a passion similar to a devotion and in whom she saw a further declination of that restoring alterity in which she had found refuge[22]:

> « Même avec une femme de passage [...] quand un Noir fait l'amour, c'est comme avec sa femme. À mouvements doux, sûrs et puissants de fauve honorant sa femelle ! [...]. Soumise, écrasée et baisée, je me venge des Blancs, de leurs petits cœurs secs ter-minés en sexes débiles. En quelque nuits, j'ai vengé toutes les femmes privées d'amant de notre famille [...] Dormez en paix, l'amour a explosé. Il me ronge le ventre. Que son sperme brulant retombe sur vos cendres, qu'il foute le feu à vos squelettes »

---

[21] « aussitôt interdit, escamoté, maudit ... intouchable » Réal, G., ibid., p. 332.
[22] It is important to underline that the "fetishization" in which Réal involves the "Black anatomy" might plausibly be assimilated to a euro-centric, colonial dichotomy. It is equally clear, however, that even if this tendency could correspond to a process of objectification of the foreign corporeality, it does not emerge on the basis of a conscious racist intent, but rather because of a self-narrative style that stands out for being primarily—and also clumsily, in a perspective of ethnic representation—plethoric (for what concerns black and white people, in equal measure), and that is also born in an historical and social context that was still far from considering certain linguistic and conceptual limits in the description of the foreign.

> (Even with a streetwalker [...] when a Black makes love, it is like she was his woman. With sweet, firm and powerful movements, those of a beast honouring his female! [...] submitted, crushed and fucked, I got revenge of Whites, of their little dry hearts that end in disabled sexes. [...] in a few nights, I took revenge for all the women deprived of a lover in our family [...] Sleep peacefully, love has exploded. It corrodes my womb. Shall his burning sperm fall over your hashes, shall it set fire on your skeletons.)[23]

Réal ecstatically describes the "wild" nature she finds in Black men, who are punctually the "winning" characters of the comparison with the whites: the description of the member, that is grandiloquently positive in the case of blacks, got "rotten" in the case of whites, becoming the withered extension of sexual taboos, of the "little dry hearts" of Europe. Black men, on the contrary, are able to honour women through sexual intercourse, and with their sexual vigour are even capable to go up the course of an oppressed female genealogy, taking vengeance for all the pleasure that has never been felt. And, as for the piece from "Les Dragon du Sexe", ejaculation has again a thaumaturgic role: the masculine vital stream vigorously erupts in a death context and vivifies it, starting a purifying fire.

Nevertheless, we note that the soothing and positive nature of the sexual intercourse is accompanied by concomitant allusions to brutality and subjugation. Réal claims to be "submitted, crushed", describes a love that explodes, but while corroding her womb. This peculiarity also returns in this passage:

> « D'abord il me le donne à regarder dans le silence, cuisses écartées, debout sur le sol de la chambre comme une statue de cruauté. Ses dimensions surnaturelles réduisent mon corps au sommeil, à l'attente, l'acte se passe en adoration et en prière. On peut être sacrifiée avec joie à une lame de telle beauté. »
> (At the beginning he just let me watch it in the silence, thighs wide open, standing in the room like a statue of cruelty. His supernatural dimensions induce my body to sleep, to anticipation, and the act continues in adoration and prayer. You can be sacrificed with joy to a blade of such beauty.)[24]

Réal describes the lover standing above her as a sort of a Christological entity who miniaturizes her and induces her to

---

[23] Réal, G., *Le Noir est une couleur*, op.cit., p. 97-98.
[24] Réal, G., ibid., p. 7.

veneration. Furthermore, the final idea of a positive self-sacrifice completes the construction of an atmosphere charged with ritualistic undertones, that of a sexualized liturgy with at its centre the "Sacred Black". Few lines later, in the same text, the author writes:

> « J'ai bu à la pointe de ton sexe une liqueur au gout de soufre et d'ammoniaque, je me suis abreuvée aux sources salées de ton ventre, aux grains de raisin bleu de ta poitrine. [...] J'ai crié. J'ai hurlé, j'ai agonisé sous la morsure de ta lame d'ébène [...] tu m'as tuée, tu m'as ressuscitée, et je n'en finis pas de revenir à la vie, dans le limon de nos jouissance mêlées, entre tes deux pythons noirs qui m'enserrent. »
> (I drunk, at the tip of your sex, a liquor flavoured sulphur and ammonia. I watered myself at the salted source of your bowels, at the blue grains of your chest. [...] I screamed, I cried, I agonized to the bite of your blade of ebony. [...] You killed me, you resurrected me, and I don't stop coming back to life in the limo of our mixed bliss, between your two black phytons that tighten me).[25]

We see, again, the juxtaposition of pain and pleasure: the body of the lover resembles a dining table which food is characterized by a repulsive and yet esoteric and attractive flavour, from which Réal draws — docile and mesmerized. The sexual act kills her and brings her back to life. The "Black" serves again its task of a renovator, giving rise to a palingenesis that annihilates and then rebuilds. The "phytons" presence, in my view, is also meaningful of the religious atmosphere with which the piece is overflowing. Réal — in the umpteenth overturning of abjection — reborn in sin, returns to herself by lying herself down to the serpent. Christian religion (that Réal had always attacked) is therefore incorporated and reutilized in the process: The author becomes a reversed mystic, who — through pain and pleasure equally — does not refuse the body but instead runs towards it, following a path that will brings her to dive deep in the dark (which is the equivalent, in her personal "abjecting cult", of the Christian light).

According to Sigmund Freud, masochism — the "secular" one as much as that linked to religious self-flagellation — is related to a conflict between ego and superego, where the instinctual drives

---

[25] ibid.

diverge with moral impositions. The body, from this perspective, undergoes a suppression invariably linked to a sense of repellence toward the self. This idea—as the whole thinking of Freud, after all—has obviously been the matter of several reviews. It is interesting—in the perspective of my analysis—to interpolate the one offered by Elaine Scarry in *The Body in Pain*. In this text, Scarry "reforms" the Freudian idea of bodily denial and claims that the individual, while flagellating himself, is actually in the act of putting his physical dimension in a central position, that he is acting an hypostatization of it in order to "unhook" it from reality:

> The self-flagellation of the religious ascetic, for example, is not (as is often asserted) an act of denying the body, eliminating its claims from attention, but a way of so emphasizing the body that the contents of the world are cancelled and the path is clear for the entry of an unworldly, contentless force. It is in part this world-ridding, path-clearing logic that explains the obsessive presence of pain in the rituals of large, widely shared religions.[26]

Rather than assuming these two affirmations as necessarily contrastive, I believe that the real limit would lie in the search for an unambiguous interpretative answer for a human manifestation which triggers are certainly multifactorial and susceptible to several individual variations. Applying (with due adaptations) these two apparently incompatible analytical perspectives to the work of Grisélidis Réal may demonstrate the efficacy of their apparently impossible "cohabitation": the first form of "martyrdom" experienced by the author was that that, by proxy, her mother imposed to her. In that case, the punishment didn't consist in torturing her own body, but rather in the torturing impossibility of controlling it. Religion thus loomed over the life of the author holding the position of "co-belligerent" of the hated parent. Réal, therefore, meets the pain of the "erased" body in a way that is close to the Freudian idea of self-punishment (even though, as already mentioned, the imposition came firstly from her mother and, only later, turns into a self-inflicted stop). Once she moves away from the native environment and its rules, though, the author

---

[26] Scarry, E., *The Body in Pain – The Making and Unmaking of the World*, Oxford University Press, New York, 1985, p. 129

establishes an emancipatory sexual ceremonial which results are close to the ideas exposed by Scarry: the flesh — over which Réal has now control — becomes protagonist of a compulsory and brutalizing sexual acting. The body — precisely because it has been impregnable for so long — is now used until pain, in an unholy rituality which cancel the "contents of the world". The world I am talking about in the case of Réal, though, is that of her childhood. The "world-ridding, path-clearing logic" coined by Scarry does not correspond, here, to a liberation from the world in a broad sense: the "centralized body" of Réal rises, dies and revives (through the brutal sexual pleasure) to "delete" the specificity of one "world" only, the moral one, in order to make room for an ascension that is the equivalent of the "unworldly, contentless force" recognized by Scurry as the goal of ritualistic pain, but which — unlike the latter — is not a condition of mystical annihilation, but rather a force drenched in three-dimensionality, words and flesh. Réal, hence, suffers (and feels pleasure) not in order to ascend and forget reality, but to definitively precipitate in the hyper-concrete spaces of its denied recesses — the only ones she considers possible and true. And male virility (called, not by chance, "lame") could be interpreted as a substitute for cilice, an instrument of voluptuous torture to which "be sacrificed with joy".

2. Prostitution as a "Humanism", Re-Coded Flesh and the Irrecoverable Unity

Grisélidis Réal — from her early thirties and until the very last years of her life — has been a prostitute. It is important to emphasize, before venturing into the analysis of this phase of the artist's life, that — regardless of the climate that might surround prostitution (more or less supportive, both on a legal and social level) — the personal experience of each single prostitute stands out from any historical and statistical attempt of grouping. In this brief analysis, sex-work is considered as an experiential data included in the framework of an existence that has processed it and, ultimately, acquired it through multiple (and often simultaneous) conflicts. What stands as a fact is that the events that might cross and influence the singularity of a community or an individual (in a given moment of their history or as a consequence of it) could lead to a "knowledge" and a "consciousness" of prostitution (as of any other experience) that erodes the fixity of certain assertions about the indisputable vulnerability and lack of agency of prostitutes. Réal has talked about prostitution for decades, and in her usual way: polemic, pugnacious, prescriptive. What she never lacked in doing so, though, was the agency we quoted just above, an agency used to advocate for that society could learn a sense of understating and support toward a profession that — as she stressed out multiple times -could be called so only if chosen, and that she used to describe as "an art, a humanism, a science". A vocation transformed into a job (or maybe the opposite) that allowed her to reinforce the capacity of "telling herself", and that could be considered as the last — and somehow synoptic — act of her long journey in search of an identity.

The "prostitutional" experience of Grisélidis Réal began in the sixties in Munich, as narrated in "Le Noir est une couleur". It all started as a casualty, as a circumstance treated — at the beginning — only as a repulsive necessity. After years marked by a strongly conflictual perception of her condition of sex-worker, Réal embraced the idea of it as an act of self-determination and social support that deserves respect, heading toward almost three decades of activism.

> « Chacun des hommes qui vient ici est unique, et je les aime de plus en plus même si c'est dur, insupportable, terrible et qu'ils viennent déverser en moi non seulement leur sperme, mais aussi leurs fureurs, leurs douleurs, l'amertume, la douceur, le désespoir des pauvres et des blessés. »
>
> (Each and every man that comes here is unique, and I love them all more and more even if it's hard, unbearable, horrible and even if they come here to pour into me not only their sperm, but also their furies, their pains, their disappointment, their sweetness, their desperation of poor and bruised.)[27]

These words help us to understand the profound ambivalence that Grisélidis Réal recognized in her work, the inextricable *summa* of

---

[27] Réal, G., *La Passe imaginaire*, Vertical, Paris, 2006, p. 253.

love and misery that she felt to receive and return: being a prostitute, for the author, means to "use yourself, to awfully ripping yourself apart"("on s'use, on se morcelle terrible-ment"), but—at the same time—the overwhelming charge of humanity with which she feels to be put in touch through prostitution allows her of feeling herself crossed, filled by the vastity of the "elsewhere" she has always chased. Prostitution represents, for Réal, another instrument to re-affirm the idea that the "truth" of existence can only be realized within the synthesis—or else in the concomitant manifestation—of harsh but/and exhilarating conditions, which overcome her in their dimension saturated with duplicity and—precisely for this reason—reality.

An ambivalence that returns in a sort of "semantic clarification" that Réal makes when she writes "Je les aimetous, mais je nc suis pas amoureuse." that may be translated in English as "I feel love for them, but I'm not *in love* with them." In this linguistic "sophistication" the author stresses again the coexistence of an all-embracing drive towards her work, and the fact that—at the same time—it is *still* a work—re-affirming herself as "wide open" but/and precautionary "closed". She once again wants to say that the encounters with all the desperate, love seeking, filthy men she receives may represent a consuming, awful circumstance, but that, simultaneously, she is fulfilled in serving their loneliness and—in some occasions—she is drawn by them into a physical rhapsody that sublimates in the chance of "exceeding" herself and her individual barriers, of endlessly duplicate herself:

> « Vous restez vous-même, mais en même temps, vous appartenez à d'autres, j'étais moi-même tous les corps des autres qui étaient venus là. J'étais non seulement leur corps, mais leur sexe, leur âme, leur race, j'étais devenue totalement multiple. C'est magnifique. »
>
> You are still yourself but, at the same time, you belong to the other, I was myself and also all the bodies of those who were there. I was not only their bodies, but their sexes, their souls, their race, I was completely multiple. It was beautiful.[28]

---

[28] Hennig, J.L., *Grisélidis Courtisane*, op. cit., p. 118.

Clearly, clients occupy a central role in the idea of prostitution that Grisélidis Réal develops. Once she has abandoned the ultra-negative perception she had of them in the first period of work in Germany—in which she painted them as a depersonalized "stain", indiscriminately described as alien and rapacious -, the author gives back to them three-dimensionality and human significance. Hence, these men—always painted as the faceless demand that produces the prostitution-supply, which is in its turn trapped in certain dichotomic narratives—acquire in Réal's words a voice, and one that looks like hers:

> « Comme je le disais hier à un journaliste de La Suisse, il y a dans la Prostitution deux démarches à la fois contraires et complémentaires : un défi, une autodestruction (car on s'use, on se morcelle terriblement) et une tentative d'échange et de reconstruction des rapports humains sur un mode différent : estime, amitié, complicité et reconnaissance de la même frustration sexuelle chez l'autre, donc fraternité, puis qu'on est les victimes et les révoltés de la même injustice. Cette injustice qui est la même au départ pur tous, clients et prostituées (et leurs femmes aussi d'ailleurs), éducation morale et chrétienne étriquée : défense d'avoir un corps, interdit d'en jouir et de faire jouir les autres. Chair: Péché. »
>
> (As I said yesterday to a journalist of *La Suisse*, in Prostitution there are two drives that are complementary and opposite at the same time: a challenge, a self-destruction and an attempt of exchange and reconstruction of human relationships on a different level: respect, friendship, empathy and the recognition of the same sexual frustration in the one in front of you, because we are all the victims and the insurgents of the same injustice. This injustice is the same at the beginning for everyone, clients and prostitutes (and client's wives, also), moral and Christian petty education: impossibility to have a body, ban to enjoy yours and to help the others to enjoy theirs. Flesh: Guilt.)[29]

In the construction of sense that supports her idea of "vocational prostitution", the unsolved debt of childhood presumably occupies a fundamental space. A debt that the author, as usual, links to the flesh, and to the label of "guilt" which was attached on it. In her essay called "Mama's Baby, Papa's Maybe", Hortense J. Spillers investigates the influence of slavery on gender dynamics in the Afro-American community. Spiller, in doing so, establishes a

---

[29] Réal, G., *La Passe imaginaire*, op.cit., p. 17.

precise conceptual distinction between "flesh" and "body". "Before the body" she writes "there is the "flesh", that zero degree of social conceptualization that does not escape concealment under the brush of discourse"[30]. According to this idea, flesh represents the "concrete" predecessor of the body, a territory that is still free from symbolic connotations and in which, through manipulation, a complex compartment of signs is inscribed. This process led to the creation of the body, a symbolic entity which is the result of the manipulations carried out on its "zero-degree". The perspective introduced by Spiller is interestingly concordant with the identity evolution of Réal. We have previously encountered passages in which the author refers to the sensation of being equipped with a dead, killed body, and of how that murder was imputable to the dense network of interdictions that were inscribed — precisely — on an innocent and "sign-less" flesh. According to this view, Réal has thus tried for her entire adult life to let her non-body- an intolerable symbolic corpse — recede to its previous stage, reviving her original flesh (evocatively, her memoir should have been titled "Chair vive", which means "Alive flesh" in English, but the editor later decided to change it in "Le noir est une couleur", "Black is a colour"). This need for liberation is thus finally completed — and "professionalized" — through prostitution, which also increases and actively involves the collective connotation given by Réal to her personal traumas. The way in which Réal "narrates" prostitution stands as decisively far from the usual chronicles that involve sex-working, not so much on a factual level, as in the "emotional" tale of the prostitutional experience, usually outlined as solipsistic, victimizing, informed by the creation of the dyad client-prostitute, which elements build upon each other although being antagonists. Politically speaking, the author busily works for that sex-work gets to know a "moral recovery" in the social space, and, by doing so, she finally recognizes this space: she does not deny it as she has done during the first phase of her "identity war", but instead tries

---

[30] Spiller, J.H., "Mama's Baby Papa's Maybe", in *Diacritics*, Vol. 17, No. 2, *Culture and Counter-memory: The "American" Connection*. (Summer, 1987), pp. 64-81, p. 71.

to establish a dialogue with it, showing to be opened—now- to an idea of reality that could consider negotiation as an option. This reconsideration emerges clearly in his excerpt from a television interview dating 2002:

> P.R. : Vous vous êtes toujours battue contre la morale
> G.R: Non, contre les abuses de la morale. Il faut une certaine morale, une certaine dignité dans la morale. Mais il faut pas de l'hypocrisie dans la morale
> (P.R.: You have always fought against morality
> G.R.: No, against the abuses of morality. It is necessary to have a certain morality, a certain dignity in morality. What is not necessary is to have hypocrisy in morality.)[31]

Morality is thus no longer "crucified" but, on the contrary, repeatedly (and positively) quoted in reference to prostitution. What stands as permanently despicable, for Réal, is the aberration of morality, that is the inappropriate use of it as a tool for repression and persecution (always in this regard, there are several passages in which the author makes a clear distinction between the adjectives "moralising" and "moral"). Therefore, a counterpart still exists. The substantial difference comparing to the past, though, is that Réal no longer circumscribes this enemy to the "White" society, does no longer rigidly thinks of it as innately and consciously possessed (and controlled) by the "White", but rather suffered by the "White", interiorized by it, calcified in it. Prostitution prompts the author to a new reconsideration of borders, those of the "Black" of which she had done her centre. This new, open perspective brought her to the point in which categorical schemes still persist, but not as granitic and reciprocally exclusionary as in the past, and especially no longer aprioristically assigned according to racial and social criteria: sexual ban and body annihilation are all things that certainly manifest themselves in the "acceptable" society in which Réal is born and raised. The difference, now, lies in the fact that she takes in account—by choosing to communicate with it—the "corrigibility" of this same society, the existence of a common background of human, neutral equality—that "We" she repeatedly

---

[31] Television interview by Pascal Reberez to GrisélidisRéal (2002).

used in "Les Dragon du Sexe". Good and Evil don't have geography anymore, but are rather signs—fossils—of an ancestral separation, (forcefully) succeeded to a condition of entropic purity: "We are all mortals from our birth" she wrote in her "medical testament", two month prior her death "and devoid from every added filth". Prostitution have thus served as an instrument, for Réal, to trying erode what she thought was the "hypocrisy in morality": she has politically acted on the proscenium of a social space by which she was certainly still disappointed, but that she has later learned to consider as part of a borderless, wounded humanity.

The sense of loss towards an atavistic unity constantly returns in Réal writing, especially during the last days of her life. In one of the last letters contained in "Les Sphinx"—a collection of correspondence written during the period of her cancer—Réal writes:

> « J'ai découpé pour vous dans le nouveau numéro de L'Illustré d'hier ce magnifique reportage sur le Cirque Zingaro, ce spectacle de Chevaux dressés au « naturel » qui vous va si bien, je ne me lasse pas d'y penser, de l'admirer. Je vous le donne bien sûr. Il y a là des correspondances et une complicité évidente entre la force et la vérité du cheval à « l'état brut » avec cette pureté, cette volonté d'Être, d'exister, peu importe qu'on soit homme, femme ou cheval … il faut « bander », danser, s'amalgamer aux violences primitives de la Nature et de ses impératifs VIERGES. »

> (I clipped for you (Jean Luc Henning, the recipient of the letter A/N), in the new number of L'illustré, this magnificent reportage about the Cirque Zingaro, this show of horses in their "natural state" that you love so much. I can't stop thinking of it and admiring it. I am going to give you these clippings, for sure. There is an evident match between the strength and the truth of the horse "in the wild" and this purity, this will of Being, of existing, no matter if you are male, female or horse … You must "get it hard", dance, mingle with the primitive violence of Nature and its virgin imperatives.)[32]

On the eve of her "last deliverance" (this is how she called her death), the author returns to all the "Commandments" that have ruled over her existence, building a retrospective in which gipsy culture, bestiality, violence and Nature gravitate all together,

---

[32] Réal, G., *La Passe imaginaire*, op. cit., p. 243.

representing the imperative of being. Réal, using her compelling "it is necessary" ("il faut"), suggests that humans should raise, and to do so she uses the verb "bander", which in French precisely refers to the act of achieving an erection – the old healing act of liberation she recognized in virility and that, here, involves men and women as a whole. She thus affirms, once again, an identity that has been able to realize itself despite (or maybe thanks to) an unceasing "combat", thanks to the capacity of always standing in the apparently irreconcilable incoherence of her multiples faces, thanks to the will of celebrating the truth hidden in the aporia of the world and of her own personality.

« Every face of ours has two visages», she wrote in a letter "behind which they hide, because the only true one, the inner one – imperceptible – remains unknown."[33]. For Réal, therefore, "being" according to all the possibility suggested by her interiority has corresponded to one, realizable (and probably approximate) "truth". Another possibility, however, has always loomed over her personal narration: the "impossible" one, that in which, precisely, all the multiplicity she thought inhabited herself and the others existed as "virginally" summed and stable: The "Great Night of origins" of which she talked in "Le Noir est une couleur", that in which the human "fraction" was animal harmony, perceivable but not completely recoverable. An idea of unity she has lightly touched but never actually realized, and that also returns in her thoughts about death:

> « La vie et la Mort sont magnifiques et se donnent la main dans l'invisible, elles jouent à saute-mouton pardessus le Mur de Planck. [...] Le mystère reste entier, indéchiffrable, préservé. On peut masquer la mort de tentures solennelles, mauves, noires, pourpres et or ... elle n'en reste pas moins inexplicable ... entière dans sa nudité originelle. »
>
> (Life and Death are magnificent and they hold their hands in the invisible, they play leapfrog over the Planck Wall [...]. The mystery remains intact, indecipherable, preserved. We can dress up death with solemn shades,

---

[33] « Toutes nos faces ont deux visages derrière lesquels elles s'abritent, car la seule vraie, l'intérieure, insaisissable, est inconnue.» (ibid., p. 243).

mauve, black, purple and gold ... it is no less inexplicable, and entire in its original nudity.)³⁴

Life and death, reunited under the scientific metaphor of the zero-moment of creation (in which everything was one), represents an inscrutable compendium that—for de-formation, we could say—Réal would not have defined as (catholically) divine; and that, in an interview, she evokes in the form a "Grand Master", the culminating and unknowable sum of all those men that have been—for an entire life- the fragile, cruel and freeing Gods of her personal *pantheon*:

> Alain-Pierre Pillet : Qui aimez-vous ?
> Grisélidis Réal : Tous les hommes, et pourtant je préfère l'Inaccessible. l'Interdit, le seul Grand Maître des violences oni-riques, celui à qui l'on n'a accès qu'en esprit en sachant qu'il nous est dérobé pour la vie et l'éternité .
> (Alain-Pierre Pillet: Who do you love?
> GrisélidisRéal: Every single man, and yet I prefer the Inaccessible one. The Forbidden one, the only Grand Master of dreamlike violence, that to whom you can only have access through spirit, knowing that he has been stolen from us for all our life and eternity.)³⁵

Notes

A/N: Every French quotation in the present chapter has been translated by the author.

---

³⁴ Réal, G., *Les Sphinx*, op.cit. p. 301
³⁵ « 7 questions d'Alain-Pierre Pillet à Grisélidis Réal », in *Pris de Peur* n°7, 8-04-1998

Bibliography

Bhöm, T., Kaplan, S., *Revenge: On the Dynamics of a Frightening Urge and Its Taming*, Karnac Book Ltd, London, 2011.

Butler, J., *Bodies That Matter*, Routledge, New York, 2011.

Butler, J., "Can one lead a good life in bad life?", lecture delivered in occasion of the award received during the Adorno Prize, Frankfurt, 11 September 2012, in *Radical philosophy* 176 (November/December 2012).

Butler, J., *Gender Trouble, Feminism and the Subversion of Identity*, Routledge, New York and London, 1999.

Corona, D., "Critica letteraria femminista", in *Dizionario degli studi culturali*, Cometa, M., Meltem, 2004.

Chodorow, J., N., *Femminilemaschilesessuale*, trad. di Adriana Bottini, La tartarugaedizioni, Milano, 1995.

Chodorow, N., J., *Feminism and Psychoanalytic Theory*, Polity Press, Cambridge, 1989.

Cixous, H, Gagnon, M., Leclerc, A., *La venue à l'écriture*, Union Générale d'Editions, Parigi, 1977.

Davidson O'Connell, J., "The Rights and Wrongs of Prostitution", in *Hypatia*, Volume 17, No. 2, Spring 2012, pp. 84-98S.

Davis, K., "Intersectionality as Buzzword: A Sociology of Science Perspective on What Makes a Feminist Theory Successful", in *Feminist Theory*, April 2008.

De Beauvoir, S., *Il secondo sesso – II. Esperienzavissuta*, trad. di Cantini, R., Andreose, M., Casa editrice Il Saggiatore, Milano, 1965.

Diaz, B., *L'épistolaire ou la pensée nomade*, Parigi, Press universitaire de France, 2002.

Douglas, M., *Purezza e pericolo*, ed. il Mulino, Bologna, 1993.

Foucault, M., *Sorvegliare e punire*, trad. di AlcesteTarchetti, Einaudi editore, Milano, 1976.

Friday, N., *Mia madre, me stessa*, Milano, Mondadori Ed., 1980.

Gerassi, L., "A Heated Debate: Theoretical Perspectives of Sexual Exploitation and Sex Work", published on final edited form as, *J SociolSoeWelf*, 42(4): 79-100, 2015.

Genette, G., *Seuils*, éditions du Seuil, Paris, 1987.

Gilfoyle, T. J., "Prostitutes in History: From Parables of Pornography to Metaphors of Modernity", in *American Historical Review*, February 1999.

Glucklich, A., *Sacred Body: Hurting the Body for the Sake of the Soul*, Oxford University Press, New York, 2001.

Hennig, J.L., *Grisélidis Courtisane*, Verticales, Paris, 2011.

Hershatter, G., *Dangerous Pleasures: Prostitution and Modernity in Twentieth-Century Shangai*, University of California Press, Berkley, Los Angeles, London, 1997.

Hirsch, M., *The Mother/Daughter plot: Narrative, Psychoanalysis, Feminism*, Bloomington: Indiana U.P., 1989.

Irigaray, L., *Sexes et parentés*, Les édition de minuit, Parigi, 1987.

Jovovic, J., *L'Intimité épistolaire (1850-1900), genre et pratique culturelle*, Cambridge Scholars Publishing, Newcastle upon Tyne, 2010.

Kauffmann, V., *Lettres ouvertes, in L'épistolarité à travers les siècles – geste de communication et ou d'écriture*, Franz Steiner Vergalstuttgart, 1990, pp. 58-67.

Kristeva, J., *Poteridell'orrore*, trad. Scalco, A., SpiraliEdizioni, Milano, 1981.

Kristeva, J., *Stranieri a se stessi* trad. Serra, A., Giangiacomo Feltrinelli Editore, Milano, 1990.

Kristeva J., Goldhammer, A., "Stabat Mater", in *Poetics Today*, Vol 6, No. ½, *The Female Body in Western Culture: Semiotic Perspectives*, pp.133-152, Duke University Press, 1985.

Martinez Reventòs, M.D., "The obscure Maternal Double: The Mother/Daughter Relationship represented in and out of Matrophobia", in *Atlantis* XVIII (1-2), 1996.

Mc Call, L., "The Complexity of Intersectionality" in *Journal of Women in Culture and Society*, 2005, vol. 30, n.3, The University of Chicago Press, 2005.

Monticelli, R., *The Politics of the Body in Women's Literatures*, I libri di Emil, Bologna, 2012.

Monticelli, R., "Oltre lo specchio: politiche e poetiche di genere e delledonne", in *Moderna* XIV 1-2, 2012.

Réal, G., *Le noir est une couleur*, Verticales, Paris, 2007.

Réal, G., *Les Sphinx*, Verticales, Paris, 2006.

Réal, G., *La passe imaginaire*, Verticales, Paris, 2006.

Réal, G., *Mémoires de l'inachevé*, Verticales, Paris, 2011.

Réal, G., « Se prostituer est une acte révolutionnaire » in *Marge*, n.13, Novembre-Décembre 1977.

Rich, A., *Of Woman Born: Motherhood as Experience and Institution*, W W Norton & Co Inc, 1995.

Rich, A., *Blood, Bread, and Poetry*, Selected Prose 1979–1985, W.W. Norton & Company, New York, 1995.

Scarry, E., *The Body in Pain–The Making and Unmaking of the World*, Oxford University Press, New York, 1985.

Spivak, G. C., "French Feminism in an International Frame", in *Yale French Studies No. 62, Feminist Readings: French Texts/American Contexts* (1981), pp. 154-184.

Walkowitz, J. R., *City of Dreadful Delight – Narratives of Sexual Danger in Late Victorian London*, The University of Chicago Press, Chicago and New York, 1992.

White, L., *The Comforts of Home: Prostitution in Colonial Nairobi*, The University of Chicago Press, Chicago and New York, 1990.

Videography
Documentaries

« Grisélidis, une courtisane libertaire » in *Les Oubliés de l'Histoire*, Dir. Jaques Malaterre, arte tv, France, 2017.

Muerte de una puta, dir. Harmonìa Carmona, Spain, 2006.

Belle de Nuit – autoportraits, dir. Marie-Ève de Grave, Belgium, 2017.

Interviews

Interview by Pascal Reberezto Grisélidis Réal, published on *www.notrehistoire.com – ensemble pour l'histoire numérique de la Suisse romande*, and originally appeared in the show *Les grands entretiens* on RTS (2002).

Radio interview to Grisélidis Réal on "Radio Suisse Romande" (RSR), 10-09-2004, published on https://www.youtube.com.

A Place Not Our Own: Gulf Emigration and Bordered Lives in Benyamin's *Jasmine Days*[1]

Priya Menon

> You know how it is when you arrive in a new place and feel like you don't belong there? That hesitation to reckon with a new geography. That knowledge that this place is not mine, these ways of talking are not mine, these silences are not mine, this etiquette is not mine. So many new things to absorb. And the place also takes time to accept the new person. Often you have to meet the place on its own terms. Sometimes you have to work hard to earn your little corner in it. Till that place becomes yours, till you find your equilibrium there, there will be a gap between you and the place.
>
> Benyamin, *Jasmine Days*

Generally referred to as the Gulf, the GCC States consist of six countries of the Persian Gulf — i.e. Bahrain, Kuwait, Oman, Qatar, Saudi Arabia, and the United Arab Emirates. Since the *discovery* of oil in the late 20th century, these States have employed a large expatriate labor force, primarily from the South and Southeast Asian countries of India, Pakistan, Philippines, Sri Lanka and Nepal to fulfill manpower requirements for its booming hydrocarbon industry. Statistics tell us that more than half of the total population of the Gulf are such expatriates (Ahmad, 2011). This kind of mass emigration has not only allowed for the rapid economic expansion for the Gulf and 'sender' countries, but at the same time it has also contributed to various vivid and diverse cultural productions in the arts and humanities. Yet, the current dominant discourse on Gulf diaspora is primarily filtered only through the plasma of labor and its rights, let alone any cultural representation of them in narratives of significant political events,

---

[1] This work was partially supported by the Fulbright Scholar Program under the Fulbright-Nehru Academic and Professional Excellence Fellowship 2018 during which I have been affiliated with The Centre for Development Studies, Thiruvananthapuram, Kerala. This work began during my fellowship and since it also benefited from valuable comments that an anonymous reviewer has generously provided.

such as the Arab Spring that shook much of West Asia in the beginning of the twenty-first century. In what ways do the arts and humanities, especially the cultural production of narratives that create sites of interpretation, enhance our understanding of the bordered emigrant-native, individual-social, and political-artistic dyadic discourse on Gulf emigration? Much of the existing scholarship in the area is currently linked to the institutional analysis of economic, sociological, political and legal spheres of Gulf diaspora—mainly to tackle human rights abuses of the notorious Kafala sponsorship system of contractual labour that endows sponsors-employers (Kafeels—native Gulf citizens) with extraordinary powers over the migrant workers. These institutions expose instances of exploitation of Kafala ranging from mistreatment in the workplace to trafficking into situations of forced labor, and even death while trying to escape. Political and legal approaches to these problems are justifiably focused on seeking institutional solutions to labor rights abuses. Journalists, politicians, human rights advocates and legal practitioners who work on these issues are all driven by an important instrumental desire to change the climate of abuse and establish fair practices by influencing just policy making through advocacy. And, no doubt, the legal, socio-economic and political consequences associated with labor rights are numerous—both for the Gulf and also for the South and Southeast Asian countries that dominate the migration charts. For instance, while a top 'sender' country like India boasts of an exceptionally high economic remittance rate from the Gulf, India also registers an alarming suicide rate among Gulf expatriates and their immediate families. Yet, peculiarly, every year the number of emigrants from here to the Gulf continue to rise. Why do so many seek expatriation to these Gulf States? More particularly, what causes this exodus when the host country is partially hostile? How do they register their presence during a political upheaval in the host country? How do they disseminate information about their lives in the Gulf? How are their experiences registered in the cultural and literary fabric of their respective countries? How might one unearth the histories of a land that does not encourage/let alone allow expression of dissent? More importantly, how can everyday lived experiences of emigrants be made evident for a larger audience within the context of political rebellion and uprisings? Important as the acts of investigation and documentation of the socio-political, legal, and journalistic aspects are of Gulf emigration and diaspora, so are the poignant narratives of literature that represent and interpret the emotions and imaginations of these migrant experiences (Menon, 2020).

Cultural production of narratives that create sites of interpretation can also work alongside the institutional approach to Gulf emigration discourse to reveal vital links between what Homi Bhabha (2018, p. 8) calls the "human affect—the intersubjective realm of suffering and survival—and the aspirational mission of establishing human progress in practices of migration". For Bhabha (2018, p. 9), the human affect is "that whole set of emotional and imaginative non-visible forms and forces of life that relates to psychic identifications and its complex dependencies created by some form of materiality" (e.g. the way in which one relates to territorial displacement in one's life by constructing a whole narrative on how to deal with the fact that one is being stamped foreign). He claims that "out of the affective realm associated with distress of migration is born the imaginative desire to overcome, to survive, to make retributions and restitutions, to apologize, to reconcile, to even find joy—and to represent in dance, music, literature, and art—the lives and times of "others" who are hidden from history or are its victims" (2018, p. 7). Thus, while the existing discourse on Gulf emigration may contribute to institutionalizing a formal *archive* on Gulf emigration, its *affective* presence—the human experiences that complements these institutional practices, work alongside to provide a *counter-archive* that not only act as testimony to history by imaginatively recording it, but also to provide aspirational goals to creatively transform human relations and historical practices. Not just focusing on the simplified citizen-emigrant binary, this counter-archive is also informed by the quotidian everyday lived reality of generations of emigrants in the Gulf that involve multiple experiences—such as forbearance in the face of being stamped foreign, quest for ways of belonging despite being temporary, solidarity exhibited in creating communities, and agency (limited as it may be) displayed in the will to survive and sometimes even to thrive. Thus, practitioners and performers of the arts and humanities are not just 'record keepers' of the legal and political state(lessness) of migration, but are also interpreters of the human affect, — of the varying relationships between cultural meaning and social values in the Gulf as they shape civic agents who contribute to the creation of public opinion and the definition of communal interest. Creative writers of Gulf diaspora—Benyamin, Deepak Unnikrishnan, Hansathika Sirisena, Saud Alsanausi, André Naffis-Sahely, Tahmima Anam, to name a few—articulate aspirational values through the empathetic act of interpretation, by transforming the material elements of a known and shared world into an instructive aesthetic experience. When writing on the Gulf Diasporic conditions, they not only initiate an evaluation of the socio-economic situations that force emigrations in the first place, and in turn, challenge the coherence of the existing system of global capitalism but also recognize the human affects of territorial displacement. Acts of interpretation thus "allows for our aspirational goals to creatively transform human relations and historical practice" (Bhabha, 2018, p. 9) apropos the Gulf. An analysis of Benyamin's *Jasmine Days* succeeds in breaking down the arbitrary disciplinary borders between the humanities and social sciences by shaping a site of interpretation using the affective, human and historical raw material of the (non)-citizenry politics in the Gulf.

Benyamin's commitment to empathetic interpretation of the human affect of Gulf diaspora is profoundly grounded in social context and human discourse—language, dialogue, narrative, and symbols all come together in his extraordinary prize-winning[2] text, *Jasmine Days*. Set against the backdrop of the 2010 Arab Spring, *Jasmine Days* explores multiple migratory experiences of various South Asian nationalities in the Gulf

---

[2] Benyamin received the inaugural 2018 JCB Prize for Literature.

States—Pakistanis, Indians, Filipinos, Bangladeshis as they commingle with the local Arab (non)citizenry at the City's Radio station owned by Broadway Communications. Each emigrant group is projected as civil society. However, even when the characters are firmly rooted in their own nationalist or religious or familiar clique, they seldom belong: Sameera Parvin, the protagonist of the novel, is a young woman, a recent emigrant from Pakistan who enjoys the newfound freedom of being employed as a Radio Jockey, but must negotiate her allegiances when confronted with her 'other' alliances—family, friends, and colleagues; who fall on opposite sides of the revolution for political reform in her adopted land which in turn, create a break with her social affiliations. However, Sameera's ability to construct a narrative allows her to be a civic agent providing us with a counter archive of the revolution. Additionally, Benyamin's use of adeft narrative technique prompts us to investigate the multiple subject position that a Foucauldian author-function assembles, equipping him with numerous frames of narratives—where authors, translators, editors deliberately challenge assertions of a single author-creator as producing one dominant truth, "where fiction begins on the first page (Benyamin, 2018). This makes visible a dynamic contradiction in the text to be set as its creative loci—where emigration gets altered into the constructive craft of narrating—and at the same time bears the burden of distance and separation. Rather than wipe away the various authors of this text, I want to propose that the historically specific figure of Benyamin helps yoke-together various discursive strands.

Benyamin contextualizes *Jasmine Days* in the broader history of the Arab Spring of the 2010s when the original *Mullappooniramulla Pakalukal* was written and published by him in Malayalam[3] in 2014. Historical precision is not typically allied with the world of fiction; yet Benyamin has repeatedly insisted in being inspired to portray life as he observes it[i]. He began writing

---

[3]   Refer to Goat Days that describes the real life events of a Malayalee emigrant worker tortured under the duplicitous Kafala system in Saudi Arabia.

this Malayalam novel during his exile in the Gulf State of Bahrain, when a series of anti-government protests, uprisings, and armed rebellions spread across the Arab world that sought democratic freedom from the minority autocratic Sunni monarch: "It [the text] comes from my own experience of living in a Middle East country like Bahrain for so many years," Benyamin says in an interview (2018). The context of the publication of the novel is important because it explores various dimensions of a seminal moment in the history of the Gulf States and its representation in a narrative form that offers a cultural site of interpretation of the above defined human affect. Benyamin's specific status as an emigrant in Bahrain during the revolution provides us with a view of his political commitment when he says that he has "often wondered how the people could live through a dictatorial government, and if they didn't desire democracy. And then, the revolutions happened. The Arab Spring happened" (2018). Yet, in *Jasmine Days*, Benyamin doesn't name a country. It is simply called the 'City' — "It needn't have a name," Benyamin says, "it shouldn't be specific, for it can be any Middle Eastern country" (2018). In seeking such a generality, a continuing pattern to be found behind the specific detail of the setting, Benyamin's writing correlates with the Aristotelian conception of poetic truth. For Aristotle, poetry is a medium that explores the universals and hence retains the deepest kinds of truth. This idea of poetic truthfulness — that within this text, the characters and their actions can be found in any City, has certainly moved Benyamin to present the identifiably *true* though undocumented narratives of a plethora of diverse lives in the Gulf States during the Arab Spring. Publishing the novel post-Arab spring and playing with a self-reflexive form of narrative technique — a la Marquez, thus, aided him to create a text with political themes that are clear to his astute readers. Readers draw many parallels between the names of characters (Ali makes an oblique reference to the human rights activist, Abduljalil Al-Sangac), places (The Pearl roundabout was an actual square in the heart of Bahraini protest) and dates (14 February 2011 is the day the actual protests began) mentioned in the novel and the actual political revolution of 2010s in Gulf States, which was caused by many factors—resentment of autocratic monarchies, rising tensions between Sunni and Shia Muslims, gendered violence in the façade of revolution, and overrated power of social media to name a few. In fact, the chapter entitled "The Donkey Cart and the Mercedes" reenacts the 2011 scene in Tunisia which is said to have triggered off the Arab Spring when a street vendor, Mohamed Bouazizi killed himself after being hassled by state police officers who tried to shut down his business without providing any other alternative means of living. His suicide by self-immolation electrified Tunisian protesters, who captured and transmitted the events through their cell phones which inspired anti-government protests in neighboring countries such as Bahrain (Ryan, 2011). The resemblance of these events in historic annals and in Benyamin's fictive *Jasmine Days* is deliberate where two brothers, one an engineering student and the other a medical student, selling fruits and vegetables in a cart, are violently attacked by the police for "bringing shame to the country and its ruler by riding a donkey cart through such an important road, one used by foreigners and tourists" (p. 85). We are told that the next day the younger brother "immolated himself in front of the mayor's mansion just as the mayor was exiting his car" (p. 85). Such a commentary which plays with a historical fictive perception, a deliberate commingling of political and historical reality of the state is purposeful in order to challenge the literature-politics, fact-fiction boundaries to ultimately announce the universal value of such a text that self-reflexively chronicles the quotidian everyday lived reality of an albeit arguably a "failed revolution"[ii].

Set in the City, *Jasmine Days* is a labyrinthine structured *mise-en-abyme* narrative that questions reality through multiplicity of perspectives—both in form and content. From the outset, we are told that the text, *Jasmine Days* is Benyamin's translation of the original, *A Spring without Fragrance* written by Sameera Parvin in Arabic. The narrative voice gains more agency as Sameera dedicates the book to her father, Baba. Yet the reader is made aware through certain absence-presences that the book she is reading—*Jasmine Days*, is a translation by Shahnaz Habib of

Benyamin's Malayalam novel entitled *Mullappoonira-mulla Pakalukal*. Furthermore, throughout the text, we see Sameera addressing a friend, whom we later learn is her editor—Javed, with whom she even shares a private joke that the reader is not (yet)[iii] privy to in her *Afterword*: "Dear Friend, for remembering me in my time of need, for listening to this story with an open heart, here is a doughnut from me! (I hope that this small joke will remind you of the old Sameera, the one I hope to recapture soon). Yes, today, I am opening the door to a new life (2018, p. 258). In an interview with Narayan for *Hindustan Times* (2018), while explaining how he came to write *Jasmine Days*, Benyamin reveals his affinity for the works of Marquez; in doing so he indirectly sheds light on the kind of textual sensitivity he demands of himself and his readers: "Some of the translations are better than original works. Marquez always says that Rabassa's translations are better than mine. Like that, this one also [is better]". Benyamin's affinity to Latin American writers find an echo when Efrain Kristal in his book on the translations of Borges claims that "even as he compared many translations to their originals, Borges insisted that the aesthetic value of a translation does not depend on its relationship to the original" (23). More significantly, that Benyamin assigns himself the role of a translator allows us to agree with what Eduardo González (2005) asserts in his work "Creatore vs. Traditore: Borges, Reiss and Others on the Translator's Role" that all creators are translators; and that the creators-translators are:

> "those who devote much of their lives to the task of conveying culture, history, feelings and emotions from one language to another, from one conglomerate of people to another, from a part of the body of humanity to another part of the same body" (p. 95).

By inserting himself in the novel within the "Translator's Note," the character-Benyamin tells us that, initially, when he was asked to write a novel about the City he was reluctant: "to be honest, I was afraid of the consequences (p. 261); but when he read through Sameera's text he is immediately "drawn to its orbit" (p. 261) and thinks that "it was the novel that [he] would have written if [he] had the guts to write it (p. 263). He goes on to say that it was by "accident that the book ended up in [his] hands (p. 261) and that he is actually ghostwriting for Pratap, a Malayali journalist from Canada who had already acquired permission to translate Sameera's *A Spring without Fragrance*. The character-translator Benyamin goes on to reveal the privileged positioning of a writer:

> We are hardwired to share the good that happens to us. If we see a good movie, we want to tell a few people about it. If we hear a good song, we want our friends to listen to it. What's the point of making delicious food if we want to declare it to the entire world? A good book is like that. If we read a book that shakes us we have to share that experience. Soon I was obsessed enough to ask Pratap to seek permission from the book's editors to translate it [...] Whoever the story belongs to, the language is the writer's. You cannot sell language. We decided in the end that I would write Pratap's story as a novel. (263)

Thus, by agreeing to be a ghostwriter, Benyamin collapses the border between the various author-translator figures as he seems to confirm the inevitability of figuration in any mode of representation. A ghostwriter is really an absence-presence that signals a non-present presence in the text. Jacques Derrida (1994, p. 100) claims that 'the Specter, as its name indicates, is the frequency of a certain visibility. But the visibility of the invisible'[4]. Then, Derrida's concept of spectrality, can be used here to argue that Benyamin's goal here is to declare that so called authors, just as their characters — are also translator because they function as spectral figures, non-present presences, representing the intersections of Gulf history and the popular tales of it through which they establish a creative relationship between place, history and memory. Thus, as the unofficial translator of a historic event in the Gulf States, Benyamin taps into the layers of coordination between the individual memory of the storyteller and the collective memories of various narrations captured in numerous telescoping frames — that of Sameera's story, of Javed's possible degrees of edits, of Pratap's copyright conditions, of the Malayalam translation by Benyamin mixed with his formal text

---

[4] Please refer to the NPR Special Series entitled "Bahrain: The Revolution That Wasn't" (Jan. 2012).

of Shahnaz Habib's translation—all repeating itself infinitely to ultimately produce multiple sites of interpretation of various existential, intersubjective dilemmas that emerge from the affective realms of the paradoxes of personhood.

If *Jasmine Days* succeeds in dramatizing the borders and boundaries of form to be reflexive of its medium, to what extent does it explore the tensions between exile and affiliation? What are the possibilities of civil society when creative individuals are confronted by group ideologies in the context of a public political uprising such as this revolution? In *Jasmine Days*, the primary means of transportation can be seen functioning as a trope to regulate communication and social relationships. Sameera's journey to the Radio Station begins and ends on a bus—in what she calls a "Cattle Class Mercedes" (p. 18). The general nature of her experiences during her travel exemplifies collective emigrant behavior in the Gulf and helps us to comprehend nuances of that civil society. While the Toyota minibus that "looks good from the outside, [but] the inside is a different story" (p. 18) functions as a pivotal trope that collects characters and delivers momentum to the story, it simultaneously produces experiences of alienation for the individuals within the group. The ruler of the City and his establishments are not present; the passengers gathered in the bus are a collection of different emigrant groups—dominated by the Malayalam Mafia[iv] but also includes people from Sri Lanka, Philippines and Pakistan that share a common bus route in their the journey of emigration. This is an imagined location of civil society, where power supposedly reposes with the endless chattering jibes of Malayalam Mafia and with Yunus, the driver; but only to the degree that he delivers the service of transportation as dislocation. The bus quickly becomes the site of resentment where Sameera finds herself targeted as it becomes a cacophonous battle ground that the Malayalam Mafia controlled through unending gossip and strange scuffles with the ultimate goal to proclaim that "India was the most amazing country in the whole world" (2018, p. 21). Initially, non-Indian Shahbaz, Hasan and Sameera are the targets of the Malayalam Mafia's unfounded resentment because, reminiscent of Freud's argument about "the need to hate an outsider in order to establish group identity⁵" (Adorno, p. 137), in this case, what binds the society of haters is the presence of the questionable category of *outsiders*. What does this microcosm of the various emigrant social groups suggest by these daily ritualistic trips? The small sorority of non-Keralans comes about as a shield against the larger group that insists on exclusive behavior by speaking only in Malayalam: the hostilities and hatred are unfathomable. The bus ride becomes a contentious space because nothing prepares Sameera for the perplexing vehemence of their fellow expatriates. In effect, the emigrant community of the bus is established in and through the act of hating together. Extending the confusing behavior of the Malayalee Mafia's antagonism is the absence of sharing a common language:

> As soon as I got into the minibus, I could hear their annoying chatter, their voices like stones in a tin can. They were experts in speaking exclusively in Malayalam, without using even a single word from Hindi or English, so that the rest of us might not even guess what they were saying. Later they even started a radio programme based on this. I would plead with them, 'Aren't you tired of blabbering in your own language all day? Why not give it a rest now? And they would retort, 'That was for the public, this is just for us.' (Benyamin, 2018, p. 20)

For Sameera, there are no overt codes provided with which to master such social systems. The social language and code are indecipherable: neither Sameera nor the young men who become her ally have any way of knowing what motivates the silent rage in the bus. However, when the revolution hits the streets of the City, the emigrant community represented by the workers at the Radio Station are terrified and collectively escape from the riotous mob where "car[s] sped by us from opposite direction, without waiting for their turn" (p. 173) lead them all less to their liberation than to anxious conformity: the emigrants join the "Ass-Lickers' Rally" (p. 142) so that they, too, can participate in the events taking place around them—even though they will never

---

5   Perhaps fleshed out more fully in Benyamin's upcoming translation of *Al Arabian Novel Factory*, the "twin novel" to *Jasmine Days*.

belong. The sudden development of this bond between the Malayalee Mafia and Sameera is shaped through a shared experience of fear. Here, associations are molded precisely as they both encounter the aggressive revolutionaries, which the novel signifies as being fundamentally estranging: more than volunteering alliances, the novel lays bare an encounter for a common pursuit of shelter in the midst of a public existence marked by violence.

Moreover, alienation is oxymoronically augmented by modern but fractured instances of communication, which ironically weakens the expatriate social bond. Facebook and Twitter—dubbed as "train[s] to hell" (p. 55), become exclusionary tools whereby characters stumble through the revolution, struggling to decipher incomplete messages: obscure comments, vague references, and oblique remarks of exclusion:

> Facebook was a forbidden fruit in our household. The men of the house called it the ticket booth for the train to hell. But apparently, those tickets took only women to hell. Our men were free to delight in Facebook as much as they wanted, while we women sat patiently in heaven (p. 55).

Despite the modern means of communicative tools available at hand, its gendered and limiting nature underscore Sameera's helplessness to ultimately predict the devastating loss of her Policeman father and her revolutionary friend, Ali Fardan. Messages received during the revolution are equally unclear and ambiguously stated without a specific sender: when Farhana, Sameera's cousin, spots a notice pasted outside their home—the Taya Ghar, apparently from "Young Revolutionaries of 14 February" (p. 149), the private chaos of their lives are sharpened by the undisclosed identity of a specific sender and by the threatening tone of the notice: "who pasted this on our door? I shouted at Farhana as if she was guilty. Poor girl, what did she know. I was, in fact, more terrified than she was and was taking it out on her (p. 149)." Later on when all of Taya Ghar goes silent on Sameera, withholding information of her Baba's brutal murder, the readers sense that the narrative technique employed by Benyamin colludes in denying us complete information, so that we share Sameera's doubtful obliviousness in a world of family, neighbors and friends who seem to discern something they hint at but hide. Only at the end does the novel reveal the secret everyone else seemed to be in on—Sameera's father was killed by none other than her best friend, Ali Fardan. In another instance, Sameera encounters a hostile gaze from a native woman who was clearly enraged at the emigrant community for upholding, albeit inadvertently, the oppressive monarchical regime: "It was not merely resentment, it was a mix of envy, self-pity, helplessness and desperation. Her eyes were saying, 'Look at you, travelling in a fancy car, getting rich in my own country, while I have to take this service bus in this heat. You are responsible for my misery" (p. 130). Analogous complications with communication inside established groups (family, friends, neighborhood, nation) often lie at the root of the emigrant experience of alienation in Benyamin's novel, as if the social were undeniably the location of this dehumanization.

However, it would be deceptive to propose that practices of intimate and authentic relationships are absent in Benyamin's text: Sameera's long nights filled with friends and music with the "String Walkers"—her guitar loving friends, are a prime example of an attempt at genuine civil society. The friendship shared by Ali and Sameera, along with Sameera's relationship with her father—Baba, provide the cornerstone for the architectonic unity in *Jasmine Days*; therefore, it is essential to explore the position of these characters apropos each other, their various affiliations and the modes in which their subject formation is tied in with the respective social codes. The rapports between Sameera and Ali on the one hand; and on the other, Ali's allegiance to the Shiitevi cause of political reforms, are based on various differences and social distance.

Benyamin constructs his characters as outsiders to act as critical voices that slide in and out of their associated group identifications. Sameera is a favored member of Taya Ghar, where she successfully influences decisions made by her Sunni father, uncles and aunts; yet, she is ostracized for allegedly having an affair with the Shia, Ali. Similarly, Ali having born and raised in

City is a member of the majority Shia population and is a true citizen; yet he is considered a "second class"and experiences discrimination for "not belonging to the ruling Sunni's" (p. 62). Ali and Sameera work at the same Radio Station. Their friendship begins when together they defend group action as superior to a one-man show when the Malayalam Mafia's claim that "the most beautiful game in the world was cricket" (p. 44). Sameera's argument foreshadows the root of the political unrest that will envelope the City: I said that cricket is a one-man show and it is the man of the match who usually wins the game. But in football, you can see the beauty of teamwork. And finally, I argued, the pleasure of winning as a team is much bigger than the pleasure of winning for oneself. (p. 45). We soon begin to see the possibilities of social formations in Benyamin's fiction when Ali and Sameera are drawn together in constructing an imaginary place—complete with post-offices, villas, small villages and streets:

> The next day he invited me to be the postmaster of his 'Shia village,' an imaginary place in a Facebook game called City Villa. I accepted and invited him to be the police officer in my village called 'Lahore Gali'. Thus, two City villa freaks stopped being strangers in the same office [...]. He visited Lahore Gali and helped me harvest carrots or deliver goods to the bakery [...]. Till then, the two of us, with our different languages, cultures, and religions, had nothing in common. But now we had a Facebook dream to build together. (p. 45).

Ali is focused on bringing his virtual world to reality through a path of revolution and the need for political reform. Benyamin's political and ideological stance toward the protest movements is established as a dominant implication fornative, migrant and stateless citizens during the revolution which is here foreshadowed and later encoded along the terse lines articulated by the numerous Facebook/Twitter status updates by Ali: "Your Majesties, Excellencies and Highnesses: we spit on you" (p. 104); "History will judge you. These streets will not forgive you" (p. 144); "Today's news is tomorrow's history. Let's make news!" (p. 152). Also, Sameera do not belong to the emigrant majority that stay away from the revolution; her sympathies are with the cause of political reform, yet she is called out by a middle-aged protestor: "pointing his finger at me, he said "[...] you shameless foreigners, you are dogs eating the leftovers of this government. Till you leave, this country will not get better" (p. 129). Working under a Kafala contractual system that removes any agency foreign workers may have, emigrants are indeed "ready to work on meager pay [...] making the government so arrogant" (p. 129). Here we see that even though Sameera's sympathies to Ali's cause give her privileged access to the sphere of revolutionary actions, she remains an outsider. Additionally, Ali's affiliation with his music group—the String Walkers too comes under duress when he is determined to play "Hawk of Lebanon," a popular song of revolution, but the group did not want "to bring politics into our music" (p. 145). Sameera is confused when Ali stubbornly walks out: "There was nothing left to say. We had believed that even as the country fell to pieces around us, even as communities broke down, music would keep our little band strong and tight, like a taut string on a guitar. But even our miniature world was in ruins now" (p. 146). Ali's vacillating position problematizes the group's harmony—he is their friend and participates in all the sessions, buthe cannot eschew the space that separates a revolutionary's alertness from engagement with a social body such as the String Walkers. Ali's ideological idealizations do not allow him to establish deeper connections and commitments as he elides into becoming a puppet at the hands of revolutionary ideologies.

That the discussions Ali have on the revolution is utopic is made clear as it traces the ideologies of dream, revolt and festival that permeate the entire narrative. In the chapter entitled "The Hawk of Lebanon," Ali recounts of his recurring dream that haunts him lately: an animated crowd drags "the ruler of the country" to sodomize, torture and ultimately shoots him to death but when the identity of the gunman is revealed to Sameera as Ali himself, she is shocked and "begins to fear Ali as if he were an alien from another planet" (p. 70). Like the numerous protesters who actually marched in Bahrain at the Square of Pearls in 2011, *Jasmine Days* feature protests through recitation of poetry, chanting of sad slogans and singing of revolutionary songs. Dreams, music and song become instrumental in the political crisis that rebels against the archaic structures and the authoritarian monarchies of the contemporary Gulf autocratic society. Later on, a curious reader will learn in historic annals that the Shia protesters indeed marched to dream-like discipline using sad songs and music as their creative excrescence. Thus, in history and in fiction, they find their way toward what Michel de Certeau calls "the irruption of the unthought," (Sorensen 1999, p. 384) where dream and revolt merge to yield a space that offers a productive intertextual resonance to reveal the homogeneity between so-called history and fiction. The site of protest with its evocation of music and song to express dissent, along with unleashing the powers of eros—which gets expressed when they are jokingly cited as "condom revolutionaries" that the leaders of protest rightly dismisses, suggest that the revolutionary dreams in the text has a shot at a possible victory, but only with a fictive combination of imagination and action:

> Friends, this is a protest full of celebrations. Three or four pairs of young people have got married here in this protest camp. Others have got engaged. Yet others are celebrating their anniversary here [...] This is a protest that emerged from our common humanity. Anything human is welcome here. We are not afraid of human nature [...] This is not a protest for lifeless statues. This is a protest for ordinary people, human beings with bodies and needs. That's what makes it a human protest (p. 137)

The protestors are staging a way of living which has firm roots in the world of purposive action; yet it is a performance, a stirring up in order to disband routine and convention. Nevertheless, as the end of the novel makes regretfully certain, nothing has been accomplished, except for the many sacrificial deaths, especially of Baba; and the arrest of Ali. The accomplishment, however, is in Sameera's return to Pakistan before the country gets to hear that she has written a novel documenting the Arab Spring. Besides, the text tells us that revolution is suppressed, the group scatters, its traces to be read not only in Sameera's *A Spring without Fragrance* but also in the future book that Benyamin hints at the end. The reader anticipates the sequel, having had a glimpse at the text through "A Preview Chapter from Al Arabian Novel Factory: Coming out in 2019" (p. 265). As an epilogue, the preview confirms that politics as representation that provide creative sites of interpretation will have the power of provocation even if it ends up calling into question its ultimate realization.

Eventually, it is Sameera's atypical status as an emigrant majority (without power) belonging to the Sunni minority (that has power) that endows her with a distinctive insight that ultimately creates and holds this novel together. For after all, it is her condition of 'insider's outsideness' (Bhabha, 1995, p. 14) that enables her to fully engage in the representation of the quotidian lives lived during the rebellious revolution in her novel, *A Spring without Fragrance*. Her commitment made to writing—escaping the country to reach it to safe hands, offers us an understanding into the various relationships between and across borders of separation as she remains the privileged point for Benyamin to empathetically affirms the role of artistic innovation in creating spaces of interpretation. Then, in many ways, Sameera's engagement with innovative artistic representation of a historical moment is similar to Ali's desire for creating anew his old land. In the end, however, what comes to fruition is Sameera's text proclaiming that artistic practices can be considered more unsettling than Ali's activism, as it attempts to challenge its own conditions of existence within its own domain—a quality that the revolutionaries eschew as made clear by the voice of an old man in the text: Even "a four-year old [can make you] believe things by repeating them again and again. So imagine the kind of thing we would believe if sooth talking politicians and religious leaders kept talking to us, insisting that they alone have the truth. Our biases and beliefs have a lot to do with what we row up hearing. And that's what happened to Ali" (p. 232). Yet, Ali expresses relevant socio-political responsibilities of a dissident and progressive citizenry. Can the socio-political obligations expressed by Ali and artistic innovation exhibited by Sameera be brought together in the text? What links the revolutionary culture to creative production here through negotiations between self-reflexive, critically informed writing and the demand for a democratic state without surrendering the power of one or the other? We have no answers as we are threatened with an *aporia*.

However, Diana Sorensen's discussion on the author-function (1999, p. 384) as that which "actually assembles but never resolves statements and positions which stem from the disparity of historical change" will help us acknowledge that a dynamic reading of this text can be achieved not by advancing a resolution but by engaging in a creative dialogue that will forever vary. Thus, the only potential resolution is deferred by the Benyamin author-function: It is those many prospective readers of "Al Arabian Novel Factory" who will variedly interpret this text, which has resulted from an abstract but creative attempt at providing a site of interpretation of the human affect that aid in erasing the borders between the native and migrant, the individual and the group, the writer and the translator.

Notes

i. Refer to Goat Days that describes the real life events of a Malayalee emigrant worker tortured under the duplicitous Kafala system in Saudi Arabia.

ii. Please refer to the NPR Special Series entitled "Bahrain: The Revolution That Wasn't" (Jan. 2012).

iii. Perhaps fleshed out more fully in Benyamin's upcoming translation of *Al Arabian Novel Factory*, the "twin novel" to *Jasmine Days*.

iv. Malayalam Mafia is a playful name given to a group of Malayalees— natives of the southern Indian state of Kerala.

v. The Shia majority of Bahrain remains under the autocratic rule of a Suni minority monarchy, and hence the protests led by the Shiite cause of democracy.

References

Adorno, W. Theodor (1991). "Freudian Theory and the Pattern of Fascist Propaganda", Ed., in *The Culture Industry*, J. M. Bernstein. London: Routledge.

Ahmad, Attiya. (2011). 'Beyond Labor: Foreign Residents in the Gulf States', Ed. *Migrant Labor in the Gulf*, Mehran Kamrava and Zahra Babar. Doha: Center for International and Regional Studies, Georgetown School of Foreign Service Qatar.

Benyamin (2008). *Goat Days*, Trans. Joseph Koyippally. New Delhi: Penguin.

Benyamin (2018). *Jasmine Days*, Trans. Shahnaz Habib. New Delhi: Juggernaut.

Bhabha, Homi. (1995). "Unpacking My Library Again", *Journal of the Midwest Modern Language Association* Vol. 28, p. 14.

Bhabha, Homi. (2018). "Migration, rights, and Survival: the importance of the humanities today", *European South*, Vol. 3, p. 7-12.

Chris, (July 27, 2018). "*Of 'Jasmine Days' and revolution: Writer Benyamin speaks to TNM about art and society*, Retrieved from https://www.thenewsminute.com/article/jasmine-days-and-revolution-writer-benyamin-speaks.

Derrida, Jacques. (1994). *Specters of Marx: The State of the Debt, the Work of Mourning, and the New International*, Trans. Peggy Kamuf. New York: Routledge.

González, Eduardo. (2005). "Creatore vs. Traditore: Borges, Reiss and Others on the Translator's Role" *Confluencia*, Vol. 21, No. 1. Denver: University of Northern Colorado Press.

Kristal, Efrain. (2002). *Invisible Work Borges and Translation*. Nashville: Vanderbilt University Press.

Menon, Priya. (Anticipated Jan. 2020). "'*Pravasi* Really Means Absence': Gulf-*Pravasis* as Spectral Figures in Deepak Unnikrishnan' s *Temporary People*," *Journal of South Asian Studies* (accepted publication)

Narayan, Manjula (Nov. 2018). "Revolution and the Immigrant Life," *Hindustan Times*, Retrieved from https://www. hindustantimes/videos/of-revolution-and-the-immigrant life.

Ryan, Jasmine. (2011). "The tragic life of a street vendor", Al Jazeera. Retrieved from https://www.aljazeera.com/indepth/features.

Sorensen, Diana. (Mar. 1999). *From Diaspora to Agora: Cortázar's Reconfiguration of Exile Author*, MLN, Vol. 114. pp. 357-388.

Challenges and Resistance to the Partition of Bengal: Impact of Baul and Marafati Oral Tradition

Sharmistha Chatterjee Sriwastav

In 1905 Lord Curzon divided Bengal by separating and foregrounding the eastern, Muslim dominated Bengal and Assam, from the Hindu predominant, smaller part of West Bengal along with Bihar and Orissa. The colonial rulers cited the reason asdifficulty in administering a province so vast and huge in length and breadth. The people in Bengal did not take this Partition in the right spirit and amidst widespread protests; the Partition had to be revoked in 1911 although Bengal had to subsequently give away Bihar and Orissa, which were given the rights of independent and separate provinces. As a seeming punishment to the audacity of the Bengalis, the British shifted the capital of their empire from Calcutta to Delhi. Bengal could never recover its former glory, although the British could never crush the spirit of its people.

1905 was a crucial year with the subcontinent being at the peak of Nationalism and the Bengali intelligentsia (primarily educated, Hindu, upper class) putting in all their efforts to prevent the vivisection of the two communities (the Hindus and the Muslims) in the name of Partition. At that time, 'Nationalism' of the Bengalis had not become synonymous to 'communalism' (in the words of Joya Chatterjee)[1] which it was to become in the 1940s leading to the

---

[1] Jaya Chatterjee in her book, *Bengal Divided: Hindu communalism and partition, 1932-1947* published from Cambridge University Press (1994), explains how, in the years between 1930s and 1940s Nationalism became communalized. In her words, "The relationship between Indian nationalism and communalism is complex and ambivalent, both in terms of ideology and political practice. Recent studies have argued that nationalism in India cannot be regarded as the 'other' of communalism. The opposite of communalism is secularism, which separates politics from religion. Admittedly, many aspects of Indian nationalism were not in this sense secular: nationalist campaigns often manipulated religious imagery and issues to win popular support. Nor did Indian nationalism have truly secular ideological and philosophical

final Partition of Bengal. Among the many nationalists and thinkers who saw the possibility of destroying hierarchy and creating a broader milieu of inter-faith and inter-community understanding in the free-state was, Rabindranath Tagore with others like Bipin Chandra Pal, Satish Chandra Mukherjee, Manoranjan Guha Thakurata, Aswini Kumar and others. One of the significant events which resulted in the rescind of the 1905 Partition was undertaken by Rabindranath Tagore in the form of 'Rakhi Bandhan Utsav'. Tagore travelled beyond the homes of individual brothers and sisters, thrust himself upon the public domain and proclaimed the fraternity of the Hindus and Muslims in Bengal. The 'bandhan' or the ties were to be between the two communities, (the 'petals of the same flower', in the words of Kazi Nazrul Islam). Tagore's efforts were to once again establish that, Bengal consisted of the unity of the Hindus and Muslims who had lived in the land cheek by jowl for centuries.

It is in this year , at the dawn of the Swadeshi movement, which was launched to protest against the Bengal Partition of 1905, Rabindranath composed his historic , patriotic song 'Aamar Sonar Bangla, Aaami Tomae Bhaalobasi' [O my golden Bengal, I love you] (later to become National Anthem of Bangladesh). Critics trace the origins of this famous song to one of the popular *Baul* songs of Gagan Harkara, 'Aami kothaae paabo taare' [where do I find him/her]. Later on Tagore composed another extraordinary patriotic song 'Je tomae chaare chaaruk aami tomaae chaarbona ma' [let those who want, leave you, I am not going to leave you mother] based on the tune of Harkara's other song 'O mon osaar maayaae bhule robe kata kaale emni bhaabe' [O heart , how long will you be forgetful in this way, entrapped by the numbing, worldly

---

underpinnings. Nationalist thought tended to share the colonial view that the basic unit of Indian society was the community as defined by religion. The 'secular' nationalist ideal was *sarva dharma sambhava*, that is, the equality of all communities and the spirit of accommodation between them. Yet most nationalist thinkers tended to describe national identity in religious terms, and to equate being an Indian with being a Hindu. This was particularly marked in Bengal, in the writings of Bankimchandra Chattopadhyay, Aurobindo Ghosh and Swami Vivekananda and in the brand of 'extremist' nationalism they inspired.

attractions]. Incidentally Gagan Harkara (1840-1910) and Gosain Gopal (1869-1912) were disciples of 'Lalan Fakir' or 'Lalan Sain' (1774-1890)[2] who composed over hundred *Baul/Sufi* songs on eclectic themes, including love and amity between people of diverse religions and communities. Gagan Harkara knew a lot of songs and was an itinerant singer. It is from him that Karunamoy Goswami collected *Sufi* or *Baul* songs for printing in the 'Haramoni' section of 'Probasi Patrikaa' (a patriotic periodical printed from 1901 onwards, for about 60 years). One may guess that Tagore must have heard Lalan's songs initially from Gagan although there is historical evidence of Tagore having met Lalan in person.

Supratip Debdas of Indian Baul Search Academy, records in his book *Lalan Fakirer Gaan*, (*The Songs of Lalan Fakir*, 1410 [2003, English Calender], pages 20-21) Sachindranath Adhikary's (Sachindranath was the accountant of the Silaidaha estate) anecdote titled "Lalan Fakirer Sange Molakat' ("A meeting with Lalan Fakir") which is about Rabindranath's meeting the Fakir :

> Apparently, one morning around 1311 (Bengali Calendar), the poet was at his study table in his Silaidaha house. During this time, a group of his subjects came to meet him and talk about their problems. All of them were from the other bank of Gorai river belonging to the Cheuria village near Kushtia. When Rabindranath had finished with them, it was already 11.00 a.m. Among the group of subjects who sat in rows on the benches, was an old man, sitting right at the back. He seemed to have no petition. He did not say anything nor did he ask. Only, the old man continued to gaze at the poet in rapt attention, throughout the entire span of time. Although the poet looked at the gentle face once or twice and showed an interest to listen to him, the cacophony of the crowd prevented him from doing so. After having pleaded for about three to four hours, the crowd went away in the same way as they had come.
> Thereafter the poet went upstairs for taking a bath and having his lunch. At this moment, his eldest daughter showed him a strange walking stick. It was not a sophisticated one, but a crude villager's prop...so queer was the *laathi*.

---

[2] According to Professor Abul Ahsan Chowdhury, one of Lalan's disciples Malam Shah gave Lalan around 16 *bighas* of land at the Cheuria village. In this donated piece of land grew Lalan's *Aakhra* (place of congregation). Local disciples of the artisan class build a spacious East open hut, made of straw. The straw house had balconies on all four sides to enable Lalan stay as well as continue his *Sadhana*. Next to this, Lalan himself built another straw house, where he sang and prayed. It is here where he was buried at his death. (Chowdhury *Lalan Shah* Bangla Academy Dhaka p. 21).

Constant contact with oil and water had made the stick black as ebony. The hilt of the stick was bent like the mouth of a snake...and lo! The hilt has been made to resemble the snake's mouth perfectly, with a variety of decorations. Rabindranath enquired, "whose *laathi* is this"? But neither the servants nor the guards could say anything about it.

Finally Haider Mian, an armed-guard from Cheuria said, "*Hujoor*, this stick belongs to Lalan Fakir, a man from our village."

It is said that Rabindranath was astonished to know that Saiji had visited his home. The poet had heard a lot about him but had not seen him. After hearing from Haider Mian, Tagore immediately sent after Lalon Fakir. The rural singer and the poet struck a chord immediately. After a long discussion, Lalon sung with his *ektara*,

Aami ekdino na dekhilaam tare,-
Aamar barir kaache aarshinagar,
Taate ekparasi basat kore...
[I didn't see him even for a day,-
Aarshinagar is close to my home,
There stays this neighbour of mine ...]

Rabindranath was touched with the sincerity of the song of this unknown, illiterate village poet. Songs followed with their myriad moods and tones. That was the beginning of a lifelong paradisiacal relationship between the two.

(translation and abridged version, mine)

The song sung by Lalan Fakir when he met Rabindranath for the first time is translated and enlisted as Song number 36, by Abu Rushd in his book *Songs of Lalon Shah* published by Bangla Academy (1990). What should strike the readers immediately are the rapport and the intimacy that the few lines are able to build between the listener and the singer, the educated and the illiterate, the elite and the subaltern. We might never know whether Lalan specifically composed this song for Rabindranath, but for the moment the 'neighbours' were the Poet and Lalan himself, to be tied in an everlasting tie. It is this utter hypnotic attraction of the diction and the arrangement of the diction in a garland of meaning that smites the listeners of *Baul* songs to this day. These songs appeal to their hearts, ultimately creating a harmonious relationship between the singer and the audience.

Recognizing the richness of Lalan's songs and the *Baul* tradition the 'Bengal Renaissance' borrowed heavily from the oeuvre and spread the message of inter-community faith and love as an integral part of 'Nationalist' movement, to be used as an antidote against the divisive policies of the British and the advances of Hindu Nationalism. While the general tide of thought after 1905 was spearheaded by the elitist Bengalis who slowly but surely became a mouthpieces of Hindu interests, at the cost of neglecting the feelings of the majority Muslims in undivided Bengal, there flowed a subterranean current of a subaltern discourse in the form of folk songs and folk culture. The *Baul* and the *Marafati* movement was a part of this alternative 'Nationalist' discourse which spun the dream of a utopia based on universal love and brotherhood. When orthodox votaries of Hinduism championed discrimination on the basis of caste, community and gender, these subaltern counter-discourses included all and sundry: In the thoughts of Lalan, who believed in the 'religion of Humanity' or 'Manab-Dharma':

> In earthly waters
> Grow a great variety of fishes,
> And yet the lord of the world
> Remembers every fish.
> (translated Rushd, ll 11-14 Song 23)

The unlettered Lalan and his disciples often composed songs which were allegorical like the above, yet stalwarts like Rabindranath read deep, Upanishadic meanings in them.

The literary world of the late nineteenth century and early twentieth century in Bengal was fraught with contradictions. Those works which claimed to invoke a rich pre-colonial past were actually pushing forth a 'hard Hindu identity, defined in and by its conflicts with the Muslim as a marker of rising nationalism.' (Sengupta 13) Bankimchandra's novel *Anandamath* (1882) or Rangalal Bandopadhyay's long Kavya, *Padmini Upakhyan* (1858) are early examples of the growing sense of difference visible at this phase of Nationalism catapulted through a plot of Hindu- Muslim animosity. Such attempts were to take larger proportions in the later writings. Another issue which became one of the pressing subjects of the period was the question of woman's identity in the patriarchal world. The discourse created by this world, set for its women the impossible, superhuman ideal of becoming as divine and pure as the 'Deshmatrika' (The nation as divine mother, as in Bankim's *Anandamath*). Confronted with an impossible metaphor of becoming an asexual divinity, women felt being robbed of life and freedom. Rabindranath's novels *Chokher Bali* (1902) and *Ghare Baire* (1916) depicted such women's lives at the cusp of the two centuries, caught between tradition and the pull of modernity. In 1905, Rokeya Sakhawat Hossain's utopic novella *Sultana's Dream* allegorically alluded to the Muslim woman's sense of isolation and oppression at home and in the public sphere by the domination of patriarchy.

While mainstream literature continued to portray the skirmishes of caste and gender, the oral and alternative narratives were completely at peace with these differences. According to Akshoy Kumar Dutta, the noted Brahmo reformer and scholar, there were no less than 56 Vaisnavite or semi-Vaisnavite sects during the years 1870-80 in Bengal[3]. A majority of these sects were founded by members of the discriminated castes among the Hindus and the excluded Muslims (as explained, in the elitist nationalist discourse). Sujata Mukherjee in her research article observes:

> Fusion of Islamic and non-Islamic beliefs undoubtedly influenced the growth of the ideas of a large number of sects including the Auls, Bauls, Sahajiyas, Fakirs, Darbeshis and other wandering saints and minstrels. In the mid- 18th century, an Aul named Alakh Shah preached neo- Platonism as well as Hindu- Muslim unity and spread influence over Auls and Bauls of Dacca, Mymensingh, Chandpur and Barisal Districts. Popular religious cults centring round the personality of individual leaders grew up whenever any Brahminical guru initiated people belonging to low castes. It became a common practice of orthodox sections to ostracise and denounce them as "Sahajiya". (612)

These popular cults repudiated caste rules and idolatry. They considered the figure of a 'guru' as the spiritual teacher and also the 'shaman' or the medicine man who could cure diseases. Among the Bauls too, the 'Guru' or 'Murshid' is conceptualized as the

---

[3] The above data is furnished by Sujata Mukherjee in her research article, "Popular Sects and Elite Culture in Nineteenth Century Bengal: Some aspects of Interaction and Assimilation." page III/20.Mukherjee cites the following book as the source: Dutta, Akshoy Kumar. *Bharatbarshiya Upasak Sampradaya*. Vol.1 (1st edition. 1870) Reprint. Calcutta. 1987.

spiritual guide who mediates between this world and God. Members of these sects carried out many esoteric yogic practices which continue the traits of Sahajiya-Tantric tradition. Such practices accorded high position to women who were treated as partners, equals or 'Adyashakti' or the 'Universal female principle' in the physical sense. Most of these cults repudiated Brahmanical religious rituals and practices and opted for liberal, eclectic beliefs contained and disseminated through their songs. Thus as a challenge to the growing rift between communities and caste discrimination within Brahminical tradition, Lalan sang:

> Everyone enquires about the caste of Lalon,
> Lalon replies he cannot differentiate one caste from another.
> If circumcision is the mark of a Muslim
> What happens to its womanhood
> The Brahmin may be known by his sacred thread
> But how about their women-folk?
> Some sport a garland, others an amulet
> Does that alone set apart a Hindu from a Muslim.
> (Rushdll 1-8, song 73)

This powerful song addresses all possible aspects of exclusion and discrimination- that of caste, community and also of gender.

Around 1894, it was again Tagore who was vociferous against the neo-orthodox dogmas which became the parameters of Hindu Nationalism and literature of the times. In this year, in a lecture to Bangiya Sahitya Parishad, he emphasized the alternative and real ideology of Literature in an essay titled 'Bangla Jatiyo Sahityo' (Bengali National Literature):

> The word *sahityo* (literature) originates from the word *sahit* [from the Sanskrit root meaning to be together, author]. If we take its etymological meaning, then the word Sahitya carries within it the idea of Unity. This unity is not just between ideas and expression, between languages, with one text and another; it is the coming together of man and man, between past and present, between the far and the near: a veritable intimacy of connection that is only possible through literature and through nothing else. In a country where literature is scant, the people are not united in a lively bond but separated from each other. (qtd. Sengupta 14)

As an alternative to the narrow parochial interests of mainstream literature, Rabindranath Tagore, early coming to know of *bauls* and *fakirs* (who composed the *Baul* and *Marafati* songs at Kushtia in Nadia District, undivided Bengal), first brought the *Baul* songs, their lyrics and melodies to the attention of the 'bhadralok' or the educated gentry of Bengal. These songs/poems began to be collected soon after Tagore had published about 20 songs of Lalan Fakir in the Bengali journal, the *Probashi* in 1915. A series of *Baul* poems and fragments were translated by the poet in his *Religion of Man* (being Hibbert Lectures of 1930) and delivered in Oxford:

> I would not go, my heart, to Mecca or Medina,
> For Behold, I ever abide by the side of my Friend,
> Mad would I become, had I dwelt afar, not knowing Him,
> There's no worship in Mosque or Temple or special holy day
> At every step I have my Mecca and Kashi, sacred in every moment.
> (Anonymous)

> That is why, brother, I became a madcap Baul,
> No master I obey, nor injunctions, canons or customs
> Now no man-made distinctions have any hold on me,
> And I revel only in the gladness of my own welling love,
> In love there's no separation, but commingling always,
> So I rejoice in song and dance with each and all.
> (by Narahari)[4]

Rabindranath's choice of these songs/poems in simple, rustic parlance, not only discusses an alternative religion based on love and unity, but hint at an alternative utopia- an imaginary nation based on 'Manab Dharma' or the religion of humanity and love, where the only pursuit is one of truth. It is to be noted that the origin of the word *Baul* is synonymous with 'a madman or a madcap' as expressed in the first line of the song by one Narahari. The etymological roots can be traced to Hindustani *Bawla* or *Baura*, (in the modern deviated sense of 'colloquial' Hindi: *Awaaraa*) from Sanskrit *Vatula*. With their long flowing robes, white or ochre in colour, their hair tied to a bun on top of their heads, with a one stringed instrument (*ektara*) and anklets round their feet, these

---

[4] The two songs, one anonymous and the other by Narahari are cited from the research article "Hindu-Muslim Baul and Marafati Songs in Bengali Literature" by Chaterji, Suniti Kumar and Chatterjee, Suniti Kumar. Indian Literature, Vol. 15, No. 3 (September 1972), pp. 26-27.

itinerant singers were a common sight before Partition in Bengal. In their songs is a manifestation of the composite culture and spiritual yearning of India; handed down orally and practiced in 'Akhras' (now at Kushtia and Nadia) these songs discuss an amalgamation of beliefs (as explained earlier) derived from Islam, Vaishnavite, Tantric and Buddhist Sahajiya tradition, thus attacking the very principle of 'neatly drawn borders'.Usually, this composite type of religious poetry or songs composed by the Muslim Bengali has two common names *Baul* songs and *Marifati* or *Marafati* songs. Predominantly, the first name *Baul* comes from a class of religious mendicants who have both Hindus and Muslims among them, who worship the one, true God, although they may indulge in figures of Hindu mythology and Muslim symbolism to describe this Godhead. These mendicants profess to be above limitations of caste and sectarianism (as evident in Narahari's song). Hindu *Baul* sare married according to their own customs and do not follow any Brahmanical codes and orders. Muslim *Bauls*, sometimes referred to as Fakirs naturally use a larger Muslim vocabulary of Persian and Arabic words in their compositions– but not always. When the atmosphere is predominantly Muslim, with references to Sufi lore, these *Baul* songs are known as *Marifati* (or *Marafati*) songs, from Ancient Arabic *Marafat*, meaning 'Inner Knowledge'. However, even *Marafati* songs can have Hindu Yogic or Vaishnavite (Radha-Krishna or Chaitanya) allusions and references.

Lalan Fakir's or Lalan Sain's (as he was referred to) songs, sometimes manifest all these idiosyncrasies. While Song 1 refers to both Allah and Noah, Song 3 refers to Prophet Muhammad, Song 11 and 12, refer to Quran and Murshid; Song 39 refers to both Ram and Rahim; Song 53 refers to Varanasi and the Lord, while song 54 refers to 'my Lord, dark of complexion,' hinting at Lord Krishna. Song 69 specifically refers to Lord Krishna: 'Who has not succumbed to Krishna's charm?' By the time the listeners/readers reach Song 70, the bewilderment reaches its peak. Song 70, talks of the 'possessed' at 'Nadia' and of 'a fellow' very strange 'to whom caste differences get ignored.' One who utters the name of 'Hari' and (as the song finally reveals), 'The one who embraces everyone/Calls himself Chaitanya.'[5]

Recurrent images of 'blindness', 'forest', 'prison' 'cage', 'raw bamboo' , 'house' refer to the pain and ignorance of being trapped in the human body and life, whereas images of 'alert physician', 'clouds', 'illumination' 'garland', 'bird of paradise', 'crossing', 'moon', 'looking–glass' 'bridge of Diamond' refer to man's redemption by God from pain and suffering and the final return to the Almighty. The other important, set of images, juxtapose a world of carnality and the male-female union as a path to this salvation. There are references to 'female organ' as well as the 'male', 'catch(ing) the fish', not 'touching the water', 'fabled snake', of a 'jewel' in Song numbers 33 to 76, hinting at the esoteric and alternative sexual practices. In such practices the female becomes as important as the male in the ritual of the search for divinity through sexual union, thus offering freedom, choice and equality to the female which is absent in the greater and orthodox world of the Hindu, Muslim communities. The significance of the female could be further endorsed by citing the Vaishnavite imagery in the song by a Muslim *fakir*, Ali Raza (Song no 402, in Professor Ahmad Sharif's book, *Muslim Kabir Pada- Sahitya*):

> Where can I conceal you, O Love,
> When can I conceal you?
> Through the strong fire of love even the body of my love sweats,
> The three worlds are burnt into ashes.
> Your love is a precious jewel, what strength have I to keep it on?
> The whole world has a right in it.
> The three worlds are as a sacrifice to her
> Who knows how to preserve this previous love,
> She is indeed the really beloved one, happy in her success;
> She that is without love is dead in life,
> Beginning or end, no good to her. (ll 1-10)

Again, it is possible to discern in Lalan's songs a strange, irreconcilable blending of Arabic/ Persian and Hindustani words. Songs 39, 60, 61 or 62 (from Abu Rushd's collection)in original Bengali contain words as, 'janam', 'aasman', 'daria', 'fikr', 'hujoor',

---

[5] All song numbers refer to the anthology by Rushd, Abu. (1990). *Songs of Lalon Shah*. Bangladesh, Dhaka: Bangla Academy.

'qabulati', 'tufaan', 'qudrati', 'khuda', 'hayaat' contradicted with Sanskrit/Bengali/Hindustani words in the same poems/songs as, 'bhram', 'khsiti', 'jal', 'hutashan', 'bhasma', 'amrita', 'rasik' ,'sujan', 'gagan' and so on. Thus, Lalan's songs could be grouped under the *Marafati* tradition sometimes with a predominantly *Sufi* atmosphere. Song 39 could be quoted in original to show the amalgamation of opposites in search of God and the ignorance of the human engaged in the process:

> Ke kothaa koe re dekhaa daenaa.
> Nare chare haater kaache khujle janam bhar melena.
>
> Khunji tare aasman jami,
> Aamaare chinine aami,
> E bhison bhrame bhrami,
> Aami konjon se konjona.
>
> Ram-rahim boleche je jon,
> Khsiti jal ki bae—hutashan,
> Sudhale taar onneshon,
> Aamae murkho keu bole naa.
>
> Haater kaache hoe naa khabar,
> Ki dekhte jao dilli-lahore,
> Seraj shah koeLalon re tor
> Sadai moner ghor gelona.

Abu Rushd translates the song as the following:

> I can hear His voice but cannot see Him.
> After the frantic search of a life-time one cannot find him.
> I look for Him in the sky and on the earth
> I do not know what I am
> and move in delusion.
> Who am I and what is He?
> He may be Ram, He may be Rahim,
> He may be water, He may be fire,
> but this fool is never told the truth.
> You do not know what happens in your own hamlet,
> Why then go to Delhi and Lahore?
> Seraj, the friend, says "Your mind, Lalon,
> will never be illumined".

This song, a perfect example of *Baul* heterodoxy, is also an alibi to bring the opposites together, 'Delhi and Lahore', 'Ram and Rahim' in search of the eternal. Lalan's songs further present a conversational, colloquial style of the common man to his friend and protector, Seraj. The essential simplicity, artlessness and inclusive character of these songs which defy categorization, got an appeal among the subaltern masses and spread as a counter discourse to both native and foreign divisive forces.

It is easy to reject the role of these abstract, allegorical songs in 'Nation' making, but the *Baul* songs did have a concept of a 'eutopian' place, the good place, which is practically achievable as opposed to 'utopia', the distant dream. It is possible to equate the *baul/fakir's* dream of an egalitarian society as a substitution of the concept of 'Nation', as a 'socially constructed community, imagined by the people who perceive themselves as part of that group' (Anderson 6-7) much in the same way as Kazi Nazrul Islam or Jibanananda Das composed poems and songs about Bengal's society, topography and demography. Song 98 [Supratip Debdas, Indian Baul Search Academy, *Lalan Fakirer Gaan*, (*The Songs of Lalan Fakir*)] of Lalan sketches and dreams of a good place of future; a Nation where there would be no communities and castes: "emon samaj kobe go srijon hobe/jedin hindu- musalman- oudhya- christianjaati-gotra naahi robe." [When will such a society be created/where hindu-muslim-buddhist-christian community- castes would not be there?]

The allegorical nature of the *Baul* songs often rendered them incomprehensible to people who were not aware of such practices and resulted in serious linguistic as well as semantic and conceptual deviation. They could be compared to a mass of amorphous materials which often resembled mazes or cryptic puzzles. It is this protean or androgynous nature of the songs, and the assumed carnality coupled with it, that drove the Brahmanic Hinduism and Shariati Islam to describe them as Heretics or 'Sophists' in the classical sense of the term. For the fundamentalists such practices were blasphemous and therefore the *Bauls* and *Fakirs* were hounded and marginalized. But the real objective of these syncretic sects through their reverse practices was and is, to return to their own self which is 'sahaja' or inborn in nature (i.e love, compassion, amity and kindness). The path adopted, indicates self-introspection and self-realization by shorning artificial rituals and therefore 'Sahajiya'. After the introduction of the British colonial rule in the 2nd half of the eighteenth century, the Sahjiyas in Bengal began to face special problems. The government eyed this syncretic tradition with suspicion and a possible obstacle to their policy of 'Divide and Rule'. It was easy to brand this diffused group as anti-socials, miscreants or dacoits. Without the support of the majority of the population they were easily incarcerated, tortured and killed.

The Letter Copy Book of the supervisor of Rajshahi at Nattore, (Mr. Boughton Rous), January 1770, described the Fakirs and Sanyasis as 'pernicious tribes' (Sanyasi and Fakir Raiders in Bengal 41). Early in 1772, a certain Majnu Shah sent a petition to Maharani Bhawani of Nator, at that time the largest Zamindar in Bengal to win her sympathy in favour of the *Fakirs*. Among the many things mentioned in defence of the *fakir* tradition and rituals the petition also mentions how the British harassed the itinerant beggars and singers,

> [...] Nevertheless last year 150 Fakirs were without cause put to death. They had begged in different countries and the cloaths and victuals which they had with them were lost.... Formerly the Fakirs begged in separate and detached parties but now we are all collected and begged together. Displeased at this method they [the English] obstruct us in visiting the shrines and other places- this is unreasonable. You are the ruler of the country. We are Fakirs who pray always for your welfare. We are full of hopes. (Sanyasi and Fakir Raiders in Bengal 47)

The intensity of such oppression mounted after the suppression of the great Sepoy Mutiny of 1857-58, post which the British assumed direct control over the Indian affairs by the British Crown-in-Parliament,

> As a part of the new comprehensive policy of domination, the colonial rulers decided to initiate moves to divide the united forces of opposition in order to forestall any repetition of the experience of the Sepoy Revolt. Consequently, the British Viceroys and Provincial Governors embarked upon a cynical policy of playing with the Hindu- Muslim religious diversities among the Indians, pitting one community against the other....theBauls of Bengal Began to experience organized onslaughts from

the orthodox Shariati Islamic leaders in the closing decades of the nineteenth century. The maulanas and mullahs concentrated their offensive against the presentation of syncretic philosophical songs by the Bauls as well as the Sufi Fakirs...Similarly Hindu orthodox leaders at Calcutta came out with satiric song processions variously criticizing the Bauls and the Fakirs for their syncretistic inclinations. (Dasgupta 81-82)

A Bengali tract, *Baul Dhangsher Fatwa* written by Maulana Riyajuddin Ahmad of Rangpur towards the beginning of twentieth century (second edition reprinted in 1925) contained specific instructions given by the maulana to his followers. The instructions ordered the organization of militant committees in each district to crush the *Sahajiya Bauls* and *Sufi Fakirs*. Notwithstanding the organized onslaughts, Riyajuddin's tract mentions some sixty lakh *bauls* in the early decades of the twentieth century, still engaged in propagating their songs and dance and spreading the message of love, harmony and brotherhood in the villages of undivided Bengal.

Perhaps, to a section of the educated gentry, these rustic, mendicant singers symbolized a perversion of culture and heritage. Their activities which were unpredictable, threatened the neat borders, hierarchies and paradigms much in the fashion of Bakhtin's, 'carnivalesque' where the lower orders challenge and berserk societal norms. It could be that these heterodox sects were detrimental to the few in power, who wanted the largest political representation for themselves after independence. But at the hindsight, the *bauls* and *fakirs* were aiming in their local, unpolished parlance, exactly the same that a few constructive individuals like Tagore were dreaming for Bengal and the country:

> Where the mind is without fear and the head is held high
> Where knowledge is free
> Where the world has not been broken up into fragments
> By narrow domestic walls
> (Gitanjali 35 ll 1-4)

In this regard, Tagore's observations in the introduction to Muhammad Mansuruddin's rare collection of Baul songs entitled *Haramoni* is worth quoting:

> The elites in our country who call themselves educated have been exploring tactical measures for Hindu- Muslim amity out of their own compulsions. They have taken the training of history in schools which are alien to us. But the real history of our country bears testimony to the devotion for synthesis which has been shared by the common people as the innermost truth in their emotional depths. This devotion can be located among the Bauls-their syncretistic tradition emerging as a common heritage of both the Hindus and the Muslims who came close without hurting each other. Such a confluence did not end in a meeting or a committee. This blending has produced songs. The language and music of these songs is melodious with a suavity which is untutored and natural. The voices of both Hindus and Muslims have converged to make the songs resonate as a chorus, without giving anybody a chance for provoking a confrontation between the Koran and the Puranas. This confluence is the real reflection of the Indian civilization, while the confrontation exposes the uncivilized edges. (qtd Dasgupta 82)

It is true that the Partition of Bengal could not be averted, but the Baul songs and tradition are a testimony to the sincere attempts to deter Partition, continue and preserve the essence of Bengali culture and ideology—the belief in inclusiveness, acculturation, unity and amity. These songs/poems remain as fantasies today in official narratives. As Lacan (and Freud before him) has reminded people, that the event of trauma, by its very ambiguous nature, recedes to the background while fantasies based on it overpower individual and collective psyches.

In spite of all aggression and hatred and an utter refusal to offer any space in the meta-narratives, in spite of attempts to shirk the *Baul* way of life as a fantasy, the *Baul* and *Marafati* tradition have survived all odds. The aspiration of eutopia (good place) for all (a unified Bengal), post 1947 and even 1971, has ultimately yielded to 'heterotopic' spaces in reality, where these subalterns have made 'things different'[6] (Walter Russell Mead). Hounded down as heretics, these marginalized people continue to challenge societal and religious domination by congregating yearly at *Dolpurnima* in Kushtia (Bangladesh), *Joydev Mela* at Kenduli (Nadia, India) or *Poush Mela* at Shantiniketan (India) to spread the message of

---

[6] Mead, Walter Russell uses this expression to describe 'Heterotopia' (originally a concept of Foucault) in his Journal Article, Trains, Planes, and Automobiles: The End of the Postmodern Moment. (1995/1996). *World Policy Journal.* 12 (4). pp-pp.13-31. https://www.jstor.org/stable/40209444.

'Manab Dharma' or 'the Religion of Humanity'. Following Sri Ramakrishna's belief in his 'Kathaamrita' that the *Sain* or the *Baul Guru* is a person of supreme perfection and the congregation of followers, most divine and pure in their aspirations, *Bauls* and *Fakirs* have indeed proved their mettle by carrying their music far and wide. In an interview taken by Madhurima Dey, published in 'The Sunday Statesman' on 7th July 2019, Purna Das Baul reiterates the true meaning of the sect:

> I often call it the art of knowing people and touching their souls. *Baul* is the bridge that connects humanity and the creator of nature… It is an amalgamation of *dharma* and *sadhana*. …*bauls* are wanderers; they wander from place to place, singing songs in pursuit of happiness and captivate the life of other beings and not just their own life. The iconic *ektara*, which they carry, symbolizes their nomadic life and their sacrifices to get closer to other human beings and God. (01 8th Day)

Purna Das is however severe about the modernization of *Baul* music and culture: "It is not easy to become and remain a *baul*; it takes a lot of dedication, devotion and sacrifice. *Baul* Music cannot be produced inside air conditioned recording studios." On being asked about sects with whom the Bauls identified outside West Bengal today, Purna Das promptly continues, "In the Sindh province of Pakistan, they are called Sufi singers *alan fakir*. These *fakirs* have many similarities with *bauls*. Even their dress code and way of singing are similar to ours" (01 8th Day). The last answer of Purna Das during these times of intolerance, perhaps makes the philosophy and intention of this continuing, oral tradition, crystal clear. Like all sane art forms, *Baul* and *Marafati* is about bridging borders and finding sameness among differences.

References

Benedict, Anderson. R.O'G. (1991). *Imagined Communities: Reflections on the Origin and Spread of Nationalism*. United Kingdom, London: Verso.

Chatterjee, Jaya. (1994). *Bengal Divided: Hindu Communalism and Partition, 1932-1947*. United Kingdom, Cambridge: Cambridge University Press.

Chatterjee, Suniti Kumar and Chaterjee, Suniti Kumar. (1972). Hindu–Muslim Baul and Marafati Songs in Bengali Literature. *Indian Literature*, 15 (3), pp-pp. 5-27. https://www.jstor.org/stable/23330736

Chowdhury, Abul Ahsan. (2009). *Lalan Shah*. Bangladesh, Dhaka: Bangla Akademi.

Dasgupta, Atis. (1994). The Bauls and Their Heretic Tradition. *Social Scientist*, 22 (5/6), pp-pp. 70-83. https://www.jstor.org/stable/3517903

Debdas, Supratip. (1996). *Lalan Fakirer Gaan*. India, Kolkata: Indian Baul Search Academy.

Dey, Madhurima. (2019, July 07). 'Baul is a way of life'. *The Sunday Statesman: 8th day*, p. 1.

Mukherjee, Sujata. (1996). Popular Sects and Elite Culture in Nineteenth Century Bengal: Some Aspects of Interraction and Assimilation. *Indian History Congress*, 57, pp-pp.612-623. https://www.jstor.org/stable/44133366

Rushd, Abu. (1990). *Songs of Lalon Shah*. Bangladesh, Dhaka: Bangla Academy.

Sengupta, Debjani. (2016). *The Partition of Bengal: Fragile Borders and New Identities*. United Kingdom, Cambridge: Cambridge University Press.

Sharif Ahmed. (1961). *Muslim Kabir Pada- Sahitya*. Bangladesh, Dhaka: Dacca University.

Sanyasi and Fakir Raiders in Bengal. Chapter V: The Raids Increase, 1770-1772. United Kingdom, England and Wales: Taylor and Francis. pp-pp.41-49. http://www.southasiaarchive.com/Content/sarf.144355/211618/005

Bordering the Screen: Separation Themes in Popular Film and Television

Amanda Rutherford and Sarah Baker

Contemporary film and television continue to expand on themes of borders and walls within their narratives, creating ever-growing interest in popular culture. These storylines delve into cultural anxieties surrounding ideas of the threat of war and terrorism, alienation and isolation, consumerism and loss of individualism, as well as religion and apocalyptic events. Film provides a visual platform to explore these current real-world concerns and utilises boundaries and walls as dividers between that which is deemed to be the safe and secure, from the unknown 'other' in the form of zombies, infected animals or humans, foreign species or those considered to be of lower class or social standing. This chapter investigates the trope of boundaries and walls found in film and television such as *The Colony* (2016-2018), *Game of Thrones* (2011-2019), *The Walking Dead* (2010-2018), *The Hunger Games* (2012-2015), *Zoo* (2015-2017), *Blade Runner 2049* (2017), *The Maze Runner* (2014), and others where the threat of separation is at the forefront of human existence. These examples from popular culture are utilised as a means to explore the advantage given to those behind the wall or separation divider, as well as to showcase the alienated, viral, disadvantaged or poverty stricken who are often left behind. These fears are teased out and recreated into several genres such as horror, science fiction, post-apocalyptic, thriller and dramas with many receiving huge success and fame. The physical boundaries and barriers are examined and how they manifest into modern representation for everyday contemporary society.

To contextualize the current real-world anxieties in film and television, one cannot ignore issues such as the influence and effects of the current political climates across the world, such as Global Warming and environmental concerns, as well as problems surrounding the raised levels of surveillance and the constant threat of deteriorating economies, cultures and societies. The heightened apprehension and fear created through these current and real threats to humankind inspires producers of film and television content to explore the possibilities of a collapsing world, from various viewpoints and degrees of degradation, as a representation and means to voice these concerns across the screen. It is interesting to note however, that these representations in film and television are often reflected by walls and boundaries, where a distinguishable border is established to isolate the unwanted or feared, in order to preserve what is considered to be the 'chosen' or 'untainted' individuals, worthy of redemption. As current global concerns are brought to the fore there appears to be a 'mirroring effect' seen on screen, with multiple scenarios presented to view all possible outcomes of the real-world fears surrounding the events. Furthermore, is it pertinent to consider the possibility that these borders and walls found in film and television may in fact be providing an ongoing stream of potential solutions to the perceived dilemmas faced in modern times, providing a basis for political advantage, control and power on a global scale.

An example of this can be seen by looking at the Trump ideology for America in the run up to the 2016 election. Media coverage promoted patriarchal principles encouraging Americans to stand together for the wellbeing of their country and kin, and to cast aside foreign labour and products. To achieve this, it would be necessary to create distinct boundaries and walls and include stringent regulation of migrants into the country. One of Donald Trump's most controversial policies was the proposal, which created a division in both the media and the general electorate, of constructing a wall along the Mexican border. The American/Mexican border measures approximately two thousand miles in length with about six hundred miles of this currently comprising of physical man made barriers (de Monchaux, 2016). In reality the existing barriers could easily be severed as they are mostly made of chain-link, so to effectively close the entire border between the countries would require a massive cost, and to serve what purpose? Is it possible that the creation of the wall along the

Mexican border echoes popular film and television tropes seen prior to this time, like that of the thirty-foot tall wall built in *Doomsday* (2008), to control the 'Reaper' virus from spreading through Britain from Scotland; or the seven hundred-foot high and three hundred mile long solid ice wall isolating Westeros from the north in *Game of Thrones* (2011-2019), which was built to keep the undead White Walkers out? Trump has consistently iterated that America needs to be purified or cleansed of migrants in order to regain the strength and power to the American people as part of the 'Make America Great Again' campaign. The Mexican migrants being likened to the 'infected' or undead who seek to bestow their virus upon the American people.

Diener and Hagen (2013) suggest that territorialization is made up of two main processes, the division of land between the social entities, and the resulting social implication that the separation means. In order to keep Americans 'safe' it was thus essential to reclaim American territory by closing the borders, thus Trump issued Executive Order 13769 in January 2017, which permitted a travel ban on seven largely Muslim countries. This raised the level of concern and the urgency of the ban was spurred on by the San Bernardino terrorist attacks in December 2015 and the Orlando shootings at the gay nightclub *Pulse* in June 2016, which were carried out by individuals of Muslim descent, giving a means to instill fear that the Muslim community at large are to blame for crime within the American borders, even though no correlation exists. We suggest that it is the combination of the physical separation and then associated symbolic meanings that generate the power of boundaries and separation in popular culture texts. Walls and barriers, physically separate space marking boundaries and territories but also symbolically splits people into classes and demarcated space. They are not only physical symbols, but psychological emblems of alienation and self-division.

Historically, there have been many walls that have taken prominence in history and the collective consciousness, and it is prudent to assess these barriers in terms of their impact on modern society, by contrast and comparison. In mapping the association and relevance to popular film and television, it can be argued that these narratives which are viewed as a form of entertainment, are able to explore the hidden anxieties and fears of the real-world, which are frequently felt in times of uncertainty and stress. The Bible, one of the oldest texts ever written, talks of the walls of Jericho and Jerusalem. The Jericho wall was built some eight thousand years Before Christ (BC) (Kenyon, 1960) as a defense against flooding and way to fortify the city; and the wall of Jerusalem, built in the sixteenth century to surround the old city, and is approximately forty feet high and eight feet wide containing thirty-four watchtowers and nine gates. These walls resonate with popular films like that of the *Hunger Games* franchise (2012-2015) in that the city of 'Panem' is protected by similar majestic barriers with watchtowers and large gates. Panemis referred to by President Snow as the "beating heart" of the dystopian America in *The Hunger Games: Mockingjay*–Part 1 (2014), with the surrounding districts providing all requirements to fulfill the needs of the city and the people within it. The result of this is that the people within the Capitol Panem are excessively fed and nourished whilst others are deprived and left with barely enough food to survive.

The expansion of borders and border control displayed in popular culture mirrors the growth seen in real world examples. Diener and Hagen (2012, p. 9) suggest:

> In sum, as of 2011, approximately 12,500 miles (ca. 20,000 kilometers) of the world's borders are marked with walls or fences and an additional 11,000 miles (ca. 18,000 kilometers) host noticeable security enhancements such as surveillance technology and patrols.

The template for this expansion in popular culture appears to emerge out of a direct and growing public concern surrounding emerging and current political viewpoints, and the continuing instability on a global scale. United States President George H.W Bush when speaking before the United States Congress in 1990 stated that this was an era of a new world order which was emerging on the base of new greater international cooperation and based on values like freedom, justice and peace. More recent key events like the September 11th terrorist attacks in 2001, the effects of the United States 2016 general election for example, and the fall out of Brexit in 2016, appear to highlight the growing concerns over the use of territory namely borders and controls. As the 1990s ended, the "rhetoric of a frictionless globalized world, the free movement of money, goods and people (Luckhurst, 2017) disappeared and in the new millennium there has been an extraordinary expansion of wall-building projects. This seems to largely be in reaction to the anxiety created by open borders and human flows of populations. Diener and Hagen (2012, p. 5) suggest that "today, perhaps more than ever, the rise of cross-border processes, patterns, and problems, often lumped together under the term "globalization," challenge established notions of territorial sovereignty" .However, the definitions and means of examining the patterns that emerge around borders and boundaries are often fluid and difficult to assess. Furthermore, Haselsberger (2014, p. 505) suggests that the definitions around borders are complex:

> They are multifaceted, multilevel and interdisciplinary institutions and processes transecting spaces in not only administrative and geopolitical but also cultural, economic and social terms (Donnan & Wilson, 1999; Newman, 2003; Paasi, 2005; Popescu, 2012; Scott, 2012; Van Houtum, 2011; Wilson & Donnan, 2012a, 2012b). Borders either confirm differences or disrupt units that belong together by defining, classifying, communicating and controlling geopolitical, sociocultural, economic and biophysical aspects, processes and power relations.

Popular film and television texts link walls with a dystopian and often apocalyptic representation that seems to echo periods in history such as of one of the most iconic modern-day walls of all time, the Berlin Wall. The collapse of the Berlin Wall suggested that the story of separation and repression was coming to an end and that the new promise of globalization was to see the world more interconnected and freer than before. The fall of the wall was meant to suggest optimism for freedom that never quite came to fruition. The "unprecedented geopolitical changes of the late 1980s and 1990s, most notably the collapse of the Soviet Union, the fall of the Berlin Wall, and the proliferation of regional trade blocks (EU, NAFTA, ASEN, etc.) compelled a broad reassessment of border functions, practices and meanings" (Diener & Hagen, 2013, p. 60). It was, however, the collapse of the Berlin wall that signaled the new era of globalization, that has since been the driving force of the new representations of tensions in popular culture of walls, boundaries and population divisions.

Notwithstanding the stark contrast in size, a surprisingly similar parallel exists between the Berlin wall and the makeshift barriers and compounds seen in most zombie narratives such as *28 Weeks Later* (2007), *The Walking Dead* (2010–2019), *World War Z* (2013), *Z-Nation* (2014–2018), *Fear The Walking Dead* (2015–2019), to name a few, where a world which is now free of barriers has become nothing short of a nightmare. The once peaceful depiction of the world as a free and open global channel of growth and prosperity now becomes the sight of death and destruction, where mere survival becomes the most one can hope for, yet unachievable alone. To live one must rally together with others building walls as tall as possible with scraps of metal, wood or any object large enough. Lookout towers and manned, armed guards rotate duties to ensure the joint safety of all, and as such the acquired freedom is little different to imprisonment.

The Berlin Wall was designed to prevent the mass migration of Eastern bloc citizens to the West, and erected when the rise of nuclear armament put the USSR and America against each other in a cold war. This was a key turning point in international relationships and mass nuclear weapon production, and effectively the world was gathering pace to be able to destroy itself in an apocalyptic nuclear event. Public distress and anxiety was extremely high during this time and we argue that this spurred an increase in the production of film and television narratives of apocalyptic events and disasters. These productions often included themes of separation and isolation, war and terrorism, the loss of individuality and faith in the post-apocalyptic world.

Setting up Walls and Increasing Boundaries: The Threat of War and Terrorism

The Berlin wall was built in 1961 to separate both physically and ideologically the West and East parts of Germany after world war two. The border zone itself became the "iconic setting for many spy thrillers, from John Le Carre's *The Spy Who Came in from the Cold* (1965), to Stephen Spielberg's *Bridge of Spies* (2015)" (Luckhurst, 2017).

Walls and barriers, throughout history and film, have been erected primarily as a means of identifying the physical territorial boundaries, differentiating one space from another. Diener and Hagen (2012) suggest that they also create separation on a political level, or for economic or social division. From the political front, the threat of war and terrorism has been a constant concern to both governments and public, creating a raised concern and need for protection and surveillance between factions and countries.

After the terrorist attacks on the United States on September 11th 2001, the reality and vulnerability of America left the world reeling. The terror from this act of terrorism became the extreme focus of countries on a global scale, and simultaneously film and television have seen a string of films that present societies as divided, such as *The Minority Report* (2002), *V for Vendetta* (2005), *The Space Between* (2010), *Zero Dark Thirty* (2012), *White House Down* (2013), *The Fifth Estate* (2013), *Snowden* (2016), *The Angel* (2016), *London Has Fallen* (2016), *The 5th Wave* (2016), *Designated Survivor* (2016–2019), *Sand Castle* (2017), and *12 Strong* (2018), to name a few. This effectively marked a new phase in post-apocalyptic films. There is also an increase in productions based on high levels of surveillance of both individuals and large populations, like *Eagle Eye* (2008), *Paranoia* (2013), *Closed Circuit* (2013), *Eye in the Sky* (2015) or *The Colony* (2016-2018) where intrusive and divisive governments set a patriotic agenda that is often militaristic and repressive. In these films, renegades and militants are often down trodden rebellious armies fighting for freedom. The walls and boundaries that are put up, are there to hold power over the populations and generally maintained by military control. Often there is resistant presentation to those who are initially portrayed as criminal or militant. The terrorist attacks of the 2000s have resulted in several political leaders across the world seeking to increase control of territorial borders.

The Great Wall of China is another example of the extent to which nations will go to protect themselves from intruders. This wall was started in the seventh century BC to protect from invaders from the north (CBC News, 2012), and became a collection of man made barriers which were later joined to create a total of 13 170 miles of wall (CBC News, 2012), and one of the seven wonders of the world as the longest man made wall on the globe. In the popular film narrative, the science-fiction adaptation *The Great Wall* (2016), explores life protecting the barrier to human safety from alien monsters, with several armies permanently stationed on the top in order to be ready for attack. The anxiety surrounding the threat of losing all to a foreign nation is explored with scenes of monsters in their thousands scaling the massive wall by piling one upon another to get to the top, while the humans desperately attempt to save it from being overrun.

In *World War Z* (2013) a similar representation is witnessed as Jerusalem city and the wall become central to the plot as a place of sanctuary for the Israelites and Palestinians within its massive walls. Marshal law is declared as zombies are infecting millions of people across the globe, and the safety of being behind this great wall lifts spirits and the people begin to sing. This false sense of security is quickly lost as the singing attracts zombie hordes that climb upon each other to get high enough to breach the top, and effectively infect those on the other side. These stories resonate with the contemporary fears of terrorists invading seemingly impenetrable borders, and the ensuing suffering brought to entire nations; the evocation of conscious thought about the ramifications of the enemy 'scaling the wall'. As such, walls erected across borders need to be continually enhanced and upgraded by governments or leaders; prioritizing the most advanced technology available to ensure strength and durability. The question remains as to the cost and affordability of this enhanced security, and if in fact these borders can provide the safety sought, as acts of terrorism continue to occur. Diner and Hagen (2013) concur with this idea, stating that "the borders themselves are changing as new walls, fences and observation towers seem to emerge daily" (p. 61), but the net effect remains constant –a fear of being overrun by something or someone.

Frequently, there is massive inequality seen in the populations and the futuristic societies are seen in factions. In many of the films, such as *Divergent* (2014), *Insurgent* (2015) or *Allegiant* (2016), there is a mixed sense of who is really the enemy much akin to the feelings surrounding terrorism and acts of war in contemporary society. A key trend that comes across in all the popular cultural texts we analyse however, is that borders constructed to keep people excluded or contained are permeable filters and their efficiency or utility is largely carried out subjectively. "Their specifics are shaped by legal, governmental, historical, social, political, and economic circumstances" (Diener and Hagen, 2013, p. 66). Even within structures, there is varying permeability, and these sites become the area of space that are contested in the narratives. The Divergent series mentioned here explores the ideas of trying to create a better or pure society, and question who the real enemy might be, with the narrative setting out a massive wall which serves to protect those within it from hostile beings beyond. People within the futuristic walls have formed factions based on human virtues, providing essential services to the whole community. Although the society is initially depicted as a perfect example of how harmony can be achieved, is it soon clear that there is a corrupt leadership and hidden agendas. Popular culture texts are very good at potentiality and suggesting what the future may hold (Gurr & Polka, 2015), and these films showcase the consequences of social division in modern society where issues of threat and survival come to the fore. War and terrorism are not necessarily found to be coming from outside the borders of neighboring countries, but rather from within the very heart of the people that are being protected. The leaders in the Divergent films are constantly chasing down 'Divergents', who fit the parameters of all the individual factions and are thus considered a high threat to the harmonious system. Bail (2008) says that whilst boundaries between countries create a division in terms of social groups, "the conceptual distinctions used to construct notions of "us" and "them" are an equally important component of social identities" (p. 37). These factions within the narrative of the Divergent franchise show that the outside enemy at times is lost to the internal violence and terrorism that ensues within the wall. Thus, the wall is rendered impotent and incapable of protecting those people within who have relied on it for their safety. The leaders are seen injecting the population with a serum to clear their memory, rendering them much like zombies, so whilst the population are led to believe that outside of the wall is where the danger lies, it is the danger within that is far greater. It is only later revealed that this post-apocalyptic city of Chicago is merely a part of an external experiment, controlled from outside of the wall by a group of scientists who seek to slowly restore places like Chicago to their former glory days. The experiment is deemed a failure when the humans within the walls are not performing according to prescribed requirements, and the premise continues as a fight to ensure this external eradication does not happen, forming tensions and sites of contestation that are seen both in contemporary society and in popular film and television.

Another example of terror originating from within the barriers can be seen in the six action horror films of the *Resident Evil* franchise (2002–2017), which is loosely based on the gaming series of the same name, the division or border is seen at Raccoon city, which sits as the entry to an underground genetic research facility called the Hive, owned by the Umbrella corporation. Although they produced and sold commercial products, the core business was that of bio-weapons research, specializing in viral weaponry, and thus the hive had highly advanced security, surveillance and arms to ensure that no unauthorized individuals could enter. The problem however emerges that it is not the outside world posing the threat, but the contamination which has occurred from the deadly T-virus created within these walls. There were many employees and animals on site who have been compromised, and now the underground containment units are full of human and mutated animal zombies whose sole desire is to eat human flesh. Essentially this is a tale of war and terrorism where the borders and barriers have failed because the evil is already living within the 'safety' of the walls, and when the fear and panic ensues it is far safer on the other side.

Alienation and Isolation

The very purpose of walls is to separate groups and societies. They are often positioned as defensive structures and shown as impenetrable barriers, however, the symbolic meaning attached is as powerful as the actual wall itself, operating as "gestural markers that serve more social, psychological and symbolic purposes. They help a culture to define itself by keeping what its not at bay" (Luckhurst, 2017). These barriers and borders can thus be considered in terms of the perceived need for people to erect separation devices between smaller regions, like that of state separations within countries, or communities within suburbs. In some instances, these divisions are created on a house-by-house basis on the same suburban street.

There are many instances in the past of barriers and boundaries created to alienate and isolate people from one another within countries. Segregation was officially mandated in 1913 through the Natives Land Act in the Union Parliament of South Africa (Apartheid's roots, 2013), where black coloured people were made to leave the land and move into reserves, and their property sold cheaply to the white minority (Apartheid's roots, 2013). Apartheid, or 'seperateness' in the white Afrikaaans language of South Africa, continued into the 1990s, and is one of the clearest cases of isolation in practice where under white minority ruling, racial segregation was enforced. This alienation ensured that people of dark skin were severely marginalized by their white leaders and included practices such as using them as a form of cheap labour, especially in the mines and on farms (Wolpe, 1972). Dusk to dawn curfews were also enforced, where black people were to be arrested if found walking the streets at night under the guise of ensuring safety from guerrilla warfare. Sadly, these individuals were often severely assaulted or killed by security forces (Mushonga, 2005) even though they presented officers with their passbooks for verification as non-guerrilla members.

In the popular television series called *The Colony* (2016–2018) similar tropes of alienation and isolation are followed within a once unified community. Los Angeles has been divided into sectors with great walls that are highly weaponized and monitored after the invasion of the planet by an alien nation. Much like the British lead apartheid regime in South Africa, the wealthy and elite have been separated under the guise that they can provide knowledge and assistance to the new rulers, while the majority of people are kept within their own 'reserves', controlled by the authoritarian regime. These people are subject to extreme levels of surveillance from the elite including cameras in all locations including homes and workspaces, and armed drones which serve to enforce the curfews at night. The army called the Red Caps is employed to maintain order and to ensure that no acts of warfare or terrorism occur against the new establishment. This oppressive dystopian regime shows how most citizens have been alienated and targeted as dangers to the established rule, where the penalty for disobedience is arrest and a trip to the 'Factory', never to return. There is no proviso for sickness and all medication for these people has been stopped as they are deemed unworthy of assistance. These tropes parallel those of apartheid where the expendable people of colour formed a cheap labour force and were denied basic human rights.

Van Der Werff (2017) suggests that *The Colony* portrays the idea that violence is often expected in resistance, as the narrative showcases both the extreme measures that the Bowman family themselves will go through in order to save their family from the 'Factory' and to what extent oppression creates resistance within the different sectors. People begin to join the cause when they realise that those in power are not concerned with their needs or well-being, and the guerrilla war tactics turn into a civil war. This once again resonates with South African history and the long war to equality that was fought, but it can also be likened to other large movements against discrimination across the globe such as the fight for women's rights, gay rights and religious rights.

Historically, America and Mexico have had several disputes, including the battle regarding the annexing of Texas to America in 1846 (Immigration Mexican, n.d), and through the Great Depression of 1929–1939 when America deported approximately one million Mexicans across the border even though sixty percent of them were American citizens, as a way to exclude them from the welfare programme (Largest Mass Deportation, 2019). In more recent times the 1954 'Operation Wetback' programme saw the American military authorized to remove all un-papered Mexicans from the country as Mexico had advised of a shortage in labour. This brought about both the removal of tens of thousands of people, including many with American citizenship, but also a perception of the Mexican immigrants as "dirty, disease-bearing and irresponsible" (Largest Mass Deportation, 2019, n.p). In the climate, President Donald Trump could arguably be looking at historical events as a means to cleanse and free America of people of Mexican decent, still wrapped in the misconception that these people are lower in value than his fellow Americans.

In this respect there are similarities to be drawn from films such as *The Purge* franchise (2013-) where the wealthier Americans are far more capable of affording high-grade security, weapons and walls than the lower earning class and as such these poorer people—much like the Mexicans living in America today, become the target for extinction in an annual purging. Naturally Trump could not legitimately authorize a purging of all Mexicans and undesirable immigrants into America however the building of a wall between the borders and the psychological terrorizing of Mexicans by authorizing the 'Family Separation Policy' in 2018 which effectively separated children from their parents at the border created untold distress, with no policy in place to return the children to their families (Rhodan, 2018). The fear and terror experienced by these young children runs a close similarity to the narrative found in the *Maze Runner* (2014) where the film begins as the character Thomas arrives in a box that brings teen boys to an isolated forest where they have built a makeshift society, not unlike the manner in which Mexican children are brought to the detention centers. The boys are trapped there with no clue as to how they got there, and the only way out is through the maze. The walls refer to the boundaries of the Maze surrounding the Glade, and they are 200-300 feet high. In reference to the child detention facilities, these children too have no way to escape, locked behind a maze of walls and security, not knowing if or when they will be able to go home.

Consumerism and Loss of Individualism

Blade Runner 2049 (2017) may be considered a good example of consumerism gone awry with no space effectively free from ubiquitous advertising and technological promotion in this futuristic dystopian world. Humans and replicants are so similar that it is hard to differentiate them from one another — a replication of the human form to display how far technology has advanced. They live within the giant wall, created as protection from the altered weather patterns and elements, caused from what could be argued as the result of capitalism and consumerism which created Climate Change and Global Warming. Luckhurst says that "the rhetoric of internationalism and free movement across borders has become hemmed in by the simultaneous construction of physical barriers that often serve deeply symbolic ends" (2017, n.p). There has often been both a positive and negative view of how globalization could positively impact the world. On one hand, there was the view that globalization would bring economic efficiency and technological gains that would lead to a rising standard of living, while on the negative side that economic decline in developed countries would lead to waves of impoverished immigrants that were going to flood into more economically advantaged countries. Both these views were situated around a new world order, with boundaries that were porous, and permeable (Diner and Hagen, 2013). In *Blade Runner 2049*, the projected view via the advertisements and technological advancements portrays a positive outlook for this global impact, however the altered climate and depictions of severely disadvantaged people depicts the harsh reality of a commodity growth and dependence crisis.

The collapse of the Berlin wall was covered extensively by worldwide media as a herald not only to the changes in the west, but as the rise of globalization which ushered in a world where boundaries were being collapsed, especially economically. Rguig (2016) says after the fall of Berlin Wall, a metamorphosis of the world began, opening an era of interrelations and global exchanges. The fall of the Wall symbolized the rise of new forms of capitalism, and the world rejecting the lack of freedom that the wall had symbolized. Whilst the world celebrated the demise of the Berlin wall and the increased openness and global freedom this brought to those who were previously marginalized, an increase in accessibility and connectivity in communication and trade encourages higher consumerism, as individuals become easy targets for propaganda and consumption. Said (1993, p. 7) says that "the earth is in effect one world, in which empty, uninhabited spaces virtually do not exist". Globalization and surveillance in modern society renders no space truly vacant or free from access or visibility, and perhaps it is the notion that freedom results in loss of individualism that has resulted in a new wave of construction of borders and walls in an attempt to stop the intrusion of other cultures and nations from imposing their ideas and viewpoints onto communities and countries.

The Walking Dead (2010-2018) has been on the popular culture horizon for several years and speaks to the concerns about consumerism and neoliberalism. Based on the comic book series written by Robert Kirkman, the drama portrays life in the months and years following a zombie apocalypse. Rick Grimes wakes up in a hospital to find that the world as he knew it has disappeared, much like the start of the narrative in *28 Days Later* (2002). Most people have turned into zombies who feed off humans, changing them into the undead once bitten, and the remaining untainted people are constantly on the move for a safe and secure home. The zombie narrative has often been compared to tropes of consumerism, where the result of the 'Hypodermic Needle' effects (Lasswell, 1927) of advertising, promotion and propaganda constantly full all areas of our human life through digital media, social spaces and into individual homes via television and radio. This creates desire and the subsequent need to purchase products and services in excess of actual requirements, rendering humankind to become a type of unthinking purchasing body, devoid of reason or brains, mindless slaves of consumption. *The Walking Dead* narrative feeds off these cultural fears of becoming the zombie–devoid of individual thought and reason.

In this series, a hard examination is given of what has become of humanity, presenting the zombie as a "metaphor for social decay" (Schott, 2010, p. 62). A key trope is that all the comforts and security that the survivors have become accustomed to have gone, and in order to survive, people need to work together against both the zombies surrounding them, and other humans attempting to take their meagre items of protection, food and water. The only way to avoid this 'decay' is by building walls and compounds to isolate and exclude those of danger lurking outside the boundaries. These boundaries are mostly manufactured from recycled materials, the items which have been left as waste in the new apocalyptic world, and as such can be likened to global environmental movements and principles of re-use. Perhaps Mother Nature could not sustain the high levels of consumption and has delivered a means to stop humanity from destroying the earth. These films allude to the idea that in order to save the planet a reversal back to the basic elements of food, water, and shelter are required by all people. In terms of our contemporary society, the narrative can serve to warn of the extent of consumerism, where individual thought has been replaced in a dangerous path to destruction. The walls and boundaries in *The Walking Dead* however, do not always provide a clear-cut demarcation of assistance, and the 'Terminus' for example is promoted as a place of sanctuary with large fences to keep the un-dead out. Unfortunately, it is also a location, inhabited by an unstable community, that set out to kill those people who have sought refuge there. This community behind the walls are cannibals, slicing human flesh into food for the BBQ. Walls are used here to both secure and contain, yet this television series shows that in reality the barriers contain as many problems lurking within the walls as they do outside. The show "addresses the essential concerns of dramatic pathos: the struggles, losses, and emotional traumas experienced by the human protagonists" (Lowder, 2011, p. 10).

After the September 11 terrorist attacks in 2001, there was a transition to a period where security became the major importance and multiple walls blossomed in the increasingly globalized world. The move to globalization and subsequent creation of walls was a paradigmatic shift influencing politics, geography and international relations (Rguig, 2016). Popular culture film and television reflect these cultural anxieties, and the proliferation of texts that have walls, or boundaries as a central trope or centrally located in the plot are symptomatic of the tensions that exist since the first waves of globalization and demonstrate tensions around war, terrorism and security, and even the threat of apocalyptic events. In the post-apocalyptic film *Mad Max: Fury Road* (2015), the Citadel represents these modern-day fears where the need to be impenetrable has resulted in the city being built upon the tops of the mountain with sheer cliffs dropping below. This ensures that the select few are removed from potential threat or harm from the 'others' who live below or invaders, and to maintain the power and control the water supply is operated and controlled within the raised city with the working-class dependent on those in power above to supply them—an effective representation of modern-day America.

Religious and Apocalyptic Events

Some of the most popular forms of popular culture are films and television series that deal with post-apocalyptic events and survival. Post-apocalyptic events appeared to grow in public consciousness after a string of high-profile attacks and disasters like the Tokyo sarin nerve gas attack in 1995, the American World Trade Centre in 2001, London Bombings in 2005, 2006 Mumbai train bombings, 2014 Pakistan school shooting and bombing, 2015 Paris shootings and bombings, the continuous terrorism in Iraq to name but a few (Johnston, 2018). These attacks are often both brazen and unprecedented, with many being caught on film, with the images spreading around the world instantaneously. These atrocities are addressed in popular film and television narratives like that of *Warcraft* (2016) where the walls of Azeroth are suddenly attacked by the Orc invaders who have fled their dying world; or the Zoo series (2015–2017) where humans are in danger as the animals have been infected with the Triple Helix Virus that changes their behavior and causes them to hunt and attack in isolated groups or packs—much like planned terrorist attacks where specific locations and times are selected, the animals are capable of reaching into all areas of human life from wild animals to family pets and birds. All of humankind is thrown into panic as there seems nowhere safe to go, and this representation of terrorism can be used to address current world fears and concerns. As the story progresses, the main protagonists are urgently trying to find a cure and are seen in the Pangaea Command Centre desperately trying to reinstate the high-voltage electric fencing surrounding them as they are being hunted by extremely ferocious hybrid animal creatures.

There are other forms of creatures in popular television shows that are restrained by giant walls. The most popular of them all would be the towering wall in HBO's *Game of Thrones* (2011–2019), which is based on R.R Martin's book series *A Song of Ice and Fire*. In the fantasy world of *Game of Thrones*, the great ice wall stretches east to west across the north border of Westeros, and for most of the series guards against "would-be revenant barbarians, zombies, and other monstrous outlanders" (de Monchaux, 2016, p. 4). The Wildlings who live behind the wall have often attempted to scale it, however few ever survive as it is a treacherous climb, and the summit of the wall is patrolled by the Night's Watchmen. It is however, the act of terror which is launched by the undead Night King, upon Viserion the zombie-dragon, that brings on the final apocalyptic event as the wall is destroyed and the un-dead march in.

It is not merely the human attacks in the modern-day society that are a cause of social anxieties regarding apocalyptic events. Natural disasters in many ways pose an even greater concern as there is no stopping or predicting when such an event may occur. On 26th December 2004, a massive 9.1 magnitude earthquake and tsunami destroyed the coast off Sumatra killing an estimated 230 000 people (Indian Ocean tsunami, 2004); in January 2010, Haiti experienced a catastrophic earthquake which killed over 250 000 people and displaced over five million others (Haiti earthquake: Facts, 2010) and a cholera outbreak; Russia experienced a loss of 56 000 people in the same year due to the heat causing raging fires; and August 2005 saw Hurricane Katrina hit landfall on Florida and

Louisiana, America causing catastrophic damage to property and 1833 fatalities. This has led to some of the most haunting images captured on news, with dead bodies littered along the streets, and survivors placed in stadiums like a post-apocalyptic film. There is no wall or boundary capable of wearing an onslaught of this proportion and proved that nature cannot be contained.

Frequently, the borders and walls in film and television narrative contain the tropes of danger that face survivors and are filled with imagery of building new lives from the waste and ashes (Gurr & Polka, 2015). These end of world scenarios emphasize the desperation and terror in characters by framing scenes with religious artefacts and prayers. In *Fear the Walking Dead* (2015-2019) for example, La Colonia has an outer fenced boundary and then an inner wall barrier as protection from the dangers outside. The wall was built to protect the inhabitants from the zombies, but the second was to protect them from the other surviving humans by placing zombies between the two barriers. For Griselda Salazar, these measures are not enough to protect them, and as a deeply religious woman she has built a small grotto with a statue and rosary beads as a place for her constant prayer. She encourages many to pray in the hope of survival and salvation. Later in the series Celia Florez who looks after the 'Plantation' is seen to be serving the Christian rite of Communion to the people, although in this case she is poisoning them in order to assist them to become zombies so that she can look after them in their un-dead state, as she believes it to be a part of human 'passing' to the afterlife. There is a grotto in the Plantation for daily prayer and photos of those who have passed.

Conclusion

Historic borders and barriers like that of the Berlin wall, The Great Wall of China, and the Wall of Jerusalem have created spaces of security and safety usually for those to whom the walls belong. Those excluded or on the other side of these borders feel fear and trepidation of the future to come and are often powerless to rise and defend themselves. In popular film and television, both sides of these borders are often explored to address and dissect possible outcomes and ways forward for those on both sides of these barriers. The modern-day tropes around end of world prophecies, general global uncertainty and the rise in globalization form the prototype for the images of contemporary walls and boundaries, which are used in film to negotiate them. These texts connect to cultural anxieties surrounding War and Terrorism, where present-day attacks are frequent; the feelings of being alienated or isolated from family or country; the effects of consumerism on contemporary society and how this creates a loss of individualism; and the prophecies of religious and apocalyptic texts.

These texts in film and television all present borders and boundaries as sites of contestation within popular culture, as a stage for the borders to perform as part of the mise-en-scene, creating order and spaces where action may take place, "wherein actors and observers must work at making borders intelligible and manageable and must do so in order for the drama to proceed" (Wilson & Donnan, 2012, p. 19-20). Borders and boundaries are places of actual and symbolic control as well as locations where people continue to negotiate and contest their place in life, and general life chances. On one side of a boundary, a person may be elite and wealthy, while on the other side, they may be poor and impoverished. But as the promise of globalization spread throughout the world when the Berlin Wall came down, these texts demonstrate that progress has been anything but linear, and borders and boundaries continue to be fought over, and repositioned in a number of popular culture texts.

Reference

Apartheid's roots: The Natives Land Act. (2013, June 21). *The Independent in International*. Retrieved from https://www.theindependent.co.zw/2013/06/21/apartheids-roots-the-natives-land-act/.

Bail, C. (2008). The Configuration of Symbolic Boundaries against Immigrants in Europe. *American Sociological Review*, 73, 37-59.

De Monchaux, T. (2016). The Walls Before Trump's Wall. *The New Yorker. Culture Desk*. Retrieved from https://www.newyorker.com/culture/culture-desk/a-wall-is-not-always-what-you-think-it-is-trump.

Diener, A. C., & Hagen, J. (2012). *Borders. A very short introduction*. Oxford and NewYork: Oxford University Press.

Gurr, B. & Polka, B. (2015). *Race, Gender, and Sexuality in Post-Apocalyptic TV and Film*. London: Palgrave Macmillan.

Great Wall of China even longer than previously thought. (2012, June 6). *CBC News*. Retrieved from https://www.cbc.ca/news/world/great-wall-of-china-even-longer-than-previously-thought-1.1263111.

Haiti earthquake: Facts, FAQs, and how to help. (2010). World Vision. Retrieved from https://www.worldvision.org/disaster-relief-news-stories/2010-haiti-earthquake-facts.

Haselsberger, B. (2014). Decoding borders. Appreciating border impacts on space and people. *Planning Theory & Practice*, 15(4), 505-526. DOI: 10.1080/14649357.2014.963652 To link to this article: https://doi.org/10.1080/14649357.2014.963652.

Immigration...Mexican. (n.d). *The Library of Congress*. Retrieved on August 20, 2019 from https://www.loc.gov/teachers/classroommaterials/presentationsandactivities/presentations/immigration/alt/Mexican2.html.

Indian Ocean tsunami: Facts, FAQs, and how to help. (2004). World Vision. Retrieved from https://www.worldvision.org/disaster-relief-news-stories/2004-indian-ocean-tsunami-facts.

Johnston, R. (2018). Worst terrorist strikes—worldwide. *Johnston Archives*. Retrieved from http://www.johnstonsarchive.net/terrorism/wrjp255i.html.

Kenyon, K. M. (1960). *Excavations at Jericho: The architecture and stratigraphy of the Tell*. British School of Archaeology in Jerusalem.

Largest Mass Deportation in American History. (2019). *History.com*. retrieved from https://www.history.com/news/operation-wetback-eisenhower-1954-deportation.

Lasswell, H. D. (1927). *Propaganda technique in the world war*. New York: Peter Smith.

Lowder, J. (2011). *Triumph of The Walking Dead: Robert Kirkman's Zombie Epic on Page and Screen*. London: Ben Bella Books.

Luckhurst, R. (2017). What walls mean from Hadrian to Trump. *BBC. Culture*. Retrieved from www.bbc.com/culture/story/20170502-what-walls-mean-from hadrian-to trump.

Mushonga, M. (2005). Curfew and the 'man in the middle' in Zimbabwe's War of Liberation with special reference to the eastern border areas of Zimbabwe, 1977-1980. Retrieved from https://www.codesria.org /IMG/pdf/Mushonga.pdf?464/b62295d97167b09e9fc56f51ba28d64 fc89bb99e.

Rguig, M. (2016). The geopolitics of new frontiers (walls and fences...). LegalVoxfr. Retrieved from https://www.legavox.fr/blog/miloud-rguig/geopolitique-frontieres-nouvelles-murs-clotures-20486.htm.

Rhodan, M. (2018). Here Are the Facts About President Trump's Family Separation Policy. *Time*. https://time.com/5314769/family-separat ion-policy-donald-trump/.

Said, E. (1993). *Culture and Imperialism*. The T.S Eliot Lectures at the University of Kent 1985. New York: Knopf/Random House.

Schott, G. (2010). Dawn of the digital dead: The zombie as interactive social satire in American popular culture. *Australasian Journal of American Studies*, 29 (1), 61-75. Retrieved from http://www.jstor.org/stable/ 41054186.

Van Der Werff, E. T. (2017). Colony, USA's alien invasion drama, is accidentally the most relevant show on television. *Vox. Culture*. Retrieved from https://www.vox.com/culture/2017/2/2/14447258 /colony-usa-season-2-review.

Wilson, T. M. & Donnan, H. (2012). *A companion to border studies*. London: John Willey and Sons.

Wolpe, H. (1972). Capitalism and cheap labour-power in South Africa: from segregation to apartheid, *Economy and Society*, 1(4), 425-456. DOI: 10.1080/03085147200000023 To link to this article:https://doi. org/10.1080/03085147200000023 Published online: 28 Jul 2006.

Film and Television Cited

Blum, J., Bay, M., Form, A., Fuller, B., LeMercier, S. (Producers). DeMonaco, J. (Director). (2013). *The Purge*. [Motion Picture]. United States: Blumhouse Productions.

Blum, J., Bay, M., Form, A., Fuller, B., LeMercier, S. (Producers). DeMonaco, J. (Director). (2014). *The Purge: Anarchy*. [Motion Picture]. United States: Blumhouse Productions.

Blum, J., Bay, M., Form, A., Fuller, B., LeMercier, S. (Producers). DeMonaco, J. (Director). (2016). *The Purge: Election Year*. [Motion Picture]. United States: Blumhouse Productions.

Blum, J., Bay, M., Form, A., Fuller, B., LeMercier, S. (Producers). McMurray, G. (Director). (2018). *The First Purge*. [Motion Picture]. United States: Blumhouse Productions.

Fine, K., Fine, T., & Howell. (Producers). Fine, T. (Director). (2010). *The Space Between*. [Motion Picture]. United States: TSB Films.

Fisher, L., Shabazian, P., & Wich, D. (Producers). Schwenke, R. (Director). (2016). *Allegiant*. [Motion Picture]. United States: Red Wagon Entertainment.

Mitchell, D., Mitchell, G., & Voeten, P. J. (Producers). Miller, G. (Director). (2015). *Mad Max: Fury Road*. [Motion Picture]. United States: Warner Bros Pictures.

Molen, G. R., Curtis, B., Parkes, W, F. & de Bont, J. (Producers). Spielberg, S. (Director). (2002). *Minority Report*. [Motion Picture]. United States: 20th Century Fox.

Silver, J., Hill, G., & The Wachowskis. (Producers). McTeigue, J. (Director). (2005). *V for Vendetta*. [Motion Picture]. United States: Warner Bros. Productions Limited.

Wich, D., Fisher, L. (Producers). Burger, N. (Director). (2014). *Divergent*. [Motion Picture]. United States: Red Wagon Entertainment.

Wich, D., Fisher, L., & Shabazian, P. (Producers). Schuentke, R. (Director). (2015). *Insurgent*. [Motion Picture]. United States: Red Wagon Entertainment.

Representation of Incarcerated Women in *Orange is the New Black*: An Intersectional Feminist Approach

Sharmistha Das

Although the term 'culture' is not discreet in its definition it can be understood to mean a meaningful wholeness constructed by the dynamic interplay of languages, customs, beliefs, knowledge, and collective identities and memories developed by the members of distinct social groups. The process of cultural meaning-making can be understood by exploring individual and group communication that finds expression in and through social narratives, ideologies, practices, tastes, values, and norms that are embedded in collective representation and social classifications. A wide range of disciplines and methodologies have evolved overtime to document and analyze the production, diffusion, reception, evaluation, and application of cultural meaning across institutions, organizations, and groups, and also to understand the role of culture in the differential production of racial, ethnic, and class groups, inevitably generating inequalities and group boundaries. Literature, History, Sociology, Anthropology are some of the broader disciplines; whereas Feminist Studies, Cultural Studies, Postcolonial Studies, Media Studies are some of the theoretical methodologies that are concerned with depicting, analyzing and questioning the process of cultural formation and how it functions in the(re)production of public order and social control. Representations—text, performance, photography or media—are social constructions or cultural mediations that reflect and (re)present reality. These are powerful tools that shape knowledge in favour of, or against the ethics of established discourse.

This chapter purports to analyze the much acclaimed media text *Orange is the New Black*—a Netflix original and the longest running American media series of 2013. *Orange is the New Black* assembled a protean cast representing a swath of the population generally excluded from popular mainstream television. Loosely based on a memoir, of the same title by Piper Kerman, (2010) that documents her custodial experiences in a federal prison in Danbury, Connecticut *Orange is the New Black* has been written and produced by Jenji Kohan. Modeled on the genre of comedy- drama the show follows its protagonist Piper Chapman (the televised form of Piper Kerman) and her struggles to understand her surrounding environment in the fictitious Litchfield penitentiary which houses a wide variety of criminalized women. Incarcerated within the borders of the prison wall are women of color, black, white, Latino; sexually deviant women, lesbians, homophobes, trans-genders, drug abusers et al. Piper Chapman, the white educated upper class figure serving a sentence of 15 months for her past association with drug laundering, is initially appalled at the crude forms of racism, sexism, classism practiced within the prison boundary. The show records her reaction, negotiation and finally her acquired wisdom of the US Prison Industrial Complex (PIC refers to the intertwining of Government, the penal apparatus and capital interests) (Artt and Schwan, p 5). It would be pertinent here to note that Piper Kerman has garnered useful attention as a prison reform advocate after her memoir *Orange is the New Black: My Year in a Women's Prison* was successfully adapted into this television series as it could distribute her critique of the American PIC to a much larger audience. Kerman actively advocates for better living conditions for the incarcerated women and also to influence the PIC to attend to the damaging effects that the imprisoned mothers leave on their families and communities. The Prison Communication Activism Research and Education Collective (PCARE) have called out to scholars of multiple disciplines to challenge the cultural presumption that drives the PIC. *Orange is the New Black's* popularity can be measured by the fact that the show captured 13 Emmy nominations in 2014, winning in the category of 'outstanding casting for a comedy series'. In 2013 it was honored with a Peabody Award for Excellence in quality storytelling. And it has maintained a 93% approval score across the first three seasons on the popular media-ranking database, Rotten Tomatoes (Netflix is not evaluated by Nielson ratings which are only designed to measure advertising based television, Suzanne Enck and Morrissey). The show and the individual cast members have received multiple awards, including two comedy ensemble awards from the Screen Actors Guild and the Female Comedy Actor award for Uzo Aduba (who played the role of Suzanne Crazy Eyes).Although Netflix does not disclose viewing numbers, Netflix's chief Content Officer Ted Sarandas called *Orange is the New Black* the streaming services most watched show (Birnbaum 2016). Netflix's global reach, spanning members in more than 190 countries, contributed to the series' ongoing impact (Sarah Artt and Anne Schwan).

Orange is the New Black's unquestionable commercial success has garnered unexpected critical attention leading to a spurt of scholarly articles that discussed the show's treatment of race, class, sexuality and also the way it has represented the American prison system. Open-access sites such as FLOW: A Critical Forum on Television and Media Culture, and In Media Res has been flooded with criticism emerging on *Orange is the New Black*. Criticism on *Orange is the New Black* mostly got channeled into two contrary directions. One group talked of the debate on female incarceration that the show successfully generated and that contributed in formulating the idea of prison as a site of registering resistance and agency. Whereas the other camp focused on the show's failure to address structural inequality, as it depended and developed on the perspective of a privileged white upper-class woman prisoner, and also that by using Netflix as a media platform, the show is conscripted by its own representational strategies, legitimizing the institution of mass incarceration as the only cure for the social deviants. To quote some of the responses: (a) "the buzz has been increasing about the show's varied portrayals on screen, ranging from racial and sexual diversity, to trans-characters and beyond" (Walkey, 2013) and (b) "The show brought incarcerated women into America's living rooms, where viewers can embrace the characters as people with strengths and flaws" (Gwayne, 2013).

Quotations from the opposite school: (a) "...deeply flawed representations of women and the PIC" (Doyle, 2013) and (b) "The show's depictions of black and Latina women constantly threaten to veer into all too familiar tropes and stereotypes" (Charlton,

2013). Responding to such concerns Jenji Kohan in an interview with NPR's Fresh Air explained that she used Piper as her 'Trojan horse', enabling more complex conversation about race, gender, class, and sexuality in a medium that would typically preclude such topics and characters: "you are not going to go into a network and sell a show on really fascinating tales of black women and Latino women and old women and criminals. But if you take this white girl, this sort of fish out of water, and you follow her in you can then expand your world and tell all those other stories. But it's so hard to just go in and try to sell those stories initially" (Gross, 2013).

What is indicative of *Orange is the New Black's* potential to unite the popular and academic spheres is the range of responses that the show has generated—from the rigidly academic scholarly interest to the more socially engaging activism, both functioning to ensure greater human rights for the minorities and the spread of a fruitful critical awareness on issues of female incarceration. The series has a strong official social media presence and its fan base is active on Twitter. Cast members such as Dascha Polanco (Dayanara Diaz in OITNB) and Laverne Cox (Sophia Burset in OITNB) made high profile appearances in campaigns to support racial and sexual diversity and several cast members made prominent appearances at the protests that followed the death of Eric Garner, a movement that became known on Twitter by its # *I can't breathe* (Jordan, 2014). These forms of real life activism by the cast members were often viewed cynically as commoditization of resistance that used protest sites as publicity tropes. But it would be unfair to debunk these activities as mere publicity stunts, for actors such as Cox who is also a trans-woman of color was hailed in the cover page of Time (June 9, 2014) for her socialist activities. Cox has also appeared in conversation with feminist scholar and activist bell hooks who noted the impact of *Orange is the New Black* on black women empowerment. *Orange is the New Black* has indeed brought to the fore a wider public debate on PIC stimulating a genuine social change on the issues of how criminalized women came to be viewed. Jenji Kohan's assertion that for her: "Entertainment is Activism" (Mc Clelland, 2015) holds ground insofar as how it has raised tele-viewing from a living room leisure activity to a mode capable of exerting socio-political agency.

This chapter will study *Orange is the New Black* from an interdisciplinary approach and show how the series translates into praxis the Foucauldian ideas of the modern prison—the effects of disciplinary power, surveillance and the law on the individuals and their bodies. Situated within the socio-feminist epistemology, this chapter would also conduct a qualitative content analysis to explore the themes of race, class, gender and sexuality, not disparately but as part of an intersectional chain in relation to the women characters within the series. I would try to show how *Orange is the New Black* departs from many other mass media depictions of criminalized women in the way it brings to light the racial demographic realities of women prisoners in trying to address structural inequalities, often implicating the socio-economic injustices perpetrated by the American Penal System. In trying to understand this media text, this chapter would refer to the epistemology of Media Representation Theory in order to understand the material conditions behind the inter-linked processes of production-viewership strategies. How far *Orange is the New Black* problematizes its stance, with regard to conforming to stereotypes or resisting the hegemonic notions of social classification and normativity will be the final critical concern of this chapter.

The critical discussion on *Orange is the New Black*, in this chapter will begin by situating this dramedy (comedy-drama) within the frameworks of cultural criminology—the broad theme that the series deals in, and the new media Netflix, the structural platform that gives visibility to this media text. In modern times, the concept of cultural criminology refers to the increasing systematic attention that many criminologists now give to popular culture constructions, especially mass media constructions, of crime and crime control (Ferrel, 1999). Cultural criminologists have shown how the media represents a constructed reality of crime, crime control and criminals; as entertainment, infotainment or even news media are predicated on the demands of viewership. How meaning is constructed and appropriated within and between media and political formations, audiences and illicit subcultures around matters of crime and crime control are explored by scholars of criminology. And there is no denying the power that mass media representations have in shaping and influencing the audiences' ideas and perspectives in matters related to crime. Crime has been a fundamental theme in American media, evolving as an ongoing construction of inter-textual image driven media loops. Early examples would be films like *The Great Train Robbery* (1903), *Scar Face* (1932) and *The Big House* (1930) whereas some of the more recent examples would be *The Hole* (1960), *The Godfather* (1972) and *The Shawshank Redemption* (1994). The most popular occurrences and themes within the prison film genre includes escapes, resistance to authority, violence and masculine control, and the promotion of idealized characterizations of heroic men at the centre of exceptional events such as riots, escapes and the release of dangerous criminalized individuals (Chermak 1998; Levenson 2001; Whodarz 2005).

In television, both in Entertainment and Infotainment, the most popular genres of content are crime and violence, depicting lives of the incarcerated within the crime and justice genre shows. Infotainment is reality-based television that purports to portray reality through marketing of edited and highly formatted real life information with the assumption of exposing the viewers to real facts of the world. But most of the time the representation becomes a highly exaggerated interpretation of a narrow and edited portion of truth. Over all, this genre provides entertainment through sensationalizing real stories about crime and justice, typically through realistic police narratives, interviews or actual video footage. In contemporary mass media, reality-based crime shows have become more popular because they shift news to entertainment, while still being viewed as credible and realistic (Surette, 2015). As Television is a widespread and most used form of communication that is both accessible and entertaining, it becomes a popular and reliable source of knowledge about the criminal justice system for the public. Surette (1998) estimates that roughly 25% of primetime entertainment television programs featured crime themes as their main focus between the 1960 and 1990. The soaring popularity of crime-prison-criminal content can be indexed by some of the highest rated crime shows that has been aired in the recent past viz. *Hawaii Five O, The Sopranos, Sons of Anarchy, Arrow, Breaking Bad* and *Criminal Minds.*

Regardless of the growing popularity of these kinds of shows the media representations of them have been partial or even distorted. Whatever the domain might have been; news, entertainment, films or online, media, in general, tends to represent the most dangerous aspects of prison life that constructs an environment premised on violence, torture and the ugliest of living conditions. These make individual transformation seem impossible, thereby implicitly supporting the harshest of punishment as retributive justice meted out to the extreme criminals. Motivated as they are by their need to entertain above all else, it is only the sensational and the compressed version of reality that gets typically displayed; reinforcing stereotypes (mis)leading the public into consuming constructed versions of reality. The 'spectacle' of representation blurs the bordering line between fact and fiction, real and the fake—thereby generating a parallel secondary version of the penal institution and the incarceration experience within the criminal justice system. My analysis of *Orange is the New Black* purports to show how this dramedy in its representation of the incarceration experience differs vastly from the above discussed 'types'. The original series aired on Netflix on July 11, 2013 in all regions where Netflix is available—the United States, the United Kingdom, Canada, Ireland, Latin America, Brazil and the Nordic countries (Goldberg 2013). It was then aired on broadcast television in New Zealand and Australia later that year (Goldberg 2013). Netflix, the newest and the fastest growing domain differs from the traditional television as it is based on online mediatizing and has revolutionized the concept of viewership-entertainment. Netflix allows viewers to watch multiple episodes in rapid succession as it provides its own original programming which are released all at once and this is related to the viewership phenomenon 'binge watching' which develops through contemporary streaming services. Netflix is better equipped to provide exclusive quality content as compared to traditional television as Netflix's production does not need to cut to commercials for sharing advertising space within the main programme. The Netflix producers are not dependent upon the 'pilot system' since all episodes are released all at once and there is no risk of the show getting shelved owing to low initial viewing figures. Additionally, these types of release are not reliant on cliffhanger endings to make the audiences come back for more the following week and hence allows for more integral narrative modes. Jenji Kohan explains how binge-watching impacted the production of the series as: "we could string out the moments and let a character fall away for a few hours because if you are binging then you will see them again in a few hours" (Ma 2016, p. 1). *Orange is the New Black's* atypical content was bolstered by the platform of Netflix, whose marketing system is subscription based, making it commercially viable of supporting innovative programming.

The theoretical framework and the epistemological position that inform the analysis of this chapter are formulated on intersectionality that is part of the extended notions of socialist feminism and multiracial feminism. Feminist criminologists have argued for a need to address the different needs and experiences of women convicts before their entering the penal system, particularly with regard to their exposure to violence and politics. How and why they came in conflict with the law and how far their post-incarceration experience would be determined by the specificity of their race, gender, ethnicity, sexuality and class have been the basic thematic premise of *Orange is the New Black*. The show's portrayal of female prisoners and the American PIC have shown that these apparently discrete segments of culture actually overlap while determining their incarceration experience.

Intersectionality was first introduced and later popularized by Kimberly Crenshaw (1989) and Patricia Hill Collins (1990) respectively, and has its roots in several intellectual traditions like socialist feminism, race and ethnic studies, and postcolonial feminisms. Kimberley Crenshaw used the term intersectionality to bring to the fore the black women's experiences within a 'single axis' framework of feminist theories, anti-discrimination laws and anti-racist politics. Crenshaw argued that feminist theory was fundamental and exclusive that ignored the intersections of race and class within the basic trope of women's operation. She illustrated this idea through an analogy of traffic.

Discrimination, like traffic through an intersection may flow in one direction, and it may flow in another. If an accident happens in an intersection, it can be caused by cars travelling from any number of directions and sometimes, from all of them. Similarly, if black woman is harmed because she is in the intersection her injury could result from gender discrimination or race discrimination (p. 149).

Similarly Collins argues that "cultural patterns of operation are not only interrelated but are bound together and influenced by the intersectional systems of society such as race, gender, class and ethnicity" (p. 42). Given the fact that *Orange is the New Black* incorporates multiracial characters who are mostly fraught with layered characteristic dimensions, intersectionality evidently becomes the most appropriate approach of analysis for two broadly identifiable reasons; (a) a female prison house in North America operating within its PIC functions through four interrelated domains of power: structural, disciplinary, hegemonic, and interpersonal. Intersectionality as an analytical mode claims that systems of race, social class, sexuality, gender, nation, ethnicity, and age form mutually constructing features of social organisation that shape women's experience and are in turn shaped by them; (b) intersectionality allows feminist criminology to examine issues of social justice from a more inclusive and cohesive perspective that would lead to a better understanding of the circumstantial causes that led to the crime committed. It also provides insights into the political and social circumstances as intersectionality is aligned with theories of knowledge and power, and more specifically with the relationship between power and knowledge production. Collins (1990) argues that this type of analysis emerges when abstract thought is joined with concrete action, which aims to reduce marginalisation and subordination (p. 29). *Orange is the New Black* as a media text includes the perspectives of individuals who are normally marginalised and excluded in the production of knowledge and in doing so challenges the existing power relations and also subverts the political practice and stereotyping commonly associated with media tropes.

This study so far analysed how media representations take part in producing cultural meaning and as cultural artifacts themselves are influenced by the existing cornerstones of culture — society, politics, ethics, economics, race, religion, education, and law. It has discussed *Orange is the New Black's* performative role as a media text, the diverse responses that it has generated, the commercial success and the critical acclaim that it has garnered. And then it has discussed the theoretical frameworks and the analytical tools that would be used in analysing this media text. The concepts of cultural criminology, the online new media platform Netflix have been discussed as factors that have been responsible for shaping the content and treatment of the show. The next section of this chapter will focus on the issues of sexuality and race as the binding content of OITNB (the first three seasons), along with a preliminary description of its plot and some of the important characters.

Plot

Piper Chapman is a law abiding, public relations executive living an upper middle class life in New York with her fiancé, friends and family. Piper, living a normal life, suddenly finds herself in a complex situation as her shady past infringes on her present. Almost 10 years back she had been in a lesbian relationship with a girl named Alex Vause who worked as an international drug smuggler. But Piper gets convicted for her decade old crime of transporting drug money for her criminal girlfriend. She transported a suitcase carrying drug money across international borders for Alex and now after 10 years she gets convicted for that crime and is sentenced for 15 months. She would need to serve the tenure in a minimum security federal prison in Litchfield. Although it completely disrupts her present life and future plans, she takes the trial in her stride, dons the prison orange suit and makes her way through the correction system, making friends with many unusual, eccentric and unexpected people she meets within the prison boundary. In fact the 30 something Piper becomes the most felicitous inmate of Litchfield prison who espouses the ideals of the egalitarian, colour blind, neo-liberal American ethics, championing the cause of multiculturalism. In the promotional trailer for *Orange is the New Black* Piper Chapman is seen sitting across from her wealthy mother, who is in the visitation room of the prison, claiming responsibility for her own act of crime: "I am no different than anybody else here. I committed a crime. Being in here is nobody's fault but my own". Season 1 focuses on Piper and how she struggles to acclimatize with the new environment, inviting both friends and enemies with her poise and neutral behaviour. Season 2 begins with Piper waking up in solitary confinement and getting shifted to an unknown place which she later realises to be Chicago. Piper discovers that she had been taken there to testify in the trial of Alex's drug boss Kubra Balik. She returns to Litchfield after a short while where the main character of season 2 has shown up threatening to take control of the drug contraband that is secretly run within the prison. She is Yvonne Parker, infamously known as Vee. The third section of this American comedy drama is more expansive, where in all its 13 episodes the representation includes multiple diverse characters, their past experiences (shown through flashbacks) and what led to their crimes along with their present day relationships. This study will primarily engage the first three seasons of *Orange is the New Black* and analyse its select content to examine the complex ways in which power relations operate within a female prison.

Main Character(s) Development

Piper Chapman

Piper Chapman (Piper Kerman's TV alter ego) is the main character in *Orange is the New Black*. Piper is young, white, has blonde hair and blue eyes. She replicates the ideal woman of the media who should be thin, beautiful and blonde. No wonder that Piper earned nicknames like 'blondie', 'Taylor Swift', 'Lindsay Lohan', 'Dandelion', and 'College', all often sarcastic references to her appearance and background. When Piper enters the prison she is a naïve, progressive, neo-liberal, non-racist white woman. But as the show develops Piper's struggles with the harsh environment hardens her into becoming devious and manipulative. This is evident in her plot to have Alex re-incarcerated and prevent Stella's release. Piper's class privilege earns her undue power which she uses in starting a business to sell used underwear online (season 3), twisting the exploitative structure of the whispers prison sweatshop to her own advantage. Her motivational speech to her 'Orange sisters' to rebel against patriarchy and its infused self hatred and 'make a reek to last a thousand years' (season 3, episode 8) is one of the remarkable moments of the season. Piper's characteristic courage seems to stem from her privileged position of a white woman, with a network of friends and family who visit her, help her by sending money from outside. But these cannot offset the struggles that she has to wage through; as she cries out that she has been "starved out, felt up, teased, stalked and threatened" by the other woman (season 1 episode 4). She goes to the extent of expressing her concern over the uncertainty of a place to live in and a job to sustain her after she gets her release from the prison. This concern of Piper is representative, in the sense that it voices the collective concern of most women convicts about the uncertainty that marks their post-incarceration life — the problem of reintegrating themselves within society and family. Prior to entering Litchfield Piper got engaged to Larry Bloom, a heterosexual bond that reconstructs her sexual orientation shielding off her lesbian past with Alex Vause. In the very first episode of season 1 Piper clarifies in an explanation given to her family: "no I am not *still* a lesbian." But throughout the series she conducts herself as a self-professed bisexual who simultaneously loves Alex and Larry both. Within her incarceration experience Piper very consciously refuses to be identified within a discreet sexual identity. This conscious hybrid positioning of Piper's sexuality within the prison border is ambitious as it has the potential to engender agency that disrupts the established socio-cultural order. This intra-diagetic strategy of questioning the establishment turns the fictional Litchfield prison into a space where feminist agency and praxis are made possible.

By providing its protagonist with at least relative intermittent agency the series proposes alternatives that move away from the demonized criminal women or the passive victim types to be found in androcentric narratives, the polyphonic and multiplicity of micro level practices of agency in *Orange is the New Black* denounce and work against the homogenizing, dehumanizing practices of the prison system (Morales and Menendez, 10).

Alex Vause

Alex Vause, a Caucasian woman coming from upper middle class background, is a thirty-something bisexual womon who has been sentenced to Litchfield as an international drug smuggler. Piper's former lesbian partner, Alex admits that her only skill is in "moving massive amounts of heroine" (season 1 episode 12).

Tiffany 'Pennsatucky' Doggett

Tiffany Pennsatucky Doggett, a Caucasian heterosexual woman from lower class background, is in her twenties and is convicted of murder. She is Piper's primary antagonist in season 1. Tiffany is shown as a religious extremist and homophobic who has been used as a character filler to make Litchfield seem horrible and dangerous.

Carolina 'Red' Reznikova

A Heterosexual woman in her fifties coming from lower middle class background, whose nature of offence is not exactly known, Carolina within the Litchfield prison is shown as a powerful woman who ruled the kitchen with an iron fist. She is a self determined mother figure to the other younger women of the prison, and once starved Piper for using drugs (season 1 episode 2).

Suzanne 'Crazy Eyes' Warren

She is an African-American lesbian women struggling with her mental health issues yet compassionate and friendly to those in need, such as when Piper was being troubled by Alex she stood by her. She has big and bulgy eyes and is treated differently by others possibly because of her race.

Tasha 'Taystee' Jefferson

Twenty something heterosexual African-American women from lower class background, Tasha admits that she has always been in some form of institution her whole life; beginning from an orphanage, group home, to Juvenile penal institution and presently Lichfield. An intelligent woman Tasha provides a lot of comic relief with her mockery of the white inmates and is, in general, a friendly girl, and is convicted for drug trafficking.

Dayanara 'Daya' Diaz

A twenty something Spanish women, heterosexual and from lower back class background, she is serving a sentence for drug related charge and is in Litchfield along with her mother Aleida Diaz who is charged of the same crime. Dayanara is a responsible character whose pregnancy and childbirth within the Litchfield borders represents the trope of motherhood in custody.

Poussey Washington

An African-American lesbian woman from middle class background Poussey, sentenced for dealing marijuana, is depicted as humorous, honest, thoughtful and one of the Litchfield's most likeable woman.

Sofia Burset

Sofia is an African-American transgender woman, in her forties, who before entering Litchfield was a firefighter, husband and a father. Sofia in order to pay for her gender reassignment surgeries committed credit card fraud that lead to her incarceration. Although Sofia is often subject to transmisogyny from the other woman she is bold and vocal about her gender status and is overall presented as friendly who enjoys doing her and others' hair and makeup.

Gloria Mendoza

Represented as the leader of the Hispanic women (Latin American descent), Gloria is made the kitchen in-charge after Red is removed from that post for smuggling in Contraband. It is revealed that Gloria suffered domestic abuse in her early life and that makes hair look for a pseudo family inside Litchfield, and she does become a pseudo mother to many of the Latina girls. Some of the other characters are Carrie 'Big Boo' Black, Brook Soso, Yvonne 'Vee' Parker, Leane Taylor, Sister Jane Ingalls apart from some other minor characters. Sam Healy is the prison guard, who is both a correctional officer and an inmate counselor. Mr. Healy is a 50 year old heterosexual Caucasian man who is overtly homophobic.

As has already been discussed, female representation in media is generally narrow and restricted in the sense that they are based on certain stereotypes tied to gender, race, sexuality and class. Several media critics have referred to these types of media representations of women as promoting ideological persuasions that convince consumers that certain behaviours are innate for different groups of people and present culturally constructed norms of gender, race, class, and sexuality as natural rather than performances we have learnt to adopt through societal education and expectation (Pozner 2010, p. 98). But *Orange is the New Black* with its diversified content ushers in a radical though identifiable genre of crossover television programming that represents women prisoners in strategically complex and messy ways so as to reproduce the characters as active subjects with potential for transformation, playing out their narrative of resistance against the disciplinary practices of the penal institution. They embody counter ideological statements with an ambition to reorient the stereotypical televiewer's consumption and expectation. Foucault conceived power as a dynamic that creates new possibilities, produces new things, ideas and relations, and this is akin to what feminists call empowerment (Mclaren 2002, p. 41). The final episode of the third season is one of the most remarkable examples that illustrate the value of women coming together in a prison context.

The women in the prison escape through an opening in the fence to enjoy their time at the lake and beach nearby. The characters, putting their differences aside, enjoy the moment forging a bond that is deeper in its resonance. For example, Daya and her mom Aleida, who blamed each other throughout the first two seasons, over Aleida's poor parenting and Daya's physical intimacy with the prison guard John Bennett issuing her pregnancy, embrace each other on the beach. Some other notable friendships that have surfaced on *Orange is the New Black* are those between Taystee and Poussey, Gloria and Aleida, Big Boo and Doggett. Notwithstanding the severe antagonisms that developed between Piper and Doggett, Leane and Soso, Red and Vee the instances of the women's solidarity and friendship make *Orange is the New Black* confer to the new Faucauldian precept of female friendship as an agentic practice. *Orange is the New Black* incorporates a broader array of friendships that defy the racial divide imposed upon by the prison system. In the show's first season, friendship emerges between Sofia and Sister Ingalls both of whom are viewed as outcasts in the Litchfield prison, Sophia being the only transgender woman and Sister Ingalls the only nun.

Orange is the New Black depicts a multiplicity of body types that include a range of characters with overlapping gender (e.g. trance, masculine, femme, butch), sexuality (e.g. lesbian, queer, heterosexual, heteroflexible), class (e.g. working, upper middle) and racial and ethnic identities (e.g. African-American, Caucasian, Dominican, Puerto Rican). *Orange is the New Black* reverberates with overt representations of lesbian sexuality that does serve the purpose of raising the sensational quotient but more importantly makes a statement that disrupts hegemonic classifications of sexuality and identity. *Orange is the New Black* displays a variety of different sexual acts, which is in line of literature that states that masturbation, consensual sex and coerced sex is part of the landscape of women's prison (Pardue et al, 2011). Several scenes within season 1 to 3 present lesbian sexual acts based on desire and enjoyment. These occur in various locations within Litchfield such as the shower, chapel, and the unoccupied rooms. As the main character there is an enormous emphasis devoted to discussing

Piper's sexuality. It is clear that Piper's sexuality is complex and ambiguous, and it is shown through both visual and contextual cues that Piper shifts between her attraction for her would-be-husband Larry and her former lesbian lover Alex, also feels it for another female inmate Stella (season 3 episode 9), and voyeuristically enjoys the steamy scenes between Nicky and Morello (season 1 episode 1). She describes her sexual preferences as changing through 'phases' and 'at times' and explains to her friends that "you don't just turn gay, you fall somewhere on a spectrum, like a Kensey Scale" — to demonstrate that there cannot possibly be a specific indicator to one's sexual identity. Piper's non concession towards labeling herself as specifically heterosexual/lesbian/bisexual brings home the idea that homogeneity of sexual identity is a socially imposed myth. Representation of female bonding as erotic and growing out of love or the need for bodily pleasure presents a challenge to another media stereotype where women are often portrayed as 'gold diggers'. This 'gold diggers' trope is strongly rooted in heteronormative understandings of womanhood wherein, women are encouraged to position men at the centre of their lives given that heterosexual relationships for women are traditionally viewed as the most important type of relationship in a woman's life (Taylor 2012). This trope is exemplified through the character of Lorna Morello. In the third season she is shown as cultivating a hobby of writing erotic letters to the men in the prison, who are mostly employees, and then manipulating them into giving her extra privileges and money. Morello exploits her good looks, charming personality and attractive body to her advantage thwarting the disciplining practices of the penal system that seeks to suppress female bodies as 'docile'. This evolution from *docile bodies to active bodies* (my emphasis) disrupts the gender hierarchy within the prison structure. *Orange is the New Black* foregrounds lesbian sexuality whose hermeneutics is based on a contextual probability — subverting traditional expectations that position women as passive and submissive. Suzanne in season 3 writes a science fiction erotica book called *The Time Hump Chronicles* that becomes a huge hit amongst the inmates who even write fan letters to her. The show contests heteronormativity of network television and seeks to engage the audiences who identify themselves as either straight or gay/lesbian to explore the fluidity that inhabits a more complex sexual position vis-à-vis a wider range of gender performances practised within various class, racial and ethnic positions.

The nationalist ethos of contemporary United States is based on a multiculturalist rhetoric that lays claim to a national culture of inclusivity that purports to promote social justice and equality. A cultivated practice of colour blindness and meritocracy seeks to erase the differences between black, white and coloured people who, apparently, compete on equal terms in an open market, claiming responsibility for individual acts of consumption, accumulation, and deviation. This neo-liberal idiom of multiculturalism, however, fails to acknowledge the deeper structural and racial inequalities that permeate American society at every level. This paradox, which notionally celebrates difference and inclusivity and in actuality practices discrimination based on class and colour is the strategic standpoint of *Orange is the New Black*. Jenji Kohan's multiculturalist approach is dictated by her choice of genre—the space of a prison that houses female convicts who have all been convicted by law, irrespective of their race and class, in proportion to the measure of their respective crime. *Orange is the New Black*'s diversity oriented programming is founded upon a casting system that effectively forges a departure from the 'blindcasting' model which deliberately overlooks the auditioning candidates' race/ethnicity. The traditional practice, on the contrary, had been to explicitly specify the role's desired race/ethnicity before auditions. But in the blindcasting model producers refrain from designating a racial preference for available roles, allowing productions to practice racially diverse casting without acknowledging structural difference as part of a show's content (Warner 2015, p. 635). Showrunners like Shonda Rhimes have been blindcasting since the early aught, a practice Kristen Warner has called a 'public relations miracle' allowing networks to address accusations of racial and cultural disparity on television, all the while evacuating the specificity of experience (p- 634). But given the setting *of Orange is the New Black* in a women's prison, Kohan's award winning casting director, Jennifer Euston does the opposite of blindcasting. Euston has claimed that diverse casting rather than blindcasting would enable the show to address the racial and structural inequalities refusing to whitewash a black woman's struggle as universal rather than particular.

White privilege has been predominantly presented through the character of Piper Chapman. In the very first episode she is offered a toothbrush by another white woman Lorna who tells her "we look out for our own..." (season 1 episode 1). When a similar situation arises in season 3 episode 2, Vee, a black woman, is sharply taunted by Laura, a white, who tells her: "one of the black girls didn't come round when you got in? that's a shame" (3.2). The sub-spaces within the Litchfield penitentiary like the cafeteria, dormitories, and bathrooms are clearly segregated where each inmate sits only with her clan. When Piper was awaiting initial room assignment, Nicky comforted her by saying that she will send her to "'the suburbs' with the other white people" (season 1 episode 3). Another obvious instance of racial privilege is when Piper is granted furlough in season 2 to visit her dying grandmother. On previous similar occasions Poussey and Sofia were denied any such leave of absence when their mother and father respectively, were fatally ill and dying. Reflecting on this Poussey comments, "Chapman ain't got no strife in her life, but bitch gets the red carpet laid out for her" (season 2 episode 8). To which Piper unsympathetically retorts: "I guess white privilege wins again. And as a speaker for the entire white race, I would like to say that I am sorry that you guys got the raw deal, but I love my fucking grandmother (season 2 episode 8). Piper who is otherwise known for her felicitous and non-discriminatory behaviour is unable to grapple with the systemic racism within the prison system.

The Women's Advisory Council (WAC) is an elected body within the prison where representatives of each race interacted in occasional meetings with the correctional officer Healy. Nicky explains this concept to Piper, "you can only vote within your race or your group. Look, just pretend it's the 1950's, it makes it easier to understand" (season 1 episode 6). The racist comments that everyone indulges in with laughs and giggles implicate the densely racist environment that an American prison generally has. Lorna explains, at the white women's table what she knows about the Hispanics: "They live like 20 people to one apartment, they have more kids then even the Irish... they are dirty, they are greasy, and they are taking our jobs (season 1 episode 6). Black women Taystee and Poussey raise hilarious laughter in the table when they talk of stereotypical wealthy white activities such as sushi, yoga, wine tasting, setting up hedge funds, being vegan, viewing documentaries and really having quiet sex at 9:00 p.m." (season 1 episode 6). At one of the Hispanic tables, the black people are described as "smelly, stupid, and lazy, but they ain't got different bones" (season 1 episode 6). These conversations, all framed in a comical manner, reinforce the existing nature of race-relations in America, busting the myth of its idealized inclusive culture.

Orange is the New Black's tagline is "every sentence tells a story" and throughout the 39 episodes of the first three seasons the incarcerated women's lives are represented as diverse, unique, and yet relatable. The stories of black, white, Hispanic, Latina, Asian women are told giving sufficient insight into their past lives as the focus has been less on their actual crimes and more on the material circumstances of their lives. The episodic unfolding of the individual storylines, through the strategies of flashback and present experiences, alternating, the depiction has been a humanized account of these criminalised women, each spaced within specific socioeconomic challenges. In season 1 a woman officer tells Piper: "I just want you to know that as far as I am concerned you and me are the same, the only difference between us is when I made bad decisions in life I didn't get caught." (1.7), implying a fundamental commonality that characteristically binds women. The micro-landscape of the prison in *Orange is the New Black* addresses issues such as a fluid sexual (non)identity, hegemonic and structural oppressions leading to intersections of inequality, the present American penal system, stimulating and complicating the audiences' views on these serious social concerns. *Orange is the New Black*, if not revolutionary, does have the potential to challenge stereotypes tied to race, class, gender, and sexuality in spite of its realistic premise that cannot bypass the elements of racism, sexism and other institutional prejudices that do exist within a prison narrative. But the show definitely succeeds in generating broader public discussions on women prisoners, raising a conscientious awareness on matters of systemic oppression and control which make the mutual precepts of individual freedom and responsibility appear inconsistent in practice.

References

Birnbaum, D. 2016. "'Orange Is the New Black': Jenji Kohan, Cast Talks Season 4, Diversity, Binge-Watching." January 17. http://variety.com/2016/tv/news/orange-is-thenew-black-season-4-jenji-kohan-1201681782/ (accessed February 14, 2016).

Charlton, T. F (2013, September 3). "Orange is the new black," and how we talk about race and identity. RH Reality Check. Retrieved from: http://rhrealitycheck.org/article/2013/09/03/orangeis-the-new-black-and-how-we-talk-about-race-and-identity/

Chermak, S. M. (1998). Police, courts, and corrections in the media. In F. Bailey & D. Hale (Eds.), *Popular culture, crime, and justice* (pp. 87-99). Belmont, CA: Sage Publications.

Collins, P. H. (1990). *Black feminist thought: Knowledge, consciousness, and the politics of empowerment.* Boston, MA: Unwin Hyman.

Crenshaw, K. (1989). Demarginalizing the intersection of race and sex: A Black feminist critique of antidiscrimination doctrine, feminist theory and antiracist politics. *The University of Chicago Legal Forum, 140,* 139-67.

Doyle, S. (2013, Sept. 9). Orange is the new black roundtable, Part 3: The final work on OITNB (oh, and Larry). In These Times: With Liberty and Justice for All. Retrieved from http://inthesetimes.com/article/15552/orange_is_the_new_black_roundtable_part_3

Enck, Suzanne M., and Megan E. Morrissey. 2015. "If Orange Is the New Black, I Must Be Color Blind: Comic Framings of Post-racism in the Prison-Industrial-Complex." *Critical Studies in Media Communication* 32 (5): 303-17.

Fernández-Morales, M., Menéndez-Menéndez, María Isabel. When in Rome, Use What You've Got: A Discussion of Female Agency through Orange Is the New Black. Television & New Media, vol. 17, 6: pp. 534-546, First Published May 5, 2016.

Ferrell, J., & Websdale, N. (1999). *Making trouble: Cultural constructions of crime, deviance, and control.* Hawthorne, NY: Aldine de Gruyter.

Foucault, M. (1975) 1995. *Discipline and Punish: The Birth of the Prison.* New York: Vintage.

Goldberg, L. (2013, April 30). Netflix sets premiere date for Jenji Kohan's Orange is the New Black. *The Hollywood Reporter.* Retrieved from: http://www.hollywoodreporter.com/live-feed/netflix-orange-new-black-premiere-date-jenji-kohan-448610.

Gross, T. (2013, August 13). Orange creator Jenji Kohan: "Piper was my Trojan horse." Fresh air.Podcast retrieved from http://www.npr.org/templates/transcript/transcript.php?storyId=211639989

Gwynne, K. (2013, September 6). "Orange is the new black" author: Prison wastes time, human potential and money. Alternet. Retrieved from: http://www.alternet.org/progressive-wire/orange-new-black-author-prison-wastes-time-human-potential-and-money

Jordan, C. 2014. "'Orange Is the New Black' Cast Join #MillionMarchNYC." *The Wrap*, December 14. https://www.thewrap.com/orange-is-the-new-black-cast-join-millionmarchnyc/ (accessed October 30, 2015).

Kerman, P. (2010) 2013. *Orange Is the New Black: My Time in a Women's Prison*. London: Abacus. Kohan, Jenji. 2013. *Orange Is the New Black*. Netflix. Lionsgate Television.

Levenson, J. (2001). Inside information: prisons and the media. *Criminal Justice Matters, 43*, 14-15.

Ma, W. (2016, June 17). How Netflix develops its original content. *News*. Retrieved from: http://www.news.com.au/technology/home-entertainment/tv/how-netflix-develops-its-original-content/news-story/ec4029dde1b28c657e7792e80755f885

McClelland, M. 2015. "'Orange Is the New Black': Caged Heat." Rolling Stone, June 12. http://www.rollingstone.com/tv/features/orange-is-the-new-black-cover-story-caged-heat-20150612?page=2 (accessed October 30, 2015).

McLaren, M. A. 2002. *Feminism, Foucault, and Embodied Subjectivity*. Albany: State University of New York Press.

Pardue, A., Arrigo, B.A., & Murphy, D.S. (2011). Sex and sexuality in women's prison: A preliminary typological investigation. *The Prison Journal, 91*(3), 279-304.

Pozner, J. L. (2010). *Reality bites back: The troubling truth about guilty pleasure TV*. Berkeley, CA: Seal Press.

Surette, R. (1998b). *Media crime and criminal justice: Images and realties*. Belmont, CA: Wadsworth.

Surette, R. (2015). *Media, crime and criminal Justice: Images, realities and policies* (5th ed.) Stamford, CT: Cengage Learning.

Taylor, A. (2012). *Single women in popular culture: The limits of postfeminism*. New York, NY: Palgrave Macmillan.

Walkley, A. J. (2013, August 23). Bi-erasure in orange is the new black. HuffPost Gay Voices. Retrieved from http://www.huffingtonpost.com/aj-walkley/orange-is-the-new-blackbisexuality_b_3799037.html

Warner, K. 2015. "the Racial Logic of *Grey's Anatomy*: Shonda Rhimes and Her 'Post-Civil Rights, Post-feminism' Series." Television and Media 16 (7): 631-47.

Wlodarz, J. (2005). Maximum insecurity: Genre trouble and closet erotics in and out of HBO's OZ. *Camera Obscura, 20* (58), 58-105.

Tracks and Borders: Railways in Ray's *Apu Trilogy*

Sandip Mondal

There is another implication of this focus on borders in terms of borderness. Whileit is clear that borders do not independently exist as self-evident entities in the landscape, in that they are fashioned out of particular epistemologies that vary across time and space, it is also the case that once constructed (which includes all the various associated bordering practices, both formal and informal), borders can take on thing-like qualities, both in practice and in people's imaginations. That has, of course, given rise to a considerable focus, particularly within anthropology, on frontiers and borderlands, where widely diverse conditions provide a variety of spaces in which people, things, places and relations can take active roles in what goes on in such regions (Donnan and Wilson 1999, 2010; Roitman 2005). Borders provide the possibility of making different, perhaps additional, worlds—or, to use Viveiros de Castro's (2004) understanding, they could generate and reflect many possible ontologies. In that sense, borders are not only epistemological entities, they are also ontological ones—epistemologies made real, in a sense (Green, Sarah 580).

Ever since its entry into the domain of academia in the late twentieth century, Border Studies/theory had been deployed as an acumen to understand political implications of 'fences' as manifest in different forms of cultural texts. Such political understanding definitely involves the issues of state, nation, family and their relation with individuals/subjects which in turn define the identity of all concerned. Due to the political situation of the exponents of the theory of border and their stand amenable to their position coupled the problematic geographical location of their space they live have made this school of thought pondering over the issues of partition, immigration and reclaiming of lands. The understanding of the politics and culture of Mexico so overtly expressed in the writings of Gloria Anzaldua and her contemporaries, has been deployed to examine the similar situation like the partition of India, the fall of Berlin wall in 1991 Perhaps this over-emphasis border studies on the aspects of external reality has often made it overlook the dynamics of the inner reality, of human mind and sensibility affected by the seen and the unseen 'fences' of culture and politics. In this dialectics of the seen and the unseen 'fences' crucially stands the track of railways emerging in Europe in the 1820s and spread all over the world within fifty year. The country's first railway, built by the Great Indian Peninsula Railway (GIPR), opened in 1853, between Bombay and Thane. A British engineer, Robert Maitland Brereton, was responsible for the expansion of the railways from 1857 onwards. The Allahabad-Jabalpur branch line of the East Indian Railway had been opened in June 1867.

Primarily conceived of as a mode of conveyance and a marker of modernity, railways seem to connect spaces; spaces of variety, binary and symmetry. Such connections, across the world, amenable to the negotiation of country and city, of rural and urban, contributed to the growth of the nations all over the world from the mid nineteenth century onwards. As an offshoot of the European Industrial Revolution, railway, when reached the colonized spaces of Asia and other continents, continued with similar cultural and ideological implication as they did in the West. However, the differences are not invisible either. Designed primarily as an agency to move soldiers and European officials railways in the third world colonized countries also brought in a cultural progress and modernity which of course was an unintended byproduct.

However, the unintended aspects of early railways in India fostered the modernity from towards the middle of the nineteenth century. The crux of such modernity lies in the negotiation of country and city; reaching out to the city with raw materials for industry in cities and outskirts, commodities for the city markets and of course young learners for the academic institutions was a common code of such negotiation. City, on the other hand, reached out to the country in the form of finished product materials sent by the country itself, goods and commodities of foreign lands, institutions, services and most importantly enlightened human resources with languages and the thoughts of the Western epistemology. Railways played an important role in this process of reaching out, an unmistakable tool for the negotiation of country and city. Conceiving of railways as a mode of communication and as an agency of assimilation would rather represent the railway track as a vertical axis that moves along a definite topographical space without any obstacle and resistance. Such an absence of any obstacle for the journey of the railway track vis-à-vis the train would mean a similarity between the country and the city particularly in terms of culture. But neither the country nor the city, despite the possibility of being linked through railways, have been fully accommodating of the other. The gaps and lapses existing between two spaces and resistance, anxiety and desire experienced by individuals have also come into play when it comes to the relationship between country and city especially through the agency of railways. Such an understanding would however represent the railway track more as a horizontal axis than as a vertical axis which divides and disconnects rather than connecting and communicating. This vertical axis now functions more like a barrier, a border; a metaphorical and a cultural one. One must undergo the pains and sufferings, the desire and the dilemma while crossing it as this border is amenable to a rite of passage.

When it comes to the modernity of pre-independence Bengal, railways play an important role in negotiating the country and city. The first railway to be established in Bengal is between Howrah and Hooghly in 1854. A parallel track of railways was established from Sealdah to the eastern part of Bengal, running along the river Ganges, would suggest that railways, in its nascent stage of development functioned as a conduit between the villages/suburbs and the city of Kolkata rather than connecting Bengal with the rest of the country.

Once this negotiation of the country and the city settles in the public consciousness, it starts reflecting in late nineteenth and early twentieth century Bengali literature; travelogues, novels, memoirs, short stories and even poetry. One such writer who brought this issue of negotiation of the country and the city the agency of railways, symptomatic of modernity itself, is Bibhutibhushan

Bandyopadhyay (1894-1950) This article will focus not so much on all the writings of Bandyopadhyay that explore the issue of railways as a marker of colonial modernity as it would on the three films made by Satyajit Ray, *Pather Panchali* (1955), *Aparajito* (1956) and *Apur Sansar* (1959) better known as *Apu Trilogy* based on the novels of same title written by Bandyopadhyay. Hence, the references of railways discussed are presented more as a visual trope/code rather than as verbal ones. However, the literary and the cultural understanding of Bandyopadhyay vis-à-vis the Bengali community is well rendered in the film adaptations of Ray.

In many cultural texts across the world railways have been associated with modernity and mobility. Train, however, does not merely signify physical mobility; it comes along in many cultural texts with other connotations, the loss of faith, fragmentation, alienation and distance of all sorts. Chiefly functioning as a metaphor of journey from agrarian to the industrial, from country to city, from possible priesthood to an urban profession, train in the trilogy also suggests the psychological nuances of the characters concerned and their engagement with society in the context of modernity.

But when it comes to considering train as a narrative component in *Pather Panchali*, we are immediately and reductively drawn to the famous train sequence with the image of the *kaash*[1] flowers. But the story of train and railways begins much earlier than this 'iconic' representation of train.

Suggesting the possible future convergence of the inner world and the world outside, the family and the city it all begins as an aural scheme in an evening. While the female members of the family, including Durga are busy in evening chores, and Harihar, most importantly, in writing a jatrapala, as he, besides being a priest, was also an aspiring playwright, Apu suddenly hears the noise and the whistle of a train running far across the village. He immediately plans with Durga that they would go and watch the train someday. This sequence as an embryo of the later

---

[1] A plant of the grass family, mostly seen growing along rivers. It is famous for its dry white flowers weighing light.

development of the reference of trains continues to inform different stages of the narrative in the entire *Apu Trilogy*.

Train in the trilogy is not presented just as a metaphor of physical and psychological mobility. Movement and stagnation often jostle for space in the trilogy. Train as a trope is often placed in the dialectics of movement and stability; of life and death. Despite its episodic structure *Pather Panchali* in terms of the visual, the narrative anticipates the rondo pattern, the organic growth of a film that Ray would apply in his later films.

Placed structurally in the middle of the film, train comes along with the fast pace of life when the villagers, children, Apu and Durga gain a rhythmic promptness, a momentum during the festival—*Durga Puja*[2]. The rhythm of the visual suddenly assumes this fast pace of life with editing becoming faster and the subjects on screen gaining a sporadic momentum. Most pertinent in this context is the performance of *yatra*, a festivity rite emulating which the next day perhaps Apu first confronts the train while going to find out the lost calf with Durga. It is in this moment of fast movement that the train suddenly appears with even faster pace.

A close analysis of the mise-en-scène of the sequence would lead us to infer the other meaning to be fully developed in later sequels. The train which was coming from the right side of the frame from the point of view of Apu and Durga suddenly appears from the left side of the frame. It suddenly evokes the point of view just in the opposite direction of the point of view of Apu and Durga; that of the audience, the camera or some other person not yet introduced. The camera, emulating that perception, has suddenly moved to the other side of the railway track while Apu and Durga, left with a sense of awe, remain on the other side as if startled by an epiphanic moment. Railway track thus, being symptomatic of border, suggests a number of antinomies, of childhood and youth, of innocence and knowledge, pain and pleasure all of which together define the dynamics of modernity. Given that the image of a running train suggests the culminating point of fast rhythm, it is followed by a foreclosure of all sorts of mobility temporarily. The

---

[2] This festival of Bengal revolves round the worship of Goddess Durga.

pace of life for the characters concerned suddenly becomes slower. While coming back home, with the calf and the experience of the train, Apu and Durga suddenly discover the Indir aunt lying dead in the village street.

The final tempo of the film, in keeping with the rondo structure, corresponds to a slow rhythm, visually recreated in the form of slow cutting, slow movement of objects on screen and camera to imply and anticipate all other unpleasant elements in the film and the entire trilogy; as the death of Durga.

Train in *Aparajito*, is introduced primarily on auditory level as in *Pather Panchali*. However unlike *Pather Panchali*, which projects a distance of several shots and sequences between train as an auditory referent and the visual one, *Aparajito* refers to the auditory referent immediately followed by the visual one. This sequence, moving beyond just an experience of modernity, acquires meaning, in terms of a more esoteric relationship between human sensibilities and train. Sarbajoya, while in a dilemma over whether to accept the job of governess in Dewanpur or to go back to the village with Apu, suddenly stands in favour of the latter option as she thought the previous one would spoil all future possibilities for Apu. And she decides to go back. Immediately followed by the sequence where Sarbajoya is requested to accept the join the job of a governess permanently, in a scene she suddenly discovers Apu in a position of servility and decides that she would go back to the village. And this is suggested simply by the whistle of a train which merges with the visual image of the train in the shot the follows immediately. They are coming back to the village. This return to the country is suggested by a shot taken inside a train crossing the river Ganges in Benaras. Given the motif of journey, as explored in this *Apu Trilogy*, each train journey is a ritual of crossing a border, a rite of passage for an experience, a new life.

Apu in *Aparajito* is not rooted in one single topographical space. He becomes subject to mobility and in turn modernity. Starting his journey at Nishchindipur at the end of *Pather Panchali* to *Kashi*, and then to another village of his maternal connection, Monsapota, he finally settles in Kolkata only to come back pretty often to the village to see his mother. The more he becomes a subject to mobility the more he grows up as a loner, as artist of a bildungsroman.

Along with this line of argument that Apu matures as a loner, Apu travels alone on the train to Kolkata in the second tempo. Apu, thus developing the narrative/visual code that started in *Pather Panchali* moves to the other side of the railway track, the city. During his journey Apu is shown to toy with a globe implying that he is about to know and explore he primarily reaches via train. Apu is always caught between mobility and stasis as primarily implied in *Pather Panchali*. This is thoroughly corroborated by Apu when he deliberately misses a train to stay with his mother for a few more days.

The third reference to train is for more suggestive and in continuation with the meaning already formulated by previous motifs of train. Sarbajoya waits for Apu in ill health; she listens to the whistle of the train again going far across the village as in *Pather Panchali,* from left to the right side of the frame while Apu has moved to the other side of the track which suggests that Sarbajoya now equates her perception with that of Apu. But it is something more than an equation of perceptions. It is about the dilemma of choosing between two spaces, when conceived of in contradictory terms—the urban and the rural. However with all his rural connection severed at the end of *Aparajito*, Apu in the last sequel of the Trilogy is bound to remain confined in an urban space with only the memory of the rural space and the desire to go back there.

In *Apur Sansar* train does not so much recur as a metaphor of mobility, it appears, as of an urban space; a space that Apu, in different ways, is desperately trying to adjust with. If we consider the entire trilogy as an organic composition, if not a musical one then in the final tempo of the trilogy disparate visual and aural tropes conglomerate for resolution on an idealist level rather than on an empirical plane. *Apur Sansar* offers many modes of urban conveyance, not just trains. While the train links the rural with the urban, the horse driven tram and the electric tram are transported within the urban space. Apu with the memory of the rural space is more comfortable in dialogue with the urban transports once he is married to Aparna. In this short phase of adjustability Apu is not seen to be drawn so much by the memory of the rural. He rather graduates to accepting the modes of urbanity. But underneath the narrative development in terms of Apu's maturity Ray is equally concerned with portraying the difference between the rural and urban cultures, in which Apu places himself as the hero of a bildungsroman fiction. Apu's growth runs parallel with the development of indigenous cultural forms into ones informed by colonial modernity. This is evident in the coalescing of the two sequences with the aid of the technique of fade in and fade out which remains almost invisible. The implications of *yatra* in *Pather Panchali* now mature into a modern cultural art form, cinema. The last shot of *Bhakta Dhruva*, a film Apu and Aparna went to watch together, fades into the image of the window of a horse-tram implicating the movement of individual, community and cultures to the domain of modernity. Immediately follows the sequence in Sealdah station. Aparna is leaving for her father's place in a matured stage of her pregnancy. Ironically this is the last meeting between Aparna and Apu with the train now becoming an ironic metaphor of separation. A few shots later Apu reads the later in his journey home on a tram symbolising his life in motion only to be thwarted by the news of the death of Aparna with trains moving slowly in the background of the mise-en-scene.

Had this film ended here all the modes of transport, as tropes, would have remained separate from each other without being mingled in a single organic whole. Immediately after this, like *Pather Panchali,* all things halt and the elements and the experience of life become stuck in a stasis. The railway track is no longer a mark of mobility, the empty track in the mise-en-scene is now a metaphor memory and sense rupture in human minds.

But emulating the structure of an elegy, the grief of Apu transcends to a higher plane reached through the piety of nature. Once Apu decides to leave the city and start for the unknown we once again confront the images of train and train journey. The rhythm of editing becomes fast once again with images of trains running even faster. Fast movements of a train justify such psychological transcendence represented by a fast movement. Trains no longer suggest motion and mobility on physical and cultural level. It is represented as a metaphor of how Apu transcends the plane of grief to sublimate that into nature. This poetic resolution almost in Coleridgeian vein is possible when one crosses the chaotic phase of the assimilation of the disparate as Apu has crossed the physical mobility through different modes of transport to reach a plane of transcendence. The image of river comes thrice in the film and poses as an antithesis to train. River appears in an image seen through the window of the room on their wedding night. It also reappears with exactly similar visual and aural implications when toward the end Apu once again travels from city to village to meet his son. Once placed in a village Apu with the agency of his son visits the leitmotif of his memory and desire and their meaning and the meaning of life are drawn from the interaction between all modes of transports of modernity on one hand and rive, as a universal and archetypal one on the other.

Border entails the stories of estrangement; estrangement from individuals, places and experiences. But with an unmistakable irony, embedded in the very notion of itself, border brings forth the narratives of unification in the plane of memory, recollection and desire. All cultural texts, dealing with ideas of 'border' attempt to restore that originary unification. The notes of alienation, anxiety and desire, associated with the railway track as a 'border', primarily established in the *Pather Panchali* and then re-experienced and revisited in *Aparajito*, seem to resolve in the father-son unification in the end of *Apur Sansar*. This unification however, rather than being just a literal one of father and son, is symptomatic of many metaphorical ones; of individuals of land, memory and desire, death and living and so on that one can experience beyond the domain of binaries, made separated through lines and borders.

Bibliography

Bordwell, David and Kristin, Thompson. *Film Art: An Introduction*. New York: McGraw Hill, 1996. Print.

Caughie, John, ed. *Theories of Authorship: A Reader*. London: Routledge, 2001. Print.

Ellis, C. Hamilton. *Railways*. London: Peebles Press, 1974. Print.

Green, Sarah. "Sense of Border." Wilson 577- 584.

Lapsley, Robert, and Michael Westlake. *Film Theory: An Introduction*. New York: Manchester University Press, 2006. Print.

Ray, Satyajit. *My Years with Apu*. New York: Viking, 1994. Print.

Turner, Graeme. *Film as Social Practice*. London: Routledge, 2007. Print.

Wilson, Thomas M.and Hastings Donnan (Ed.) *A Companion to Border Studies*, Chichester: Blackwell, 2012. Print.

Wollen, Peter. *Signs and Meaning in the Cinema*. London: Secker & Warburg, 1972. Print.

Oceanic Borders:
Climate Refugees, Borders and Extinction in the Necrocene

Oriol J. Batalla

The last two decades have been marked by an increase on the mainstream cultural and political *ethos* promulgated by the economically-rich countries towards a greener "sustainable development" through the *logos* egology can spread through factual data and analysis affecting the *pathos* of societies. In a world dominated by a *Capitalomania,* paraphrasing Zea's *nordomania* (Zea, 1986), and the strategical execution of its power (Foucault, 1975), where there is an influence and the episteme of perceiving the economically-rich areas — mostly but not exclusively North America, Europe and Australia — as the superior entities in the global order due to their economic, strategical, political, mass-media and cybernetic influence, control and power (Cajigas-Rotundo, 2007; París, 2013; Mbembe, 2016; Latour, 2017), the contemporary world has become "one marked by the globalization of markets, the privatization of the world under the aegis of neoliberalism, and the increasing imbrication of the financial markets, the postimperial military complex and electronic and digital technologies" (Mbembe, 2017:3), and, in an Orwellian manner, also dominated by fear -of the "other", of a different system, of a revolution- to solidify political power (París, 2013), together with an exploitation of crime and discrimination of subalterns in order to execute a control on populations (Chomsky, 1997). Furthermore, cyberculture and development of new technologies and media, production of consumerism-based subjectivities, and the transition to an immaterial post-Fordist economy have led to the hegemonic globalization and abysmal expansion of capitalism in a global scale (Cajigas-Rotundo, 2007). In this turmoil, a new, unprecedented, eerie environmental, ecological, political and cultural crisis is threatening, not only the economically-poor, neocolonized countries, but also the economically-rich and politically privileged countries. Paradigmatically, environmentalists in influential and powerful positions have advocated for a "techno-fixing" of the current issue, so as to trigger a future so called "green growth" through "green technology" (Kallis, 2018). The dichotomy here is that capitalism, cause of most of the inequalities in the modern and contemporary world and booster of the Capitalocene (Moore, 2016), an age dominated by the geological agency of capital accumulation which has led to the becoming of Nature of a set of objects outside Humanity with a monetary value, is included within the environmental and ecological conservationist discourse without being challenged. In this dialectic between Nature and Humanity, not only natural ecosystems per se are found, but also members of human societies ``such as peoples of color, most women, and most people with white skin living in semicolonial regions" (Moore, 2016: 91), what Moore (2016) coins as the *Law of Cheap Nature*. Therefore, the planetary order is divided between the beings subjugated into the Law of Cheap Nature (exploited) and Humanity, the ones outside of it (exploiters).

As Bellamy and Diamanti (2018) shed light upon in line with what has been previously said, "by almost every projection, the simple reproduction of existing systems of production and distribution, to say nothing of their growth, will doom the planet to a host of ecocidal developments" (Bellamy and Diamanti, 2018: x). Nonetheless, even though it will be due to the ecocidal nature of Capitalism that the planet will be facing an unparalleled environmental crisis, such politics of accumulation and the hegemony of a profit-over-society agenda will also develop towards the extinction and direct perishing of peoples, cultures and societies both from environmental catastrophes, such as the rising seas, ocean acidification or desertification; and discrimination based on capital power. Bearing this in mind, here I want to advocate for the *Necrocene* narrative, a twist within the Capitalocene theorization as an alternative to the Anthropocene discourse, in order to frame the current geopolitical age and ecological catastrophe.The Earth is currently facing the Necrocene epoch, a geological age triggered by Capital mass-accumulation which "reframes the history of capitalism's expansion through the process of becoming extinction" (McBrien, 2016), not only of species, but languages, peoples, resources and the (de)construction through pollution. The Necrocene sheds light upon the reality of the Sixth Extinction, visible on the notorious decline in amphibian numbers and disappearance of species in the last decade (Kolvert, 2014), but also, as the Necrocene narrative points out, the extinction of societies and cultures through direct or indirect influence of Capitalist accumulation upon them. Everything is affected by an entity that triggers extinction of everything it touches upon, absorbs everything it can colonize and turns it into a monetary product, creates inequality through economic growth and inflation—or what is wrongly named as "development"- in a "brutal state of affairs, profoundly inegalitarian -where all existence is evaluated in terms of money alone" (Baidou, 2001; in Fisher, 2009: 5), creating a "business ontology" (Fisher, 2009) presented to all societies as the ultimate reality and the ideal of progress and welfare.Even climate-change denialists such as Donald Trump and his administration—although neoliberal to the core—seem to unconsciously bend to the catastrophic fate of the planet by wanting to expand the US borders to other planets in opposition to the US immigration policies, mostly based on what I consider a *capitalist racism*, a racism that is not anymore solely about race but about culture and purchasing power (Mbembe, 2016) and the epistemic realization that race discrimination is used by the strata thathave control of certain powers in order to benefit those who are supporting the devaluation of humanity, non-human entities, those who offer low-cost labor and to get rid of those who are said to be useless or not beneficial for the system (Mignolo, 2008). As Marcuse (1964) well exemplifies, the "other" is seen by the State as the "enemy", which works as a cohesion element and triggers society to a defense state towards a common target, therefore, becoming a binder for social stability (Marcuse, 1964).

The Necrocene is already affecting, amongst other entities, the peoples from islands and coastline areas. The current estimates of sea-level rise rates predict a human cataclysm by the end of the 21st

Century which will change our perception of our global reality in a catastrophic event never acquainted before, disvaluing the prediction of future events through previous knowledge (Pilkey et al, 2016), which will affect between 25 million and 1.4 billion people by 2050 (Brown, 2008, in Parenti, 2011; Geisler & Currens, 2017). As Parenti highlights,

> even if all greenhouse gas emissions stopped immediately [...] there is already enough carbon dioxide in the atmosphere to cause significant warming and disruptive Climate Change, and with that considerably more poverty, violence, social dislocation, forced migration, and political upheaval. Thus we must find humane and just means of adaptation, or we face barbaric prospects (Parenti, 2011: 212).

In this situation, as Cajigas-Rotundo (2007), Cohen et al. (2013) and Kallis (2018) amongst other scholars have proposed, there needs to be a switch from the paradoxical "green" sustainable development, which acknowledges the false possibility of sustainability within unlimited Capitalist mass accumulation, since there cannot be equality for all the living entities in the voracious and unequal reality of Capital accumulation, towards a more "prismatic ecology" (Cohen et al, 2013). Current environmentalist politics and policies do not adopt measures related to what Levi R. Bryant (2013) nomenclates as "Black Ecology", an environmental justice and theory that leaves aside the green and "comforting homeostatic conception of nature" (Bryant, 2013: 292) in order to draw attention to the issues of race, gender, discriminated minorities and peoples disproportionately affected by the current environmental crisis triggered by capitalist mass accumulation.

Whatever color it might be, the reality in which the Earth and humankind find themselves right now can be coined as the *Necrocene Realism* (Batalla, 2019), paraphrasing Fisher's "Capitalist Realism" (Fisher, 2009), in which there is not only the widespread sense of a Capitalist logic and order that does not allow humankind to view a coherent alternative to it, but also acknowledges -even dooms the planet I would say-whether it is consciously or not, the existence of an Environmental and Political Crisis worldwide. The Necrocene is present everywhere and ontologically triggers our perception towards the Zizekian realization that nowadays it is easier to think about the end of the world than to grasp a feasible end of Capitalism (Zizek, 2018). Nonetheless, as Fisher (2009) helps us see through, when we manage to challenge the inconsistency and incongruences of Capitalist system, the entity as a whole can be put into question because it brings to the surface that "capitalism's ostensible 'realism' turns out to be nothing of the sort" (Fisher, 2009: 16). From a Prismatic Political Ecology, Neo-Anticapitalist and Environmental Humanities lens, in this chapter I will try to explore the ethical global conflict of the climate refugees of islands and coastlines within the Dark Hyperobject of the Necrocene related to the concept of (b)order and the dialectic it predicts between locality and globality. The term climate refugee "describes a person who is forced to leave their home or community due to changes to the local environment, such as rising sea levels, drought, famine, or other effects of Climate Change (National Geographic Society, 2012; in Tetrick, 2018). The latest evaluations of sea-level rise rates forecast a human catastrophe never acquainted before in human history by the end of the 21st Century which is bound to challenge and modify the perception of our global reality due to the exhaustion of certain resources, disappearance of big chunks of land and a consequent massive movement and flux of people (Pilkey et al, 2016). Seas, oceans, islands and coastlines affected by the Necrocene and the Sixth Extinction, and the human responses to such situation, are an interesting item of analysis since they have belonged to the magic, mysterious, mystical and aesthetic veneration enclosed in the human imaginary throughout human history and cultural representations, and signified the realities of the Earth in a scale that humans are able to grasp. It is also crucial to acknowledge the signification of the oceans as a natural border that also borders political life since humans are a terrestrial species and, thus, not able to build huge populations offshore.In an age where Planetary Boundaries (Stockholm Resilience Center; Rockströem et al., 2009) and their singularities—in the Deleuzian sense—based on the formation of constellations of knowledge (Deleuze on Foucault, 1985-86)will shed light upon the different singularities that define and frame the different force relations and "power" (Foucault, 1972), therefore affecting the current environmental and political global crisis, bordering and limiting international actions -just like a Velázquez painting and his use of light to stress and highlight the important parts and singularities of the narrative and leading to the realization of power/knowledge relations outside the diagram-, the idea of a physical border is as present as ever when it comes to people's movement yet useless when approaching the contemporary environmental crisis since nature obviously follows a different time-space logic (Diener & Hagen, 2012). Bearing this in mind, this chapter aims to produce fruitful narratives for an alternative thinking of the current environmental and political global turmoil regarding, in this case, island and coastline refugees in the Necrocene epoch, towards a Degrowth transition.

The Dark Hyperobject of the Necrocene Realism

In this situation of environmental, social, cultural and political uproar without precedent, it is important to highlight that the most common understanding of human reality in mainstream thought, politics, culture and media is based on a colonial past and present and the ontological border of the Dark Hyperobject of the Necrocene Realism. Still, crucial for this realization is to recognize *what* a common hyperobject is. Devised by Timothy Morton (2013), the concept of hyperobject refers to "things that are massively distributed in time and space relative to humans" (Morton, 2013: 1), such as Global Warming, Plastic Pollution, the Biosphere or the concept of Planet Earth (Batalla, 2019), and share some common traits: All of them are Viscous. This means that they do not stick to the concepts of outside or away and, as Morton (2013) exemplifies, "just as radioactive materials: "The more you try to get rid of them, the more you realize you can't get rid of them." (Morton, 2013: 36). They are also Molten in time and space, in the sense that they stretch, bend and reshape on time to such an extent that, even though hyperobjects surround us, we as humans are not able to grasp their limitations, becoming ontologically and phenomenologically eerie (Batalla, 2019). Morton also indicates that "the recognition of being caught in hyperobjects is precisely a feeling of strange familiarity and familiar strangeness" (Morton, 2013: 55). Just as in a scuba-diving immersion, hyperobjects surround and pressure, and alter your perception of time and space, just like the ocean. However, humans are independent agents from the water surrounding them. Even if humankind can be framed as a hyperobject, it is trapped and entangled within others too. In addition, hyperobjects are considered to be Nonlocal and Phased, since they tend to be part of a "high-dimensional *phase space*" (Morton, 2013: 70) that unables humans to identify them holistically from an "ordinary" 3D human perception. To conclude, hyperobjects are thought to be Interobjective, meaning that the insight we might get from such entities is never delivered and felt straightforwardly but "only as mediated through other entities in some shared sensual space" (Morton, 2013: 86). This means that they might not be phenomenologically or ontologically perceived in a direct way, but that they might be able to be visible when mediated, devised or factualized through other means — data, time-lapse images or electronic microscopes for instance-.

If we account on Latour's idea that the difference between natural and cultural in terms of agency is inexistent and his assumption that every single entity must be regarded as an actor as long as it has the ability to act (Harman, 2016), hyperobjects should be treated as agents on other objects whether they are perceived or not or whether they act directly or indirectly upon such objects. Thus, if we consider such traits, they can be equally applied to the concept of the Necrocene. To my understanding, the Necrocene is a conceptualization that unfolds many hyperobjects from it, such as Climate Change, Inflation or the Sixth Extinction. All these agents meet the core traits of hyperobjects: they are viscous, molten, nonlocal, phased and interobjective. Nonetheless, perhaps when tackling such colossal matters that touch upon and affect everything that surrounds and builds up our reality, but we have not reached a way to quantify them or they are built by other hyperobjects, we might be dealing with a bigger, much larger entity which might attach to a different logic. In this light and bearing in mind what has been said so far, here I would like to suggest the concept of *Dark Hyperobjects* (Batalla, 2019). These entities are constrained within the same characteristics of the common Morton's hyperobjects stated before. Nevertheless, they are "dark" just as Dark Matter and Dark Energy. Dark Matter refers to components of our surrounding reality and universe that are not visually tangible but obey the elementary definition of matter: anything whose energy density scales with the inverse cube of scale factor. It is said to constitute around 85% of the matter of the entire universe but humans, due to our lack of relevant knowledge and technology to mediate such an entity, have not been able to directly quantify or perceive it (CERN, 2019). Dark Energy on the other hand is thought to accelerate the expansion of the universe which will eventually retreat (CERN, 2019) and, according to the CERN,

> Dark Energy makes up approximately 68% of the universe and appears to be associated with the vacuum in space. It is distributed evenly throughout the universe, not only in space but also in time—in other words, its effect is not diluted as the universe expands. The even distribution means that dark energy does not have any local gravitational effects, but rather a global effect on the universe as a whole. (CERN, 2019).

Dark Hyperobjects are therefore "dark" since humans have not found yet a way to perceive them or quantify them as a whole entity, and, even though they might not be as even as Dark Energy, also affect our entire reality due to their sucking and viscous agency. The Necrocene Realism belongs to such recognition. It is viscous and it affects our reality as a whole, since it affects everything it contacts, creating a strange unfeasibility and recognition that it is almost impossible to get rid of it, not only ontologically, but culturally, politically and economically due to the capitalomania and the lobbied and manipulated system it governs the Planet in our age. It is also molten, in the sense that its limitations in time and space are unknown and so its ability to grow or collapse in a precise or certain way. Predictions can be made and statistics have been proposed in certain matters belonging to the Necrocene. However, the entity itself bends and reshapes through time and space without showing its limitations. The Necrocene is also nonlocal and phased. That is, it does not belong to a 3D perception of reality and, hence, it does not allow humans to understand it holistically. Finally, it is also interobjective. We can perceive it through other hyperobjects such as Climate Change, Media Control or our ontological conception of the Earth and Environment. Through a deconstructivist perception of such issues, the realization and existence of the Necrocene Realism can be made. In addition, Dark Hyperobjects and, consequently, the Necrocene Realism, are "dark" in Morton's conceptualization of "darkness" in *Dark Ecology* (2016). For Morton (2016), thinking "dark" means to be in an ecognosis, which is "like knowing, but more like letting be known. It is something like coexisting" (Morton, 2016: 5). Dark Hyperobjects are therefore an ecognosis: they let us know their existence is real through their hyperobjectical characteristics. When this happens, we enter in the loop of knowing: the strange becomes known and what used to be casual turns out to be eerie at some point (Morton, 2016). In other words, and applying it to the Necrocene Realism, this eerie entity is not eerie anymore. We have become used to its existence in our reality and, consequently, we do not question it. Yet, we cannot see the entire object. As a final statement, worth is considering that it is, in fact, the darkness of capitalism that makes the Necrocene "dark" itself. This, consequently, begs the question of "how can we quantify capitalism and the influence it has had, has and potentially will have on every single entity subjugated to it?" (Batalla, 2019: 64). It is in fact this question what drags us to the realization of the darkness and eeriness of the Necrocene Realism.

Even Global Warming diehard logical, interpretative and implicatory denialists (Cohen, 2001 in Almirón & Talfalla, 2019), such as Donald Trump's administration, notorious for their rejection of theUS Fourth National Climate Assessment (2018) which detailed that Climate Change will cost the US hundreds of billions of USD, plus irreparable health issues on the US population (UFNCA, 2018), seem to unconsciously subjugate to the reality of the Necrocene and the catastrophic future of the Earth in the long run. By starting to build an eventual US colonizing mission to Mars, together with the foundation of a Space Force which will constitute the sixth branch of the US Defense Department to have an

"American dominance in space" (Hamill, 2018), it is worth considering that such politics and policies may be an unconscious path of acknowledgement of the current global crisis, dooming the Earth and all living species by planning a settlement outside the planet, which will clearly be only available for sociopolitical/economic privileged people. Climate Change has been brought into scientific and geopolitical discourse and actions by denialism and populism, discourses in which the oligarchy has given up a common ontology and reality of the Earth and life on it (Latour, 2017). Such issues reflect on the idea of losing grip of our reality (Morton, 2010) and the crucial question of "how much nature can we do without, to what extent simulations of nature can replace 'the natural'" (Heise, 2003: 60).

Bearing this in mind, the Necrocene Realism that we can acknowledge as part of our reality is "dark" in the sense that cannot be visualized, yet, in a Dark Matter/Dark Energy metaphorical motion, globally affects our reality, same as dark matter and dark energy might be composed and therefore affecting subatomic particles, dragging and sucking everything into the canopy of Capitalist accumulation. It keeps on expanding without knowable limits until its collapse. Capitalism constitutes a solid dark hyperobject under the umbrella of the dark hyperobject of the Necrocene. It is in fact the ontological, phenomenological, cultural, political and ecological darkness of Capitalism is what makes the Necrocene dark, due to its impossibility of quantification. With its Chthulu tentacles (Haraway, 2015, 2018), it infects and affects everything from the tiniest to the biggest elements of our surroundings through its "gluttonous sight" (translated from Cajugas-Rotundo's concept of *Mirada Glotona*). That is, all of them are affected by the Necrocene Realism and its politics of existence, a Dark Hyperobject constituted of other objects—some of them hyper as we have seen—which shapes, rules and modifies life of human and non-human agents of the Earth right now.

Island and Coastline Climate Refugees in the Necrocene

In the paradigm of the Necrocene Realism, crucial is to explore the conception of space and border. In this light, borders and migration seem to be co-implicated in the operation of spatial distribution (Novak, 2019), co-constituting "fluid fields" (Brambilla, 2015: 26) that derive towards "an ongoing and situated b/ordering process" (Novak, 2019: 78) of the Earth. Consequently, and even though the process of bordering might seem natural in humanity, due to the reality that borders are not natural phenomena but human-made and only culturally valued within humankind (Diener & Hagen, 2012), we can state that borders are not evenly distributed, since they are anthropologically constructed according to social, political, cultural and economic influences and claims (Brambilla, 2015). Thus, borders and bordering fall into the dichotomy of hospitability/hostility (Bulley, 2017), a division between "us" and the "other". As Paasi et al. well established, "whereas business people, elite travelers, and prosperous tourists, for example, cross relatively soft borders regularly without difficulties, migrants and particularly asylum seekers often face the hard side of borders and bordering practices" (Paasi et al., 2019: 19). Movement and migration are politically triggered when it comes to restricting or allowing mobility to those who are said to be lacking the needed credentials for legitimate travel, interventions framed by "the climate of perpetual insecurity and dehumanizing discourses that are particularly marked in the world's wealthiest and powerful states preoccupied with the threat of globalterrorism and the 'migration crisis'" (Jones, 2016 in Bianchi & Stevenson, 2019: 166). Although a disappearance of borders in the near future is not a feasible option regarding the political, cultural and identitarian agency of them and bearing in mind the self-shepherding social and spatial distribution of humankind coined as the *Human Zoo* (Sloterdijk, 2009) which can be perceived in different civilizations throughout human history (Longo, 2018), I consider basic to acknowledge that borders and bordering processes have helped to delimitate the concept of the "other" and "stranger" -going back to

Marcuse's idea on the "enemy" as the stranger (1964), affecting the colonized, economically-poor and subjugated beings within the category of Nature—exploited and discriminated entities—in the Law of Cheap Nature, leading to a capitalist racism based on economic power and categorization of the land in the global episteme of the territory confined within certain borders. As Altvater (2007) points out, Nature is "not *value*-productive, because it produces no commodities to be sold on the market.... [I]t is labor which turns nature into commodities (Altvater in Bellamy & Diamanti, 2018: xxiv).

In a contemporary era in which the neoliberal open bordering processes has only benefited the global privileged (Sassen, 2019), excluding most of the peoples victims of exclusion, discrimination and environmental catastrophes, yet borders seem to be cybernetically inexistent under the canopy of global control of mass media and influence on information, what is at stake in this work is the situation of Climate Change refugees of islands and coastlines. Globally, around 10% of human populations are distributed throughout the coast, live within a mile from the shoreline and below 10 meters in elevation (Byravan & Rajan, 2015), hence, share some similar concerns (Larzus, 2012). However, and due to the current global environmental and ecological crisis, some islanders have been labelled as the first Climate Change refugees, migration of which has been triggered not only by a sporadic or a series of natural or environmental catastrophes but by the human-induced Climate Change and its variety of consequences (Larzus, 2012). As Pilkey et al. (2016) clarify,

> There is one important difference between political and environmental refugees. Political refugees tend to move as individuals or groups that share a fear of persecution from a shared ideology, religion, war, or another driver. In the future, entire villages, towns, or island nations could flee sea-level rise, regardless of their differences or likenesses. (Pilkey et al., 2016: 128).

That is, climate refugees are victims of the new era the Earth is facing in the shape of the Dark Hyperobject of the Necrocene and here we can see how this central issue- singularity- sheds light upon and makes visible in a Foucauldian way the different relations of force and, therefore, power that define such problem (Deleuze on Foucault, 1985-86). There is no direct persecution in this case due to cultural conflicts or war but the reality that the homeland of these populations will disappear, in this situation amongst many others concerning climate refugees, undersea. However, as we will see, the Dark Hyperobject of the Necrocene is always gliding above all these issues, infecting or causing them, from increasing the sea surface temperature leading to ocean acidification, to developing towards protectionist anti-immigration policies due to a capitalist racism linked to the Necrocene and the Law of Cheap Nature that has become in an ecognosis (Morton, 2016) motion, a common practice and accepted in global politics. As Paasi et al (2019) highlight "the growing number of migrants echo complex social and environmental problems, wars and conflicts, natural disasters (droughts, floods), famines, daily amenities, and livelihoods" (Paasi et al., 2019: 21) and also the necessity of better possibilities and global politics. In the specific turmoil of the Dark Hyperobject of the Necrocene and the environmental crisis that the planet as a whole is facing, which will affect between 25 million and 1 billion people by 2050 as pointed out by an assessment of the International Migration Organization, acknowledging that "as is already the case with political refugees, it is likely that the burden of providing for climate migrants will be borne by the poorest countries -those least responsible for emissions of greenhouse gases" (Brown, 2008, in Parenti, 2011: 173).

In this paradigm, islands and coastal regions must find creative alternatives to overcome or, at least, palliate the effects of global Climate Change such as sea level rises, ocean acidification and sea surface temperature when it comes to migration and resource management (Lazrus, 2012), yet acknowledging that without an alternative to accumulation and the *gluttonous sight* (Cajigas-Rotundo, 2007) of capitalism there is no feasible option in the long-run. The delimitation or natural bordering agency of the sea will disappear since, as Meehl et al. (2007) shed light upon, sea level rise is likely to accelerate in the 21st Century, with an increase of approximately 18-59cm above 1990 levels (Meehl et al., 2007).Having said that, not only members of Nature—exploited according to Moore's Law of Cheap Nature-such as the peoples of low lying islands and coastlines such as Bangladesh—which is estimated to have around 75 million people affected by 2100 (Byravan & Rajan, 2015), Kiribati—likely to be the first complete exodus due to Climate Change (Tetrick, 2018), the Marshall Islands, Shishmaref, Nunavut or the Maldives who are likely to become or already becoming environmental refugees due to the inhabitability of their lands and extinction of resources due to the increase on storms, cyclones, rises on sea surface temperature, ocean acidification and consequent extinction of ecosystems, and the shortage of drinking water (Merone and Talt, 2018) boosted by human-induced Climate Change triggered through mass-accumulation (Larzus, 2012; Pilkey et al., 2014), but also members of Humanity—privileged areas and people—are starting to be affected or will be affected by human-induced Climate Change and the effects of it on their surrounding or coastal seas and oceans. For instance, cities such as New York City, Miami, Amsterdam or Barcelona, privileged and economically-rich metropolis and valued within the global order, are on the verge of facing the drastic effects of this crisis, yet they have the resources to start applying some short term palliative measures to such wound (see Pilkey et al. "New and Old Amsterdam" and *Barcelona Pel Clima* reports). In a global scale, such phenomena will trigger the infamous melting of ice sheets and permafrost in the Arctic, a spread of hit-related diseases to previously colder areas and migration of invasive species to other ecosystems (Larzus, 2012), since nature does not rule under the same logic as humanitarian cultural and political borders. It seems that the delimitation between privileged and non-privileged starts to blurry here. Nonetheless, the effects on the peoples living at that time in such locations not be the same as the effects this will have on the peoples living in targeted economically-poor areas since, as Pilkey (2014) highlights, "those that contribute the least to the human causes of sea-level rise will be hurt the most" (Pilkey, 2014: 3).

In other words, the Necrocene is already affecting not only non-human species but also human beings and it will eventually affect the economy, culture and life of both privileged, economically-rich and exploited or depicted-of-value entities alike since, as mentioned before, nature does not stick to the same logic of delimitation and border as humans culturally and politically have. Therefore, the environmental chaos and Sixth Extinction will not discriminate regions according to their political borders or purchasing power. However, it is obvious that within the canopy of the Necrocene and the holistic injustice of it, the ones that will be affected worse regarding humankind are most likely to be the peoples of regions where their direct contribution on the global environmental catastrophe has been infimal in comparison to the big, multinational, colonial and industrial powers. As Pilkey et al. (2014) state,

> There are so many inequities in this crisis. The developing coastal countries are beginning to demand monetary assistance from the larger polluting countries for the retreat process and compensation for their suffering. Island nations such as the Maldives and less-developed coastal countries like Bangladesh are demanding a halt or at least a reduction in the production rate of greenhouse gases. These nations believe (perhaps correctly) that those that contribute the least to the human causes of sea-level rise will be hurt the most. Unfortunately, even if we reduced the production of CO2 tomorrow, it would have little effect on the rate of sea-level O2 rise in this century (Pilkey et al, 2014: 3).

Thus, climate refugees can be established within the confines of what Mbembe outlines as "superfluous humanity" (Mbembe, 2016:3), human agents that are not even worth exploiting by the system, who are left abandoned or pressured to be erased from an area, subjects who might be perceived as a setback for the accumulating motion of Capitalism.

Furthermore, it is also fundamental to comprehend that, although the "Objective 4" of the UN *Global Compact for Safe, Orderly and Regular Migration* of 2018 accredited for the first time that "climate, environmental degradation and natural disasters increasingly interact with the drivers of refugee movements" (UNHCR, 2018), and it stated that "refugees and migrants are entitled to the same universal human rights and fundamental freedoms, which must be respected, protected and fulfilled at all times" (UN, 2018: 2) and the fact that all migrants and refugees should be facilitated with the right documents, visas and registration (UN, 2018), it also acknowledged that residency and citizenship could be rejected at a local and national level (Batalla, 2019). This UN report also highlights that "migrants and refugees are distinct groups governed by separate legal frameworks. Only refugees are entitled to the specific international protection as defined by international refugee law" (UN, 2018: 2), without any mention to climate refugees—or any other nomenclature annexing to such idea—from coastal and island populations affected by sea-level rises which was labeled as "scientifically and legally problematic" by the Intergovernmental Panel on Climate Change in 2014. Yet, as Merone and Talt (2018) postulate, "to classify these people as migrants is erroneous, as a migrant is defined as someone who has voluntarily left their country of origin and can return any time; for those displaced by climate disruption, return would likely not be feasible" (Merone and Talt, 2018: 508). This brings back the idea of the Dark Hyperobject of the Necrocene Realism: it is in our consciousness infecting the way we behave and perceive the world. This report rings the alarm of a refugee crisis as a consequence of the environmental catastrophe that the Earth is already facing. However, it does not give international protection by law to the human (and non-human) beings affected by it, nor does point a finger to the real agency to blame and to long-term solutions to a planet in unrepairable decay due to the different economic pressures and lobbies that hold the system as an unchallenging entity.Crucial here is to consider Australia's and New Zealand's relation with prospect climate refugees from the Pacific Small Islands, such as Kiribati or Tuvalu, areas which are likely to disappear around 2050-60. Interesting is to consider the situation of a Tuvaluan family that was denied access to New Zealand by the court due to the effects of Climate Change because their claim did not attached or "fit" the 1951 Refugee Convention which did not and does not acknowledge the state of Climate Change refugees (Ferris, 2017, in Tetrick, 2018). Without acknowledging any climate refugee migration booster in their migration law and policies, and having one of the strictest immigration agendas, the people affected by the current environmental crisis, who are not just facing an environmental catastrophe but the loss of their homeland and an eventual loss of their culture, have really low or almost no option to get into Australia or New Zealand if they are not "merit-based" promoted or have any family ties inside the country (Merone and Talt, 2018). If these people were given credit as refugees, not as migrants, they would have access to live and work in Australia, even though the setbacks in terms of language and access to employment and healthcare are noteworthy (Murray and Sally, 2005). Refugees usually go inlands and collaborate in Australian much-needed non-metropolitan jobs due to its shortage of labor (Australian Red Cross, 2018), yet as we can see they are facing massive setbacks in order to pursue livable conditions outside their homeland.

What we can extract from this situation is that the Dark Hyperobject of the Necrocene is present everywhere, from a tangible local and international crisis to an unconscious behavior. It triggers a capitalist racism based on the fear of the "other" which is seen as the "enemy", referring back to Marcuse (1964), extremely useful for populist politics, the protection of the system and the lobbies and to trigger the Deleuze/Foucault (1985-86) knowledge light towards the relations of Power they want society to perceive, such as the "us" and "other" we have at hand here, ignoring the reality concerning their societies.In addition, as Abel et al. (2019) point out, "if Climate Change does induce conflict, then indirectly Climate Change also contributes to forced migration" (Abel et al., 2019: 53). There is an inadequacy in the current vocabulary, nomenclatures and political/ economic/ social/ cultural discourse when approaching the global environmental crisis, inputs that will lead towards further unknown social and political conflicts on top of the ones already happening. Thus, we can speculate that the agency of this Dark Hyperobject is also a bordering one.

Conclusion: From Ontological to Physical Borders

Borders and bordering processes are everywhere. They dominate our life and the way we perceive our reality. They delimitate spaces, make us behave in one way or another or condition the way we live.

Let us think about an apartment: Every door in the apartment borders one space from the other, making a difference between a bedroom, a bathroom and a living room. In one of the houses, there is also a gym, a studio owned by a painter and even a mini disco. With this example, you can see how ordinary spaces border our reality and the patterns of behavior that are supposed to take place within them. Now imagine a big building with different flats and different apartments with different rooms. Let's say there are three different flats. In the lower one, only people that are said to be "dangerous" or "superfluous" can live. The conditions do not stick at all to the "welfare state" order imposed by the oligarchy. In the second flat, working people live. They are tied to their job whether they like it or not because they are anchored to the cage of capitalism. In the third and last flat, not a lot of people live. Most of them are rich and feed — consciously or unconsciously — the illimited expansion and consequent regress of capitalist systems. They own data, media, politics and the economy, elements that will help expand certain ideas and beliefs according to the necessities of the system, without questioning it. From this quick sketch, it is clear that our society, whether we want to admit it or not, is divided in these different strata dominated by the strategic agency of power and society (Deleuze on Foucault, 1986). Behaviors, concerns and resources are different from one to the other. Consequently, our lives are also bordered by the social role we play in our certain environment and the system that makes these strata strictly based on "the not-quite-natural, not quite- social space that had come to be called 'the economy'". (Mitchell, 2014: 234), which dictates the values of the current planetary order. These lives are also bordered by politics and the binaries contemporary politics unfold: bare life/political existence, zoe/bios and most important exclusion/inclusion (Agamben, 2013). This politicization of life is in fact politized through capital, shedding light upon the contradiction that the imposed dialectic connection between democracy and capitalism is clear as ice in contemporary politics, where private tyrannies acquire total control over all the aspects of life, both human and non-human (Chomsky, 1997).

If we go back to the problem of the coastline and island climate refugees in the Dark Hyperobject of the Necrocene, the issue of bordering is threefold. In the local sphere, the sea keeps its bordering agency, both ontological—one might say mystical or mythical—and physical. It borders the movement of coastline, but specifically of island communities to a claustrophobic realization that their land is being swallowed by its surroundings. The sea also makes us grasp that their physical agency, connected with the human limitations of life on it without access to a mainland, is also extended to the political international sphere. Here the second problem of bordering in this situation arises. International organisms and communities have not acknowledged yet the necessity of giving setback-free asylum to the not-recognized climate refugees from coastline areas and islands, especially the ones that do not have the economic resources "merit-based" grants or familiar linkages to a more secure land. Most of these impediments are purely based on a fear of the "other", seen as the "enemy" (Marcuse, 1964) or "superfluous" (Mbembe, 2013). Wariness, fear and the eternal dream of a utopian future without wars, material woes and happiness is now intertwined with the unknown, the eerie and the ecognosis (Morton, 2016) of what was familiar and no longer is, wisely used for the populist propagandists of the neoliberal democracies of the "free-market" to bias societies, defending the system and the "international and national interest"—protecting the opulent majority over the masses—of the "tolerant society" with full blast and violence if necessary (Chomsky & Dieterich, 1997). This leads us to the realization of the existence of a capitalist racism, which helps the political order shed light upon the relations of power they want society to see towards the dialectic of the us/other-enemy and, thus, dissuade the mere appearance to the real social/political/environmental conflicts inflicted by the inconsistency of capitalism in their societies. This capitalist racism and the recognition that the political, economically privileged lobbies might be fighting heart and soul to keep the system as it is no matter the planetary costs in human and non-human agents drag us to the awful truth that there is a bigger logic infecting everything at its reach, creating extinction of human and non-human beings alike: the Dark Hyperobject of the Necrocene Realism. This dark hyperobject borders every single part of our reality. We are inside it. We are part of it. From culture to the environment, the Necrocene has modified everything at its reach to the extent that a different imaginary or ontology outside accumulation is nothing short of impossible nowadays due to its infecting tentacles which have been playing part of our metaphysical, ontological, phenomenological, cultural, political, economic and environmental lives and relations for centuries. Accumulation is the center of the discourse and the main cause of greed and consequent extinction of everything you can imagine, yet the lobbies and economic elites protect it and bias public opinion towards this realism. We are physically and ontologically bordered and, although bordering processes and relations of force and consequent power are seen in many areas of our everyday life, the politics of bordering go beyond the local, the national or the international when we look at the bigger picture and the core cause of bordering conflicts in the contemporary/cyber age. That is, these politics unfold and at the same time empower the Dark Hyperobject of the Necrocene Realism and the solidification of it without questioning its inconsistencies, inconsistencies that are hidden behind the opposition between us/other-enemy in this specific case of the climate refugees, conflicts that do belong to the political and cultural anthropocentric notion of border but also to the different logic of borders when we tackle non-human agents, agents that do not stick to human conceptions of time and space but to their own.

The Contemporary age is confined in a global system in which profit and accumulation are prioritized and extreme populist nationalism and locality and reinforcement of human borders and anti-immigration agendas do not match nor understand the logic of natural ecosystems and environments, and the public debate and politics have been infected by the Necrocene Realism since the 1980s when the oligarchy and ruling social strata stopped leading and "began to shelter themselves from the world" (Latour, 2017: 1). Furthermore, and connected with the will of reformulating nature in order to protect capitalist accumulation without challenging the foundations of "development", accumulation or contemporary sustainability and the objectification of nature as natural capital and labor as human capital (Cajigas-Rotundo, 2007; Moore, 2016), injected into our ontological understanding of our reality—it being the Necrocene Realism— by the leading lobbies, how can we expect a global understanding and policies that acknowledge the current yet unprecedented reality of the Earth and humankind? Here, I am not saying or giving too much credit to the so-called "privileged", since they are part and victims of the Necrocene Realism as much as the rest of us. Nevertheless, a systematic attack towards such agents will never provide a source of change. We are currently facing what Beck (2002) coined as the *boomerang effect*, which is characterized for being an age in which security, welfare, certainty and confidence of both humankind and capitalist development are lost, developing into the dialectic of such characteristics. The current epoch in the Global North—if there is so—has been driven by a considerable collective mainstream ethos towards certain issues concerning race, gender or, in our case, sustainability and the environment. Nonetheless, there is a misconception when it comes to really pointing to the agent who is to blame for most of the environmental, social and political catastrophes since 1492 (Moore, 2016) or even before (Batalla, 2019). As Fisher (2009) states, "the cause of the eco-catastrophe is an impersonal structure which, even though it is capable of producing all manner of effects, is precisely not a subject capable of exercising responsibility" (Fisher, 2009: 66). In other words, it is easier to turn the blind eye and mentally slave our thoughts to the Necrocene Realism by saying that there is no direct responsible for the social inequalities, bordering problems and the environmental crisis that our generation is facing for the first time in human recorded history than enclosing mass-accumulation to the reality it has played through colonialism, neocolonialism and exploitation of human and non-human agents that has led the planet to the Sixth Extinction, the first mass extinction of the Earth caused by a single species.Thus, and considering the previous assumptions and the reasons why economic and political lobbies—the oligarchy—do not even think about turning the system upside down and challenging its view and consequent inequalities and inconsistencies, global politics, deliberately or unconsciously, fail to acknowledge the proper solutions in the long-run due to the darkness of the Necrocene Realism. Even the Planetary Boundaries proposed by the Stockholm Resilience Center and Rockströem et al (2009), which I believe they should be taken into consideration by every country in the world right now in order to limit and (b)order environmental and ecological politics, although claim for a reduction on the production and consumption of certain goods, do not directly state what is the core cause of such production and mass-accumulation and consequent cataclysm and extinction. There is a fear of pointing mass-accumulation and the political and economic lobbies for what is happening. Almost anybody in the mainstream agenda has directly claimed that any solution from within capitalism, although palliative and "useful" to certain extent for our current generation, is inconsistent in a humanitarian and ecological sense in the long-run.

This chapter has tried to critically think about borders considering the current politics of the contemporary and the environmental and humanitarian turmoil the Necrocene and its Realism have brought to our perception of reality, politics and society using the conflict of the Coastline and Island climate refugees. The Necrocene Realism works as a heuristic to drive us through the different issues tackled here. In this light, and to add my humble opinion to this matter, to radically reorganize our society both mentally and spatially, the aim should be to "both diminish systematic domination and suffering and encourage systematic compassion" (Heckert, 2002: 6) from within Morton's loop (2016), reversing the eerie and reshaping value and what is at stake when we define it. When value is not based on accumulation and the central discourse of profit and "development" is no longer in the center of our ontological, political, cultural and economic reality, such as in both communism and capitalism, alternatives that both show that the system is inconsistent and morally wrong and provide interesting changes that could palliate the current global situation in the long-run -with a global will of doing so, of course—appear in the popular discourse. However, proposing radical alternatives to capitalism to mainstream political agendas and elections is still an electoral suicide (Kallis, 2018), linked with, as mentioned in the introduction of this work, the Zizekian paradigm that it is easier to imagine the end of the world than the end of capitalism (Zizek, 2018). We are bordered, both physically and ontologically, locally and globally under the canopy of the global border of the Dark Hyperobject of the Necrocene Realism.

Acknowledgement

Some of the content of this thesis has been inspired by my MA Thesis *Planetary Catastrophism: Rethinking Hyperobjects, Extinction and Politics in the Necrocene* (University of Amsterdam/UvAScripties, 2019).

References

Abel, G., Brottrager, M., Cuaresma, J.C., & Muttarak, R. (2019). Climate Conflict and Forced Migration. *Global Environmental Change*. Vol. 54, 239-249.

Agamben, G. (2013). Introduction to Homo Sacer: Sovereign Power and Bare Life. In Timothy Campbell & Adam Sitze (Eds.) *Biopolitics: A reader*. (pp. 134-144). Durham/London: Duke University Press.

Almiron, N., Talfalla, M. (2019). Rethinking the Ethical Challenge in the Climate Deadlock: Anthropocentrism, Ideological Denial and Animal Liberation. *Journal of Agricultural and Environmental Ethics*. Vol. 32, 255-267.

Batalla, O. (2019). *Planetary catastrophism: Rethinking hyperobjects, extinction and politics in the necrocene epoch*. (MA Thesis). University of Amsterdam, Amsterdam. [expected to be published before December 2019 in UvAScripties]

Beck, U. (2002). *La sociedad del riesgo: Hacia una nueva modernidad*. (Jorge Navarro, Daniel Jiménez & María Rosa Borrás Trans.). Barcelona/Buenos Aires/México: Paidós. Originally Published 1986.

Bellamy, B., & Diamanti, J. (2018). Materialism and the critique of energy. In Brent Ryan Bellamy & Jeff Diamanti (Eds.) *Materialism and the critique of energy*. (pp. x-xxxvii). Chicago/Alberta: MCM Publishing.

Bianchi, R., & Stevenson, M. (2019). Tourism, border politics, and the fault lines of mobility. In AnssiPaasi, Eeva-KaisaProkkola, Jarkko Saarinen & Kaj Zimmerbauer's (Eds.) *Borderless worlds for whom: Ethics, moralities and mobilities*. (pp. 155-172). London/New York: Routledge.

Brambilla, C. (2015). Exploring the Critical Potential of the Borderscapes Concept. *Geopolitics*. Vol. 20, No.1, 14–34.

Bryant, L. (2013). Black. In Jeffrey Jerome Cohen (Ed.), *Prismatic Ecology: Ecotheory beyond green*. (pp. 290-310). London/Minneapolis: University of Minnesota Press.

Bulley, D. (2017). *Migration, ethics & power: Spaces of hospitality in international politics*. London: Sage.

Byravan, S, & Rajan, S. (2015). Sea Level Rise and Climate Change Exiles: A Possible Solution. *Bulletin of The Atomic Scientists*. Vol. 71, No. 2, 21-28.

Cajigas-Rotundo, J.C. (2007). La biocolonialidad del poder: amazonía, biodiversidad y ecocapitalismo. In Santiago Castro-Gómez's & Ramón Grosfoguel's (Ed.) *El giro decolonial: Reflexiones para una diversidad epistémica más allá del capitalismo global*. (pp. 169-193). Bogotá: Siglo del Hombre Editores.

Chomsky, N., & Dieterich, H. (1997). *La aldea global* (Esteban Montorio Trans.). Tafalla: Editorial Txalaparta s.l.

Chomsky, N. (1997). Globalización, Educación y Democracia. In Noam Chomsky & Heinz Dieterich's (Eds.) *La aldea global* (Esteban Montorio Trans.). (pp. 13-44). Tafalla: Editorial Txalaparta s.l.

Cohen, J. (2013). *Prismatic Ecology: Ecotheory Beyond Green.* London/Minneapolis: University of Minnesota Press.

CERN. Dark Matter. *CERN.* Retrieved from https://home.cern/science/physics/dark-matter. (Accessed 6 June 2019).

Deleuze, G. (2014). *Michel Foucault y El Poder: Viajes Iniciáticos I* (Javier Palacio Tauste Trans.). Madrid: Errata Naturae Editores. Originally published 1986.

Diener, A., & Hagen, J. (2012). *Borders: A Very Short Introduction.* New York: Oxford University Press.

Dieterich, H. (1997). Introducción. In Noam Chomsky & Heinz Dieterich's (Eds.) *La aldea global* (Esteban Montorio Trans.). (pp. 7-12). Tafalla: Editorial Txalaparta s.l.

Fisher, M. (2009). *Capitalist realism: Is there no alternative?.* Hants: O Books.

Foucault, M. (1972). *The archaeology of knowledge and the discourse on language.* (A.M. Sheridan Smith Trans.). New York: Pantheon Books.

Foucault, M. (1975). *Surveiller et punir : Naissance de la prison.* Paris: Éditions Gallimard.

Geisler, C., & Currens, B. (2017). Impediments to Inland Resettlement Under Conditions of Accelerated Sea Level Rise. *Land Use Policy.* Vol. 66, 322-330.

Sonic Acts. (2015, November 25) *Graham Harman: Morton's Hyperobjects and the Anthropocene* [Video File]. Retrieved from https://vimeo.com/153480982. (Accessed 5 June 2019).

Hamil, J. (2018, June 2018). President Donald Trump Wants his Space Force to Conquer Mars and Dominate the Heavens. (2018). Metro News UK. Retrieved from https://metro.co.uk/2018/06/19/president-trump-wants-conquer-mars-dominate-space-7644464/. (Accessed 6 June 2019).

Haraway, D. (2015). Anthropocene, Capitalocene, Plantationcene, Chthulucene: Making Kin. *Environmental Humanities.* Vol. 6, 159-165.

Haraway, D., & Clarke, A. (2018). *Making kin, not population.* Cambridge: Prickly Paradigm Press.

Heckert, J. (2002). *Maintaining the borders: Identity and politics.* The Anarchist Library.

Heise, U. (2003). From Extinction to Electronics: Dead Frogs, Live Dinosaurs and Electric Sheep. In Cary Wolfe's (Ed.) *Zoontologies: The question of the animal.* (pp. 59-81). Minneapolis/London: University of Minnesota Press.

IPCC. (Intergovernmental Panel on Climate Change). (2014). Fifth Assessment Working Group II: Impacts, Adaptation, Vulnerability. Geneva: IPCC.

Kallis, G. (2018). *In defense of degrowth: Opinions and minifestos.* Open Commons.

Kolvert, E. (2014). The Sixth Extinction. In Elizabeth Kolvert's (Ed.) *The sixth extinction: An unnatural history.* (pp. 4-22). New York: Henry Holt & Company, LLC.

Larzus, H. (2012). Sea Change: Island Communities and Climate Change. *Annual Review of Anthropology.* Vol. 41, 285-301.

Latour, B. (2017). *Down to earth: Politics in the new climatic regime.* Cambridge: Polity Press.

Longo, M. (2018). *The politics of borders: Sovereignty, security, and the citizen after 9/11.* Cambridge: Cambridge University Press.

Marcuse, H. (1964). *One-Dimensional man: Studies in the ideology of advanced industrial society.* Boston: Bacon Press.

Mbembe, A. (2017). *Critique of black reason.* (Lauren Dubois Trans.). Durham/London: Duke University Press.

McBrien, J. (2016). Accumulating Extinction: Planetary Catastrophism in the Necrocene. In Jason W. Moore's (Ed.) *Anthropocene or capitalocene?: Nature, history and the crisis of capitalism.* (pp. 116-137). Oakland: PM Press.

Meehl, G., Stocker, T.F., Collins, W., Friedlingstein, W., Gaye, A.T., ... Zhao, Z. (2007). Global Climate Projections. In Susan Solomon, Dahe Qin, Martin Manning, Zhenlin Chen's (Eds.) *Climate Change 2007: The Physical Science Basis. Contribution of Working Group I to the Fourth Assessment Report of the Intergovernmental Panel on Climate Change* (pp. 747-846). Cambridge/New York: Cambridge University Press.

Merone, L., & Talt, P. (2018). 'Climate Refugees': Is it Time to Legally Acknowledge Those Displaced by Climate Disruption?. *Australian and New Zealand Journal of Public Health.* Vol. 42, No. 6, 508-509.

Mignolo, W. (2018). Racism as We Sense it Today. *PMLA.* Vol. 123, No. 5, 1737-1742.

Mitchell, T. *Carbon Democracy: Political Power in the Age of Oil.* London/New York: Verso Books, 2011.

Moore, J.W. (2016). Introduction. In Jason W. Moore's (Ed.) *Anthropocene or capitalocene?: Nature, history and the crisis of capitalism.* (pp. 1-11). Oakland: PM Press.

Moore, J.W. (2016). The Rise of Cheap Nature. In Jason W. Moore's (Ed.) *Anthropocene or capitalocene?: Nature, history and the crisis of capitalism.* (pp. 78-115). Oakland: PM Press, 2016: 78-115.

Moore, J.W. (2016). *Anthropocene or capitalocene?: Nature, History and the crisis of capitalism.* Oakland: PM Press.

Morton, T. (2016). *Dark Ecology: For a logic of future coexistence.* New York: Columbia University Press.

Morton, T. (2013). *Hyperobjects: Philosophy and ecology after the end of the world.* Minneapolis/London: University of Minnesota Press.

Morton, T. *The Ecological Thought.* Boston: Harvard University Press, 2010.

Novak, P. (2019). Borders, Distance, Politics. In AnssiPaasi, Eeva-KaisaProkkola, Jarkko Saarinen & Kaj Zimmerbauer's (Eds.) *Borderless worlds for whom: Ethics, moralities and mobilities.* (pp. 72-87). London/New York: Routledge.

Paasi, A., Prokkola, E., Saarinen, J., &Zimmerbauer. (2019). Introduction: Borders, Ethics and Mobilities. In AnssiPaasi, Eeva-KaisaProkkola, Jarkko Saarinen &Kaj Zimmerbauer's (Eds.) *Borderless worlds for whom: Ethics, moralities and mobilities.* (pp. 18-37). London/New York: Routledge.

Parenti, C. (2011). *Tropic of chaos: Climate Change and the new geography of violence.* New York: Nation Books.

París, C. (2013). *Ética radical: Los abismos de la actual civilización.* Madrid: Editorial Tecnos.

Pilkey, O., Pilkey-Harris, L., & Pilkey, K. (2016). *Retreat from a rising sea: Hard decisions in an age of Climate Change.* New York: Columbia University Press.

Refugee and Asylum Seeker Facts. (2018). Australian Red Cross. Retrieved from https://www.redcross.org.au/refugees-facts. (Accessed 30 Jul 2019).

Retrocés de les Platges: Augment del Nivell del Mar. Barcelona Pel Clima.Retrieved from http://lameva.barcelona.cat/barcelona-pel-clima/ca/com-afectara-el-canvi-climatic-barcelona/retroces-de-les-platges-augment-del-nivell-del-mar. (Accessed 6 June 2019).

Rockström, J. Steffen, W., Noone, K., Persson, A., Chapin, F.S., Lambin, E., Lenton, T.M.,... Foley, J.. (2009). Planetary Boundaries: Exploring the Safe Operating Space for Humanity. *Ecology and Society.* Vol. 14, No. 2. Art. 32, 1-33.

Sally, B., & Murray, S. (2005). "Hurdles to Health: Immigrant and Refugee Health Care in Australia". *Australian Health Review*. Vol.29, No.1, 25-29.

Sassen, S. (2019). *Expulsions: Brutality and complexity in the global economy*. Cambridge: Harvard University Press.

Sloterdijk, P. (2009). Rules for the Human Zoo: a response to the Letter on Humanism. Environment and Planning D: *Society and Space*, Vol. 27, 12-28.

Tetrick, S. (2018). Climate Refugees: Establishing Legal Responses and U.S. Policy Possibilities. Scholarly Horizons: *University of Minnesota, Morris Undergraduate Journal*. Vol. 5, No. 2. Art. 8.

The Nine Planetary Boundaries. Stockholm Resilience Centre. Retrieved from https://www.stockholmresilience.org/research/planetary-boundaries/planetary-boundaries/about-the-research/the-nine-planetary-boundaries.html. (Accessed 6 June 2019)

BBC. (2018, November 28) Trump on Climate Change Report: "I Don't Believe It". *BBC News: US & Canada*. Retrieved from https://www.bbc.com/news/world-us-canada-46351940. (Accessed 6 June 2019).

United Nations. (2018). *Global Compact for Safe, Orderly and Regular Migration*. United Nations.

Zea, L. (1986). *América Latina en sus ideas*. México: Unesco, Siglo XXI.

Žižek, S. (2018). *Living in the end times*. London/NewYork: Verso Books.

Fuzzy (B)ordering: More than Human Agencies and the Ethics of (Dis)avowal

Ratul Nandi

The Great Divide

It was not until very recently, late 1980s to be exact, French Philosopher Michel Serres, sensing the inefficacy of the dominance and arrogance of human species to foresee the dangers of a life out of harmony with its non-human counterpart, called for a greater integration of human life with the variegated forms of life that are not human. Serres believes that we must now sign a 'natural contract' with the earth to bring balance and reciprocity to our relations with the planet that gives us life. Serres, as it turns out, is evidently not a great admirer of Enlightenment model of "Social Contract"[1] which he sees as uncompromisingly anthropocentric. Impatient with the dualistic framework that splits the entire existence of life into humans and its others, he uncovers the origin of such dualism in the 'institutionalization' of knowledge production during the nineteenth century, which he terms as "Modern Constitution". Bruno Latour, exploring further what Serres meant by the term, has clearly revealed how the Modern Constitution has created two distinct ontological zones, that of human beings on one hand, that of non-human on the other. This epistemological divide arises from a longer-standing set of interlocking metaphysical dualisms: notably, between culture and nature, man and beast, mind and body, spirit and matter. The act of separation or bordering of human and non-human has become the underlying structuring principle of our systems of knowledge to such extent that it largely goes unquestioned. At a time when the

---

[1] Eighteenth Century views that persons' moral and/or political obligations are dependent upon a contract or agreement among them to form the society in which they live.

humanities and social sciences are exploring and churning out significant bulk of newer critical, theoretical, and philosophical approaches to decenter the human in favor of a 'nonhuman turn', one needs to move beyond the question of efficacy of border to see how the idea of 'border' itself becomes an ironical edifice trapezing relentlessly between similarity and difference, making the relationship of the human and its others rather unusual, paradoxical and politically viable. As Latour has evinced that the great divide we draw between human and animal or between human and nature in the first place, as part of our unconscious inheritance of the great Modern Constitution, never existed in the first place. What we need perhaps, to echo both Serres and Latour, is a draconian shift in our mental landscape to see how our conceptual borders are at bottom are sabotaged and deconstructed from within.

Paradox as New Norm

Certainly the time in which we live today is underlined by an intense awareness of how our planet is heading inevitably towards an apocalypse. This recognition is so telling that it has made humans realize how far they have messed up their own planet, exhausted its resources and led it inevitably towards the brink of a disaster, an 'end'. The situation has triggered the panic button which obviously made us lift our own parochial anthropocentric barrier and open up to the 'more than human' agency as a new ethical imperative. But in trying to foreground a more 'non-human' ethics, our ethics have become more anthropocentric than ever before. Ranjan Ghosh aptly says:

> Interestingly, our understanding of nature has become even more anthropocentric than in the past. This anthropocentrist approach probably persists in a different way even where human intervention ironically fosters the perpetuation of nature. This nature, however, has lost some of its primitive diversity and seemingly inviolate independence. It is a human regeneration of nature — pastoralization with clear anthropomorphic ends — implying human continuity and the domination of nature for a human cause. Likewise, the exploitation of nature is for human advantage, and is more often about survival than obvious economic ends. Human "progress"

has reached a momentum that is difficult to reverse, and the damage done to nature is irreversible and inexorable. Sequestering nature from human intervention is clearly impossible, hence the need to create a new nature (Ghosh, 2012, 4-5).[2]

The paradox of a 'new nature' stems out of the fact that even though the humans tacitly comprehend the moment of crisis they have expedited and brought upon themselves, they nevertheless attempt to radicalize their own legal structures in order to help secure a green future for a generation not yet born. The paradox of the situation is inherently *aporetic* in the sense of rights and prerogative being claimed in the name of somebody or something non-existent. This is indeed a strange spectacle in which we are both made to accept the 'end' of nature out of hand, and must challenge its destructive unfolding in a certain manner to safeguard the existence of our race and that of the entire biotic community. Between death and life, experiencing nature now is indistinguishable from experiencing the im-possibility or the in-between. As Derrida constantly reminds us, impossibility is not the simple reverse of possibility but poised between the both.[3] Our experience of nature and our politics of nature in many ways are mediated through such irony and double-binds. We see ourselves as protectors of all living organisms against extinction, on one hand, while at the same moment we are hardly ridden with guilt when using preventive measures to make sure dangerous forms viruses, bacteria, even mosquitoes are kept in check, on the other. Are we not the same doting owners of pets who routinely consume meat? Our concentrated drive to save any remaining stretch of green on earth must somehow rely on our latest human technology, an idea the English Romantics greatly decried. Putting ourselves into conformity with such a 'new' nature means to go on living without being too panicked about the confident scientific predictions of extinction of the planet and its inmates. For sure, the glaciers are melting, the ozone layer is thinning and the Global

---

[2] See Ranjan Ghosh, Globing the Earth: The New Eco-logics of Nature. (*SubStance* 41, Johns Hopkins University Press, 2012 1 2012): 3-14.

[3] Derrida's role is vital in the entire cannon of Environmental thinking today, even though he has not written anything worth related to the discipline.

Warming signaling unnatural escalation: yet this apocalyptic prediction is neutralized by the consoling human technology, the death-defying system to overcome the radical finitude of the earth. So the 'end' of nature here is not to be equated mistakenly with the 'demise' of nature. Rather it is the death of our pristine, unalloyed 'Nature' which has served as a homeostasis to minds afflicted with a frugal pursuit of global and industrial economy. The nature we experience today is a 'zombified' nature: neither alive, nor dead but paradoxically poised between the two.

Anthropocene and the End of Nature

The untarnished nature is very often pitted against humanity and its destructive practices, creating, as it does, a rupture between humanity and nature. The result is, in the Romantic writers, the external nature is elevated into a moral norm which police against impure desires that turn towards fatal industrial growth. This, in turn, prepares ground for the emergence of a transcendental subject who could bridge the gap between mind and matter. This is obviously at issue in many a William Wordsworth poem wherein nature would anchor and guide the purest thoughts of a privileged poetic persona to overcome the wounds inflicted by the industrial economy. Poems of William Wordsworth almost transform ordinary persons, objects and sites of his Lake District almost into a picturesque spectacle of an eco-tourist advert, a romantic fallacy that Timothy Morton identifies with what he qualifies as a kind of 'aesthetic consumerism'[4]. Such an understanding of nature inevitably endorses the attitude of dualism that, for the Western thought, is foundationally destructive: nature on the one side, human on the other. For Wordsworth, the value of nature rests on its capability to lend weight to development of the poet's identity. He purposefully uses nature "as a fodder for his model of creative imagination and solitary individualism" (Hess, 2016, 58)[5]. Though

---

[4] Timothy Morton, *Ecology without Nature: Rethinking Environmental Aesthetics.* (Cambridge, MA, and London: Harvard University Press, 2007).

[5] Scott Hess, Three "Natures": Teaching Romantic Ecology in the Poetry of William Wordsworth, Dorothy Wordsworth, and John Clare, Romanticism,

in a way different from Wordsworth, the same old echo of mind-nature spilt informs the romantic wilderness tradition one associates distinctively with Thoreau and his experiment in the Walden Pond. But the question now being asked, with the human dominating and controlling every inch of our planet, how long can we clutch dependably on to the lexicon 'wilderness' which is synonymous with 'untouched land'. Climate, rain, snowfall, biosphere, sea, land: there is practically nothing which eludes the clasp of humanity. This is of course the thesis of Bill McKibben's well-known book, *The End of Nature*. McKibben posits a calculus of nature greatly un-natured by human technology at a massive scale:

> The idea of nature will not survive the new global pollution—the carbon dioxide and the CFCs and the like. This new rupture with nature is different not only in scope but also in kind from salmon tins in an English stream. We have changed the atmosphere and thus we are changing the weather. By changing the weather, we make every spot on earth man-made and artificial. We have deprived nature of its independence, and that is fatal to its meaning. Nature's independence *is* its meaning without it there is nothing but us (McKibben, 1990, 58).[6]

McKibben's allusion to human over lordship upon nature ties in with the broad geological epoch that envelops us today, an epoch named the Anthropocene. Although we are officially in the Holocene epoch, which began 11,700 years ago after the last major ice age that label, as some experts say, is outdated, some experts say. They argue for "Anthropocene" — from *anthropo*, for 'man', and *cene*, for 'new'—because human-kind has caused mass extinctions of plant and animal species, polluted the oceans and altered the atmosphere, among other lasting impacts. The elementary logic of the Anthropocene is that human beings have become synonymous with a geological force and this realization has an obvious impact on our environmental vocabulary. Today we are reluctant to call anything as 'Pure Nature' because we have come increasingly to realize that in a pristine and unadulterated way perhaps there is no place left on the planet which is free from human interference.

Ecology, and Pedagogy www.rc.umd.edu/pedagogies/commons/ecology/hess/hess.html. December 2016, 16.
6   Bill McKibben, *The End of Nature*. (New York: Anchor Books. 1990), 58.

Nature today has lost its 'aura' as the distance between human and non-human has significantly collapsed. With the collapse of distance between the human and the non-human comes greater disciplinary contamination. The events like the Anthropocene or the Global Warming have not only questioned the purity of borders between the disciplines within the Humanities and Social Sciences but also in interesting ways have challenged the very idea of our broader paradigms of Natural Science and Human Science in the first place. In fact, the idea that science is fast becoming another metanarrative anchoring our holistic understanding of what nature is is doing the rounds. In truth, the nature we know today is broadly the nature revealed to us by science. By the word nature, the scientists aim at a reification of nature which seeks to view the natural world as something which could be torn out of its immediate human meaning and be impassively studied, observed and formulated. In contrast to the scientific orientation of nature as a reified object, the humanities and social sciences deliberately employ a reading strategy which would disclose the natural science as yet another interpretative mechanism and not so consecrated and timeless as it itself professes. As Timothy Clark observers, the "scientists find themselves increasingly recruited to form advisory panels on all kinds of issues, from Climate Change to radiation levels or the design of fishing nets. Such pressure takes people well beyond any pretense that scientific work is merely factual or apolitical" (Clark, 2011, 149-50).[7] The intention of this kind of reading technique is to show how the idea of 'construction' is built into the very premises of any scientific inquiry as demonstrated so effectively by the likes of Bruno Latour and Donna Haraway. The originality of Latour lies in his act to destabilize the dualities of fact and value, a distinction that embeds the very notion of human as a modern thinking being. He argues:

> What is safe level of radiation from nuclear tests in the Nevada desert? What is the safe level of radiation from nuclear tests in the Nevada desert? What

---

[7] Timothy Clark, *The Cambridge Introduction to Literature and Environment* (Cambridge University Press, 2011), 149-150.

is the amount of carbon dioxide an industry may be allowed to release safely in the atmosphere? (Latour, 1991, 19).[8]

Donna Haraway, similarly, deconstructs the dominant scientific paradigm believing '[t]he detached eye of objective science is an ideological fiction'.[9] In her monumental work like *Primate Visions* (1989), she strives to expose how the dispassionate rhetoric of science inadvertently falls back on the conventional cultural assumptions from which it desperately endeavors to shy away. Haraway is against using terms like nature and culture separately as much as she rebuts accepting the domains of science and culture as distinct fields. Her preference is instead using a term like *natureculture* which emphasizes the falsity of separating the one from the other.

Politics of Speaking for

Even though the idea of the anthropocene stands as dissolution of the binaries of human and non-human, there is also a widespread consensus that it has eventually led to a very stringent form of ethics and politics in our time, one which readily anticipates a border between human and it's others. This is largely because, according to the prevalent opinion, our ethical imperative to act in the interest of nonhuman agents is based on the lexicon of 'Saving' the nonhuman other. The drive to 'save' eventually takes the form of a politics of preservation which in effect remains 'all too human' in the sense that it is only through the mediating agency of the human that the ethical obligation of saving can reach its fruition. A case in point is the initiative taken by some philosopher-activists to consider a new platform for animal ethics. The admirable project of practical ethics advanced by Peter Singer, Tom Regan and many others primarily center around the idea of extending the notion rights to the animals on the perceived signs of intellect and

---

[8] Bruno Latour, The Impact of Science Studies on Political Philosophy: Science, Technology, and Human Values 16.1 Sage Publications, London (winter 1991), 3-19.

[9] Donna Haraway, *Primate Visions: Gender, Race, and Nature in the World of Modern Science* (Psychology Press, 1989) 213.

emotions of the apes which qualify them to claims of subjectivity. The force of animal ethics as demonstrated by Singer draws its energy from the idea that the human should include the nonhuman animals into the 'community of equals' which comprise both animals and the human.[10] The primary aim is to bridge the ostensible border between the human and the animal by appealing to the principle of 'sameness' between the two. The observation posits that similar beings should receive similar moral consideration. Though captivating and revolutionary in scope and attempt, the type of applied ethics advocated by its practitioners does not succeed in foregrounding an ethics for animals *per se*. In its avowed bid to speak for the nonhuman animals, since they cannot speak for themselves, the ethics as such inadvertently stages the advent of human *cogito* as a mediating agency. This unfortunately ends up in a fiasco as the ideal of dislodging difference between human and its animal other is compromised and the borders between them, apparently contested by the animal rights philosophers, once again find themselves retained. As already argued, the same holds true for much of the nature criticism in circulation today. The predominant idea is that nature is a pristine entity which determines the physical and psychic wholeness of human beings. Hence, the crucial task is to rediscover our roots back in nature from which we have distanced ourselves only at our own peril. The task of effacing the border between human and nature ironically ends up rupturing it even more. As with the animal ethics, the question of ethics of nature also is undercut with ironical double-bind between the urgency to 'save' it from the overarching human intervention, and the melancholic recognition that the desire for preservation counterfactually reinforces and keeps the binary in play. So the desire to speak for other supposedly 'muted' non- human agencies is never as simple as ordinary act of speaking because in 'speaking for' it takes on a

---

[10] This particular view is underscored by a principle of 'sameness' which opens onto an idea of a shared 'capability' or 'I can' of both human and animal. The observation posits that similar beings should receive similar moral consideration.

certain valence wherein speaking automatically becomes a little more hegemonic and thereby, political.

Border, Ethics and Contingency of Irony

It would not be perhaps a cliché to say that in the recent past the idea of a border has been viewed with considerable skepticism especially when it concerns the boundary between the human and the more than human. One of the crucial and distinguishing features of our current doing of humanities and social science studies in twenty-first-century is the way the recent flood of multiple intellectual and theoretical developments from the last decades of the twentieth century that expressly served to minimize the efficacy of (b)ordering or border-thinking between the human and more-than-human agencies. The prevailing idea of Posthumanism seems to be that the humans are deeply prosthetic, amalgam of disparate parts, which are not very unalloyed themselves. However, let us also not forget that Posthumanism, in trying to forge a new understanding of the nonhuman other, too stands accused of fetishizing the human. In trying to obliterate the human from the discourse for something 'post', it inadvertently stages its return. As a result the idea of a border between the human and the more than human remains a rather fuzzy one; a principle which is simultaneously contested and retained, dead yet very much alive, living in a state of suspended animation.

But the question then arises if 'bordering' remains very much an anthropocentric project, should not the counter move to 'dis-border' the binary (between human and its others) be the only ethical response as an inherently anti-humanist gesture? Is it at all possible to consider even 'anti-humanism' without human, let alone humanism? A substantial bulk of academic writing on environmental and animal studies today, following the lead of Poststructuralism, are dedicated to the task of un-working the *logos* of the human as the only viable ethical injunction of our time, a time of intense ecological emergency. The rallying cry of these critical thinkers against their express anti-humanism draws from the fact that humans are not special but just a tiny part of a complex network of biotic and non-biotic entities of which no final knowledge is possible. The trivializing of the human subject follows the articulation of toxic impact the human modes of living on this planet have unleashed. The history of human existence on earth has demonstrated the violence it wrought on the planet, how it catalyzed the extinction of species. One would agree with Neil Evernden that as a race the humans are potentially more destructive than the locusts are, since the locusts could only cause a temporary upset to crops. But the question is if humans are the chief pollutants of this planet why not be rid of them? This seems as impossible as thinking with nothing to think with. The situation here is inherently ironical: we need to keep 'human' both part and a part of our system of inscription. This is in short the very way of being human. Therefore, it will be unwise to blame humans for wittingly or unwittingly precipitating in the extinction engine. Claire Colebrook calls attention to the Anthropocene epoch, which remains a stark reminder of the massive scale violence inflicted on earth by the humankind, yet she remains skeptical in imagining any event that would have been less violent and more earth-friendly than the anthropocene. "counter-anthropocene", says Colebrook "would be a thought-experiment".[11] This ironic interchange between the earth, the nonhuman and the human race has reinvigorated the conceptual frontiers between the human and the more than human agencies. On one hand, we need our own systems of signification because we cannot push us beyond the limit of the self towards an objective no-where locus to be able to assess the predicament of the earth. On the other hand, this timely effort is self-defeating: our systems of cognitive and conceptual mapping are exactly responsible for picturing the dreadful end-of-the–world event. An awareness of this irony keeps our ethics of the border(ing) grounded as it stays in-between the two extremes: unwarranted anthropocentrism and illusion of non-anthropocentrism or biocentrism. Indeed, attaining the between-

---

[11] Dialogue on the Anthropocene between Claire Colebrook and Cary Wolfe, event at HKW, Berlin, January 12, 2013. https://technosphere-magazine.hkw.de/p/Is-the-Anthropocene-A-Doomsday-Device-LmpR41HMoQBq8564jrmTy

ness should become a political or ethical necessity and must inform whatever conceptions of the non-human animal or environment one wants to practice or safeguard today.

References

Bate, Jonathan. (1991). *Romantic Ecology: Wordsworth and the Environmental Tradition*. London: Routledge.

Bakhtin, Mikhail. (2010). *The Dialogic Imagination: Four Essays, edited by Michael Holquist*. Austin: University of Texas Press.

Benjamin, Walter. (1969.) *The Work of Art in the Age of Mechanical Reproduction*. Edited by H. Arendt. New York, Schocken.

Colebrook, Claire. (2012.) A Globe of One's Own: In Praise of the Flat Earth. *SubStance*.Vol- 41, Johns Hopkins University Press.

Clark, Timothy. (2011). *The Cambridge Introduction to Literature and Environment*. Cambridge: Cambridge University Press.

Di Leo, Jeffrey R. (2013). Can Theory Save the Planet? Critical Climate Change and the Limits of Theory. *Symploke* 21, no. 1. University of Nebraska Press.

Dialogue on the Anthropocene between Claire Colebrook and Cary Wolfe. https://technosphere-magazine.hkw.de/p/Is-the-Anthropocene-A-Doomsday-Device-LmpR41HMoQBq8564jrmTy.

Ghosh, Ranjan. (2012). Globing the Earth: The New Eco-logics of Nature. *SubStance* Vol. 41, Johns Hopkins University Press.

Haraway, Donna. *Primate Visions: Gender, Race, and Nature in the World of Modern Science*. New York: Psychology Press.

Hess, Scott. (2016). Three "Natures": Teaching Romantic Ecology in the Poetry of William Wordsworth, Dorothy Wordsworth, and John Clare. (www.rc.umd.edu/pedagogies/commons/ecology/hess/hess.html).

Latour, Bruno. (1991). *The Impact of Science Studies on Political Philosophy: Science, Technology, and Human Values*. London: Sage Publications.

McKibben, Bill. (1990). *The End of Nature*. New York: Anchor Books.

Miller, Hillis, J. (2012). How To (Un) Globe the Earth in Four Easy Lessons. *SubStance*, Volume 41. Johns Hopkins University Press.

Serres, Michel. (1990). *The Natural Contract*. Michigan: University of Michigan Press.

Wood, David. (2006). *The Step Back: Ethics and Politics after Deconstruction*. Albany: SUNY Press.

Wotham, Simon Morgan. (2010). *The Derrida Dictionary*. London: A&C Black.

'I alone ... was on both sides':
The Hyphenated Self in Hélène Cixous's *Reveries of the Wild Woman*

Rajarshi Bagchi

Place is latitudinal and longitudinal within the map of a person's life. It is temporal and spatial, personal and political. A layered location replete with human histories and memories, place has a width as well as depth. It is about connections, what surrounds it, what formed it, what happened there, what will happen there. (Lippard, *The Lure of the Local: Senses of Place in a Multicentered Society* 7)

The thinking that addresses the 'undecidable' is the thinking of tolerance, the thinking that does not sever, the thinking capable of concavity, of turning in on itself to make room for difference. The undecidable thinks all the possibilities, all the positions. (Cixous, *Rootprints: Memory and Life Writing* 83)

The first two entries for the word 'border' in the *Oxford Dictionary and Thesaurus* (Elliott 77) define it as "edge, boundary, or part near it" and as "line or region separating countries" respectively. The interesting thing to note in these definitions is the cohabitation of the contrastive ideas of 'nearness' and 'separation'. A border is a kind of Derridean *hyphen* which connects even as it separates two wor(l)ds. Transgression is therefore structural to any border, including that of binary opposites like self/other, home/abroad, human/nonhuman, etc. In his text, "Restitutions of the Truth in Pointing", Derrida comments that the "line [*ligne*] is already a tracing [*tracé*] of coming and going between the outside and the inside" (Gaston 50). The 'shadow lines' of any border are therefore *always, already* in motion, re-producing it into a *liminal space*[1] which keeps-erases itself. It is this operation of *trace* which makes every border into a site of intense conflict and contestation, especially for those living in the undecided in-between.

---

[1] A term introduced by the anthropologist Victor Turner to describe "a space of transformation between phases of separation and incorporation. It represents a period of ambiguity, of marginal and transitional state... A space of in-betweenness" (Dyk 9).

This chapter explores the onto-ethical and political implications of such a hyphenated existence, caught between moving (b)orders of nationality, race, class, and gender. If we consider the self to be our most intimate *home*, the discussion then spirals out to issues of roots and routes—to cultural hybridity, transnationality and the postcolonial condition at large. The self/home as *hyphen* thereby becomes an ontological commentary on "the migrant condition of between *here* and *there*, a liminal space of *betweenness* and transition, where internal and external worlds, here and there, past and present, intersect" (Dyk 6). The chapter attempts a comparative study on selfhood and agency by taking up Homi K. Bhabha's postcolonial idea of the culturally *hybrid* subject and juxtaposing it with the French feminist thinker HélèneCixous's anti-phallogocentric conception of *feminine* 'self/s'. Finally, the chapter engages with Cixous's diasporic auto-fiction, *Reveries of the Wild Woman: Primal Scenes*, in order to explore how a hyphenated existence affects one's self-identity.

I.

To begin with, notice the hyphen in the word "self-identity". The hyphen seems to draw a border between the two terms 'self' and 'identity', setting them in motion: Are 'self' and 'identity' contiguous or conflicting concepts? Is there a simple binary, a hierarchy, or a continuum between them? How do they align and engage with binaries like personal/political, subject/object? And so on. The interface of self and identity, symbolized by the hyphen, forms the thematic motif of many a diasporic narrative, including Cixous's *Reveries of the Wild Woman*. Derived from the Greek *huphen* which means "together", the punctuation mark of hyphen becomes a spatiotemporal marker of transit when analysed from a philosophical-theoretical perspective. It is the *chronotope* (Bakhtin's term) of the hybrid, between neither and either, a sign of liminality, a bridge which joins and preserves the chasm.

It is significant to note that the French un trait signifies both 'a line' and 'a trace'. We know, pace Derrida, that trace is not just any mark but one signifying absentpresence. Trace signifies a ghostly presence: everything that inflects the present while itself remains absent. The trace thereby prevents a closure in the meaning of the present, keeping it incomplete and open-ended, displacing the possibility of a full presence onto an interminable deferral. Trace, therefore, always already destabilizes the presence of the present by supplementing (Derrida's term) it with a simultaneous lack and excess of signification.

An awareness of this supplementary dimension of any delineation or [b]ordering is to be found in postcolonial analyses of the 'double vision' engendered by a diasporic, transnational condition. "Not surprisingly", Leela Gandhi comments, "diasporic thought finds its apotheosis in the ambivalent, transitory, culturally contaminated and borderline figure of the exile, caught in a historical limbo between home and the world" (132). Bhabha, for instance, finds the play of identities, positions and temporalities caused by cultural dislocation to be challenging and empowering in equal measure. The ethical dimension of such a position is underlined when Bhabha comments, "This interstitial passage between fixed identifications opens up the possibility of a cultural hybridity that entertains difference without an assumed or imposed hierarchy" (*The Location of Culture* 4).

II.

Over the years, Bhabha has remained topical for problematizing easy binaries between "difference and identity, past and present, inside and outside, inclusion and exclusion" (ibid 1). As a poststructuralist thinker of cultural and national identities, he tries to locate the interface of power and desire, knowledge and performance in a mode of colonial discourse analysis. Through his critical use of concepts such as mimicry, hybridity, liminal space and ambivalence, Bhabha has presented the complex negotiations which go on between the colonizer and the colonized, between the self and the other in the act of shoring up a secure identity.

What is of interest here is that such negotiations are primarily linguistic. Speaking about the crucial engagements between the transnational and the translational, Bhabha mentions how "[t]he transnational dimension of cultural transformation—migration, diaspora, displacement, relocation—makes the process of cultural translation a complex form of signification" (ibid 172). The complex negotiations between language, agency and subjecthood will be highlighted later in the chapter, especially while exploring Cixous's conception of 'feminine writing' and the 'new woman'.

We are born and brought up in the womb (the prison-house?) of language. We learn to think, express and act our being and becoming in it. And yet, language is never 'ours', we cannot *own* it in any sense of the term. Language is a home which always produces a sense of not belonging anywhere, something Bhabha calls a state of *unhomeliness* (ibid 9). From a diasporic perspective, such unhomeliness produces a new (dis-)orientation, since the lack of a 'home' is *supplemented* by an excess of it—having had to move beyond the confines of his nation/culture, the *hybrid* subject is set up for what Bhabha calls an uncanny, *vernacular cosmopolitanism*. Bhabha thereby characterizes unhomeliness as a rite of passage for "extra-territorial and cross-cultural initiations" (ibid 9) which is symptomatic of our postcolonial/postmodern condition.

However, as a real *and* metaphorical condition, such unhomeliness/vernacular cosmopolitanism is apt to open "ways of living at home abroad or abroad at home" (Bhabha, "Cosmopolitanisms" 587). Belonging as/and displacement, which is constitutive of the hyphenated self, is therefore not limited to the diasporic condition. It stretches like a skin, hyphenating the inside and the outside, the familiar and the unfamiliar in us. Bhabha reminds us, "To be unhomed is not to be homeless, nor can the 'unhomely' be easily accommodated in that familiar division of social life into private and public spheres" (*Location* 9).

As David Huddart points out, "Bhabha's work explores how language transforms the way identities are structured when colonizer and colonized interact, finding that colonialism is marked by a complex economy of identity in which colonized and colonizer depend on each other[….] [I]mportantly, he (i.e. Bhabha) develops a linguistic model of this agency" (2). In this context, Bhabha speaks of Charles Taylor's concept of 'minimal rationality' which "takes us beyond merely *formal criteria of rationality*" (*Location* 177). He uses

Taylor's concept to posit how the enunciative practice, in contrast to epistemological reference, is a more dialogic and less hierarchical register for subject-formation.

According to Bhabha, the subjects of cultural hybridity are not monolithic formations. They remain *in process* in the 'present', changing with the changing context(s) of enunciation. Thereby neither the subject is theorized as being prior to social organization nor does society subsume the subject's individual 'difference' into a homogenous 'totality'. Such subjects thereby problematize and disturb what Derrida calls *occidental stereotomy*—the ontological 'borders' of binaries like the originary and derivative, inside and outside, subject and object, etc.

Bhabha affirms, "My purpose in specifying the enunciative present in the articulation of culture is to provide a process by which objectified others may be turned into subjects of their history and experience" (ibid 178). Such enunciations thus become a "liminal form of signification that creates a space for the contingent, indeterminate articulation of social 'experience' that is particularly important for envisaging emergent cultural identities. But it is a representation of 'experience' without the transparent reality of empiricism and outside the intentional mastery of the 'author'" (179). In view of the above, Bhabha asserts that the "contingent and the liminal become the times and the spaces for the historical representation of the subjects of cultural difference in a postcolonial criticism" (179).

III.

Bhabha's assertions in favour of a polyvalent and hybrid subject have been criticized as being historically naïve and politically vacuous, bringing him into the firing lines of many a hostile commentator. Aijaz Ahmad, for instance, severely reprimands Bhabha by observing that the idea of hybridity "which presents itself as a critique of essentialism, partakes of a carnivalesque collapse and play of identities [...] remarkably free of gender, class, identifiable political location" (286-287). The critic claims:

> Such premises preclude, I would argue, the very bases of political action [. . . .] [A]gencies are constituted not in flux and displacement but in given historical locations. History does not consist of perpetual migration, so that the universality of 'displacement' that Bhabha claims both as the general human condition and the desirable philosophical position is tenable neither as description of the world nor as generalised political possibility.
>
> [. . .] Most individuals are really not free to fashion themselves anew with each passing day, nor do communities arise out of and fade into the thin air of the infinitely contingent" (Ahmad 288-289).

In a similar vein, Benita Parry finds Bhabha's reading of postcolonial issues through psychoanalytical and poststructuralist frameworks as problematic since they allegedly turn political and ideological battles into pedantic, theoretical quibbling: 'The effect of moving agency from the subject as insurgent actor to textual performance, is to defuse resistance as practices directed at undermining and defeating an oppressive opponent' (16). Like Ahmad, Peter Hallward has his own objections to Bhabha's notion of a generic, postcolonial condition of hybridity. According to Hallward, such a concept homogenizes specific, empirical subjects and their particular forms of agency, reducing them to merely derivative effects: "Escaping from a situated position relative to other positions, the post-colonial slips between *every* possible position because it refers back, immediately, to that *one* logic that positions every possibility" (26).

Insightful as some of these criticisms are, they seem to assume a strict binary divide, a neat 'border' so to say, between the historical and the textual, between the local and the global, between poetics and politics. And it is this hierarchized binary mode of thinking which Bhabha attempts to problematize through his concepts of ambivalence, liminality and hybridity. No wonder that many of these critics, in David Huddart's words, "are arguing past Bhabha, not really taking on his work on the territory it most commonly inhabits" (113). For Bhabha's 'territory' in this context is the economy of *both*, what HélèneCixous calls *tous les deux* or "all the twos" (*Rootprints* 9, 25). Speaking about the position of the *entredeux* — the space of 'in-between *and* both' where we are *always already* "in the passage from one to the other" — Cixous observes,

"One discovers the immense landscape of the trans-, of the passage. Which does not mean that everything will be adrift: our thinking, our choices, etc. But it means that the factor of instability, the factor of uncertainty, or what Derrida calls the undecidable, is indissociable from human life" (*Rootprints* 52).

It is this economy of coalition and contingency which can be codified as the economy of the *hyphen*. Talking about how the 'contingent' is not synonymous with the purely undecidable or aporetic, Bhabha comments on how its spatiotemporal economy is both situated and mobile: "The contingent is contiguity, metonymy, the touching of spatial boundaries at a tangent, and, at the same time, the contingent is the temporality of the indeterminate and undecidable" (*Location* 186). Bhabha does not simply aim to uphold the provisional over and against the essential, he wishes to question this very binary itself. His subjects of cultural hybridity are not free-floating, postmodern entities. They are rather produced in dynamic relations of interaction, dialogue and interrogation in a context of *situated enunciation*. "This hybridity initiates the project of political thinking", Bhabha notes, "by continually facing it with the strategic and the contingent, with the countervailing thought of its own 'unthought'" (ibid 64).

Furthermore, 'displacement' is not restricted to 'postcolonial' events of migrancy and diaspora. It is constitutive of cultural semiotics at large, inflecting discourses like onto-epistemology, linguistics and psychoanalysis. Julia Kristeva, for instance, traces *unhomeliness* to Freud's notion of the 'uncanny' and finds that,

> With Freud [...] foreignness, an uncanny one, creeps into the tranquility of reason itself, and, without being restricted to madness, beauty, or faith any more than to ethnicity or race, irrigates our speaking-being, estranged by other logics, including the heterogeneity of biology [...] Henceforth, we know that we are foreigners to ourselves, and it is with the help of that sole support that we can attempt to live with others (170).

Indeed, as the Freudian analysis of the '*fort-da*' event shows, the economy of displacement (inherent in the *hyphen*) is at work in language itself. Thanks to its essential metaphoric nature, language produces an illusion of presence (of the referent); which is to say, language both eliminates *and* preserves absence.

IV.

It is the economy of the *hyphen* — simultaneity of absence-presence, being-becoming — which is elaborated from a feminist critical-theoretical standpoint in HélèneCixous's conception of the feminine 'self/s'. In feminist thought, the binary pair of self/other in Western ontology is a *phallogocentric*[2] version of the colonizer/colonized binary. Conceptualizing a non-binary *feminine* self therefore becomes crucial to inaugurate an emancipatory "politics of subjectivity" (Braidotti 119). Such a self would accept and celebrate the alterity of the other through an awareness of her own multiple belongings. Feminism(s) has travelled a long way from vindicating the rights of 'Woman' to becoming aware of a border between the poststructuralist *subject-in-process*[3] and the lived experiences of empirical women. Michèle Barrett, for instance, speaks about the crucial need for "a better conception of agency and identity than has been available in either (anti-humanist) poststructuralist thought or its (humanist) modernist predecessors [. . .] to reopen in new and imaginative ways the issues of humanism" (216).

Like Donna Haraway's *cyborg* or Rosi Braidotti's *nomadic subject*, Cixous's other-oriented, feminine 'self/s' — whom she

---

[2] "A portmanteau term combining PHALLOCENTRISM and LOGOCENTRISM, coined by Jacques Derrida in his critique of Jacques Lacan in 'The Purveyor of Truth' (1975). [. . .] Although the term was intended to imply criticism it has appealed to FEMINISTS and others eager to imply a connection between male, PATRIARCHAL authority, and systems of thought which LEGITIMIZE themselves by reference to some PRESENCE or point of authority prior to and outside themselves" (Hawthorn, *A Glossary of Contemporary Literary Theory* 260).

[3] In her book *Polylogue* (1977), Julia Kristeva analyzes various signifying practices such as language, discourse, literature and painting [. . .]. In her chapter entitled "The Subject in Process", Kristeva revisits primarily Lacanian psychoanalytic theory in order to relate the evolution of the subject to the evolution of language. [. . .] What she is attempting to do is discern the actual experience of the subject, which breaks out of the enclosure of its individuality, thanks to its ability to set itself in motion, and in language expresses adynamic, signifyinglogic. [http://www.signosemio.com/kristeva/subject-in-process.asp]

christens as the 'New Woman' ("The Laugh of the Medusa" 6) — is one among the 'new and imaginative ways' of conceiving an ethical, non-hierarchical and sustainable subjectivity. *Feminine* in this context cannot be coded as the (male-defined) antonym of *masculine*. It rather suggests a non-binary, anti-phallogocentric approach. As a matter of fact, Cixous counts certain male writers and artists — Shakespeare, Rilke, Kafka and Rembrandt among them — as capable of such *femininity*. The *feminine* thereby becomes the liminal space where the subaltern may attempt to speak. It becomes a discursive site for the traditional 'other(s)' in Western culture — women, the non-Western, the migrant/colonized, the deviant, the bodily, the poetic, the unconscious, the animal, and so on.

Cixous is chiefly known as the feminist writer of theoretical texts like "The Laugh of the Medusa" and "Sorties: Out and Out: Attacks/Ways Out/Forays". These texts propose *l'écriture féminine* or 'feminine writing' as an insurgent, emancipatory practice of self-expression. It is a formidable task to schematize the vast range of Cixous's creative-critical thought and praxis. To put it synoptically, *l'écriture féminine* rethinks the inscription of the bodily vis-à-vis the textual, the relations between philosophy and literature, between politics and writing — all through explorations of a self-identity which does not conform to dominant discourses. In her theoretical and critical essays, as in her experimental plays and 'poetic' fiction, Cixous presents a self who is hyphenated with the other — in Cixous's words, a self "withagainst" the other (*White Ink* 84).

The Cixousian subject emerges as someone who is capable of multiple identifications with the other, who is gendered but fluidic, embodied but porous to the influx of the other's presence, and coherent but mobile across borders of identities. As Cixous puts it, such a subject is "a non-closed mix of self/s and others" (*The Hélène Cixous Reader* xvii). The Cixousian 'New Woman' respect(s) the alterity of the other through awareness of what Kristeva calls the self's inherent, constitutive 'foreignness' — its multiple identifications, affects and becoming(s). "I think that our human experience, a marvellous, so enriching experience, is alteration" Cixous contends, "[w]e are altered, we are altered and disaltered (*sic*) beings through the other" (*White Ink* 32). According to her, such self-estrangement is not without pain, but it is also rich in ethical and cognitive rewards.

Nevertheless, the Cixousian 'New Woman' does not produce her permeable, nonexclusive "ultra subjectivities" (Cixous, "Sorties" 84) by effacing herself or getting subsumed in the other. *She* is 'feminine' not in the traditional (androcentric) sense of passivity or self-abnegation, but by being intensely alive to the other's difference. From a woman's perspective, this difference could be represented along three axes — difference within herself in terms of conscious and unconscious processes; her difference with a man; her difference with other women. It is significant to mention here that since traditionally woman has always been the marginalized figure (be it Freud's Dora or the Medusa in Greek lore), Cixous uses the signifier 'New Woman' to designate her *conceptual persona* (Deleuze's term) of nonbinary 'self/s'. Apart from an anti-patriarchal solidarity with women, such a *feminine* subject has little to do with traditional gender/sexual categorization. This also resonates well with Cixous's concept of *other bisexuality* which refers to "the location within oneself of the presence of both sexes, evident and insistent in different ways according to the individual" (Cixous, "Sorties" 85).

The economy of the *hyphen* in Cixous's conceptualizations is highlighted by Morag Shiach who contends that the feminine self/s is not an abstract, theoretical category with no purchase on the specific struggles of 'real' women. Instead, Shiach asserts, the self-expressive poetics of the Cixousian subject can produce a 'shared identity' among women, "formed not in relation to 'woman', but rather in terms of shared unconscious patterns and forms, which are the product of shared histories worked out across shared bodies" (26). Unlike Deleuze's *becoming-woman* or Kristeva's *subject-in-process*, the Cixousian New Woman represents *both* the provisional subject-in-writing ('woman') and the empirical, historical subject (women). *She* is both historically anchored and mobile, multiple and embodied. By this double movement of the hysterical-historical, Cixous therefore *hyphenates* the sexual and textual within a broader frame of the personal-political. She thereby disturbs the discursive 'borders' separating poetics and politics, gender and genre, the philosophical and the physiological.

The simultaneity of sharing and shoring the subjective space vis-à-vis the other puts Cixous's "'impossible' subject" ("Sorties" 98) at the limits of traditional Western onto-epistemology. *L'écriture féminine*, or as Cixous emphasizes, "'so-called feminine' writing" (*White Ink* 22), could be conceived as the polyvalent language of the feminine self/s. It is this eccentric/ex-centric subject who is the protagonist in Cixous 'auto-fictional' works like *Inside* or *Reveries of the Wild Woman*. In such works "Cixous offers her reader a version of the author herself, once or several times removed. But in presenting various kinds of 'I', Cixous [. . .] would rather stress her versatile selves within a whole being than validate the 'unified' vision usually presented through biography" (Fisher 60).

V.

Described as "a meditation on postcolonial identity and gender"[4], *Reveries of the Wild Woman* is Cixous's auto-fictional account of a young Jewish girl and her family, set in the backdrop of Algeria's war of independence against French colonial rule. In her person(a) of that lonely girl, Cixous narrates the racial and gender crises she suffered as a perpetual 'outsider' (the "wild woman" of the book's title; someone who is savage, without [b]orders) in Algeria. Much of those crises stemmed from her *hybrid* identity: although Cixous holds French citizenship, she was born in Algeria. In fact, none of Cixous's Jewish parents is from France—her father hailed from a Sephardic Jewish community of Spain, her German mother had Ashkenazi roots. While living in Algeria during the anti-Semitic Vichy regime, Cixous's family lost their official French nationality and were persecuted as Jews. The cruel irony was that the French-colonized, native Arab in Algeria considered the Cixous' as French and therefore a hated enemy.

---

[4] *Reveries of the Wild Woman: Primal Scenes*. By Helene Cixous. Trans. Beverly Bie Brahic. Evanston, Illinois: Northwestern University Press, 2006. Print.

"The complexity of these origins" as Claire Boyle observes, "makes the Cixousianself irreducible to its French nationality or Jewish background, causing her [i.e. Cixous] to make a declaration of absolute hybridity in her essay 'Mon algériance'" (Boyle 71). The melancholy in *Reveries* arises from the narrator's self-ish attempts to welcome, and if possible, *become* the 'other' — namely, Arab children of her age, the "kidz Arabs" (*Reveries* 24). Experiencing that uncanny *unhomeliness* everywhere, it was the only means to forge her own identity and end a painful self-estrangement. The girl sought entry in "their" Algeria in a contra-colonizing gesture of humility and solidarity: "I wanted to be on their side [. . .] I only wanted their City and their Algeria, with all my strength I wanted to arrive there [. . .] hoping to demonstrate my goodwill" (Cixous, *ibid*).

But such an endeavour was doomed to fail, not the least because it unknowingly perpetrated the subtle violence of homogenizing the other. "It is only by understanding the ambivalence and antagonism of the desire of the Other", Bhabha cautions, "that we can avoid the increasingly facile adoption of the notion of a homogenized Other" (*The Location of Culture* 52). "[W]here there were Arabs", says Cixous's narrator, "I was hope and wound. Me, I thought I am *inseparab*. This is an unlivable relationship with oneself" (*Reveries* 24). As Bhabha points out, it is the "collaborations of political and psychic violence" which finally results not so much in "Self and Other but otherness of the Self inscribed in the perverse palimpsest of colonial identity [...] it is that bizarre figure of desire, which splits along the axis on which it turns" (*Location* 43-44). It produces that state of *unhomeliness* in Cixous's narrator, a sense of not feeling at home in one's homeland, of being a stranger in one's skin.

Reveries opens wistfully with this sense of angst and a double alienation born out of racial and gender crises. The narrator, now having moved to France, recollects her unhomeliness in Algeria which is now a more distant, and paradoxically, a more intimate *home*: "The whole time I was living in Algeria I would dream of one day arriving in Algeria, I would have done anything to get there" (3). In John Di Stefano's words, it is the "desire to leave and the impossibility of ever fully and completely returning, that marks the unique and complex position of many displaced persons today. It is the tension of knowing both worlds and never being able to arrive or entirely depart" (40). "Remembering is never a quiet act of introspection or retrospection", Bhabha observes, "[i]t is a painful re-membering, a putting together of the dismembered past to make sense of the trauma of the present" (*Location* 63).

At the heart of *Reveries*, Cixous's "unhomely fiction(s)" (Bhabha, *ibid* 12), lies *méconnaissance*. The latter is Lacan's term for 'misrecognition' in the "mirror stage", where the child misconstrues its 'image' as itself. Such misrecognition simultaneously produces identification and alienation. As Bhabha points out, "This is the basis of the close relation between the two forms of identification complicit with the Imaginary—narcissism and aggressivity" (*Location* 77). In *Reveries* we find that the girl-narrator is rejected by Arabs for being 'French'; by French for being 'Jew'; by Sephardic Jews for being 'the daughter of a German mother', the latter being a working widow and an atheist at that; the girl is alienated from her own family for showing 'abnormal' (traumatic) behaviour following her father's death; rejected even by her constant companion, her brother, for being 'a girl'. In turn, the narrator produces her own counter-identification with the Arabs and against the French.

Her selfhood is thereby smothered by what Bhabha calls "the ready recognition of images as positive or negative" (*Location of* 67), which keeps up the mode of Western hierarchized binary thinking. The hyphenation in 'self-identity' could not be more agon-izing [*agon* (ancient Greek) means "struggle or contest"]. The excruciating pain of such a torn existence could be heard in the howling of Fips, the 'mad', household dog. Cixous's family locks him up in a cage out of their sense of concern and ownership. In the course of the narrative, the dog—a gift from the narrator's father—transcends the ontic borders of the 'animal' and turns into a quasi-divine character. Fips, 'The Dog', becomes a living image of innocent victimhood—betrayed by its own people, a Christ-like figure left by the Father to suffer and pay for the sins of others.

Like Fips, the narrator too stands alone in the face of the sexism and misogyny she suffers in her Algerian hometown of Clos-Salembier. It was the "war between the sexes" in Algerian society, a "brutal crude war [...] on two fronts, on the one hand the war between the boys, same sex against same sex" (Cixous, *Reveries* 23). On the other hand it was "the war of the same against the others", the gender wars, where the narrator found herself on her own, "sisterless brotherless and friendless" (*ibid*). She says, "I am the only one who can talk about this double war for I alone in the Clos-Salembier was on both sides, as brother on my brother's side and as a girl without my brother who in this case could never have been my sister. I know what defilement is (24)."

Significantly, it is also her hyphenated self—'inseparab' *and* French, brother *and* sister—which confers on the narrator the clarity, the *double vision* of the 'outsider' perspective. It allows her to move across and displace the rigid binaries of identity, clearing up a space for the Cixousian *feminine self/s* to emerge. Jennifer Yee underlines how the perspective of such a self is formed in the *Reveries*: "For Hélène Cixous, evidently, this freedom (or marginality) of vision is maintained by constant slippage from one gender role to another, thanks here, in part, to her 'hermaphroditic' semiunity [sic] with her brother, and from one place to another in the overdefined [sic] series of exclusions, of walls, doors, and gateways that is her childhood Algeria" (199).

As the critic points out, this "slippage" is first of all semantic. In the self-reflexive narrative of the *Reveries*, it is signalled by a play of meanings effected through symbolism, allusion, intertextuality, puns and neologisms. The act of writing her troubled past becomes for Cixous a rite of passage, the opening of an old abscess. The narrative itself becomes the interpreter of the narrator's maladies, variously called as her "*Algerian disorder*" (Cixous, *Reveries* 7) or "Malgeria" —a double sickness in *and* of Algeria. That only 'writing' is the cure—the secret passageway out of the oppressive self/other binary—is something which becomes apparent to Cixous's narrator in the *Reveries*. It is particularly highlighted in the episode of the three Muslim girls joining the French lycée in Algeria where the girl-narrator studied. The narrator, who was Jewish, languished as an outcast in this school which was an all-French, anti-Semitic establishment. She is drawn to these new Muslim girls in her class: in her eyes they become the strange and true 'face' of Algeria, somewhat like the enigmatic Levinasian *face of the irreducible Other*[5] which forever eludes comprehension.

The episode evokes in Cixous the stirrings of becoming-other, which is the embryo of a future book growing in her. For, as she tells us, a book is always conceived in the womb of the self-withagainst-the-other: in the unconscious, in language, in other lives teeming in us. Such a book is magnificently imperious because it cannot be willed by the self, it decides its own arrival. The narrator describes that *primal scene* to us:

> [T]hey [i.e. the Muslim girls] instantly became all others for me [. . . .] I was with them but they were not with me, they were off in the distance no one is closer to me no one more removed. It's like a book. Before you write it it is already there, you can't talk about it, it is not there, its whole being is a little ways [sic] away very close, a few days and a few months away at the same time absolutely not before it comes into being. [. . .] To say there's a book, I feel a book invading me, I am in the clutch of a book, is madness. [. . .] In class with them [i.e. the Muslim girls], them without me, me with them in my inner life [. . .] I was in the grips of a madness I kept to myself. [. . .] I gaze into the distance to see where they are going that I am not.
> There's the book I thought [. . .] immediately after having left Algeria I would think of that book, theirs, telling myself: I have seen the book I will not write. (86).

VI.

"An important feature of colonial discourse", Bhabha points out, "is its dependence on the concept of 'fixity' in the ideological construction of otherness" (*Location* 66). By contrast, Cixous's ethical position in her postcolonial text, *Reveries*, finally brings her

---

5   For Levinas, western philosophy has traditionally defined the Other as an object of consciousness for the western subject. This reductive definition has effectively destroyed the singular alterity of the Other. Against this reduction, Levinas has asserted that the Other always escapes the consciousness and control of the western self. For Levinas, the challenge that the alterity of the Other poses to the certainty of the Self in the face-to-face encounter between the Self and the Other opens the question of ethics" (Stephen Morton, *Gayatri Chakraborty Spivak*, Routledge Critical Series 37).

closer to the Levinasian ethics of the irreducible Other, where the other is not subjected to the violence of comprehension [*prehendere* (Latin) — "to grasp"). As Cixous puts it, "It's a moving knowledge, mobile, open, capable of accepting that I cannot own the other; that is what escapes me" (*White Ink* 34). She contends that this "advancing in incomprehension, advancing towards incomprehension" is "the very movement of literature" (*ibid* 20). Cixous thereby sums up her literary ethics beautifully when she says, "Other-Love is writing's first name" ("Sorties" 99).

In its "poetics of exile" (Bhabha, *Location* 5), *Reveries of the Wild Woman* interweaves the disparate strands of being, becoming and the beyond in the texture and textuality of a limitless 'writing'. And in doing so, it becomes Cixous's auto-fictional simulation of that eternal (im)possibility of becoming-other: a book which is first and foremost *written* internally, endlessly; the interminable 'Book of You'. The "beyond" of this "third space" thereby becomes "a space of intervention in the here and now", inviting us "to elude the politics of polarity and emerge as the others of our selves. [. . .] It opens up a narrative strategy for the emergence and negotiation of those agencies of the marginal, minority, subaltern, or diasporic that incite us to think through—and beyond—theory" (*Location* 39, 181).

In the light of the above, it seems that the old question of the hyphen in post(-)colonial studies could be and should be asked in new ways. We can conclude with Yoka Van Dyk's observation that for all the (b)order and (b)ordering within and without us,

> Belonging or displacement (in relation to identity) turn out to be far more complex, fluid and multi-layered concepts than they appear at first sight [. . .] we may simultaneously experience a belonging in both places (or a plurality of experience per se), or a belonging in some ways but not in other ways, at some times and spaces, certain moments or in particular circumstances. What is subsequently of critical importance in this notion of identity and belonging—in the plural scene—is a recognition that it is perhaps not fixed or permanent. There are many sides to belonging that are constantly subjected to change, flux and multiplicity" (18).

References

Ahmad, Aijaz. "The Politics of Literary Postcoloniality". *Contemporary Postcolonial Theory: A Reader.* Ed. Padmini Mongia. New Delhi: OUP, 1996. Print.

Barrett, Michèle. "Words and Things: Materialism and Method in Contemporary Feminist Analysis". *Destabilizing Theory: Contemporary Feminist Debates.* Eds. Michèle Barrett and Anne Philips. Stanford, California: Stanford UP, 1992. 201-219. Print.

Bhabha, Homi K. *The Location of Culture.* London and New York: Routledge, 1994. Print.

—."Cosmopolitanisms" (with Carol A. Breckenridge, Sheldon Pollock and Dipesh Chakrabarty), *Public Culture* 12(3) (Fall), 577-89.

Boyle, Claire. "Writing Self-Estrangement: Possessive Knowledge and Loss in Cixous's Recent Autobiographical Work". *Dalhousie French Studies,* Vol. 68, HybridVoices, Hybrid Texts: Women's Writing at the Turn of the Millennium (Fall 2004), 69-77. JSTOR, www.jstor.org /stable/40836855

Braidotti, Rosi. *Nomadic Subjects: Embodiment and Sexual Difference in Contemporary Feminist Theory.* Second Edition. New York: Columbia UP, 2011. Print.

Cixous, Hélène. "Sorties: Out and Out: Attacks/Ways Out/ Forays". *The Newly Born Woman.* By Cixous and Catherine Clement. Trans. Betsy Wing. Introd. Sandra M. Gilbert. Minneapolis, London: U of Minnesota P, 1986. 63-132. Print. Theory and History of Literature, Vol.24.

—."The Laugh of the Medusa". Trans. Keith Cohen and Paula Cohen. *Signs,* Vol. 1, No. 4 (Summer 1976), 875-893. JSTOR, www.jstor.org/stable/3173239

—. *White Ink: Interviews on Sex, Text and Politics.* Ed. Susan Sellers. New York: Columbia UP, 2008. Print. European Perspectives.

—. *Rootprints: Memory and Life Writing.* By Cixous and Mireille Calle-Gruber. Trans. EricPrenowitz. London and New York: Routledge, 1997. Print.

—. "Preface". *The Hélène Cixous Reader.* Ed. Susan Sellers. London and NewYork: Routledge, 1994. xv-xxiii. Print.

Dyk, Yoka Van. *Hyphenated-Living: Between Longing and Belonging.* Auckland University of Technology. 2005. Print.

Elliott, Julia. *Oxford Dictionary and Thesaurus.* Ed. (with Anne Knight and Chris Cowley). New York: OUP, 2001. Print.

Fisher, Claudine G. "Cixous's Auto-fictional Mother and Father". *Pacific Coast Philology*, Vol.38 (2003), 60-76. *JSTOR*, www.jstor.org/stable/30037161.

Gandhi, Leela. *Postcolonial Theory: A Critical Introduction*. New Delhi: OUP, 1998. Print.

Gaston, Sean. *Starting with Derrida: Plato, Aristotle and Hegel*. Viva-Continuum Edition.London and New York: Continuum, 2008. Print.

Hallward, Peter. *Absolutely Post-Colonial: Writing Between the Singular and the Specific*. Manchester: Manchester University Press, 2001. Print.

Huddart, David. *Homi K. Bhabha*. London and New York: Routledge, 2006. Print. Routledge Critical Series.

Kristeva, Julia. *Strangers to Ourselves*. Trans. L.S. Roudiez. London: Harvester Wheatsheaf, 1994. Print.

Lippard, Lucy R. *The Lure of the Local: Senses of Place in a Multicentered Society*. New York: The New Press, 1997. Print.

Parry, Benita. "Signs of Our Times: Discussion of Homi Bhabha's *The Location of Culture*", *Third Text* 38/39 (1994), 5-24. Print.

Shiach, Morag. *Helene Cixous: A Politics of Writing*.London and New York: Routledge, 1991. Print.

Stefano, John Di. "Moving Images of Home". *Art Journal*, Vol. 61, No.4. College Art Association, New York, NY, USA 2002, 38-51. Print.

Yee, Jennifer. "The Colonial Outsider: 'Malgerie' in HèlèneCixous's Les rêveries de la femmesauvage". *Tulsa Studies in Women's Literature*, Vol. 20, No.2, Women Writing Across the World (Autumn, 2001), 189-200. *JSTOR*, www.jstor.org/stable/464482.

Borders in South Asia: Language, Culture and Religion from Colonialism to Globalization

Aditya Kant Ghising

The concept of 'South Asia' developed in academic circles as a result of the birth of the discipline of Area Studies in the United States. Prior to that, the region was known mainly as the 'Indian Sub-continent', which in itself had its share of ambiguity with regard to its actual constituent states. The United Nations in its geo-scheme, a system which divides the countries of the world into regions and sub-regions, states that South or Southern Asia is composed of Afghanistan, Bangladesh, Bhutan, India, Iran, Maldives, Nepal, Pakistan and Sri Lanka. The civilizational existence of South Asia, according to Shail Mayaram, emanates from the continuity of language, culture and traditions evident from Colombo to Karachi to Kathmandu to Delhi. Itsprecursor can be defined through a series of socio-cultural and post-colonial movements. This is persistent in the instances of 'cosmopolitan vernacular' mapping pre-modern to modern milieu.[1] However, the modern understanding of the region has been based on the membership of the South Asian Association for Regional Cooperation (SAARC) which indicates that South Asia is composed of eight countries, namely Afghanistan, Bangladesh, Bhutan, India, Maldives, Nepal, Pakistan and Sri Lanka. Iran is therefore not included in this understanding of the region and has been generally accepted in global politics. The genesis of Pakistan and Bangladesh has colonial roots. Most of the issues in the inter-state relations of these countries vis-à-vis the other member states of SAARC and most notably with India is clouded with this background. Colonialism has played a major role in shaping into form what we

---

[1] Pathak, D. & Perera, S. "The Poser: Mooting South Asia: Utopias and Possibilities beyond Geo-political Calculus", *Sociological Bulletin*, Vol. 64, No. 2 (May-August 2015), Sage Publications Inc., pp. 219-222.

understand today as South Asia. Apart from Pakistan and Bangladesh, the geography and geographical boundaries of countries like Nepal and Bhutan today have been a direct result of colonial policies in the various stages of its presence in the region. The Treaty of Sugauli signed between the East India Company and the King of Nepal in December 1815 (ratified in 1816) after the Anglo-Nepalese war established the present boundary line of Nepal. On the other hand, under the terms of the Treaty of Sinchula signed in November 1865, Bhutan ceded territories in the Assam Duars and Bengal Duars in return for an annual subsidy of 50,000 rupees. These are some examples of how the present geography of the region took shape during the colonial period. It must be noted that given such complexities in its very creation, South Asia today is indeed a treasure trove of culture, language, religion and tradition which have transcended borders. This of course has its pros and its cons. Spill-over effects of turbulence; political, social, economic or religious, in one state can have dramatic consequences on the other. At the same time, positive consequences of economic development in one state can prove to have immense positive repercussions on the region as a whole.As indicated by the Organization for Economic Co-operation and Development (OECD) forecast, while growth will slow in China in the near future, it is expected to stay brisk in India. Southeast Asia is also poised to maintain strong growth momentum from 2018 to 2022 due to robust domestic private consumption and infrastructure initiatives planned by a number of governments.[2] It remains to be seen whether South Asian economies can take advantage of this growth in its neighborhood.

The Complexities of Culture and Religion

The complexities in studying borders arise from the simple duality of the subject itself. While on the one hand borders can be seen as, and many parts of the world still do, a means to preserve a

---

[2] OECD (2018), *Economic Outlook for Southeast Asia, China and India 2018: Fostering Growth Through Digitalisation*, OECD Publishing, Paris, http://dx.dorg/9789264286184-en.

community's unique identity and prevent foreign influences on its culture, language, customs, rituals and traditions. In this sense they serve to protect the socio-economic and geo-political fabric of the community. On the other hand, borders are increasingly seen as connecting elements. In this sense, they may be understood as portals to a different world with a different culture, way of life, traditions, languages, etc. Ever since the beginning of globalization many countries of the world, or 'actors' as they are known in the realm of International Relations, have embraced this idea by simply opening up their markets for foreign trade. The idea here was that by doing so the positive effects of globalization and connectivity would eventually penetrate the deepest corners of society and influence its various facets thereby gradually leading to a borderless world. As witnessed in the last few years, this idea has had mixed reactions. The USA's willingness to close its borders with Mexico and the Brexit crisis has shown the darker side of globalization and its side-effects. Just like overdosing on an otherwise helpful medicine could have disastrous consequences on the human body, over-assimilation of global cultures generally has its share of side-effects. Although there may always exist exceptions to the case.

Culture and religion serve as a double-edged sword in society. On the one hand they act as a unifying force and bring people closer while at the same time possessing the power to create divisions in society and planting the seeds for a *'me against you'* mentality which has aptly been termed as 'mental borders'. There is no doubt that South Asia is a diverse region and with this diversity comes differences in culture, language, religion, rituals, customs and traditions amongst its inhabitants. Perhaps this diversity has not been explored well which has led to the birth of the idea of an alien culture as opposed to one's own. Increasing people-to-people contacts has been one of the main focus areas of the various governments in the region to eliminate this mentality. One prime example of this is the India-Nepal Treaty of Peace and Friendship signed in 1950, article 7 of which allows citizens of either country to move freely across the border as well as "*the same privileges in the matter of residence, ownership of property, participation in trade and commerce, movement and other privileges of a similar nature.*"[3] However this has had a negative impact on the Nepali-speaking Gorkhas of India and they have raised this issue several times in the form of a demand for a separate state within India with the idea that, apart from other issues, their identity as people who have been a part of British India as well as citizens of independent India is getting confused with that of the Nepalis who are residing in India since the 1950s because of this provision in the treaty. Similar dissatisfaction has been shown from various political leaders in Nepal regarding the issue. In fact in May 2018 it was set to be amended with these new developments in focus. Over the years, Bhutan and Nepal have often shown their share of cultural differences with each other as well. The mass deportation of Bhutanese-Nepalis in the 1990s has been a thorn in their relations on a people to people level as well as on a government-to-government level ever since. These issues have hampered much progress that could have been made under regional initiatives like the Bangladesh-Bhutan-India-Nepal (BBIN) initiative and may just be viewed as some of the problems South Asia as a region continues to face.

In case of Bhutan's relations with India along cultural and religious lines, one finds that in 747 A.D. a Buddhist saint by the name of *Padmasambhava* who was known in Bhutan as *Guru Rinpoche* (also sometimes referred to as the Second Buddha), came to Bhutan from India and according to tradition, founded the *Nyingmapa* sect, also known as the Red Hat sect of Mahayana Buddhism, which became for a time the dominant religion of Bhutan. Thus Indian influence played a temporary role there until increasing Tibetan migration brought with it new cultural and religious contributions. Apart from such shared cultural and religious heritage, there were other areas of interaction which developed during the British rule in India, which included several Anglo-Bhutanese skirmishes and battles that were consequently

---

[3] 'Treaty of Peace and Friendship'. Available at http://mea.gov.in/bilateral-documents.htm?dtl/6295/Treaty+of+Peace+and+Friendship accessed on 1/9/2017.

followed by treaties and agreements. It was during this period of interaction with the British, that trade between the Bhutanese and the Indians were also recorded to have taken place for the first time (1873).[4] The birth of the People's Republic of China in 1949, the takeover of Tibet the following year and the annexation of Bhutanese enclaves in Tibet led to a shift in Bhutanese foreign policy vis-à-vis India. A Treaty of Friendship between the Bhutan and India was signed in August 1949.

The European experience of regional integration in the form of the erstwhile European Coal and Steel Community (ECSC) and the European Union today has been widely appreciated by experts in the subject. In this regard while explaining the role of culture, in an article published in 1990 Karlfried Knapp writes,

> "Everybody is aware of the culture problem in contacts with far-away and exotic countries like those in the Far East or Africa, and tries to be prepared for possible cultural differences. When doing business in Europe, however, people tend to assume that no such problem exists after all, the unspoken argument might go, we Europeans all share a common heritage of Western civilization. And that is why, apart from bureaucratic regulations, it is usually only the language difference that is regarded as the main obstacle to a common market."[5]

Closer home, the people of the Maldives, Pakistan, Afghanistan and Bangladesh are predominantly Muslim and Islam is the dominant religion, Nepal and India have a majority Hindu population, Theravada Buddhism is the major religion in Sri Lanka whereas in Bhutan about two-thirds to three-quarters of the population practice Drukpa Kagyu or Nyingma Buddhism, both of which are disciplines of Mahayana Buddhism. Approximately one-quarter of the population are ethnic Nepalese and practice Hinduism. Apart from these major religions existing in the region, Christianity, Sikhism and Taoism, to name a few are also followed. This stands as being completely opposite to the general understanding of a

---

[4] Choden, T. 2011. *Indo Bhutan Relations Recent Trends*. In Perspectives on Modern South Asia: A Reader in Culture, History and Representation, Visweswaran.K (ed.). Blackwell Publishing Ltd. p. 299.

[5] Knapp, K., 1990. 'Common Market: Common Culture?', *European Journal of Education*, Vol. 25, No. 1, pp. 55-60

regional grouping like the European Union where the member states mostly share a similar culture and religion. People's religious differences have been known to influence the type of government they prefer to live under as well as the laws they follow. India happens to enjoy a unique position in South Asia with regard to culture and religion. Being a secular country and sharing borders with all of the other South Asian countries, India has been able to absorb religious differences, excluding a few instances, rather successfully. Interestingly, it was the British who, following more than two millennia of invasions and migrations from the west and north west, restored to India as a political fact the basic truth of its geography: that it is indeed a subcontinent. A 1901 map of India wonderfully demonstrates this by showing a plethora of British-built rail lines ranging in arterial fashion over the whole of the subcontinent, from the Afghan border to the Palk Strait near Ceylon in the deep south, and from Karachi in present-day Pakistan in the west toChittagong in present-day Bangladesh in the east.[6] Areas that came to comprise the nations of Bangladesh, India, Pakistan and Sri Lanka (formerly Ceylon) were ruled directly or indirectly by the British. Additionally, Bhutan and the Maldives were British protectorates and while the British did not directly control Afghanistan and Nepal, they did heavily influence both nations, essentially controlling their defence and foreign policies.[7] Even after the partition of not just the country as a geographical entity but of its people as well, West Bengal and Bangladesh follow a similar culture and language. The same is true for north Bengal, the Terai region and Nepal. In the north, Jammu and Kashmir share similar cultural traits with Pakistan as well. This has of course been overshadowed by India's strained relations with Pakistan since independence. The Tamils of South India also share some major cultural traits of Sri Lanka and the various groups inhabiting the northeastern region of India share historical, cultural and linguistic roots with the people of Myanmar. Perhaps this ability to absorb

---

[6] Kaplan, R. D., "South Asia's Geography of Conflict", Center for a New American Security, August 2010, p. 9.
[7] Snedden, S., "Shifting Geo-politics in the Greater South Asia Region", Daniel K. Inouye Asia-Pacific Center for Security Studies, April 2016. p. 4.

regional cultural traits needs to be further strengthened with more policies directed towards people-to-people contact in the region. As observed earlier, since the entire region faces similar problems and hurdles in development, such policies would go a long way in clearing misguided differences and increasing understanding of each other's geo-political motives. Along with this, the idea of sovereignty, national power and identity has largely dominated South Asian regional cooperation efforts. Sharing of resources for instance, has often been viewed as erosion of national sovereignty. Moreover since religion and culture go hand in hand with the concept of identity, it becomes important to address intra-regional understandings of the same. The similarities in culture and religion in the region need to be stressed on more than the differences in order to transcend the mental borders amongst its inhabitants if any significant progress is to be made in other areas like connectivity projects, regional economic integration projects, etc.

Ethnic and religious nationalism, with its propensity to shape relations between nation states and as a movement against the distribution of power within and between them constitutes the most unpredictable threat to nation states.[8] It is common knowledge now that South Asia is mainly characterized by its multi-ethnic, multi-religious, multi-cultural and multi-racial composition. The region has followers of the major religions of the world like Christianity, Islam, Hinduism and Buddhism along with about two dozen distinct linguistic communities. This has led many scholars to believe that South Asia faces a threat from within rather than from external sources. On the other hand, if implemented through proper policies at various levels, this diversity in various facets of life that exists within the region can also be looked at as a huge blessing with numerous opportunities for growth and development. In the case of India and Bangladesh for example, the similarities in culture, geographical proximity and almost similar physical infrastructure offer ample opportunities for mutually beneficial trade. However, the focus has to shift sooner rather than

---

[8] Smith, A.D., 1994. 'Ethnic nationalism and the plight of minorities', *Journal of Refugee Studies*, London, vol.7, no.2-3, p. 186.

later from the "border haats" and move to a higher level of economic connectivity. The same also applies to the northeastern region and the economies of Southeast Asia, through Myanmar.

Regional Economic Scenario: Cooperation amidst Conflicting Issues

Compared to India, Pakistan on independence lacked the middle-class base which could have consolidated democracy, and on its independence in 1971, Bangladesh was so mired in poverty that the maintenance of any system seems a success.[9] It is a well-known fact that India is uniquely placed in South Asia in the sense that it connects most of the countries of the region that do not have contiguous borders while serving as a vital link between East and West Asia. In today's highly interconnected global order, the demographic and economic importance of South Asia as a region cannot be over-emphasized. India has grabbed the headlines with projections that in the coming decades its economy will become one of the world's largest, but growth has been strong throughout the region. This has put a new set of pressures on political systems. For the first time leaders need to manage rapidly rising expectations.[10] According to the World Bank, South Asia is home to a quarter of the world's population and accounts for 36 percent of the world's poor.[11] In 2018 India was the world's sixth-largest economy by nominal GDP and the third-largest by purchasing power parity (PPP). The country ranks 139th in per capita GDP (nominal) with \$2,134 and 122nd in per capita GDP (PPP) with \$7,783. Since the conclusion of super-power rivalry at the end of the Cold War, the gradual shaping and reshaping of economic corridors has been one of the major focus areas in inter-state relations especially in South and Southeast Asia. The Maritime Silk Route, the Bangladesh-

---

[9] Price, G. "South Asia at Sixty", *The World Today*, Vol. 63, No. 8/9 (Aug.-Sep., 2007), Royal Institute of International Affairs, pp. 24-26.
[10] *Ibid.* p. 26.
[11] Available at: http://www.worldbank.org/en/news/feature/2018/03/15/south-asia-economicsstudents-word-toward-one-south-asia?SAR%20Facebook=SAR_FB_SAR_EN_EXT accessed on 7/8/2018.

China-India-Myanmar (BCIM) Economic Corridor and the Trans-Himalayan Economic Corridor are some examples of such endeavors. Generally economic corridors are understood as industrial economic clusters based around important transport corridors which ultimately link to global production networks and they play a vital role in strengthening the manufacturing sector, creating massive employment opportunities in the process. Although it can be argued that such linkages between countries through trading corridors have been in existence since time immemorial, in the globalized world of today the scenario has undergone some changes. The manufacturing sector has come to play a dominant role in economic development. In 1996, D. Foray and B.A. Lundvall introduced the concept of a knowledge-based economy through which they argued that factors determining the success of firms and national economies are more dependent than ever on the capacity to produce and use knowledge. The other side of this new aspect of economic growth is that innovation and technological changes have become more central to economic performance.[12] Digitalization of trade and services has now more than ever become a reality in cross border economic transactions and its tremendous future potential cannot be ignored. Apart from this, looking only at the tourism sector, promotion of cultural and heritage tourism along with religious or faith tourism in the region can be a source of massive revenue generation. An initiative like the inauguration of a waterways transit facility by India and Bangladesh in 2016 is also a welcome move. This was made possible by the Indo-Bangladesh Protocol on Inland Water Transit and Trade signed by the Prime Ministers of the two nations. According to the Ministry of Development of North Eastern Region (DONER), under this protocol inland vessels of one country can transit through the specified routes of the other country. The existing protocol routes are: Kolkata-Pandu-Kolkata; Kolkata-Karimganj-Kolkata; Rajshahi-Dhulian-Rajshahi and Pandu-Karimganj-Pandu.

---

[12] Foray, D., Lundvall, B.A., 1996. *From the economics of knowledge to the learning economy*, in Employment and Growth in the knowledge-based economy, OECD document, Paris: OECD.

For inter-country trade, four ports of call have been designated in each country. For India these are Haldia (West Bengal), Kolkata (West Bengal), Pandu (Assam) Karimganj (Assam) and Silghat (Assam). Similarly for Bangladesh, these are Narayanganj, Khulna, Mongla, Sirajganj and Ashuganj.[13]

On the other hand intellectuals and academicians have looked at SAARC as not being able to achieve its desired goals so far due to mutual distrust among the members. According to Prof. Lama, the military-centric borders such as Durand Line, Radcliffe Line and McMohan Line had actually driven a wedge permanently between the member-countries and dismantled the history and cross-cultural diversity. He stresses on a people-centric approach for the successful implementation of SAARC objectives.[14] What we find today is on the grassroots level, citizens of each of the countries that make up South Asia are facing common challenges and there is a significant level of trust and faith in cooperation for the achievement of common developmental goals and a brighter future for the region. Eradication of poverty remains high on the agenda. However at the government level, things start to change and the realities of geopolitics tend to take over. This may be attributed to the mindset that grew as a result of the experiences associated with colonialism in the region which has fostered a long and shared history of mutual mistrust and negative stereotypes, casting a shadow over cooperation efforts. Moreover, limited access to accurate information about neighboring countries perpetuates damaging myths. It may be argued that historical political tensions, trust deficit and security concerns have contributed towards the current state of affairs in the region. Along with these factors, the absence of functioning economic corridors, border-related conflict territories, high non-tariff barriers including travel restrictions and a lack of political will to strengthen and implement agreements like the South Asian Free Trade Area (SAFTA), SAARC Agreement on

---

[13] Availableat http://www.mdoner.gov.in/content/indo-bangladesh-protocol-inland-water-transit-trade. accessed on 15/1/2018.
[14] 'SAARC a failed mission, say experts'. Available at https://www.thehindu.com/news/cities/Visakhapatnam/saarc-a-failed-mission-say-experts/article 17748997.ece accessed on 3/9/2017.

Trade In Services (SATIS) and bilateral free trade and investment agreements have hampered the attempts at regional economic integration in South Asia.[15] When India proposed a SAARC Motor Vehicle Agreement during the 18th SAARC summit in Kathmandu, it was met with objections from Pakistan and no agreement could be reached. The same was done on a sub-regional level with the Bangladesh-Bhutan-India-Nepal (BBIN) grouping and the BBIN Motor Vehicles Agreement (MVA) was signed on 15 June 2015 at the BBIN transport ministers meeting in Thimpu, Bhutan. However factors like strained relations with Nepal, increase in vehicular traffic from the other nations which would affect Bhutanese truckers and environmental damage were cited as the reasons for Bhutan disagreeing to ratify the agreement. The project carried on without Bhutan and trial runs for cargo vehicles under the MVA were conducted along the Kolkata-Dhaka-Agartala and Delhi-Kolkata-Dhaka routes. The role of the Asian Development Bank (ADB) cannot be over-emphasized in this regard as it has been providing technical, advisory, as well as financial support to the BBIN MVA initiative as part of its assistance to the South Asia Sub-regional Economic Cooperation (SASEC) program. Scholars in the field have also looked at the possibility of the creation of a more vibrant common market amongst suitable and willing candidates in the region.

Scholars often see that the countries of south Asia sharea relationship of conflict and cooperation.[16] Intra-SAARC trade suffers from complex non-tariff barriers, lack of connectivity, poor infrastructure and bureaucratic red tape-ism at the borders. Even in case of foreign investment in the region, when compared to East and Southeast Asia, while FDI inflows to South Asia increased from $36 billion in 2013 to $50 billion in 2015, it is significantly less compared to East and Southeast Asia where these numbers stood at $350 billion and $448 billion for 2013 and 2015, respectively. South Asia's share in world FDI inflows in 2015 stood at a meagre

---

[15] *Trade Insight*, Vol. 12, No. 2, 2016.
[16] Sharma, N. L., "India and RegionalIntegration in South Asia: Hope for Greater Asian Cooperation", *The Indian Journal of Political Science*, Vol. 70, No. 3 (JULY-SEPT., 2009), Indian Political Science Association, pp. 907-917.

2.9 per cent whereas East and Southeast Asia attracted 25 per cent of world FDI flows.[17] This, despite the tremendous potential of developing economies in the region. In terms of logistics and connectivity, the World Bank's Logistics Performance Index (LPI) which is a benchmarking tool to identify the challenges and opportunities countries face in the performance of trade logistics, Pakistan's rank was 110 out of 155 countries in 2010, and its LPI score was 2.53. This score ranges from 1 to 5, with 1 being the worst. India's LPI score was 3.12, followed by Bangladesh with 2.74.[18] A well planned road and railway development is also one of the most urgent needs of some of the countries in South Asia. The road density for example is an indicator of the level of infrastructure development of a country. Along with road and rail, port development goes hand in hand. The cost of importing and exporting a container across borders is a significant hurdle. There is also considerable delay associated with trade between Lahore (Pakistan) and Amritsar (India) as official trade between the two countries by rail and road only takes place through the Wagah border. Furthermore, in May of 2018 *The Nation* reported that 'trade activities between Pakistan and India have slowed down in the current fiscal year of 2017-18, as the bilateral trade between the two rival nations has dropped to $1.25 billion from $2.4 billion of five years ago in 2013.'[19]

Conclusion

Although India has been included in the concept of Emerging Asia which also includes China and Southeast Asia, the regional disparities with regard to trade in goods and services have

---

[17] Ranjan, P. Coming Closer Together for Trade. *The Hindu*. Available at https://www.thehindu.com/opinion/op-ed/Coming-closer-together-for-trade/article14628676.ece accessed on 3/8/2017.

[18] Samad, G. and Ahmed, V. 'Trade Facilitation through Economic Corridors in South Asia: The Pakistan Perspective' in De, P. and Iyengar, K. (eds.). *Developing Economic Corridors in South Asia*. Mandaluyong City, Philippines: Asian Development Bank, 2014.p.160.

[19] Abduhu, S. 'Pak-India trade through Wagah border slows down'. *The Nation*. Available at https://nation.com.pk/31-May-2018/pak-india-trade-through-wagah-border-slows-down Accessed on 8/7/2018.

rendered a heavy blow to the economy of South Asia as a whole. Economic differences are aggravated by religious and cultural differences which further heighten the regional problematique. It has been difficult for South Asian countries to see eye-to-eye on major regional developmental issues, although there have been signs of peaceful relations amongst them. The need for massive projects of infrastructure development in the region seems only to be the tip of the iceberg. Mutual distrust amongst the members of South Asia needs to be eliminated for all other developmental goals to be achieved. In order for this to happen, the strains in relations amongst the states of the region need to be sorted out and the colonial hangover cured for good. The gains to be made are immense and a stable region could highly attract foreign investment as well. In this regard, one of the urgent needs of the hour is to look at borders between the countries of South Asia through the prism of borderlands and not simply as dividing lines but as connecting elements. Due emphasis must also be placed on the historical nature of relations amongst the communities living in some parts of North-East India and northern Myanmar, ranging from marriage and barter-system of trade to the complexities of inter-state relations of today guided by the process of globalization. As relations between the states improve, common national objectives like poverty alleviation should be treated more as a regional objective with national policies closely linked to regional gains. India, Pakistan and Bangladesh are the top three economies in South Asia today and in order for the rest to follow, perhaps narrow minded policies need to be shunned. Today scholars have been discussing the potential of newer forms of integration between India and her neighbors and ideas such as the development of mountain ports for boosting tourism and connectivity in the region are taking shape. There does seem to be light at the end of the tunnel although to get there, the past has to be carefully observed and respected and not seen as the only way to the future for the region to prosper.

Missing Links or the Diasporic Journey of a Rebel: A Study of H P Malet's *Lost Links in Indian Mutiny* (1867)

Debapriya Paul

In his *Cartographies of Diaspora* (1996) Avtar Brah remarks:

> The concepts of *diaspora*, *border*, and *politics of location* are immanent, and together they mark conceptual connections for historicised analyses of contemporary trans/national movements of people, information, cultures, commodities and capital. This site of immanence inaugurates a new concept, namely *diaspora space*. (16)

Written in the wake of the Indian Rebellion of 1857, almost a decade after the events in India, *Lost Links in Indian Mutiny* by H P Malet opens up one such strange 'diaspora space'. The novel begins with Yusuff's sojourn to Mecca, for Hadj. In a weirdly episodic narrative then it follows the strange tale of Hoossein ben Hassan, son of Yusuff's friend and fellow pilgrim in Hadj, Hassan, who died during the pilgrimage. Dictated by strange talismanic scroll Hoossein joins an English family as a servant, subsequently he serves in the palace of the Mughal Emperor in Delhi, then joins the thugs in their flourishing business, nearly escaping the gallows by becoming an 'approver'—a government spy and witness, against the thugs as the British administration put an end to this nefarious practice. With his scope as an approver shrinking with the sinking fortunes of the thugs, Hoossein plans to settle down in Calcutta by marrying Yusuff's daughter Ameena. But strange circumstances lead him to be abducted by unknown goons to be transported to the West Indies as plantation labour. Hoossein subsequently comes back to India in the eventful year 1857, only to be drawn into the vortex of the storm and to be hanged by the victorious British, apparently fulfilling the destiny as it was dictated by the talismanic scroll in Hossein's possession. In Malet's narration of Hoossein's life from the point of view of a former British officer in India, the protagonist's identity always remains steeped in an intersectional cusp. On one hand there is the inscrutability of fate as it has been dictated by the scroll, on the other hand there is the openness and readiness to choose what comes in life. My work intends to explore Hoossein's sojourn to the West Indies, his journey overseas, how he fares in that strange climate, and what makes him come back. I treat Hoossein's journey as one of the earliest examples of a fictional representation of the South Asian diaspora, namely the phenomenon of the indentured labour system, which has received a masterly treatment in recent years in Amitav Ghosh's *Sea of Poppies* (2008).

In the historiography of Indian Rebellion it is noted that after the failure of the uprising a lot of rebels fled to the far away countries in order to escape the British wrath. But in *Lost Links in Indian Mutiny* we have a protagonist who does just the opposite. My study intends to explore the very site of Hoossein's diasporic commitment to his native land that propels him to sacrifice himself for a 'just' cause.

In the context of the scholarly literature on diaspora, Rajesh Rai and Peter Reeves identify the problem in situating the idea of forced labour and its role in defining, especially the Indian diaspora. Following the four fold criteria as laid down by Gerard Chaliand and Jean-Pierre Rageau in *The Penguin Atlas of Diasporas*, where 'the collective forced dispersion of a religious and/or ethnic group' tops the chart, Rai and Reeves comment,

> The evolution of the term in scholarly literature has adopted a pattern where the element of 'forced dispersion' has been downplayed to accommodate a variety of migrant experiences that nevertheless meet most of the underlying principles of the diaspora condition. (1)

Although it remains debatable to what extent the element of 'forced dispersion' can really be downplayed in defining the histories of dispersed communities, one thing can be agreed upon: that each diasporic pattern has a peculiarity of its own, that

> Certainly the experience of South Asian migrant communities born out of slavery, indenture or convict labour was vastly different from that of a

contemporary South Asian migrant IT professional who finds his or her niche in 'Silicon Valley', maybe to settle into 'NRI'-dom, maybe to return to the subcontinent. (2)

In 1833, slavery was abolished in the British Empire and the other European colonial powers followed suits in the following decades. To supply the huge demand for agricultural force in the plantations in the whole of south East Asia as well as the Caribbean, the system of indentured labour was installed by the colonial government in India. This system remained in place for eighty years before it was formally abolished in 1916. Laborers, mostly from rural areas, would initially sign up for a five-year contract. Many renewed their contracts, and a significant portion chose to stay permanently, deciding to accept a piece of land or a certain payment in lieu of their right to be shipped home.Isolated from the rest of the local population, colonial rulers housed the workers in barracks and regulated their lives in almost every regard, with severe punishments for disobedience and "insufficient work." The poor living conditions and almost unlimited employer control, led historian Hugh Tinker to label the system a "new form of slavery." According to Rajesh Rai and Andrea Marion Pinkney:

> Accordingly, British officials engaged in the mass recruitment of Indian laborers; labor recruitment was also practiced by the French and the Dutch but on a much smaller scale. Those recruited signed an indenture "agreement" — vernacularized in North Indian languages as girmit — and were thereafter known as "girmitiyas" (Mishra 122). The girmitiyas were transported to British colonies as far-flung as Mauritius and Fiji to East Africa and the Caribbean (e.g., Trinidad, Guyana, Jamaica). (66)

The argument concerning the status of the girmitiyas and the improvement that the system is capable to wrought into the lives of the hapless millions, is reflected in the contemporary missionary/colonial attitude, like the one that Rai and Pinkney quotes:

> They [the indentured labours] leave India full of prejudices, utterly ignorant, and as low in the scale of humanity as it is possible to imagine such things to be. They acquire in their transmarine experience habits of thought and independence, knowledge of improved means of cultivation, a taste for a higher order of amusements, a greater pride of personal appearance, and an

approach to manliness of character rarely if ever seen in the same class in their native villages. (MF Mout, 1852, qtd in Rai and Pinkney 67)

This idea of positive betterment the indentured system can bring can also be contrasted by the scepticism and suspicion of the dehumanizing process of it, as expressed by Charles Freer Andrews.

The novel selected for present study, *Lost links in Indian Mutiny* (1867) is apparently penned by a man, H P Malet, on whom little information is available[1]. But from the evidence in the novel what can be concluded is that he was critical of this 'emigration' and he blamed the 'mismanagement' of the British Empire in India as its cause.

> How was it that [coolie] emigration was ever permitted from the British Empire in the East? True, there is a large population, and famines are frequent local visitors; but there are large tracts of food producing lands only requiring inhabitants to convert them into use from the jungles which now occupy them; great works are sometimes stopped from insufficient labour — works that could benefit people, and enrich government; the price of labour in India has more than doubled within the last twelve years; yet in the face of this great demand for labour on spot, we have suffered many thousand able-bodied men to leave a country where they were and are wanted, to go to other regions (from whence only a small portion return) to satisfy demand for labour created by our own mismanagement[2]. (93-94)

It is this mismanagement of the labour force that serves as the backdrop of Hoossein's abduction and transportation to Jamaica. Early in the novel as Yusuff returns to his native place in India after Hadj, he is surprised by the phenomenal change that has taken place during his absence at the behest of the British administration in India. His observations, particularly in the improvement of the Bheel tribe, are noteworthy. He had the dread for the deadly and

---

[1] The title page of the novel describes the author H P Malet is introduced as E I C S. what follows is a dedication page where the work is dedicated to author's mother 'Dowager Lady Malet' who may find the adventurous escape of one of her son from the Afghans and the tiger reflected under a fictitious identity. The dedication is signed by H P Malet with the date 13th June, 1867.

[2] Malet's attitude may be contrasted with the character of Benjamin Brightwell Burnham in Ghosh's *Sea of Poppies* (2009), for whom both slavery and indenture are justified as a form of "emancipation" for Africans and Asians from indigenous tyranny.

murderous Bheels since his childhood. Only being assured by his friends he undertakes the journey through the land of Bheels.

> On these representations Yusuff started. He met with no adventures; but where anarchy and ruin had been, he found people contented and happy and recovering their prosperity. The encroaching jungles reduced, cultivation increased; and the chaos which existed for only a few years, was gone.
>
> "Who has done it all?" was the repeated enquiry of the Hadji.
>
> The only reply he received was, "It is all done by James Outram Saheb Bahadoor". (50)

The reference to the 'chaos' apparently refers to the rebellion of the Bheel tribal people in the Khandesh region during 1819-25[3]. The event also serves as a suitable example for Malet to illustrate how the military skill and personal influence of an able British administrator like Sir James Outram can befriend and convert a murderous Indian tribe into an Empire building force. It is the absence of such narratives in the years preceding the Revolt of 1857, that bolsters Malet's view of colonial 'mismanagement' which is also responsible for the migration of Indian labourers to other parts of the globe.

The way the Bheels were contained and controlled presages another major achievement of the East India Company's administration in India: that of the abolition of the Thugs. And Hoossein's unwilling sojourn to the West Indies is indirectly linked with this abolition. The picaresque narrative of Hoossein's life at one point lands him with a gang of Thugs. Hoossein becomes an expert 'thugee', till the gang is chased and apprehended by the police. Among the members of his group, Hoossein saves himself by offering to serve as a government approver, an informant and a testifier against the members of his own clan. In such a position, as he earns pension from the government, needless to say, he also earns the enmity of his own countrymen. So when the British

---

[3] For details of this movement and its outcome see, 'Imperial solution of a colonial problem: Bhils of Khandesh upto 1850' in *Modern Asian Studies*, Vol 41, No. 2. pp 343-67. Cambridge UP, 2007. https://www.jstor.org/stable/4132355.

administration, confident of the fact that it has put an end to the thugs in India, dismantles the department for the suppression of the thugees, Yussuf loses his job and his life becomes vulnerable.

Apparently it is this sense of vulnerability that urges Hoossein to travel to Calcutta, the capital city of Company's government in India, with a dream to settle down in life by marrying Ameena, the daughter of his father's friend Yussuf. In Calcutta it is presumably the old enemies of Hoossein who arrange for his abduction, to be sold as indentured labour and to be shipped to the Caribbean. For Malet there seems to be hardly any difference between the system of slavery (officially abolished from the British Empire in 1833) and replced by the system of indentured labour or 'coolie'. The lineal descendant of the prophet Mohammed, Yussuf finds himself as an 'involuntary emigrant coolie', in a state of drug induced stupor, on the deck of a ship moving towards the ocean, at the break of dawn. Before Yussuf arrives on board, an unknown voice, apparently that of a white man and a veteran in slave trading, expresses his preference for the coolies over the slaves. For him coolie trading is preferred, firstly because it is officially less troublesome as 'it is cheap into the bargain' as 'it's called a voluntary departure'. Secondly, unlike the slave trade where the price of slaves varied according to their age, sex and constitution, in this new labour market the trader is paid 'by the heads'. Thirdly, the 'oriental coolies' are 'better than the regular niggers' because 'they have some civilization' (81).

Malet's perfunctory presentation of the recruiting process of the indentured labourers, on the eve of Hoossein's departure, stands in sharp contrast to the well researched reconstruction of the circumstances that lead to the departure of Deeti and Kalua in Amitav Ghosh's *Sea of Poppies*. Still the novel is capable of giving a vivid picture of the miseries the hapless, poor Indians were subjected to due to the greed of a few. Hoossein's calm and almost stoic acceptance of his fate not only makes him survive the perilous sea journey, but also earns him the distinction of serving as the apprentice to the doctor on board. Malet comments that as a former thug, it is his knowledge of corpses that makes him so indispensable for the young lad Harry, who, originally recruited as the doctor's apprentice without any idea of the medical profession, had to serve as the ship's doctor, as the real doctor backed off at the last moment. The fellow Indian workers, who almost dreaded him, give him the title 'great medicine' with which Hoossein lands in Jamaica. From a murderous thug to healer and a medicine man, Hoossein remains nonchalant to this transformation, as he feels guided by a strong sense of destiny.

In Jamaica Hoossein lands with a handsome amount of money that he earned as the doctor's assistant, and immediately after landing in Kingston, he, with the help of another Muslim living in Jamaica, obtains the job of the 'moonsif' or the overseer of a group of 'coolies' in a plantation, at a distance from Kingstown. Hoossein serves in this position for three years, during which, as Malet describes, he makes a good amount of money by working as intermediary between the workers and the management of the plantation, with help of his English speaking skills, often exploiting the sixty 'coolies' under him, by collecting 'dustooris' and pleasing and placating the superiors with bribes. Malet mentions the Bengalis who paid Hoossein to conceal 'his little delinquencies', while the Mussalman gave him contributions pertaining to religious purposes.

In the context of Hoossein's experience in Jamaica Malet digresses to launch a critique of the idea of the Abolition of Slavery from the British Empire. Though Malet attempts to remain ambivalent about the benefits of the Abolition, his account betrays sympathy for the slave-driven economy of the plantations. His suspicion of the motives behind the movement that called for the Abolition is clearly visible.

> Jamaica was a very desirable possession; no soil was more productive, few productions more lucrative. We found a slave population on it, ...When opulence and trade in due time attracted attention to the locality, it was discovered by those who had no self-interest in it, that the slaves were badly treated; that they were whipped, scantily fed, uneducated and demoralized. It was a fine opportunity for the display of pure philanthropy; so fine speeches were made, and a large quantity of agitation was supplied to get English nation into proper sense of liberality and propriety — the one in reference to interfering with matters not belonging to them; the other only extending to a shadow, called compensation, for serious losses caused by

the emancipation of the slaves, which the Great Britain, in her pride affected. (96-97)

Malet's rage not only targets the Abolitionists but also hints at the huge compensations paid by the British government to the slave owners for setting their slaves at liberty. The recent researches reveal that the complex politics that involved the negotiations for the reparations, benefitted not only the slave owners in the West Indies, but also the Abolitionists; and the capital that was obtained by these slave owning families was reinvested into the British industrial enterprises, for example, the British railways.

As regards to the slaves or 'coolies' of African or Indian origin, Malet sharp opinion labels both of them as races inferior to that of the Europeans, and only fit to serve the whites in menial positions.

> Whether England was right or wrong in emancipation, it is not my object to prove. One thing is certain—that the sweat was wiped from the brow of the African, but not from that of the Asiatic; no good can come when idleness is encouraged in any one[4]. (100)

Malet's digression is followed by an account of Hoossein's successful career in Jamaica followed by his desire to leave his job after three years and to explore the territory. In his 'idleness', Hoossein's come into contact with an 'old negro (one Sambo)' who, once was a slave but now lives a life of liberty along other such in a hillside village. Sambo invites Hoossein to be one of them, a member of their 'happy party'. Hoossein and Sambo in their lazy tour travels through an idyllic landscape for a few days before they can reach the village. From Hoossein's point of view Malet makes us see the reality of the life of the slaves after the Abolition.

---

[4] Malet's attitude of racial superiority at this point reflect the world view of the profiteering English missionary Benjamin Burnham:
Isn't that what the mastery of the white man means for the lesser races? As I see it . . . the Africa trade was the greatest exercise in freedom since God led the children of Israel out of Egypt. Consider . . . the situation of a so-called slave in the Carolinas—is he not more free than his brethren in Africa, groaning under the rule of some dark tyrant? . . . When the doors of freedom were closed to the African, the Lord opened them to a tribe that was yet more needful of it—the Asiatick. (*Sea of Poppies* 79)

> Hoossein sat down to look at the scene, rich and glorious. All around were the ample gifts of nature—a garden of Eden, tilled by the careless hands by those who once were slaves, who in their servitude had not acquired industry of ambition, who were content to cultivate to such an extent as was necessary, ...Time was passed basking in the sunshine, card playing, drinking, smoking, and an occasional fit of religious enthusiasm under the title of "Revival", (106-07)

Hoossein gets charmed into this life of degenerated idleness like the lotos eaters in Odyssey. Apparently it is the inhuman barbaric cruelty of both Hoossein and Sambo allows them to fraternize. In their mutual exchange of horrifying tales Hoossein narrates his hunting experiences as a merciless thug, where as Sambo tales of atrocities committed by the rebel slaves during the slave rebellion of 1831 in Jamaica, which is also known as the Baptist War[5]. The allusion to the rebellion of the slaves that had thoroughly shaken the prosperity and tranquility of Jamaica, is provided as an evidence by Malet, in his case against Abolition.

Although in Malet's account Sambo's culpability in the Baptist War remains dubious, it is he who tutors Hoossein about the vulnerability of the English. No wonder the chapter in the novel is titled 'The Asiatic learns a Lesson from the African'.

> Great men! Said the sable philosopher...they [the English] are not a great people, they are a narrow minded selfish race; jealous and distrustful, they are all traders and will sacrifice everything for money....they have strong laws and they are brave people, but they seldom take advantage of their bravery. They will convict a man of murder, but will decline to hang him. (112-13)

The story of the rebellion of the slaves somewhat alters Hoossein's views on the invincibility of the British colonial power. He is even invited by Sambo to forge an alliance between the Asiatic and the African that can oust the English from the island.

> Will you help us? ...See all these shall be ours, we will turn them out of it...We have no home but this; we will keep it as our own, and you, you

---

[5] For details on Baptist War see https://www.blackpast.org. For the influence of the War on the British media embroiled in the 'West Indian Question' see *Jamaican Revolts in British Press and Politics 1760-1865* by Thomas R Day (Master of Arts Thesis submitted at Virginia Commonwealth University, 2016).

were stolen from your friends and your country. Does no feeling of revenge rankle in your breast? We are ready to strike. (115)

Hoossein cautiously resists the temptation by calling the time is not ripe for such a strike. Sambo angrily reacts by calling Hoossein as useless as a tortoise. Hoossein remembers the talismanic scroll that has likened him to a tortoise and he decides to head back towards India. But one thing is sure: his Jamaican sojourn has sowed the seeds of anti-British rebellion him. Once back in India, as the later narrative shows, Hoossein waits for the cause and opportunity to strike against the British, which is ostensibly provided in 1857. Later in the novel when Ameena tries to counsel and dissuade Hoossein from fighting the English, he replies: "the Black people on the other side of the world have done it, so will we do it [overthrowing the British from India] (298). This, I presume, to be what Malet was hinting as 'lost link' in connection with the Rebellion in India in 1857. What is strange is that in the historiography as well as theories on Indian 'Mutiny' such a connection is rarely alluded to.

S D Singh in his colossal study of the novels written on Indian Mutiny comments:

> *Lost Links in Indian Mutiny* by H P Malet is a loose kind of rambling tale recounting the adventures of Hoossein during the Mutiny...The book cannot be considered impressive in any way, though it gives a fair idea of the life of those times. (40)

Singh is dismissive of the novel seemingly because it contains little reference to Indian Mutiny. However he has apparently nothing to comment about Hoossein's Jamaican sojourn and its relation to the Indian Mutiny.

In a more recent study of the literature of the Indian Mutiny, *The Indian Mutiny and the British Imagination*, Gautam Chakravarty also fails to note Hoossein's voyage and describes the novel as, 'a diffuse romance with a large cast of Indian characters [that] meanders from Company's military campaigns against the Afghans and the Sikhs to the rebellion' (5) Apparently the trajectory of a fertile British imagination suggesting a possible connection between the slave revolt in Jamaica in 1831 and the Indian Mutiny of 1857, as found in Malet's *Lost Links in Indian Mutiny*, remains unmatched in the body of narratives written in the wake of the Indian Mutiny.

For a reader of the Mutiny narratives it is interesting to note that Sambo's description of the brutal treatment meted out to their white masters and their families—the burning of houses, atrocities committed to white children, the brutal rape and the horrifying dismemberment of white women—finds an echo in the narration of the Indian Mutiny. In Malet's narrative it foreshadows what Hoossein encounters later as the Mutiny breaks out:

> The Sepoy lines were all in flames, the bungalows of the officers fiercely blazing,... they[the Indian rebels]were not contented with simple death, they hacked, they tore, they tormented. There were hissing of flames, the screams of the tortured, and roars of laughter; men demanding death, women imploring to be killed; amidst all this, there lay the mutilated body of white children. The reality of the scene surpassed Hoossein's ideas of horror, and almost eclipsed his desire for vengeance, but he went with the roaring crowd. (303-04)

It is this sense of alienation and utter confusion Hoossein that accompanies Hoossein as he tries to save Ameena, his childhood friend and now a part of the Captain Eglington's family, from the marauding band of his own rebel consorts. Hoossein is ultimately betrayed and is overpowered by the British. In the mockery of a trial Hoossein fails register a case for himself with the argument that the murder of which he is convicted is committed in an attempt to save a woman [presumably Ameena]. Hoossein is summarily hanged in a tree with one bough, just like the other rebels. In this death, which he regards as a fulfillment of his destiny as dictated by that mysterious scroll, we find something unmistakably sad. It the sadness that permeates all diasporas, as Vijay Mishra has so evocatively put it:

> All diasporas are unhappy, but every diaspora is unhappy in its own way. Diasporas refer to people who do not feel comfortable with their non-hyphenated identities as indicated on their passport. Diasporas are people who would want to explore the meaning of the hyphen, but perhaps not press the hyphen too far for fear that this would lead to massive communal schizophrenia. They are precariously lodged within an episteme of real or imagined displacements, self-imposed sense of exile; they are haunted by

spectres, by ghosts arising from within that encourage irredentist or separatist movements. (1)

The diasporic sadness of an Indian rebel like Hoossein, is to be located in the domain of, what Vijay Mishra calls the diasporic imaginary, the mourning of the impossible. From the author's point of view, Malet's narrative, in itself is case of one such mourning ;it is a mourning of a possibility of a grand material development and prosperity, that could have been shared by both the colonizer and the colonized, had it not been disrupted by the rebellions and racial conflicts, not only in India but also in the other parts of British Empire.

References

Brah, Avtar. *Cartographies of Diaspora Contesting Identities*. London: Routledge, 1996. Print.

Chakravarty, Gautam. *The Indian Mutiny and the British Imagination*. Cambridge: Cambridge UP, 2006. Print.

Ghosh, Amitav. *Sea of Poppies*. New Delhi; Penguin India, 2009. Print.

Malet, H P. *Lost Links in Indian Mutiny*. London: T Cautley Newby, 1867. Print.

Mishra, Vijay. *The Literature of the Indian Diaspora: Theorizing the Diasporic Imaginary*. London & New York: Routledge, 2007. Print.

Rai, Rajesh and Marion Pinkney. 'The Girmitiyas' Journey in Amitav Ghosh's *Sea of Poppies*' in *History, Narrative, and Testimony in Amitav Ghosh's Fiction*, ed. Chitra Sankaran. New York; State University of New York P, 2012. Print.

Rai, Rajesh, and Peter Reeves. "Introduction" In Rajesh Rai and Peter Reeves, eds., The *South Asian Diaspora: Transnational Networks and Changing Identities*. London: Routledge, 2008. Print.

Tinker, Hugh. A*New System of Slavery: The Export of Indian Labourers Overseas, 1830–1920*. London: Oxford University Press for the Institute of Race Relations, 1974. Print.

Singh, S. D. *Novels of the Indian Mutiny* New Delhi: Arnold-Heineman India, 1980. Print.

Un-blinding Doctrine and Exiting 'Molar Lines' in Arnold's *The Scholar Gipsy*

Nirjhar Sarkar

Resolve to be thyself, and know, that he/ Who finds himself, loses his misery"
— Arnold

I must create a system or be enslaved by another man's
— Blake

In a nuanced study on Matthew Arnold's "ethnographic politics", Robert Young has reminded us that Arnold's culture is a good deal more complex than mere "propagation of high culture in the service of an organicist nationalism" (Young, 1995, p. 55)[1]. Finding Arnoldian 'culture' to be a product of conflict and dissonance, of complex and contradictory experiences, Young found the proximity of Western and Oriental experiences to be a counter to the purist notion of culture. What riveted Arnold more was the wisdom in peripheral locations—its (in)appropriate behavior and knowledge, located down on hierarchy. He had deemed it necessary to incorporate what is 'outside 'or 'beyond' the realm of aesthetic within the institution of culture and never lost sight of the fact that the maintenance of established social order might also entail spatial deviance. Eager to know the margins, he shared his family's love of magic and mesmerism as it offered a joyful release from the constraints of ordinary, mundane experience. This transgressive energy of what Said calls "subjugated knowledge" had offered him critical distance from parochiality and flagrant misdirection of intellectual thought. Arnold always insisted on traffic between mobility and territorialism- the mutually enriching

---

[1] Robert Young's *Colonial Desire* famously articulates new theoretical considerations of culture as participatory in a conflictual economy-transgressive of racial lines in the context of the Nineteenth Century, in the heydays of British Empire. Here, he devotes a section on countering the over-simplified reading of Arnold's culture and its inherently syncretic nature than ordinarily conceived.

ends of the cultural spectrum. And he also staunchly believed that national culture is defined by an antithetical mixture of cultural and racial differences. The inflow and outflow of different communities and the criss-cross of their cultures have, in fact, shaped the European society since the 12th century. And its resultant syncretic traditions running counter to the standard system of knowledge have captivated the creative imagination of the Victorian artists. Functioning as mysterious, elusive 'others' the Gypsies have existed, both literally and metaphorically, on the verges of the Victorian society and through geo-temporal movement have disrupted the stable locations of identity.

The vagrancy of the Gypsy lifestyle was not only at variance with the structure and mechanism of capitalist society but also with the nineteenth century state apparatus of culture and education. The constraints and limitations of formal system in Victorian social and political life, in fact, could be uncovered by hidden discourse of Gypsy life. Robert Knox's controversial study *The Races of Man* (1850) eloquently affirmed that race was a major determinant of behavior and character and sketched the Gypsy life in terms of bestiality and free instinctuality. George Eliot's *The Spanish Gypsy* even in making reversal of child- stealing stereotype describes Fedelama's dance in terms of sexuality and sensuousness. Proliferation of racist stereotypes like these, depending on 'fixity' and "ideological construction of otherness" (Bhabha, 2012, p. 95), could only reify the national selfhood vaunted by British imperial ideology. Disruptive of such stable, coherent articulation of national identity, this strange and interesting race of Gypsy or Romaunder underscores the presence of "nation of others... gatherings of exiles and emigres and refugees; gathering on the edge of 'foreign' cultures" (Bhabha, 2012, p. 199).[2] From the mid-eighteenth to the early twentieth century the Gypsy figures in Britain were not recognized as national subjects as their foreign origins were at odds with the sedentary precepts of the nation-state.

---

[2] In his concern for discourse of nationalism Bhabha in a chapter entitled "DissemiNation: Time, narrative and margins of the modern nation" (in *Location of Culture*) points to the limitations of linear equivalence and historicist idea of nation as a cultural force and assumption of its synchronous time.

The historical construction of Gypsy identity with criminality and dirt and systematic vilification and demonization of their customs had immured them in an enclosed space. But these gatherings of scattered people and scattered communities, their myths and fantasies stirred interest in Victorian artists disrupting binary structure of social antagonism. Before Arnold, Walter Scott had already found in the Gypsy collective an opportunity for the British to learn how to recognize the fellow members of the community. Arnold, too, was a virulent opposer of the narrowness of the sectorial squabbles that had beset the educational system with its soul-killing dogmas. He knew that the abundance of directionless energy and mindless expansion could be critiqued by substantial re-working of the exemplary story of the Gypsy who had "one aim, one business, one desire;" By making forays into 'other 'terrain, Arnold reanimates the legend of Oxford scholar. Glanvil's 'pre-text' in lyrical transposition radiates alternative wisdom here to the prevailing utilitarianism of Victorian society:

> [...] Gypsy communities exhibit a fluidity that does not place itself easily within the idea of a community as a feature of the nation state. Such fluidity is a strength that binds individuals, families and wider networks together in the face of hostility within a context in which the response to such hostility within a context in which the response to such hostility may involve movement, dispersal or the concealment of identity (Bhopal & Mayers, 2008, p. 15)

Benefiting from his father's reformative zeal, Arnold as a thinker committed his ideas to overthrow the long-standing traditions. An active public figure of his day, he steered culture to remove misery, error and ennoble mankind in general. To carry forward the nation, he grew sceptic of micro-discipline of the institution- its multiple discourses, rules and striated space. In poor, Oxford Scholar's choice to embrace the Gypsy values, livelihood and practices which also becomes confrontation with the mechanism of confinement and stratification of academic learning, Arnold had found a redemptive energy from the formalism and pedagogy of the institution and a possibility of "opening of the soul and imagination" (Reports on Elementary School, 1878):

> Who, tired of knocking at preferment's door,
> One summer-morn forsook
> His friends, and went to learn the gipsy-lore,
> And roam'd the world with that wild brotherhood,
> And came, as most men deem'd, to little good,
> But came to Oxford and his friends no more. (35-40)

Freedom of thought that fleshes out in purposeless wandering and the perpetual immobility of the Gypsy scholar could inspire a question in Arnold, reminiscent of Empedocles—whether he has always been "free/Lived ever in the light of my own soul". Brushing aside shared academic values he was drawn towards the cultural aliens and peregrine lifestyles, illuminated by light of his own soul. As a sage and prophet of Victorian education, Arnold's paramount concern was to build critical opposition between man's instinctive urge to develop freely and inhibitive forces of industrial capital. And it demanded moving away from ground or foundation of Culture and its essentialist, homogenising pattern. In switching to free-roaming life, in forsaking academic glory the Gypsy may be said to be steering towards 'active individuation'—as "the nineteenth century was also a time in which writers, artists and commentators evoked a prelapsarian world of unchanging rural bliss in order to encounter the squalor of mushrooming urban life and industrial filth they encountered on a daily basis" (Taylor, 2004, p.15)[3]. Arnold begins his search for the Gypsy in the guise of a shepherd in the 'high field's corner', "moon- blanch'd green", stressing the need of leading an innocent, idyllic life. In his defter-working, pastoral convention is added further depth- it becomes a powerful exposure to the complexity and corruption of Industrial England in the Victorian age. Reconciliation between man and nature in the abiding rural scene around Oxford proves to be liberatory against the circumscribed space of University where mind and vision tend to expand in a dynamic flux of 'becoming'. Sidestepping the institutional discourses of attaining well-being

---

[3] In *Another Darkness, Another Dawn*, rather than seeing them as untouched by history, Taylor linked these outsiders (Romani, Gypsy tribe) to momentous historical phases like Enlightenment, Expansion of Nation-state, Holocaust and their offering resistance to spatial violence inherent in these epochal events.

and its regime of truth, Arnold's hero gravitates towards lore, magic of Oriental charm which interrogates the 'education of head' — so widely professed in Victorian normative ethics. Eager to form a personhood through imbibing 'other' subjects of knowledge, the scholar's venture gives vent to de-territorialisation of the knowledge system. His commitment to Gypsy styles renders rigorous codes of intellectual practices and moral behavior vulnerable. Engaging with her own political and artistic evolution vis-à-vis her 'marginality', eminent feminist thinker, bell hooks points out in "Marginality as a Site of Resistance":

> Marginality is the space [site] of resistance. Enter that space. Let us meet there. Enter that space. We greet you as liberators (1989, p. 152).

She insists that such spaces promulgate counter hegemonic cultural practice with 'radical openness' — the kind of openness that envisions alternative cultural practices.[4] For Arnold's hero, too, 'radical openness' is offered by adoption of alternative life-style; as a counter-hegemonic cultural practice it offers a way to travel out of one's place and push against the structure of ideological domination. To transform the present reality Arnold found non-striated, provincial, pastoral locations more enabling.

Pushed by oppressive boundaries and the molar/macro structure of academia, Arnoldian hero makes a radical departure to 'unaddressed' space. In the rapidly expanding industrial society all institutions were plotted in a "homogeneous metric space" (Colebrook, 2007, p. 44). Deleuze and Guattari had found society as a regime of coding which aims to bring to the fore certain fixed ways of existence while relegating other malleable ways. Refusing to be shaped by structured habits of thinking or hankering after 'intellectual throne' the Gypsy sought to be illuminated with heavenly wisdom — "Thou waitest for the spark from heaven!" Through estrangement he has sought the bliss of living with

---

[4] Bell hooks celebrates the 'margin' as a locus of 'radical openness' and its immense transformative potential which help my argument at the end that margin — such as Gypsy story in Victorian England — had the power to move beyond the border and affirm its presence as disruption. (341-343 in *Out there: Marginalization and contemporary cultures.*)

intuition; he makes a promise to return to his own folks only after endowing himself with skills and practices of the Gypsy folk. Perpetually mobile and evading, he is denied of any territorialisation in the final stanzas:

> Then fly our greetings, fly our speech and smiles!
> — As some grave Tyrian trader, from the sea, (231-232)

In charting the scholar's movement the dialectic of departure and arrival is rendered problematic — as every nomadic life is described supremely 'deterritorializing' by Deleuze and Guattari. Instead of reading the scholar's movement in terms of dualisms like inside-outside, inclusion- exclusion, we may find the tropes of 'space' and 'lines'- famously articulated in seminal study of Deleuze and Guattari, *A Thousand Plateaus* — more helpful. As both the thinkers had found life as ubiquitously segmented and every entity as segmented and classified subject, according to them, this segmentarity is of two types — rigid and supple. Rigid segmentation works through different units, mostly binaristic and exclusively disjunctive. In terms of territory they identify 'striated' and 'smooth' space as mutually exclusive and contrastive. Institutions like Schools or University are governed by a set of codes and provide the subject the assurance that the more they conform to these rules, they will be positioned in hierarchical arrangement. Such molar line is identified as "line of rigid segmentarity on which everything seems calculable and foreseen" (Deleuze & Guattari, 1988, p. 229). In a very instructive passage of his famous foreword to the *A Thousand Plateaus* (in the Paperback Edition Published in 2003), Brian Massumi succinctly expresses the differing features of 'smooth' and 'striated' space:

> [S]tate space is "striated'or gridded Movement in it is confined as by gravity to a horizontal plane, and limited by the order of that plane to present path between fixed and identifiable points. Nomad space is 'smooth' or open-ended. One can rise up at any point and move to any other. Its mode of distribution is the *nomos*; arraying oneself in an open space (hold the street), as opposed to the *logos* of entrenching oneself in a closed space (hold the fort). (XI)

The roving scholar was already 'tired' of knocking 'studious walls' and grew apathetic towards status and identity involved in academic pursuit. Because in such territory, defined also as 'state space', movement becomes confined by an order of plane or determined path which traverses fixed and identifiable points. In Deleuzian terms, in 'state-less' society work takes place in a complete antithetical way from the striated space-time of capitalist formation. Forsaking the privilege of education and wealth, 'intellectual throne' that emanates from utilitarian fervor for elite academia and popular Victorian moral assessment and decision-making, the poor scholar veered away to 'shy retreats' and 'retired ground'. Defined by movement, the space produced thus is 'smooth' where laws or logic of hierarchy do not operate but create through movement positions and lines. Averse to structured and ordered conception of existence and molar aggregate of institution, he roams without purpose and eludes contact with old mates and very fleetingly appears among the rural folks. In such a life movement is primary and the environment is non-structured and without intrinsic organization. In the analytic account of Deleuze and Guattari, "smooth space is occupied by intensities, wind and noise, forces and sonorous and tactile qualities, as in the desert, steepe or ice... Striated space is canopied by the sky as measure and by the measurable visual qualities deriving from it" (1988, p. 55). Referring to the Greek concept of open space of *nomos* (like pre-urban countryside, mountainside, plateau) they mention how such spaces were opposed to the *polis* — city' or 'town'. It is in such spaces that the ordered conception of existence could be destabilized as their secret art ran counter to dominant British culture[5]. And in such the company of the Gypsy folks a new series of desires and relations intersect to celebrate a life which is "Free from the sick fatigue, the languid doubt". It is in such imaginative quest unencumbered by traditional authorities in the rural backwaters that liberatory space may be opened up. The intrinsic boundaries of ordered academy

---

[5] In all of their major writings, Deleuze and Guattari argue that culture, like a body of water, spreads towards available space or trickles downwards towards new spaces through fissures, gaps.

life crumbles and dissolves to pave the way for nomadic distribution—for encounters where an alternative order of existence may be articulated. Gypsy's forsaking of academic life is suggestive of curative, healing touch to the afflicted generation; rather than active subjectification, it enables new lines of subjectivity through imaginative quest. As in a different context while analyzing Deluezean 'affect', Nadine Boijkovac observes:

> To truly 'have faith in this world' is to believe in the world at hand rather than an illusionary transcendence, and to discover a new 'health', one that might explode and refold damaging illusions that inhibit creativity, life and thought (2013, 20)

Arnold's diagnosis of the ills of his society pointed out through metaphors of 'sickness', 'infections' are strongly resonant of the afflicted societal state as experienced in his time. And it might have recovered 'new health' in a nomadic life which inspired the scholar in (un)learning normative ethics and whole-hearted commitment to Gypsy values.

No less than spatial grids, temporal grids are also eliminated in Arnold's poem as past and present overlap and intersect; as the poet's search for Gypsy unfolds, past and present, time and timelessness are seen to be poised against each other and lines between them increasingly blur. In re-imagining Glanvil's hero, Arnold's poem makes a smooth juxtaposition of "the timeless and the temporal, the past and the present, permanence and the change, knowledge and experience, the ideal and the real" (Gareth, 2006, p. 108). At the outset the gypsy is the centre of 'oft-read tale' whose story the poet has taken up after two hundred years—the object of local legend as an elusive figure who left Oxford associates to join the 'gipsy crew' and in rumours he still roams 'shy retreats'. Arnold's rumination engages at the outset with Gypsy's non-existence for he is one who has not yet felt the "lapse of hours":

> Two hundred years are flown...
> And thou from earth art gone
> Long since, and in some quiet churchyards laid (130-135)

But when the quest moves forward, chronologically conceived historical time is occluded—Gypsy returns haunting the space of fringe territories, roaming among innocent folks and is seen in glimpses to 'housewives' and 'children' only to disappear again. The legend is reanimated to stress the perennial 'freshness' of the Scholar's energy. He is invoked as a redeemer of the numbness and perplexity—the blights of the Victorian age:

> At some lone homestead in the Cumner hills,
> Where at her open door the housewife darns,
> Thou hast been seen, or hanging on a gate
> o watch the threshers in the mossy barns.
> children, who early range these slopes and late
> or cresses from the rills,
> Have known thee eyeing, all an April-day,
> the springing pasture and the feeding kine;
> and mark'd thee, when the stars come out and shine,
> through the long dewy grass move slow away. (101-110)

These glimpses underline the Gypsy's 'immortal lot'—one who is 'exempt from age' and who survives beyond 'Glanvil's page'; here, objective, measurable aspects of time, is surmounted and fixed, identifiable points of linear time dissolves to shed light on imperishable aspect of the Gypsy's life. Straddling between past and present, dead and living, the poem revises the legend into a site of collision between idyllic dreams and hard facts. In the organized framework the temporal continuity and its homogenisation define every single action; in contrast, Gypsy's time is listless, eternally lethargic. In the final section as the gypsy is exhorted to 'fly', to disappear from the Oxford milieu or surrounding, like the Tyrian trader who has made use of his own dark, secluded environment. These intersecting timelines are not merely evocative of nostalgia of living but experiencing what Bhabha has called 'the past-present' of migrant life. It also fleshes out the unresolved tension between reality and ideality; between perfection and change. By going into the depths of the sea— another form of non- striated space can the trader shelter himself from the blights of the 'burning plain' and in the process disrupts the flow of time. In the nomadic life time is experienced as polar opposite of the homogeneous, synchronous time—what Bhabha in his famous discussion on "The Time of the Nation" calls "gathering the past in a ritual of revival" (2012, p. 199). This arrangement and rearrangements of temporal units, navigation between different temporal planes underlines why life should not be seen 'in fixed and immobile terms' (Colebrook, 2002, XX)[6] and why an event is not merely located in time but generative of a 'new line of time' as life is always transformative. As Elizabeth Grosz observes in her introduction to *Feminism, Nature, Power:* "The force of time is not just a contingent characteristic of the living, but is the dynamic impetus that enables life to become, to always be in the process of becoming, something other than it was"(2005, p. 8). The active force of time in Arnold's elegy is not subordinated by making the event as past only; in fact, the scholar's commitment to Gypsy life is not grounded upon one single intent but on its dynamic impetus.

Quite unlike George Eliot or Walter Scott, Arnold does not portray Gypsy in terms of virtue or vice—as mere agent of morality; rather he takes up a Westerner's radical departure as a historical event and endows it with an experience of 'becoming'- gypsy. In his re-presentation of Glanvil's story, the lyric appears to be a narrative of difference and 'becoming' and not merely a story of 'difference-from-the-same'. Culture, described as process of 'growing and becoming' by Arnold himself is found also to be steering towards "perfection which consists in becoming something rather than in having something, in an outward condition of the mind and spirit, not in an outward set of circumstances" (Arnold, 1948, p.48). Living in a disjointed age, Arnold had reposed faith upon flux of change and their consequent paradigm shifts. Deleuzean formulation of 'becoming'—so central to all art experiences—is not merely a journey between two different states or terms, approaching finality. Here, in place of reaching a final state the lyric breaks off with the exhortation to 'fly'—"fly our paths, our feverish contact fly"which is not merely

---

[6] In *A Thousand Plateaus,* Deleuze and Guattari refer to life's production of 'lines of flight' where mutations and transformations occur to challenge life as an ordered consequence with a pre-given set of possibilities.

eluding but of disappearing into a distance — as 'fly' is analogous to the French term *Fuite*. It is not merely the sartorial signs — roaming in "In hat of antique shape, and cloak of grey,/The same Gypsy Wore" — that is suggestive of imbibing alternate lifestyles. Even after deserting the society he grew up in, he commits that upon learning the skill of the gipsy he will disseminate it to the world:

> And I, "he said," the secret of their art,
> When fully learn'd, will to the world impart;
> But it needs heaven-sent moments for this skill. (48-50)

Such 'becoming' is not merely imitating another entity or getting transformed by entering into the discredited zone of subculture. By crossing social fields the Gypsy has articulated a new vision of truth and faith. As a subject he has not only withdrawn from the 'majority' but also he would return after due period from the cultural location of the 'minor'. These two simultaneous movements or 'indissociable blocks of becoming' casts the experience of Scholar as a kind of 'becoming' — Gypsy of a non-Gypsy. An illustrative passage from *A Thousand Plateaus* will clarify the point further:

> Becoming-Jewish, becoming-woman, etc. therefore imply two simultaneous movements, one by which a term (the subject) is withdrawn from the majority and another by which a term (the medium of agent) rises up from the minority. There is an asymmetrical and indissociable block of becomings, a block of alliance; the two "Mr. Kleins", the Jew and Non-Jew, enter into a becoming- Jewish..." (p. 339-345)

This passage occurs in Chapter 10, titled "Memories and Becomings, Points and Ranks" where Deleuze and Guattari cite the story of Arthur Miller's novel, *Focus* and Losey's film, *Mr. Klein* to argue that the axis of transformation is in the process of how a non-Jew who becomes Jewish — one who is swept up and rent apart from the standard of measure. Much in the same way the adventure of the Oxford scholar may be called a story of 'becoming' of a non-Gypsy in relation to the White/ Western man which constitutes the majority. In navigating two different, conflictual modes of existence, the roving scholar has eliminated the notion of simple departure and arrival. Rather than inhabiting either side of the dualism, he has crossed cultural borders to live with the energies of what Deleuze and Guattari call "the intermezzo" (p. 323). Such zones may be described in the Deleuzian term as "line of Flight" — a path of mutation which relieves the subject of rigid segmentarity of 'Molar Lines' and all forms of 'territorialisation'. It is here that "life reconstitutes its stakes, confronts new obstacles, invents new paces, new alternatives" (Deleuze & Guattari, p. 500). Such lines enable the process of creative transformation after which one is no longer the same person; the impoverished scholar after being sucked up in Gypsy life never returns to the company of Oxford dons. It is analogous to the hero of Fitzgerald in *The Crack Up* who undergoes a change to emerge as 'the new person" — the one who is no longer the same subject. About Arnold's hero it may be said "his goals are not the same, nor are the values which would underpin his strong evaluation" (Parr, 2010, p. 118). Uninhibited by the institutional codes, undivided by boundaries his free-flowing energy exhibits why one's self must be conceived as constantly changing assemblage of flows. In nomadic societies productive activity proceeds under a regime of 'free action' — as underscored in apparent impracticality and uselessness of Gypsy's gesture and movement. Such life is clearly sundered from the molar organization of the state or what G. Wilson Knight had called the Dionysian power of the Gypsy life — set apart from the Apollonian power of the Oxford life. Stripping himself of greater knowledge or what Descartes calls 'rigorous knowledge' or 'systematic body of knowledge' (*scientia*) and drawn towards lesser grades of conviction or 'perfectibility of knowledge' (*persasio*), the Gypsy has chosen to confront the "competition and the battle of life" (Dyson, 1972, p. 50), the ascendancy of 'truth' over wisdom. In learning the lore and magic imagination takes wing; it offers therapeutic relief from 'sick fatigue' and 'languid doubt'. It is in living the perpetual outsider's life that "Gypsy communities exhibit a fluidity that does not place itself easily within the idea of a fluidity is a strength that binds individuals, families and wider networks together in the face of hostility within a context in which the response to such hostility may involve movement, dispersal or the concealment of identity" (Bhopal & Mayers, 2008, p. 28). In such anti-intellectual life, Arnold had found an opportunity of disruption to the conventional mode of existence, a gate-way to wholly intense, molecular life.

Art at its most creative mutates as well as experiments, producing new paradigms of subjectivity. In critical and creative thinking of his time, Arnold had always brought to the fore transformative potential of popular legends and myths. Instead of being bound by abstract concepts or dogmatic notions of culture, he was unrelentingly exploring new practices and actions and for renewal of faith in the 'darkling plain'. Because he knew that new hopes and wishes could cure the ills of his society one can overcome 'disappointments new' — as in Deleuze's account, one leaves behind the 'molar' to enter a 'molecular' phase of existence or break free of the fixed identity and conventions of over-coded life and all its blinding doctrines. Despite ubiquitous presence of ideological 'border' of class and race, Arnold had engaged with the disturbing presence of the 'foreign' and 'stranger' within the sanctum of culture. Where power only builds walls, entrenched opinions immure us in a closed space. It is 'lines of flight' — running away from regulatory lines of our lives and creating 'molecular possibilities' — that imbues the Arnoldian hero with energy to overcome the submission to system, fixed practice and make confrontation possible with what is already ordered.

Acknowledgement

All the textual quotations are derived from *Arnold-Poetical Works*, edited by C.B. Tinker and H.F. Lowry (London: Oxford UP, 1949)

Works Cited

Arnold, M. (1948). *Culture and Anarchy* ed. By John D. Wilson. Cambridge: Cambridge UP.

Beckey, T. (2004). *Another Darkness, Another Dawn: A History of Gypsies, Roma and Travellers*. London: Reaktion Books.

Bhabha, H. (2012). *Location of Culture*. London: Routledge.

Bhopal, K., & Myers, M. (2008). *Insiders, outsiders and others: Gypsies and identity*. Hertfordshire: University of Hertfordshire Press.

Boljkovac, N. (2013). *Untimely Affects: Gilles Deleuze and an Ethics of Cinema*. Edinburgh: Edinburgh University Press.

Colebrook, C. (2007). *Giles Deleuze. Routledge Critical Thinkers*. London: Routledge.

—. (2002). *Understanding Deleuze*. Crows Nest, N.S.W: Allen & Unwin.

Deleuze, G., & Guattari, F. (1988). *A Thousand Plateaus: Capitalism and schizophrenia*. London: Bloomsbury.

Dyson. A.E. (1972). *Between Two Worlds: Aspects of Literary Form*. London: Macmillan.

Grosz, E. (2005). *Time Travels: Feminism, Nature, Power*. Australia: Allen and Unwin.

Holland. E. W. (2013). *A Reader's Guide to A Thousand Plateaus*. London: Bloomsbury

Holland. W. Eug Ferguson, R., In Gever, M., In Trinh, T. M.-H., In West, C., & Tucker, M. (1990). *Out there: Marginalization and contemporary cultures*. (341-343)

Parr, A. (Ed.). (2010). *The Deleuze Dictionary Revised Edition*. Edinburgh: Edinburgh University Press.

Reeves, G. (2006). "T. S. Eliot and the Concept of Tradition". *Literary Theory and Criticism: An Oxford Guide*. Oxford UP.

Young, R. (1995). *Colonial desire: Hybridity in theory, culture, and race*. London: Routledge.

Reorganising (B)orders: Reading the Women's Writing in Colonial Bengal

Priyanka Chatterjee

In his essay, 'Our Modernity', Partha Chatterjee, while evaluating the term 'modernity' and, more specifically, dwelling on 'our' modernity, as distinct from other modernities that might exist, discusses Rajnarayan Basu's *'Se Kalaar Ekal'* (1873) ('Those Days and These Days') where, by 'those' and 'these' days, Basu meant, "the period before and after the full-fledged introduction of English education in India" (p. 4). The reason for considering 'English education' as the border that perpetuated differentiation, Chatterjee goes on to explain, is rooted in assigning a sort of privilege to this new language that opened channels of communication with and acceptance by the western world, where the world of western education and thought was considered *'nabya'* or 'new', and appealed to the sense of experimentation. *'Adhunik'* or 'modern', as we know it today, had still not made its way into the imagination of the generation, let alone the vocabulary. The 'new', therefore, stood as a disruption in the flow of time. With a close affinity with the 'new' stood another word, *'unnati'*, the nineteenth century English equivalent of which is 'improvement' or 'progress', an idea that seemed to occupy a lot of space in the discussions of the period. While marking out the areas where there had been improvement or decline, Basu pays attention to seven areas—health, education, livelihood, social life, virtue, polity, religion. Among all these areas, Basu pays particular attention to health, investing a sense of pride and faith in 'those' days when men were known for their physical capabilities, while in 'these' days the Bengali race was characterised by feeble, sickly and short-lived men. Chatterjee here poses a critical query at Basu's unflinching conviction that the 'new' that the British had brought with them had resulted in a failed harvest of feeble generation of *bhadralok*. This notion of Basu seems to be coloured by a radical nationalistic agenda which tried to discard all that is western as unsuitable for Indians who, they asserted, must look inside the treasures of their own civilization which should be hailed as supreme—thus moving from one extreme to another. Thus, Basu considers the uncritical adoption of European ways of 'modern' life, which were not only at odds with the indigenous conditions, but also did not answer the requirements of the Indian way of life, as the most assertive cause for such an outcome. Chatterjee, therefore, inferred from such a view as Basu's that, "...true modernity consists in determining the particular forms of modernity that are suitable in particular circumstances...." (p. 8).

While referring to another essay by Immanuel Kant on Enlightenment, Chatterjee points out, in a somewhat similar vein, that Kant considers that person as enlightened who having stopped depending on other's authority, becomes free and assumes responsibility for one's own action. Visualizing enlightenment as a means of negation, a sort of closure of oppressive forms through the disclosure of independence, for Kant 'enlightenment is an exit, an escape; exit from tutelage, coming out of dependence' (p. 10). Thus another important aspect of the essay has been to understand individual autonomy, freedom of thought and expression. There are areas of personal and social living where, according to Kant, freedom of thought and expression would prevail, while in other areas, the directives or regulations of a regularised authority would have to prevail. Kant separates these two spheres of exercising reason as the public, "where matters of general concern are discussed and where reason is not mobilized for the pursuit of an individual interest or for the support of a particular group" (p. 11) and the private, "which relates to the pursuit or individual or particular interest" (p. 11). In the former, Kant states, freedom of thought and speech is essential, so that when one has the proper knowledge regarding a certain thing and one is able to openly argue and express one's opinion. In the latter, such freedom is not at all desirable, as what one thinks in the private may hardly impinge upon his work, which might be governed by a legitimate authoritarian body. This notion of the 'public' and the 'private' did not gain much currency in later discussions when the private sphere was always associated with unrestricted freedom, whereas the public sphere of social relations was associated with limitations. However, Kant's idea of 'public' and 'private' seems intriguing to a point where, besides endorsing differential access to knowledge and hence, the creation of experts, thus a hierarchized system of gaining knowledge, he also states that the public domain is that domain which is not restricted by the particular and individual interest, and hence becomes the domain of free and unrestricted thoughts which tend to become the universal domain of discourse, the sphere of enlightenment.

Turning to contemplate over the idea of modernity as we comprehend it, Chatterjee points at an inherent insecurity among the discourses of the colonized, who always looked at modernity with a certain skepticism, following the imposition of the nationalistic appeal against the dominance of the west, and define it in negative terms, just as Basu did when he inferred that the 'new' era has led to the generation of a category of feeble *bhadralok*. Chatterjee argues that 'our' modernity has been so entwined with colonialism it becomes impossible for us to think that we are able to generate modernity on our own, without either becoming the consumers of universal modernity, or following the other extreme of discarding any notion of universality altogether. However, what seems to lead towards an inevitably bordered existence might reflect a completely different outlook if we zoom into the writings of the early twentieth century women writers, particularly from Bengal (for the ease of analysis, and also because Bengal formed the hotbed for nationalistic politics, of which women's emancipation through education and writing evolved as the mechanism to deal with the much debated 'woman's question' that dominated discussions of the period). In doing so it would be necessary to draw from the premise already laid down where firstly, that the idea of modernity could arrange itself around particular forms of modernity that would be suitable in particular circumstances; secondly, that modernity should mean an exit from dependence, an urge towards exercising freedom of expression; thirdly, that the public sphere could be a sphere of emancipation as a whole, since it is not dominated by particular interests and agendas and can contain freedom of expression in the truest sense, while the private sphere is be spotted by moments of restrictions, which might spill over into the public sphere, thus prejudicing its emancipatory character. This chapter intends to look into the women's writings, particularly the genre of essays and fictions, of *'shekal'* i.e. the late nineteenth and early twentieth century, to understand how these writings tried to comprehend and deal with modernity, which could not be understood as a happening or an event or a moment that could be recognized separately, but as a continuum, which internalized itself into lived experiences of women, often translating into their writings, in such a manner that the boundaries of conventional spheres of lived experiences developed perforations, marking the a continuous change within the stagnation of the everyday.

Combating the 'New': Nationalism and the Modern Times

The socio-cultural and political upheaval of the late nineteenth and early twentieth century settled itself around the most commented and contested issue — the 'woman question' as it traversed the socio-cultural economy of colonial India. The 'woman question' became the main matter of contention among the reformers and the colonial government, or those who represented the colonial authority, like the missionaries. The abject and lowly condition of women in colonial India manifested itself in myriad ways so much so that it appealed to the imagination of those for whom women eventually turned into a synecdoche for the nation. On one hand, the colonial masters, whose dominance over the colonised was based on the myth of superior racial qualities, found in women the appropriate subject for propagating their role as the savior of the brown woman from the brown man, thus upholding their civilisational grandeur. While reform measures taken up by the colonists did not receive a radically unfavourable reaction from among the natives at the very beginning, the slow transition that came over the colonised by the modern concepts of nation and nationality, made the rising nationalist leaders skeptical about being appropriated by European notion of modernity wholly. As such, they devised their own understanding of modernity, enwrapped within the nationalist agenda as stimulated by the tumultuous times of nation building, and propagated the cause of women, trying to assume responsibility for reforming the position of women from a standpoint that would befit their nationalistic goals. Tanika Sarkar, in her 'Introduction' to *Hindu Wife, Hindu Nation* (2000), notes that late nineteenth and early twentieth century colonial Bengal had witnessed a transformation of the public sphere from an 'expansive and adventurous' (p. 8) discussion of prescription and custom, to a more authoritarian, conservationist and nativist form to 'the larger material experiences of the middle classes' which 'put a closure to their willingness to question the bases of their social power' (p. 8). The Pabna riots, according to Sarkar, made nationalists out of the Bengali *bhadralok*, who felt that the privileges they had been enjoying were slipping out of control which were mostly articulated through 'the motif of loss of caste and the loss of virtue of women' (p. 16). The news that spread through the news media highlighted the precarious position of women during such upheavals, which seemed to be indirectly advocated by the state i.e. the colonial ruler. However, delving into the matter brings up a different perspective of the state altogether. Sarkar points out that not only did the state intervene in uplifting the conditions of the lower caste, especially through education, the same reform measures taken up by the state also empowered women to the extent that they too were able to undercut the privileges and claims of the Bengali gentlemen. What became apparent through these 'new' measures is that in the face of consistent insecurities that developed, the middle class Bengali *bhadralok* developed a new political sensibility that made the structures of social authority so stringent that, especially in the realms of gender relations, the trend was not only to 'conserve tradition, prescription and custom but also to construct elaborate arguments in their defence' (p. 17). Thus, while the state was perceived as the locus of violation of rights and privileges, it was also seen as the desecrator of womanly honour, an aspect that a feudal, patriarchal society found themselves obliged to 'protect'. A counter narrative, against the reformist measures taken by the state, was formulated which became more authoritarian and conservationist, but remained undisputed, a tendency which can be comprehended by the unquestioning acceptance of structural violence. What turned out to be problematic in the defence that was hence constructed is that, there was an immense weightage conferred upon indigenism, which by now had become a tool for both comprehending the 'new' times and also for differentially suppressing the import and implementation of anything foreign. Any form of resistance against it was considered as 'mimicking of the Western colonial knowledge, while status-quoism was linked to the survival of authentic norms' (p. 9), thus trying to solicit a sort of embracement of such conservationist and authoritarian indigeneity from the lower castes, peasants and women.

Partha Chatterjee in his essay, "The Nationalist Resolution of the Women's Question", while trying to trace this notion of indigenism under work, probes into the causes of the disappearance of the debates concerning the 'woman's question'. Here he tries to understand if its absence was rooted in the accepted notion that most sections of opinion in Bengal had found a satisfactory resolution of the 'woman's question' by the second decade of the twentieth century. Chatterjee points out that, a straight-forward, linear historical assumption would not allow us to understand the fact that the problem in actuality lay with the original structure of assumptions. In fact from the point of view of Bengal renaissance, questions had been raised about the strictness and consistency of the liberal ideas propagated by the renaissance and also whether the fruition of all these ideas was at all possible under colonial rule. Chatterjee states, "…the incompleteness and contradictions of 'renaissance' ideology were shown to be the necessary result of the impossibility of thoroughgoing liberal reform under colonial condition" (p. 308), an assumption that might be derived from Sarkar's argument as well.

Chatterjee infers that nationalist ideology did indeed tackle the 'women's question'. He clarifies that what Sumit Sarkar has pointed out as an absence of any significant autonomous struggle by women themselves to change relations within and outside the family during these times, is in fact embedded within the very idea of resolution of the 'woman's question'. To comprehend its workings it would be important to direct our attention to the nationalist ideology itself, which, according to Chatterjee, stood up to the new social and cultural problems, and resolved the 'women's question' in complete accordance to *its* preferred goals. He identifies two contradictory pulls of nationalist ideology in its struggle against the dominance of colonialism and the resolution it offered to the contradictions therein. The resolution was built around the separation of the domain of culture into two spheres- the material and the spiritual. The material sphere, with its emphasis on technological advancements, its claim to rationalize and reform the traditional culture of the natives, was the sphere where western civilization appeared most powerful. The Indian nationalists argued that in the process of rationalising and reforming the traditional culture of the people, it was not desirable and not necessary to imitate the west in anything other than the material aspects of life, because in the spiritual domain the east was superior to the west. "What was necessary was to cultivate the material techniques of modern western civilization while retaining and strengthening the distinctive spiritual essence of the national culture" (p. 312).

This material/spiritual distinction got further condensed into ideologically more powerful dichotomies of the inner and the outer domains, which came to be applied to the social sphere as '*ghar* and *bahir*, the home and the world' (p. 313). The outer/*bahir*/world was the material domain, the domain of the male- the public sphere. It was a space that was a mere external, where adjustments were required; but it remained unimportant in comparison to the inner world. The inner/*ghar*/home, on the other hand, remained as the true essence of life that must remain unaffected by the profanities of the outside world. Women represented this domain—the private sphere. Although this categorization was in all likeness with the western distinction of the two domains of 'public' and 'private' based on the meanings associated with productive and reproductive labour, Chatterjee argues that the conceptualization and practice of this dichotomous understanding of social and cultural life was considered as a 'new' formulation to the nationalistic mind, by using which the nationalistic struggle could be fostered. Although, by and by, this dichotomy settled itself to various connotations of the western conception of production in the public world by men and reproduction in the private world by women, for the time being nationalists prided themselves at such compartmentalization which made the world/public domain an arena where the 'European power had challenged the non-European peoples...'(p. 314). It is here that it had subjugated everyone to their superior material power. But it had 'failed to colonize the inner, essential identity of the East' (p. 314). It is here that the identity of the east remained distinctive by their superior, spiritual culture which became the inner core of national culture for the nationalists, which was crucial for them to protect, preserve and strengthen. So they adopted a dichotomous stand: 'in the world, imitation and adaptation to western norms was a necessity; at home they were tantamount to annihilation of one's very identity' (p. 314). While such duality of life was acceptable for the male, who were conceived as the warriors at the forefront of the nationalistic struggle, women's participation in this struggle for identity would be that of the sanctified alter of upholding and preserving the past, in the name of tradition. Women were not imagined to have any role to play in the public that could be divested from their role in the private domain. However, men could, or rather had to, cater to this ideological principle of selection, by which the nationalist attempted to make modernity consistent with the nationalist project.

As the 'Woman's Question' garnered Attention

Consistent with the nationalistic agenda, any western influence upon Bengali women was countered by making it a subject of social parody which found expression in every form of literature of the period. Although the creation of this idea of the Bengali woman turning into a western *memsahib* was not consistent with reality, it was basically stood out as a criticism of manners—in dressing sense, reading habits and others- which was seen as a threat to the inner sanctity of the *ghar* — the home. The changes in the ideological world of the nineteenth century are divided by Chatterjee into two parts. The first half of the nineteenth century focuses on the straightforward defense of the 'tradition' and outright rejection of the 'new'. Amidst huge ideological confusion the era moved to the end of the nineteenth century, when there was an upsurge of the discourse of nationalism which was coalesced with the previous practices. It is, then, that all attempts of 'locating the position of women in the modern world of the nation' (p. 316) became important, thus turning all attention to the debates concerning the 'woman's question'.

The emergent middle class in Bengal found themselves threatened by the various conditions and contradictions that the colonial rule had brought. In such a scenario, they were anxious of saving their homes, their inner identities. Since older norms would not be competent to bring about the desired result, new norms, which would not be prompted by western ideas alone, were needed to appropriately combat the external conditions of the modern world. It is, then, that the onus of such preservation of culture was vested on women who were transformed and almost desexed into the godlike species among the human race and would, thereby, be responsible for keeping up the sanctity of the inner spiritual space. The masculine/feminine domain was made watertight: men would bear the brunt of the outside material world while women would be the preserver of the site of inner spirituality- thus 'expressing the spiritual quality of the national culture' (p. 319). Hence, although changes in the external conditions of the life of women were acceptable, they were supposed to retain their inner spiritual (i.e. feminine) virtues. As such, social reforms that went in consistency with these requirements were desirable and perpetuated through social and cultural practices. Thus, the idea that men and women could be westernized, but with a distinction, was responsible for the way in which the relation of women with family and work was visualized.

The 'New' for Women and 'New Woman'

In fact, problems with regard to comprehending the application of these dichotomies of home/world, masculine/feminine, spiritual/material concerning the everyday life of 'modern' women emerged with the rapidly changing situation of the middle class homes. The content of these changes was not predetermined or unchanging; the only aspect which had to be ensured was its consistency with the nationalist project. Hence "the 'new' woman defined in this way was subjected to a *new* patriarchy" (p. 321). The 'New Woman' was to remain distinguished from the traditional common woman, who could be defined with negativities of moral and social parameters, and also from the westernised woman. In fact the 'New Woman' was marked by her efforts to attain superior national culture which would in turn project her freedom as a woman.

In this respect, Chatterjee cites the case of women's education which has been the most contentious subject of the 'woman's question' debate. While traditionalists rejected the idea of schooling for women, the end of the nineteenth century saw tremendous rise in women's education, due to increase in the establishment of indigenous schools, which was made possible due to the development of educative literature in Bengali language, which flourished, not only because much of the content of the curriculum was feminine and seemed untranslatable in English, but also because the need to translate it in English, the language of the external world, seemed unnecessary as women would always operate within the household where western education in any form was considered a threat. This sanitised way of offering freedom to women became necessary, as women would have to bring up able sons for the nation. Bagchi notes that, education of women fostered "to promote women with enough efficiency to uphold traditions and bear sons for the nation. Thus, Bagchi indicates that colonial Bengal threw up this 'mother-son dyad', which not only confined women inside their homes with minimal or no access to the world, but also materialized into a discourse on women's powerlessness, the only exception being the mother of the son" (Chatterjee, p. 3).

All efforts to reform the materials of education and dissemination helped shape the new literature in Bengal, which now had the 'new woman' as creative contributors, who also worked to make it accessible to women who could read only one language—Bangla. It is through these disseminations, often carried out by women themselves, that ideological understandings like women could receive formal education without jeopardising her place at home-gained enough currency. To be able to gain this education was made to look like a personal challenge that women must overcome using their will to uplift themselves. For this first generation of 'new women' in Bengal to achieve this education was to achieve freedom and to place oneself at a higher cultural ground.

Education, therefore, was supposed to inculcate in women the virtues that would help her to formulate a kind of disciplining of the household in order to equip it to face the new physical and economic condition of the outside world. She would venture into the outside world as long as she could keep her femininity intact, which in turn helped to consolidate the socially acceptable male and female behaviour. Femininity was marked by spiritual qualities in her way of life, which would bear the burden of compensating the inability of the men to inculcate such spirituality due to the trials and tribulations of the material world which was their designated domain. What went on happening unnoticed was a continuous flow of traffic of women between the two domains, private and public, despite all the strictness that was gathered to consolidate the spheres according to the ideologies of the time. While the middle class women were idealised either as mother or as goddess, in keeping with the image of *Bharat Mata* that fulfilled the nationalist agenda of women emancipation and removed all controversies regarding women's question from the public arena, education, the tool of writing opened up the private domains to create a public presence where the public world of writing and publishing became a more open space of expressing one's angst against the constriction of the private space, quite as Kant points out. The two spheres were thus created and consolidated in ways that suited this 'new' times for the 'new woman' who transformed the meanings of the public and private from the domains of the home, evidences of which are present in documents that took shape within such confines (p. 330)

The Voices from the Confines: Women's Writing in Magazines in Colonial Bengal

An anonymous essay titled *'Bangadeshiya Mahilaganer Swadhinata Bishay'* ('Bengali Women and the Issue of Freedom') was published in *Bamabodhini Patrika* around mid-May to mid-June, 1871. *Bamabodhini Patrika*, which began to be published in 1863 with the purpose of uplifting the minds of the 'new' age men and women, was the first of its kind in the country to be dedicated to women issues, trying to awaken women to wisdom and intellectuality. Such a magazine carried articles that mostly spoke of domesticity as a sacred occupation for women, who were always being encouraged to do the right thing in order to be the perfect wife, mother, nurturer or caretaker, the idea of an ideal Bengali Hindu *ramani*/woman ringing in most of the topics. This essay had been signed *'Ekti Bhadramahila'* ('A genteel woman'), a category that spoke of a transition, a change that was underway in the socio-cultural and political atmosphere of colonial Bengal, where *bhadralok* was also a newly emerging category among the urban middle class Bengalis. The essay is an interesting assemblage of propositions on women's freedom coming out from a *bhadramahila's* pen, who is supposed to reckon it as her sacred duty to be within the confines of the *andarmahal*, the innermost part of the house, where she must obligingly carry out her familial duties that have been laid down for her. With the advent of modernity, when 'new' made an ubiquitous presence, change in the lives of women brought about by education, however meager that might be, needed to be channelized in a way that the 'new' did not mean adopting the western ideals, especially in the private core of one's existence. Thus, as discussed above, tradition, indigeneity was to be preserved in those spaces that were zealously protected against the encroachment of the public world which, as was visualized, was compelled to adopt the modern western ideals of materiality. However, the effects of change within the inner sphere had to be neutralized. Reformers like Bankimchandra Chattopadhyay in his famous essay, *'Prachinaebong Nabina'* in *Bangadarshan* in 1874, pointed out that the work of a 'new woman' or *nabina* was to add an aesthetic dimension to the uninspiring daily chores and transform it into a skilled operation. Thus, education was required to fashion a *bhadramahila* who could use all her acquired skills to refurbish the household, which in fact meant that her need for mobility was derided, although subtly. The nationalistic project required women to hold base within the household where they would work towards bringing up better sons for the nation. Their need to access public spaces, which were basically considered male reserves, was thoroughly discouraged owing to male insecurities which would be further threatened by the presence of women. While patriarchy trickled down through both men and women, the 1871 essay authored by an anonymous *bhadramahila* has something different to offer.

The author advocates the movement of women out of their confines to explore the world. She admonishes the prejudices that constantly bind women's mobility. She states, "…the lack of freedom has led to the calamitous condition of the women of Bengal who from their birth till death are reduced to the existence of caged birds and beasts' (p. 5). There is a call for a curious marriage between the private and the public world of a woman's life when she writes, "what can be more pleasurable to men than to find their educated, liberated wives fulfilling the duty of looking after their families conscientiously and with care, and also being appreciated by people all over the world?' (p. 5). The union between the public and private spheres can happen only when a woman is able to first fulfil the needs of the private inner world and then look out in the public arena. This moving into the public arena cannot, however, happen without men leading the way, "I had thought that the educated broadminded wise men would dispel the sorrow-filled darkness and free women from bondage…" (p. 5), as is apt for the age in which it was being written. This desire, however, opens up another aspect of subtle realisation, "He, who is our Father and has created us, has not discriminated between men and women and has shown equal mercy or retribution to all" (p. 5), thus calling in divine providence as witness to the predestined equality with which men and women are made. Thus the notion of freedom did not lie in separating the spheres of men and women, in creating a constricted existence of the private and public world, but in creating a coalition of spheres. There is a radical understanding of 'new' which tries to overthrow the past, but rather 'new' is understood through a newness of dealing with life that has broadened its scope of comprehension by means of the changes in the social and cultural life of the mind that it has encountered. Equal status of a woman and a man is emphasized upon and it is also pointed out that a woman cannot lose her dignity only by crossing the threshold, by overstepping the borders of her existence. However, her moving out can not be without baggage. She not only needs 'educated, broadminded wise men' to help her cross the threshold, she must also prove herself worthy of occupying the public space; she must be the subject of appreciation of the world. While this implies that the crossing over for women is not an easy task asso much must go into equipping them for occupying the space, it also means that by acquiring the requisite skills, women can definitely occupy the public space, enriching the domain with their skills and practices. While this seems like settling for a conditional claim to a space, it also draws attention to the realisation that women have a mind of her own that does not quite follow the strictured restrictions of the public and the private, something that is definitely appreciated in an 1891 essay by Krishnabhabini Das.

Krishnabhabini Das in "The Educated Woman" published in *Sahitya* in 1891 writes:

> Woman was not created to be the ignorant slave or the plaything of man. As it is the purpose of a woman's life to do good to others, and to live for them, so does a woman live for herself. And the serious responsibilities that are entrusted to her demand not only a sympathetic heart, but also a cultivated mind. (qtd. in Bannerji, p. 135)

The emphasis on the possession of a 'cultivated mind' to 'live for herself', with its implicit implications of the upcoming class structure that the discourse of a *bhadramahila* was bringing up with it, also points at a shift from an earlier dependence of women on men for their deliverance to women themselves, although not completely divorced from their necessitated roles within the household which is now seen as 'serious responsibilities that are entrusted to her'. In another essay, *'Streelok o Purush'* (Women and Men) published in 1890 in *Bharati o Balok*, Das writes:

> The most dangerous and terrible barrier against equality in society and rights for women is the barbaric and odious notion that women exist only for men and they have no purpose in life except to fulfil that specific objective (p. 23).

She further states,

> "By comparing women and men with regard to their intellect, devoutness and moral sense, we can clearly perceive that the characteristic traits of both are similar. But from the dawn of civilization, women and men have led completely different lives. Educated differently, they have adopted different habits, are encouraged to work differently and thus have become skilled in different fields of work, and this is why the phrases and concepts- 'man's work', 'woman's work', 'male virtue', 'female virtue'- have become so firmly entrenched in our minds" (p. 21).

As the notion that women do not exist for men alone gains consolidation, it can also be seen that the idea of equality is being unpacked to emphasize the aspect that having separate set of skills or separate sphere of work does not imply a hierarchical existence of spheres or a radically constricted spheres. What can be visualised here is a gradual evolution of what Himani Bannerji attributes to the process of a 'fashioning of self'. This idea is intricately linked to the notion of 'inventing subjects', where social subjectivity presents itself as a two way process—of being invented and inventing itself. Bannerji suggests that while considering social subjects as "cultural and ideological objects of others' invention" (p. 3), the entire process opens up the possibility of inventing themselves as subjects within a given socio-historical context. The subject formation must be seen as 'dynamic, and sometimes purposive, constellations of both unconscious and conscious forms of cultural and ideological constructions which are connected to history, social organization, social relations and social locations of subjects (p. 3). Thus, what can, therefore, be inferred from this formulation is that, although the invention of the construct of the 'new woman' in the colonial social and cultural setup was the task undertaken by both the male intelligentsia and the colonial government, 'the women themselves sought to contribute to this formative process of their social subjectivities and agencies' in the last decades of the nineteenth century and the early twentieth century (p. 135). Women became involved in the self-making of their classes, by adopting various modes and mediums that were necessary to fashion themselves and the society through a comprehension of their social, cultural and political existence as they encountered it in their everyday lives. The print media rendered itself as the most important space for communication where while the private and public spheres merged, it also became a sphere where women exercised tremendous freedom of expression, something that was denied to them in their private spheres.

In the pages of these magazines, 'an extensive network and general fund of communicative competence' (Bannerji, p. 137) was being built among the women writers and women readers. Many women editors were involved in the process of accumulating materials, suggesting new themes and thus, generating 'new communicative modes, availing of a certain kind of facility... with the purpose of creating another social, moral and cultural space for and by women' (ibid). All of this was being done under the male gaze.

However, while these women were not wholly co-opted by the patriarchal structures within which they were operating, the texts of these women writers made them subjects and objects of their own discourse, as their texts were constructed through, what Banerji explains, using Althusser's notion of ideological interpellation. Most of these women, who tried to impact through their writings, belonged to propertied classes who, although empowered by their social positions, were subordinated by the inherent patriarchy and gendered organisation of their own classes. Yet, these women were called upon by the upper class male reformers to act to their calls for women emancipation which would be controlled by the scriptures of nationalism. According to

Bannerji, 'this amounts to the dominant ideology interpellating women to function as class subjects while that subjectivity itself is sought to be contained, managed, truncated and unauthenticated by the repression of their full social being through patriarchy' (p. 139).

From 'Woman's Question' to Gender Question in Women's Writings

Trying to conceptualise gender at multiple levels, following Sandra Harding's conceptualisation of gender, Chanda looks at the discursive practices of gender formation, as expressed through the particular genre of writing. Attempting to map the interactions of reasons, beliefs, emotions that went into creating a comprehension of gender would result in producing glimpses of visible changes both in society's thinking processes and in its practice. This very practice of writing in the periodicals by women helped to develop a discourse in which women came out from the confines of their setup, braving the censure of the traditionalists, where they confess their identities, thus establishing a public dimension of their private self. The essays that were written by women and which were published in these magazines could be analysed as narratives of change in the life practices and beliefs of women writing on issues that had direct connection with their well-being. In fact, as Banerjee points out, the language of social reform in the nineteenth and early years of twentieth century is inscribed with a discourse of 'crisis' (p. 144) and 'the new times' (p. 145), where there has been a constant allusion to change and continuity, to tradition and modernity, so that the most fundamental social formations, involving social identity and political subjectivity, lay at the stake of this change (Bannerji, p. 145). In such a scenario education became a practical, conceptual and moral aspect which made it a wide entry point into social reformation and creation of ideology (Bannerji, p. 145). Understandably the century reverberated with thoughts on education, especially women's education, which remained as the acceptable strategy for reform (Chanda, xxii) but which also became the instrument to reason out and question the present as it spanned out for women.

The essays by women are significantly directed towards critique, solution, explication of this change brought about by education (Chanda, xxi). Examining the various issues that have been discussed in the essays by the women intelligentsia has been fraught with so much diversifications, and even contradictions, that to understand a particular line of thought that might have developed within these essays would not only be a difficult task but would also be fraught with risks of wrong interpretation. Being a period of contradiction, conformation and confrontation, gender and its organisation was a practice that was performed in daily social lives and became a part of the larger social conflict. These essays do not merely address the 'woman's question' as was in vogue among the male intelligentsia of the period. These issues clearly point towards the fact that women were concerned with a kind of social reorganisation right from the beginning of their voicing forth the concerns that plagued them. What comes to the fore is that women writers seem more concerned with gender relations than with the 'women's question' alone.

While there were essays questioning the idea of spiritualism within Hindu marriages, there were essays that displayed a broader understanding of education which had to do with questioning the dichotomous understanding of male and female spheres and also the processes by which gender was constructed. In 1923, Banganari writes:

> The behaviour of the younger members may destroy peace, happiness, discipline and well-being, in a word, the attributes that make a home a home, and often this is precisely the case. Hence they must learn from a young age to uphold the respect and well-being of the family, and *this education is equally necessary for boys and girls.* And for all these years, because men are still mired in the past, because they have been given the wrong kind of education in this regard, and because, as we have pointed out earlier, they are the powerful group in the family, it is now imperative that they are the ones who should, who must concentrate on being educated adequately in this regard (Chanda, xxvii, italics mine).

What is important to note here is that the domain of 'home', which was considered an exclusive female domain all this while, is now being shifted to becoming the responsibility of both men and women who must be equally responsible for the private space to create meanings of life. In fact taking earnest advantage of men being mired in the past and prejudiced about being women even within the household, an era of overturning logic seems to have arrived when men are also supposed to be equally equipped to understand and deliver household responsibilities. Society is viewed from an informed perspective. While there could be found a number of writings by women that co-opted and disseminated the patriarchal notions at work, there are innumerable essays which constantly tried to come out from the constricted *shastric* conventions and seemed to be adequately influenced by the advent of western ideas of emancipation, where the case for women is argued from the vantage point of rationalism, and emancipation is explained on the grounds of being human.

A 1886 article in *Bamabodhini Patrika* titled, '*Streejati o Shilpakarja*' ('Women and Art') questioned the relevance of propagating a separate curriculum for women and men, where women would not be equipped with any professional training like men, but gain the basic workable knowledge of all kinds. While most reform oriented understandings of women's education at the close of the century suggested that training and knowledge for women was only to embellish themselves to better their homes or their inner selves, by 1920s women sought emancipation, not only from the confines of the homes/*griha* but also from the demands of the family, which being a patriarchal institution, legitimised the authority of a man. It was recognised that this authority of the man was legitimised not by any *shastras* but because the gender in question was that of a man. Thus, Chanda enumerates a shift in the argument of the essays when these are read diachronically. In the first phase of writing the authors were more concerned about guiding women regarding their pursuits of betterment. They were critical of the *shastric* interpretation of the religious texts which was often misused by the guardians of society to subdue women. Later these guardians of society were identified to be men, under whose patriarchal oppression women were continuously leading a precarious existence. The very idea of *bhadramahila* was also attacked by these women writers. Since education became the marker of *bhadro* or genteel behaviour, education among the lower classes was constantly discouraged, as education was always seen as a preserve of the upper classes and became an efficient tool for promoting a system that was hierarchical in nature. The *bhadramohila* or *nabyanari* (new woman) was understood, as Partha Chatterjee states, as a foil to the coarser non-urban woman, who's another significant difference with the *bhadramohila* was lack of access to womanly education or *streeshiksha*. Women's education had become quite a necessity to fulfil the *bhadralok* agenda of nationalism. As nationalism in the country turned more and more towards militancy, the 'woman's question' issues vanished from contemporary debates because, according to Chatterjee, the issues stood resolved in accordance to the *bhadralok* agenda. But "as far as women were concerned, the [woman's] question was just being posed. Education was just opening up various new possibilities, opportunities and avenues for women, many of which led to the questioning of the emergent and very *bhadralok* gender ideology which had 'allowed' women's education in the first place" (Bagchi, p. lx). Thus many women educationists like Sarala Ray, Abala Bose, Sarala Devi Chaudhurani and others directly concerned themselves with the emancipation of women's education.

Indira Devi Chaudhurani, who spoke extensively on women's education and was actively involved in carrying out reform measures in this respect, wrote a point by point counter argument to Bankim's *'Prachin aebong Nabeena'* debate in her *'Bartaman Sreesiksha Bichar'* (Present-day Evaluation of Women's Education) in 1912. In this essay she argued that whatever was coarse within women was either due to lack of education or due to half education. Hence she overturned the very method of creating a *bhadramohila* through the system of reversal, through overturning the hierarchies inherent within the educational system, thus stating that a *bhadramohila* could be an all-encompassing category provided women's education was widespread. Hence education could become the basis of social mobility, as already mentioned, where the emphasis was not on physical movement but in the mobile world of ideas and their impact.

What now emerged was a second generation of 'new woman' whose mission was to recreate the future generations of women in the image of the 'new woman' (Bagchi, p. lxi). The first generation of 'new women' were constantly engaged in the arduous task of bringing together the private and the public in a perfect balance, since they considered home as their sacred duty and the movement outside home, no matter how restricted, as an exercise of choice. Bagchi points out that just as the idea of *bhadramohila* was being developed, all the other categories of urban, modern, Indian had also started taking shape in the early twentieth century. The modern idea of the nation was slowly consolidating itself in the imagination of the colonised and along with this the identity of the 'new woman' was being refurbished for a second time, seen especially in the urban middle-class milieu of Calcutta (Bagchi, p. xi).

The most important change that could be located in women's lives was how women were instigated for being dependent on themselves for their own upliftment. Mothers were no longer only supposed to bring up able sons, but mothers were also responsible for furthering the education of their daughters who wouldn't depend on their fathers or their husbands for their educational advancement. The 'new woman' wanted to create succeeding generations of 'new women', who were to move out from their traditional roles to make their presence felt in public as well. This was somewhat problematic for men to negotiate with. As long as educated women maintained their positions inside the confines of the private domain, or struck a balance between the public and private domain, thus moving with restrictions, men felt less threatened and accepted the presence of women in public too. But when women moved out into the public to assert their rights, to make opinions, to ensure public visibility, the patriarchal fear of losing control became strong and disrupting. By this time Gandhi's advent into the political arena ensured the space for women in politics, although Gandhi's reservation against women in certain spheres was also very strong. While women were quick to respond to Gandhi's call, they also criticised it. The question of women's education had now taken a newer dimension- the problem wasn't resolved; it only found a new expression. As education had already helped women to find their voice, they now made the fullest use of their capacities and potentials. 'As such the women's question became a larger social problem and generated a dialectic which we, the twenty-first century Bengali women have inherited' (Bagchi, p. xiii).

Dealing with 'New'-ness in Understanding Work, Woman and Modernity

As the discourses around education and training for women began to gather enough currency, a new discourse around the feminine idea of work evolved. Sukhlata Rao, the eldest among the six children of Upendrakishor Raychaudhuri and Bidhumukhi Devi, writes in her 1931 essay, "Adarsha Nari" ('The Ideal Woman') published in *Bangalakshmi*, about the different spheres of woman's work:

> While some women are serving the country; some are selflessly engaged in stabilizing the home and family. Some have even dedicated their lives for eudaemonia [human welfare/happiness] without any heed of their own well-being. Some have taken up the promotion of education as their life's objective. Others have devoted their lives to the welfare of women and society (p. 251)

The strain that is amplified here is that while the sphere of women's work have expanded, allowing them to move from the confines of their homes to the larger public space, from the betterment of home to the betterment of nation, women's work is considered to be intricately connected to serving the greater good for the society and the nation. This work is definitely differentiated from *chakri* or job which has an implicit class consciousness associated with it and also an economic angle and the idea of monetary freedom; hence it is not labour. This work is *desherkaj*, work for the country, the country which requires *swadhinata* or freedom just as women do. When Gandhi, in *Harijan*, asserted that the special calling for women was the calling of the hearth, which she must never be made to forsake, Leelabati Roy, in her 1940 essay, "*Meyeder Upajukta Karmakshetra Ki?*" ("Which is the Ideal Sphere for Women's Work?") published in *Jayasree*, presented a counter argument. "The question is whether there is or there should be a special workplace for women" (p. 362), thus, once again questioning the rationale behind the very separation of the spheres of work and the skills involved therein. Santisudha Ghosh in her essay, "*Nari o Uparjan*" while discussing the new trend in the country regarding women's employment categorically states that this idea has recently evolved for "the genteel society or those who try to imitate upper middle-class society" (p. 389). The 'newness' in the idea of work does not include "the poverty-stricken people, who are not concerned about their status and gentility, do not care about this and both men and women work together to increase their earnings" (p.389). Further in the essay, Ghosh brings up the issues of women becoming self-sufficient, the reasonable demand for wages by married, unemployed women for doing the household work (note that the erstwhile unpaid, naturalised labour given into household work is being urged to be considered equivalent to paid labour), the illogical reservations against the earning of a living by unmarried woman. She states that the society requires both men and women to evolve in a way that they might be holistically contributing to its development. This idea definitely echoes that of Roy, where she states that "for the complete development of an individual, the coexistence of both these sorts of work (women's work comprising of household work and men's work comprising of nation building) is important for both men and women" (p. 363), thus completely breaking up the constrictions involved in the construction of these spheres.

This persona of the 'new woman', who had been dubbed as "westernised", "inauthentic", and antinationalist, who demanded her own economic and social independence and aspired to a citizen-individual status, has been considered as the enemy of the nation (Bannerji, 2000). In her analysis of Punyalata Chakraborty's 1964 essay, "*Ekaljokhon Shuru Holo*" (When this Era begun), which was published in *Anandabazaar Patrika*, JayeetaBagchi states that although the new individual could represent the history of his life only by inscribing it in the narrative of the nation (p. 76) modernity revealed a moment that seemed hard to grasp because of its nature of non-categorisation. Modernity encompassed that which is new, that which has absorbed the change, and also that which speaks of a continuous instability. Bagchi goes on to observe that by time, *kaal*, what Chakraborty talks about was a period when the society required to be formed by the newly educated and emancipated urban elites of both sexes. It was also an era when the inner sanctum of the house, where an essential 'Indianness' was supposed to be preserved, had become highly problematized. The inner/outer, personal/public dichotomies were no longer unclouded divisions. Through the fissures that were developing within these compartmentalised zones, the writers went beyond the unproblematic binaries of "private/public, East/West, pure/sullied, innocent/guilty, tradition/modernity" (ibid). "For a particular class in colonial Bengal the oppositional categories intermingle at a point in history extending one to the other making it impossible to dissociate them. This, for Punyalata, is modernity", Bagchi observes (76). Again in 1916, Swarnakumari Debi wrote '*Shekele Katha*' in *Bharati* where she tried to capture a particular time when the arrival of modernity was announced when women were able to come out in the public. Both the writers by using '*ekal*', this era, and '*shekal*', that era, were trying to dwell on a time frame which could both be considered as a rupture in the flow of historical time and also as a dynamic continuous process called modernity. Grappling with the question of at which point modernity began, Punyalata writes that at the end of the nineteenth century when it became an usual sight to see women out in the open, going to schools, colleges; when a new educated society had risen which intermingled the goodness of both the western and eastern civilisation, modernity might have begun. What is important to note here is the rise of an 'educated society', not necessarily of men alone, but of a class which has turned a "'static' quality through an essential historical movement into a 'dynamic process' ushering in, what we generally term as, 'modernity'" (p. 77).Thus modernity, Bagchi states, brings up an 'alliance between inner and outer, public and private, west and east, support and decision, men and women that created modernity as manifested through something called an urban educated liberal/progressive society" (p. 78). In women's discourse modernity meant marriage between public and the private, which would also act as a leveller of gender power structure.

Since modernity is such a contested issue, Chatterjee points out that nineteenth century literature is replete with various images of change. In this period of transition the outer sphere was supposed to interact with the inner sphere, where the inner sphere was no longer the undiluted realm of pure existence as was conceived by the nationalistic project. Going back to the essay of RajnarayanBasu with which this essay began, we might once again ponder over what Chatterjee argues- that these days and those days are made to stand at two opposite ends where 'lack of fulfilment' of 'these days' (*ekal*) is always compensated by creating the image of grandiose elements prevalent in 'those days' (*sekal*) which in fact is our own creation. "Those days for us are not a historical past; we construct it only to mark the difference posed by the present" ("Modernity", Chatterjee, 25). For Basu *ekal* and *shekal* were frozen periods, where the advent of colonial modernity would create no better for the present. In the nineteenth century itself, as already seen, women were already questioning the existential essences of being Indians and were coming out of its transfixed boundaries— "'today' was brought into being by 'yesterday'" (Bagchi, p. 79) and were asserting the presence of a continuum, instead of a break alone. Bagchi asserts that urban elite women were no longer talking of purifying/maintaining/preserving innate goodness through education. Tanika Sarkar points out that there was a serious and felt need for "the modern woman to write in less gendered ways and to live in a less bifurcated world, her preferred move towards more universalist modes of knowledge" (qtd. in Bagchi, p. 80), an emergence that could be noticed within the changing dynamics of the essays discussed above.

Into the Gendered Genre of Detective Fiction: Is *Bhadramahila* and Crime an Acceptable Association?

As writings by women flourished in various genres, from letters, memoirs to essays, it was fiction writing that assimilated an enduring attraction for women writers who employed the stencil of their imagination to crave out their anxieties, dreams and desires. The canvas of fiction, novels and short stories, provided them with a huge continent for experimentation while addressing the social and cultural causes in a nuanced way. In this respect, this section intends to explore the first ever appearance of a woman detective in the Bengali fiction of a woman writer in the mid-twentieth century. The colonial period in Bengal saw a huge explosion of detective fiction that was consumed with such ardent rapidity that everyone tried their hands in writing this form of fiction, although only a few were hugely successful. Sales records as well as the revelation from authors themselves could stand as proof for claims made regarding the high demands of detective fictions by writers like Panchkari De who is said to have sold around 8000 copies while Priyanath Mukhopadhyaya's original work of detective fiction *Darogar Daptar* is said to have been sold in around 217 volumes till 1912 (Dasgupta, p. 1). Yet there have been very few attempts to study such an interesting body of work as it flourished in Bengal, in particular and India, in general, during a period that coincided with the great socio-political upheaval of the time, the nationalist movement, of which detective fiction bears significant imprints.

From 1820s to 1860s Calcutta, along with other parts of Bengal, saw a veritable explosion of independent presses set up by Bengali printers in an area in north Calcutta known as bat-*tala* (the banyan tree quarter) which had evolved into a great market for cheap print publishing a range of texts (Ray, p. 8). Literatures coming out of *battala*, however, acquired enough wry of *bhadralok* readers, who considered these demeaned narratives as propagators of vulgarity and obscenity. Hence literature from these presses never found their way into the libraries of the *bhadralok* who maintained a veritable distance. These presses produced numerous texts about crimes, which were written within a social-historical context where gender was a fiercely contested terrain, often exhibiting subjects of publicly fought debates on law, sexual relations, reform, cultural, as well as, class and caste-related identities and ideas of nation. These texts could never garner support from the ambivalent *bhadralok* community, which, on one hand, projected themselves as liberals fighting for the cause of women emancipation, and, on the other hand, were paranoid about possible gendered transgressions and the use of agency by women to look beyond the given. The presence of women in crime narratives, that were mostly modeled as domestic narratives until the publication of *Darogar Daptar*, triggered responses which were based on the prevalent discursive practices, ideological assumptions and social attitudes which were latent, or sometimes, very obverse in these narratives.

As these novels projected, via their scandalous plot construction, their explorations of gendered transgressions with gleeful voyeurism, the intricacies of violence prevalent within the sanctified *andarmahals* of the *bhadro*-households, they also became instrumental in clearly pointing out the imbalance in social order, where crisis brewed in every aspect of what was thought as normal life. Crisis in social relationships, repressed rage and conflicts, were implicit within the households in a manner in which these are repressed within the psyche of the individuals and interpersonal relations which remained the prime focus of Bankim's novels that dealt with the ideas of guilt and guilty in such a way that questions of criminality refused to be sorted through tidy endings.

Crime narrative from *battala* presses, which carried evidences of hidden material which threatened to fracture the oppressive ideals of femininity and of gendered relationships as framed within socially sanctioned practices of the time, were at the same time overtly preoccupied in dwelling on the biases that informed social and cultural operations, in a way that women who dared to step out of the fold were not only derided as aberrations, but were also shown as suffering the consequences of their acts, thus making the readers, who were mostly women, weary of too much independence and too many choices. Hence, they continued to remain the grisly narratives of sensation mongering gossip that peered into the highly protected *bhadralokantahpurs*, a sacrilege that titillated, and also demeaned any overt connection between women and crime.

The Emergence of the (Male) Detective: Can Women be Detectives?

Sukumar Sen points out that detective fiction in its formal structure is bound to have come up only after the disciplinary police was created in India in 1861 by the Police Act V of 1861. This happened after the codification of criminal law occurred in 1860. The formalisation of these legalities set up the boundaries of acceptable behaviour which, in turn, became the measure of determining class, caste and religious hierarchies that became intensely complex when gender impinged upon these concerns. With such concerns making their way into society, the *bhadralok* way of life was prioritised in every aspect. The new form of detective fiction which emerged with the detective as the focal figure and the procedural technicalities in place, sought and found its newest readers among the Bengali middle class *bhadralok*.

These readers were already well conversant with the European trends of detective fiction, having read the original and the translations which were quite in vogue in colonial Bengal and also in the rest of India. These fictions invariably had an influence in the creation of the indigenous detective, who had to be maneuvered to attune with *bhadralok* sensibility. These fictions mutated themselves on their own creating versions that were informed by the local histories and contemporary conditions (Ray, p. 21). They came to reflect upon the aspirations of the middle class Bengali *bhadralok*, who was, by then, assured of the reducing possibility of emancipation through government jobs given the racial discrimination they had to constantly encounter under the British rule. Along with that Bengali masculinity had to face constant condemnation for being weak, prone to diseases and cowardly. In order to overpower their subjects with a sense of the coloniser's physical and mental superiority, the colonisers augmented a discrimination strategy based on the myth of 'martial' and 'non-martial' races. The newly educated Bengali *bhadralok* found himself absorbed in nationalistic fervour which, however, never prompted him to overturn this myth. He, instead, immersed himself in self-criticism and tried to find a way out by either craving for incorporation into the superior colonial setup through a government job or any salaried position or by becoming a health enthusiast (Dasgupta, p. 4). This led to an assertion of *bahubal charcha* at a time when it was important to consolidate their confidence in order to address the need for shaking off their physical slackness, which became immensely necessary for their participation in the national movement. There was constant talk of the need for physically strong disciplined, upper caste, Hindu male heroes (Ray, p. 40). It is in the dreams of the job deprived Bengali and the wishful Bengali health enthusiast that the idea of *swadesh* unfolded itself (Dasgupta, p. 2). Again the tremendous upheaval following the first partition of Bengal in 1905, which was an immediate trigger for the nationalist movement to gather impetus, is also marked as the time when detective fictions, featuring male detectives, started gaining popularity in Bengal almost as a wish fulfillment of the bored and beaten Bengali *bhadrochakurijibis*.

The *goyendas* or detectives became the epitome of that wishful Bengali masculinity, who was capable of decisive action, heroic valour and physical dynamism, almost conforming to the idea of masculinity as understood by the dominant discourse of coloniality (Ray, p. 39). The fictions that came out gave wings to the fantastical aspirations of the Bengali middle class *bhadralok*, who already found himself trapped within the limitations of the modern urban setup, where such physical heroics and adventures were desired, but not possible. Confined and drained by their dull, unchanging, monotonous jobs, the *bhadralok* found himself pouring over the tales featuring these *bhadralokgoyendas* "who moved with enviable freedom and imaginativeness from one act of daredevilry to the next..." (Ray, p. 41). Besides the work of a *goyenda* seemed to give shape to another aspiration- a lifetime of selfless act which would render work meaningful, as it would be for the greater good of the society, mostly for eliminating the cause of disruption in the Indian culture, much like the colonial rule. In fact the *goyendas* were depicted in a manner that they drew enough respect from the colonial authority in an attempt to create a sort of racial subversion where the *goyendas* addressed the vehemently expressed need for a ferociously self-assured, physically dynamic upper-class Bengali hyper masculinity by contemporary cultural nationalists in the face of what was seen as unrelenting colonial humiliation, that culminated in the arbitrary and insidious partitioning of Bengal in 1905 (Ray, p. 43).

What is important to note here is that, the pressures on detective fiction to develop a form of literature that would be acceptable to *bhadralok* sensibilities—teasing out the tabooed content, insisting on a hyper-masculine figure to spur their imagination- clearly rendered an incredibly popular genre of the colonial times as an exclusive domain for men- from writers to characters. This exclusivity created by the nationalistic consciousness of nation building significantly zoned women out from exploring the possibilities of the genre at a time when women writers of both fictions and non-fictions were upcoming, following a phenomenon of the fin de siècle moment in Bengal- the rise of the women writer. This scenario can easily be compared to the scenario in England of the time. In fact it has been asserted by numerous critics that detective fiction in Bengal had been inspired by English and other European fiction, although the indigenous writers did manage to create an indigenous version of the detective. This indigenous version had not completely expunged the influences of the source, but had definitely incorporated vital changes by which detective fiction in India was able to speak differently to its audience. Although literature of crime and exploration of women therein flourished in the Bengal of the period, neither men nor women writers tried their hands in creating women detectives during the late nineteenth and early twentieth century. The presence of women in crime literature of the time, like the *battala* literature or the domestic novels, was restricted to their serving either victims or as offenders. In both cases they are reduced to offending bodies which become the locus of unbridled desires, unconventional aspirations thus leading to potential or actual transgressions (Ray, p. 17).

Class consciousness had already been taken into consideration when the independent figure of the detective ultimately lodged itself in the stories of Panchkari De, Dinendranath Ghosh, Priyanath Mukhopadhayay. Not only did the writers themselves belong to the educated, elite *bhadralok* class, their creations were also developed in keeping with the *bhadralok* ideals. In such a scenario a woman detective, who would have to transgress the boundaries of acceptable behaviour and move out of the private domain, wherein her sexuality could be threatened and could transgress the norms, seemed unacceptable. Although women's education was advocated, it was never meant to equip women with any knowledge outside that was to be required outside the confines of the domestic. The domestic realm was always considered as a secondary realm of existence because although it provided the nutrition of traditional living, rooted in the past, it was not involved directly with nation building which was solely a male imperative. Asahapoorna Debi registered her extreme annoyance at the gendered bias that so overtly informed detective fictions when she wrote at the beginning of her story, "*Meye Goyendar Bahaduri*" (Bravery of the Girl Detective):

> An investigation into the interiors of the home and the world outside will bring to view the hidden fact that women have far greater expertise in matters of detecting disorders than men. Women have an intuitive power to smell crime. And if the matter is allowed to be handled by them, they can, with immense finesse excavate the source of the smell (p. 270) [Translation mine].

She asserts that women bear a '*shohojato khomota*', an innate power, of detecting crime that emanates from a curious mind that hovers around anything domestic and thus, minute and invisible, and solves issues within their private domain (Ashapoorna, p. 271). She criticizes the patriarchal idea of considering the phrase 'woman detective' with sarcasm. She scathingly criticizes the activity of many such male writers who unabashedly borrow plots and characters from a female writer (Agatha Christie) and give it an appearance of originality, when what they are doing is mere translation. In such a prejudiced atmosphere the women detective took some time to evolve. Very few women writers even tried their hands in writing detective fictions mainly because of the demands that had been placed on it by an audience who was pouring in to detective fictions because of the thrill and adventure associated with it. However, this association was possible only when there was a male figure out there, which could encourage their masculine zeal, and excite their nationalistic feelings that were on the rise during that time. Women, on the other hand, found themselves trapped in the image of mother/goddess which in fact fuelled the nationalistic mode of thought that did not allow them to easily come out of the frame.

In such a scenario, it was not before the second decade of the twentieth century that women started breaking the mould and moving out of the bordered domains, often ruffling up dichotomies and creating new spaces for asserting their new understanding of freedom and of modernity. They were called upon to share the responsibility of building the nation with their male counterparts with whom they asserted equality. No longer did they look for saviour among men, but they claimed to save themselves. Often the pressures of a demanding, constricting society severely stunted their growth, yet never stopped the forward movement, despite innumerable jolts back and forth.

Prabhabati Debi Saraswati and her Woman Detective, Krishna

What appeared as a strong male bastion was ultimately broken through by the appearance of what can be understood as the first woman detective created by a popular woman writer of the period- Prabhabati Debi Saraswati. Prabhabati Debi, now a writer who has been completely obliterated from the memory of Bengali literature, was a prolific writer of popular Bengali domestic novels of her time. Born of educated and encouraging parents, Prabhabati found herself continuously inspired to read different literatures which turned her attention to writing from a very early age. Married at nine, she published her first poem at eleven which was the age when she also published her first story, "Tommy". At the age of seventeen she published her first novel, "Amba". Meanwhile an unhappy married life led to a divorce which made Prabhabati return to her paternal home. She led a life of continuous travel and unsettlement as she moved with her family, her father being in a transferable job. During the last forty years of her life she lived in Calcutta. Not much personal details of the writer's life can be found, because Prabhabati seemed to be seriously guarded about her personal life, not allowing her professional life to find its way into her personal life that could trigger any gossip, which was prevalent for the public figure of the celebrity women writers. However, in the life of her characters the borders between the public and private domains remained ambivalent, often rendering them as objects of intense socio-cultural scrutiny. Living the lives of a teacher, a reformist, a social worker, an intellectual of brilliance, and a professional writer who has received innumerable awards, Prabhabati's writings always explored the complexity of female existence within both the urban and rural settings of independently emerging India.

In around 1940, Deb Sahitya Kutir began two detective series—*Prahelika* and *Kanchenjungha*. In what seems to be an attempt to deliver women from the atrocious deceit of the social system, to equip her with tools of delivering herself, Prabhabati presented the character of Krishna, in order to inspire the new generation of women with new ideals that could mark the beginning of an independent nation which was supposed to provide women with a new vocabulary of freedom. Prabhabati's woman detective, Krishna, appeared for the first time in the *Kanchenjungha* series in a novella that was published in 1952 titled, "Gupta Ghatak" ("The Secret Assassin") where Krishna's parents were killed by atrocious, Burmese pirate. While this story established Krishna as a woman potent with physical capabilities of adventure and mental prudence of a detective, it ended with Krishna filled with rage against Yu-yin and vowing revenge for all the personal loses and physical hardships her family and she had to suffer at his hands. In the next instalment of the series, which Prabhabati titled "Hatyar Pratisodh" ("Avenging the Murder") we find Krishna setting sail to Burma, the land where she grew up acquiring her physical and mental skills and also her social and cultural sensibilities, to avenge the death of her parents. It is only after her horrific encounter with the loss of a precious but de-tract life of Yu-yin that Krishna decides to work as a detective, a work that was still quite unlikely for a woman. However, her reason for taking up such a task was to become instrumental in delivering people from the atrocities of crime and criminality, to help in the setting up of a better society. Such egalitarian desire smacks of keeping up with the masculinised intention of the detective figure, thus creating a scope for familiarity and acceptance of the woman detective by her readers. The ambivalence of whether she takes up detection as only a service for the nation or as a profession also remains quite unresolved because in the later stories of the series she is seen to dwindle between asserting her work as service only for her near ones (a personal issue) and also accepting monetary rewards at other times.

However, it must be asserted that in the wake of rising female consciousness and the claim of women to occupy the spaces that were erstwhile not available for them, led them to mould themselves into unprecedented roles of the deliverer. In an interview Prabhabati had said, there are very few who are capable of empathy despite being in trouble themselves. There is a reflection of this empathetic nature in Krishna, who became Prabhabati's vehicle for carrying forward the idea of women's emancipation, "May this courage and determination rise in the heart of every woman of Bengal; may Bengal once again become filled with women who are brave-hearts"('Graher Pher', "The Planetary Twist") (p. 79 translation mine). Thus, just as the beginning of detective fiction in the late nineteenth and early twentieth century emphasized on the physical attribute of bravery as an important characteristics of the male detective, besides the sharpness of the mind, the woman detective was also being drawn in similar lines. Hence Krishna is named after the fiery Draupadi. That the woman detective is not divested from nationalistic agenda is clear from the advertisement to *"Hatyar Pratisodh"*, which carries the nationalistic dictate of Vivekananda, "His whose mother's voice is chained/ Weak or strong, how would he determine?" (qtd. in

Ghosh, p. 71, translation mine) Krishna too emphasizes her role as a deliverer, her dedication to the profession emanating from the zeal to work for the society. In *Graher Pher* she says, "Give me your blessings so that I can always have this strength and courage, so that I can be of use to all, and in this way may I be able to consider my birth of some worth, and thus be able to remove the bad name of Bengali women as cowards" (p. 29, translation mine) In the same novella Krishna reveals a new understanding of the abilities of women and their rightful place in society which has been constantly denied:

> With a stern voice Krishna said, "Women are humans too, *meshomashai*. I just intend to show that if educated and trained well they can also deliver work like men. For a long time women have been relegated to darkness which has not allowed them to progress. I would only want to tell them, that no more can they languish behind, they must come forward, they must work and in every field they must leave the imprint of their courage and strength. (p. 32, translation mine)

There is this constant urge in Krishna to motivate other women, not only to come out of their confines, but also to realise their true potential and courage. This modern woman claims her rightful place in public, and also wishes to be the deliverer of women in particular. In an advertisement for the Krishna series (*Sukhtara*, Baishakh 1359) Prabhabati calls upon the women of the recently independent country to equip themselves with self-defence mechanisms. The advertisement reads-

> Every book of *Krishna* series will inspire our mothers and sisters to protect themselves from the cruelties of the conspiring world. If the mothers and sisters of the independent nation tend to depend on others for their protection, like yesteryears, then that would be a matter of more shame than the inherent bashfulness which is considered a womanly trait. (qtd. in Ghosh, p.71, translation mine)

The shift from dependence on man to dependence on self is clearly visible here, an idea that the essays discussed above already projected, where this modernist movement lay in women trying to look out for themselves outside the conventional boundaries. However, such a projection again could not accept a fiercely radical stand and completely do away with the prevalent prejudices against women. The battle of occupying the denied space could not be fought in a linear fashion and witnessed moments of manoeuvring into the popular notions. Prabhabati had to adopt strategies to make her detective more acceptable. Unlike the male detectives, even Byomkesh for that matter, Krishna is unable to completely divest herself from her private life. As already discussed, she takes up the adventures of detection not to support her financially because she belongs to an upper class family with a sound economic background, but to look out for the murderers of her parents. Although detection is not uppermost on her mind, she finds herself pulled into the vortex of crime and detection by the problems that mostly trouble her family members, at least in the first few instalments of the series. While this seems to be an attempt to legitimise her taking up the unusual path of detection, she does not completely dedicate herself to it as she is a college going student who is trying to pursue her education with seriousness. The strength of mind and courage that she projects and also propagates has been instilled in her from childhood, by the upbringing of a barrister father who considered her to be his son. Hence the unprecedented courage that Krishna projects in her public life is the outcome of her being treated as her father's son, which although tends to complicate gender understandings, implicitly conforms to the conventional ideas of gender roles, where courage and strength are always considered male reserves. However, later on in the series Krishna's call to all women to shake off their effeminacy and strengthen themselves with courage appeals to that strength which has been rusting in the insides of women for many years now, which must be brought out and put to proper use. Krishna is also positioned here as an outsider, being born and brought up in Burma, coming to Bengal only after she has attained eighteen years of age. This might seem to be an adequate justification of the unusualness in the character of Krishna, who was far away from the conventional social and cultural conservative Bengali setup. In Krishna we can, on the one hand see an easy conflation of the domains of the public and the private—as a detective she cannot always have an objective take on the circumstances which lead to her detection since she mostly deals with the private affairs within the family; but, again, she takes to the streets, often unescorted, falls into trouble, carries a revolver, appears in newspaper headlines, thus often becoming the public figure. On the other hand, Prabhabati is unsure of the acceptability of such a character among the *bhadralok* readers and so, almost as a justification, she writes in the advertisement to "*Mayabi Krishna*":

> This genteel and respectable young girl, by the sheer dint of her presence of mind, sometimes by employing disguise...is achieving unparalled success....Protecting herself from the grip of the autocratic, manipulative, ferocious (male) lot, keeping her womanly obligation and respect unscathed, the novel tricks she devises to defend herself and rescue the victimised women is possible only by a highly educated and well-bred woman of class and descent. (Ghosh *Goyendanir* p. 71) (Translation mine).

The challenge here seems to be, to register her presence in public that is fraught with the constant need to legitimise such a presence in order to appear convincing and also in order to garner respect for what could otherwise risk a voyeuristic indulgence. As such she is supposed to be in a mission to protect other women, while keeping her womanly virtues intact. She must be a *bhadramahila*, a woman of character and integrity, otherwise she might not be acceptable to the *bhadralok* readers, and all of this is necessary since she is constantly blurring the borders of the public and the private in order to create an altogether different space of existence.

Women within the Ambivalent Borders of Existence

In the essay which began this article, Chatterjee observes that modernity is the first social philosophy that conjures up in the minds of the most ordinary people dreams of independence and self-rule. The regime of power in modern societies works through the individual practice of reason. However, no matter how deftly reason tries to cloak the realities of power, power is always resisted, autonomy always sought. Hence Chatterjee enumerates: "The burden of reason, dreams of freedom; the desire for power, resistance to power: all of these are elements of modernity" (p. 25). Thus modernity tends to be a dynamic process that is always resisting power. It cannot settle down, but it has to go on developing new strategies of coping with power. Modernity calls for actions that must be directed towards changing the present. Women writings are, thus, constantly grappling with this idea of change, with the need to point at the moment of change, the 'new' that is both a marker of a disruption and a continuity, and also to point at change that marks the present state of our modernity. The very strategy that women writers have used to cope with the demands of modernity at every point of its occurrence has been to comprehend the idea of freedom. In the character of Krishna, Prabhabati mirrors not what women are, but what women could aspire to be in the changing times. Krishna came up as the aspiration of the modern woman who is conscious of her rights and position, is self-sufficient, brave enough to face and overcome, even transform the trying circumstances of a patriarchal society that she has to constantly battle against. Krishna, like the woman writer of the period, is constantly grappling with the ambivalence that modernity has presented to her. For the women writer the public medium of publication allows her the freedom to resist, aspire for change, rebel against norms. She, thus, tries to create a merger of her private domain with her public domain, when her experiences within her private sphere inspire her writing for her public presence. Krishna, too, tries to motivate her public life by her comprehension of what she experiences as a woman in her private life. Of course there cannot be any simplistic understandings of these moments which are so intricately informed by our indecisiveness towards modernity, but it can definitely call for moments which blur distinctions, reorder borders, often making them shadowy presences of ambivalent import.

References

Ashapoorna Debi. "Meye Goyendar Bahaduri" in *Ashapoorna Debi-r Shukhtara-r Shera Golpo*.Kolkata. Deb Sahitya Kutir. 2016. pp. 270-282

Bagchi, Jayeeta. "Education and Gender in Nineteenth Century Bengal: An Overview" in Ipshita Chanda and JayeetaBagchi (ed.) *Shaping the Discourse: Women's Writings in Bengali Periodicals 1865-1947*. Kolkata. School of Women's Studies, JU and Stree. 2014. pp. liv- lxvii

—. "Ekaal Kokhon Shuru Holo? (When did this Era Begin)?: Mapping Modernity in Women's Discourse in Colonial Bengal" in Anirban Das, Ritu Sen Chaudhuri, Jayeeta Bagchi. *Scripting the Nation: Bengali Women's Writing, 1870s to 1960s*. Kolkata.School of Women's Studies, Jadavpur University. 2009. pp. 71-85

—. (trans.). "The Ideal Woman" by Shukalata Rao in Ipshita Chanda and JayeetaBagchi (ed.) *Shaping the Discourse: Women's Writings in Bengali Periodicals 1865-1947*. Kolkata. School of Women's Studies, JU and Stree. 2014. pp. 250-253

Bannerji, Himani (trans.) Krishnabhabini Das. "The Educated Women" in "Fashioning a Self: Educational Proposals for and by women in Popular Magazines in Colonial Bengal" in *Inventing Subjects: Studies in Hegemony, Patriarchy and Colonialism*. London. Anthem Press. 2001. pp. 135-178

—. "Inventing Subjects: An Introduction" in *Inventing Subjects: Studies in Hegemony, Patriarchy and Colonialism*. London. Anthem Press. 2001. pp. 1-17

—. "Fashioning a Self: Educational Proposals for and by women in Popular Magazines in Colonial Bengal" in *Inventing Subjects: Studies in Hegemony, Patriarchy and Colonialism*. London. Anthem Press. 2001. pp. 135-178

Bhattacharya, Swagata (trans.). "What is the Ideal sphere of women's work?" by Leelabati Roy in Ipshita Chanda and Jayeeta Bagchi (ed.) *Shaping the Discourse: Women's Writings in Bengali Periodicals 1865-1947*. Kolkata. School of Women's Studies, JU and Stree. 2014. pp. 361-366

Chatterjee, Partha. "Our Modernity". Rotterdam/Dakar: South-South Exchange ProgrammeFor Research on the History of Development (SEPHIS) and The Council for the Development of Social Science Research in Africa (CODESRIA). 1997

—. "The Nationalist Resolution of the Women's Question" in Kumkum Sangari and Sudesh Vaid (ed) *Recasting Women: Essays in Colonial History*. New Delhi. Zubaan. 1989. pp. 306- 333

Chanda, Ipshita. "Women Writing Gender" in Ipshita Chanda and Jayeeta Bagchi (ed.) *Shaping the Discourse: Women's Writings in Bengali Periodicals 1865-1947*. Kolkata. School of Women's Studies, JU and Stree. 2014. pp. xx- liii

Chatterjee, Priyanka. Book Review: *Interrogating Motherhood* in *Asian Journal of Women's Studies*, Routledge. 23:3, p. 411-416, DOI: 10.1080/12259276.2017.1349719

Dasgupta, Arindam (ed.). *Shekaler Goyenda Kahini*. Kolkata.Ananda. 2016. (All translations from here are mine unless otherwise stated).

Dasgupta, Prajnamita (trans.). "Bengali Women and the Issue of Freedom" by Anonymous in Ipshita Chanda and JayeetaBagchi (ed.) *Shaping the Discourse: Women's Writings in Bengali Periodicals 1865-1947*. Kolkata.School of Women's Studies, JU and Stree. 2014. pp. 4-6

Dutta, Jayita. "Lekhika Prabhbati: Kalantarer Upekkhai Ochena" in Tapash Bhaumik (ed.). *Lekhikader Lekhalekhi*. Kolkata. *Korok Sahitya Patrika*. 2019. pp. 20-30. [Translation mine]

Ghosh, Nirmalya. "GoyendanirShatkahan" in Tapash Bhaumik (ed.). *Bangla Goyenda Sahitya Sankha*. Kolkata. *Korok Sahitya Patrika*. 2017. pp. 70-72

Guha Thakurta, Debolina (trans.). "Women and Art" by Anonymous in Ipshita Chanda and JayeetaBagchi (ed.) *Shaping the Discourse: Women's Writings in Bengali Periodicals 1865-1947*. Kolkata. School of Women's Studies, JU and Stree. 2014. pp. 90-93

Ray, Shampa. "Introduction: Plotting Crimes: Early Crime Writings in Bangla and Their Contexts" in *Gender and Criminality in Bangla Crime Narratives: Late Nineteenth and Early Twentieth Centuries*. London. Palgrave Macmillan. 2017. pp. 1- 49

—. "Detection and Desire: Male Goyendas and their Female Bête-Noires in the Early Bangla Detective Novels" in *Gender and Criminality in Bangla Crime Narratives: Late Nineteenth and Early Twentieth Centuries*. London. Palgrave Macmillan. 2017. pp.185- 225

Roy, Anindita (trans.). "Women and Employment" by Santisudha Ghosh in Ipshita Chanda and JayeetaBagchi (ed.) *Shaping the Discourse: Women's Writings in Bengali Periodicals 1865-1947*. Kolkata. School of Women's Studies, JU and Stree. 2014. pp. 389-395

Roy, Somesh (trans.). "Women and Men" by Krishnabhabini Das in Ipshita Chanda and Jayeeta Bagchi (ed.) *Shaping the Discourse: Women's Writings in Bengali Periodicals 1865-1947*. Kolkata. School of Women's Studies, JU and Stree. 2014. pp. 15-26

Ray, Shampa. *Gender and Criminality in Bangla Crime Narratives: Late Nineteenth and Early Twentieth Centuries*. London. Palgrave Macmillan. 2017

Sarkar, Tanika. "Introduction" in *Hindu Wife, Hindu Nation: Community, Religion and Cultural Nationalism*. New Delhi. Permanent Black. 2000. pp. 2-20

Saraswati, Prabhabati. "Gupta Ghatak" in Kanchenjungha Series (Vol. 2). Kolkata. Deb Sahitya Kutir. Reprint. 2008.

—. "Graher Pher" in Kanchenjungha Series (vol. 4). Kolkata. Deb Sahitya Kutir. Reprint. 2007.

—. "Hatyar Pratishodh" in Kanchenjungha Series (Vol. 3). Kolkata. Deb Sahitya Kutir. Reprint. 2006.

Erasing the Borders: Tagore's Engagement with the Subalterns in *Sahaj Path*

Goutam Buddha Sural

In *Sahaj Path*, Tagore consciously highlights some characters who are members of the poor working class community known for their subjugated status in society. The presence of such characters cannot be ignored in the short lessons of the two parts of *Sahaj Path*. The lessons, in a way, oppose subalternization of these marginal characters, thereby challenging a hegemonic reading of the text. Almost all the members of the upper class in these short lessons do not believe or participate in the marginalization of the inferior rank of people in our society. Rather they are allowed a space of their own which, on the one hand, helps in the establishment of a convenient mutuality between the dominant and the dominated and on the other, attempts to obliterate the psychological margins between the economically weak working class and the members of the wealthy upper class.

In the beginning of his essay "Nationalism" Rabindranath pointed out India's 'race problem' and observed:

> She has made grave errors in setting up the boundary walls too rigidly between races, in perpetuating the results of inferiority in her classifications; often she has crippled her children's minds and narrowed their lives in order to fit them into her social forms; but for centuries new experiments have been made and adjustments carried out. (419)

Sekhar Bandyopadhyay in his essay "Rabindranath Tagore, the Indian Nation, and its Outcasts" published in *Harvard Asia Quarterly* 15.1 (2013) points out that by 'race problem' Tagore actually meant 'caste distinctions' (36). On the occasion of Tagore's birth centenary Dr. Radhakrishnan paid his rich tribute to the great poet. In his essay "Most Dear to All the Muses" he wrote:

Rabindranath rebelled against the orthodoxies surrounding him and traced India's fall to the clash of castes and creeds, to indifference to the disinherited of the earth. The truly religious men have intense love for the non-conformists, for the homeless and the rejected. We have suffered on account of our meek submission to social restrictions and lazy reliance on traditional authorities which are incongruous anachronisms in our age. The greatest enemies of a nation are not their foreign foes but the enemies who dwell within them. (xxi-xxii)

Tagore's philosophy of life was to exterminate 'the enemies who dwell within' us by trying to erase the psychological borders between the upper class landed gentry and the poor working class people. Rabindranath Tagore's *Sahaj Path* is a children's text; but if we do not take the same for too neat a reading, we may unravel the text to pick up threads of interesting interpretations. In doing so we may be charged with indulging in a politics of interpretations, but I feel any new reading of a text, for that matter, necessarily involves such a politics. At this point I would like to mention the observations of Lila Mazumdar which subsequently made me further interested in *Sahaj Path* and inspired me to dig into the layers of interpretations that lie hidden under the surface. Talking about Tagore's children literature Lila Majumdar observes:

> They remind one again that when the poet wrote for children, he did not merely intend to amuse them or help them to while away their leisure, but gave to them generously the costliest treasures of his mind, to make into an integral part of their lives. *They are not the baby toys* that the young reader will outgrow after a time, but possess that rarest quality of creative achievement, whose meaning and significance increase in proportion to the growth of the reader's mind. (178) (emphasis mine)

And as far as *Sahaj Path* is concerned she writes:

> One does not need to look further than his little series of Bengali primers, *Sahaj Path*, to realize how deep his understanding of the child's mind was. The fortunate learner is initiated into the mysteries of the written word, *with a wealth of poetic suggestions* and a murmuring as of music. The very act of learning one's letter becomes a pleasure. *The primer turns into literature.* (178) (emphasis mine)

In the first part of *Sahaj Path* as the child is introduced to Bengali alphabet the letters are often personified as members of the working class like rowers, labourers, reapers, drummers, cart drivers, farmers etc. As the lessons begin there is further mention of such people—Madhu Roy-a rower, Joylal-a ploughman, Abinash-a grass cutter, Harihar, a thatcher, Patu Pal-a dealer in rice, Dinanath-a cook, and Gurudas-a farmer. These characters reflect the hegemonic structure of the society yet the way their likes are portrayed speaks about the compassionate attitude of Tagore towards these people. These subaltern characters are important contributors to the different aspects of social life and they are a major presence in the two parts of *Sahaj Path*. Usually these people are kept away from the centre but Tagore gives recognition to these characters with a view to creating an impression on the child's mind about the important role that these characters play in everyday life of the society. The discourse of feudal authority is displaced in these texts and the language breathes a new consciousness.

Tagore travelled to East Bengal in 1891 under instruction from Maharshi Debendranath to look after their landed property there. He stayed in a number of villages in East Bengal and during his stay there he got the opportunity to see the life of the village people from very close quarters. He was born and brought up in the palatial building at Jorasanko in Calcutta. When he went to East Bengal it was as if a journey from the centre to the margin. He came into contact with innumerable villagers belonging to the poor working class. He himself admits that he never particularly thought about these people before coming to these villages of East Bengal. His contact with these people generated a new awareness. In his essay "Panchabhut" included in volume I of Rabindra Rachanabali, he writes:

> Theoretically I ignore these illiterate and ignorant farmers as uncivilized savages but when I actually come in contact with them I love them as my relatives. And I feel that my heart secretly cherishes a respect for them (902)*

In the same vein in a letter (No. 95, *Chhinnapatra*) Tagore talks freely about his sympathy for the downtrodden poor cultivators:

> When I see these poor farmers I feel great compassion for them—they are like God's innocent and helpless children, until God comes down to help them there is none to feed them. When the breast of the earth dries up then

they are left to tears only, again when their hunger is satiated a little, they forget their woes. Socialists advocate for the distributions of wealth the world over. I am not sure if that is really possible—but if it is absolutely impossible then God's dispensation is really very cruel and man is really unfortunate. If woe is inevitable in this world, let it be, but there should be some possibility, some ways so that the developed section of mankind can work relentlessly for mitigating this sorrow, can at least cherish some hope for bettering the condition. (204)*

The members of the upper class need a truly compassionate attitude to comprehend the other side and transcend the existing boundary. Class boundaries can not be erased but a bridge may be built to establish a dialogue, a meaningful cooperation. While there are money-sucking landlords as we find in the character of Landlord Durlav in chapter thirteen of *Sahaj Path* II, side by side there are people among the upper class who have a humanitarian attitude and feel for the plight of the downtrodden and the wretched in the society. We may cite the example of Katyayani Thakrun, the aunt of Durlav. The central character of the lesson is Uddhav who belongs to a low caste and is very poor. He had to sell whatever little landed property he had to clear his debt. Now he passes his days with great difficulty by working as a day labourer. During his daughter's marriage he caught a big fish from the landlord's pond not being aware that catching fish from that pond was prohibited. He was arrested and taken to the landlord who gave the verdict that until he paid a ten rupee fine he would not be released. Katyayani Thakrun tried to plead with his nephew but failed. She, however, mended it not only by paying the fine but also by sending largesse needed for his daughter's marriage. Finally she herself went to Uddhav's house and gave a gold chain to Nistarini—daughter of Uddhav. This goes in tandem with Tagore's vision of life, particularly as far as his attitude towards the subaltern people of the society is concerned.

In lesson 12 of *Sahaj Path*, II Doctor Biswambhar, accompanied by his servant, Sambhu is going to a distant place, Saptagram, for treating a patient. There is a detailed description of Sambhu's physical prowess in the story. On his way to this place they were attacked by dacoits—they were five in number. Sambhu alone fought with them and while two of them fled, three of them got severely injured by Sambhu's stick. The way the text describes the incident clearly points out the helpless condition of the Doctor and his complete dependence on his servant, Sambhu. Throughout the lesson the physical prowess of Shambhu has been portrayed through at least three incidents. The protagonist of the text certainly is not the Doctor but his servant. The interesting part is that the doctor now asked Shambhu to bring his medicine box. When Shambhu wanted to know the reason the doctor replied that he would treat the injury of the dacoits. And then the doctor and Sambhu jointly carried out the treatment. The significant point to note here is that even the dacoits (who are, in a way, offshoots of the feudal system) are compassionately treated as human beings by a member of the upper class.

The traffic between the rich or the elite and the subaltern in the lessons of *Sahaj Path* points to a strategy of inclusion of the indigenous rank of inferior people. Arguments may be proffered against the specific mention of the caste or class to which these people actually belong. In other words, one may disapprove of the way a child is made aware of persons like servant, sweeper, labourer, cook etc by repeatedly mentioning them in the lessons, thereby subtly planting the seed of hegemonic relationship in his mind. But the fact is that these people belonging to the inferior rank of society are a reality. By any kind of sugar coating device their role or presence in the society cannot be camouflaged. The best way to give them their due space in the society is to recognize their dignity of labour. Rabindranath has precisely tried to do this in his writings, the *Sahaj Path* being no exception. In this connection, I would like to refer to Sekhar Bandyopadhyay's observations in his essay. Referring to Tagore's essay "Nationalism" Bandyopadhyay writes:

> By associating specific occupations to different castes, the system had succeeded in "allaying for good the interminable jealousy and hatred of competition," which was the hallmark of Western societies. In this way India was able to avoid all frictions and yet to afford to each race freedom within its boundaries." In other words, he too believed with Gandhi that *varnashrama* was a harmonious system of social division of labour — uncolonized — and therefore, a unique marker of Indian difference and her civilizational superiority over the west. (36)

Judged from this angle *Sahaj Path* plays a path breaking role in decolonizing the child mind effectively by pointing out that it is wrong to discriminate the poor and the downtrodden people of society. In this connection we may consider the words of Humayun Kabir. In his essay "Social and Political Ideas of Tagore" he writes:

> Once privileges are divorced from birth or status and related to the individual's contribution to society, Tagore was not averse to distinctions among individuals. He was a practical idealist who knew that men differ in capacity and character, and equality of opportunity is compatible with differences in achievement. In fact, he held that this was one of the devices which enable society to function in a healthy manner. (146)

Tagore was full of sympathy for the poor peasants who remained excluded from the social space in their own country. In his "Address to the Staff and Students of Santiniketan and Sriniketan" he said:

> No civilized society can thrive upon victims whose humanity has been permanently mutilated, whose minds have been compelled to dwell in the dark. Those whom we keep down inevitably dragus down and obstruct our movement in the path of progress. The indignity with which we burden them grows into an intolerable burden to the whole country; we insult our own humanity by insulting Man where he is helpless or where he is not our own kin. (326)

In the second lesson of Part II we find the servant Satya acting as a social representative of his master who belongs to the upper class. Adyanath babu, the jute merchant sends his servant to the narrator, who is a member of the nobility, to invite him to attend his daughter's marriage ceremony. The point that strikes the reader is Adyanath babu himself did not come to extend the invitation instead sends his servant for the purpose. Here Satya, the servant, is acknowledged with dignity to act as his master's emissary. The narrator accepts the invitation and confirms his participation in the ceremony. On the day of the ceremony the narrator went there and saw that farmers in large numbers have come to attend the ceremony. The difference between the rich and the poor, the upper and lower class people of society gets obliterated on such an occasion.

In the very first lesson of *Sahaj Path* II Kangla is not just a menial worker; he also has the gift of acting on the stage. He is going to play the role of a 'Song' — sort of a clown in a dramatic performance *Kangsa Badh* to be staged in honour of the king of Pangshupur. One may argue to point out that by assigning the role of a clown to Kangla he is further marginalised. But the fact is that a clown is often known for his straightforward and blunt nature and Kagla who does not have urban sophistication is a pragmatic choice for the role. Besides the 'Song' is an important character of folk performances. While the 'Song' performs as a physical comic tool to amuse the audience, he is also a cultural symbol. Such a character clearly responds to the variety of culture of his time and incorporates familiar physicality and at times even steps further to offer social critiquing through colloquial references.

The third lesson is about a cleaning operation of a locality to be taken up by the boys of that locality. Elders of the locality like Rangalal babu and his elder brother will also come to join the boys. A car is being sent to them to fetch them to the spot; the interesting point to note here is that along with these people the author says that they will also be taking sweeper Bhingi with them. The coexistence of the elite and the subaltern is to be particularly noted. Almost immediately we are reminded of Mulk Raj Anand's novel, *Untouchable*. Expressing his anger about the discriminatory and corrupt attitude of the upper class people Bakha says: "They think we are mere dirt because we clean their dirt" (79). Tagore's mention of Bhingi reflects an attitude of inclusiveness. In this connection we may take note of what Humayun Kabir says in his essay already mentioned:

> Tagore believed and repeatedly declared that the caste system and its attendant practice of untouchability were among the darkest blots of Indian society. It had prevented the development of the Indian community into a unified and homogenous whole and was a major cause of the misery and humiliation which India had suffered at various times....There is a rare intensity of feeling and indignation in his writings whenever he spoke or wrote of the injustice and misery flowing from caste, untouchability or sex. (146)

During his visit to East Bengal Tagore felt empathy for the poor and underprivileged people of that place. The responsibility of looking after the family estates opened up new vistas of inspiration for him. He now came to acquire a direct and intimate experience of the wretched life led by the poor Bengali peasants. These conditions, he thought, could not be changed by appealing to the religious sentiments of the landlord, policeman or money-lender. In human society, necessity is a greater force than charity. The first requirement therefore is that people should discover the bond that holds them together as a society. Tagore's words in this connection may be taken note of. In his essay "Panchabhut", mentioned earlier, he writes:

> When I think that there are numberless people whose sorrows and sufferings, whose humanity still remain undiscovered to us, whom we only engage in work and pay them wages in return but do not give them love, consolation or respect, then I really feel that a great part of the world is still enveloped by darkness and is absolutely beyond our ken. (911)*

As a young landlord managing his family's rural estates, Tagore came to realize that the people belonging to the inferior ranks of society represent a different face of society. Another feature of *Sahaj Path* is the mutuality of relationship between the two classes of people—the inter-dependence of the upper and lower class. In lesson after lesson we find the mention of inferior rank of people who constantly assist their masters and the masters in their turn express a concern for them; in lesson six the narrator is planning to go out on a rainy day with a group to see the beauty of a stream. Kanto, the servant will accompany them. His anxiety for Kanto is clearly expressed when he says that Kanto does not have any appetite. He has come out early in the morning just after having some boiled rice steeped in cold water. Again in the ninth lesson the author's concern for a poor female singer is expressed in no uncertain manner; it is raining outside and the narrator gives instruction that she should be allowed entry inside the house. It would be cruel to keep her outside as she might get drenched by rain.

One very interesting fact of this relationship comes out in lesson nine where Shaktinath babu accompanied by his servant, Akrur went out for a hunting expedition. In the jungle they lost their way and after spending one night on a tree top, the next day in the morning they met a group of wood cutters. Saktinath babu requested the leader of the wood cutters to give them shelter in their house and give them some food. He told them that they have lost their way in the jungle. They entertained them with food, goat milk and water from the river. They took rest in their place and in the afternoon the leader of the wood cutters guided them their way to the boat. Shaktinath babu was overwhelmed by their hospitality and offered a ten rupee note to him. With folded hands he politely refused the offer saying that to accept it would be an unethical act on his part (39).

The sense of dignity that one finds in the words of the leader of the wood cutters strikes the reader immediately. It is not always that the elite or rich people are in the position of givers; there are times when the opposite is equally true. In this connection we may take note of Promothonath Bisi's observation in his book *Silaidahey Rabindranath*. As a landlord Tagore used to visit the villages on a palanquin. He narrates Tagore's experience during such visits:

> At times a Muslim subject appears and stopping the palanquin offers Rs. 2/- to the poet as a gift. When the poet refuses to accept the money the man retorts by pointing out "How would you provide for yourself unless we give you money?" A caustic truth indeed! The primary sketch of a future indigenous society flashes up in the poet's mind. The margins between his self as a landlord and that as a writer get obliterated. (43)*

It is often found that the lower-class people hold more liberal values and are more likely to help others regardless of compassion level whereas the higher-class people with greater resources are more selfish and therefore less likely to lend their hands of help in time of others' needs. The lessons of *Sahaj Path* speak of the poet's deep faith in the efficacy of maintaining a shared relationship among the people of different strata of society. Tagore's writings, even those for children, show a profound understanding of the psyche of the poor and underprivileged village folk. Tagore always believed in the assimilative power of Indian civilization. According to him India developed as 'an inclusive civilizational community' (Bandyopadhyay 36). In *Sahaj Path* Tagore wanted to create a meaningful passage between the upper and the lower class people and wanted the learner to envision a society based on mutual cooperation of all classes and creeds. In this connection we may refer to Tagore's words in his essay "Nationalism" where he pleads for removal of boundaries among the races in India:

> India had felt that diversity of races there must be and should be…but what she failed to realize was that in human beings differences are not like the physical barriers of mountains, fixed forever — they are fluid with life's flow, they are changing their courses and their shapes and volume. Therefore in her caste regulations India recognized differences, but not the mutability which is the law of life. In trying to avoid collisions she set up boundaries of immovable walls, thus giving to her numerous races the negative benefit of peace and order but not the positive opportunity of expansion and movement. (460)

He wanted a meaningful inclusion of the working class in the society through a socioeconomic integration so that they are not regarded with unfavourable regard. He always believed that a change in the psychic perspective of the upper class people can effectively erase the margins of psychological borderlands that existed between the poor and the rich, the high and the low. He was against psychological subordination of the working class people as that was detrimental to the spiritual unity and development of the nation. As I conclude I may refer to Tagore's poem "He mor chitta, punnyatirthe" (Poem No. 106 of *Gitanjali*) where he implores the members of the upper caste to set aside their psychological inhibition about untouchability so that an assimilative and unified India can emerge out of an atmosphere of mutuality among different castes and creed:

> Come O Brahmin purify your mind and hold everybody's hand,
> Come Ye Fallen casting aside the burden of past humiliation.
> (Trans. by Mitra)

These lines essentially highlight the inclusive nature of India's civilization. It is also reflective of India's unique power to absorb various cultures and emerge as the meeting place of people not only from outside the nation but also from all walks of life within the country.

*The translations of the Bengali excerpts are done by the author.

Works Cited

Anand, Mulk Raj. *Untouchable*. London: Penguin. 1940.

Bandyopadhyay, Sekhar. "Rabidranath Tagore, the Indian Nation, and its Outcasts." *Harvard Asia Quarterly*. 15.1. (2013). 34-39.

Bisi, Promothonath. *Silaidahey Rabindranath*. Kolkata: Mitra & Ghosh Publishers Pvt. Ltd. 1972. 12th rpt. 2018.

Kabir, Humayun. "Social and Political Ideas of Tagore." *Rabindranath Tagore: A Centenary Volume: 1861-1961*. New Delhi: Sahitya Akademi. 1961. 145-152.

Majumdar, Lila. "Tagore as a Writer for Children." *Rabindranath Tagore: A Centenary Volume: 1861-1961*. New Delhi: Sahitya Akademi. 1961. 172-179.

Mitra, Chandan. "Tagore's Indian Maha Manav". *The Pioneer*. Sunday, 30 July 2017. https://www.dailypioneer.com/2017/sunday-edition/tagores-indian-maha-manav.html Accessed on 07 September, 2019.

Radhakrishnan, Sarvepalli. "Most Dear to All the Muses." *Rabindranath Tagore: A Centenary Volume: 1861-1961*. New Delhi: Sahitya Akademi. 1961. XVII-XXV.

Tagore, Rabindranath. "Address to the Staff and Students of Santiniketan and Sriniketan." *The English Writings of Rabindranath Tagore*. Vol.III. Ed. Sisir Kumar Das, New Delhi: Sahitya Akademi. 1996.

—. *Chhinnapatra*. Kolkata: Visva Bharati. 1895.

—. "He mor chitta, punnyatirthe." *Gitanjali. Rabindra Rachanabali*. Vol. VI. Kolkata: Visva Bharati. 1988. rpt. 1995. 69-71.

—. "Nationalism." *The English Writings of Rabindranath Tagore*. Vol II. Ed. Sisir Kumar Das. New Delhi: Sahitya Akademi, 1996. 417-466.

—. "Panchabhut." *Rabindra Rachanabali*. Vol. I. Kolkata: Visva Bharati, 1987, rpt. 1995. 885-949.

—. *Sahaj Path I & II*. Kolkata: Visva Bharati. 1930. Rpt. 2017.

Contributors

Amanda Rutherford *is a lecturer in the School of Communications and the School of Language and Culture at Auckland University of Technology in New Zealand. She is a member of the AUT Popular Culture Centre, the Gothic Association of New Zealand and Australia (GANZA), and the Popular Culture Association of Australia and New Zealand (POPCAANZ). Her interests include Mediated Popular Culture, Fairytale, Fantasy, Gothic and Horror.*

Sarah Baker *is a Senior Lecturer in the School of Communications at Auckland University of Technology. She is the co-founder of the AUT Popular Culture Centre and a member of JMAD and the AUT Media Observatory Group. Her research interests include political economy, current affairs television programmes, and popular culture focusing on the Gothic, sexuality and gender.*

Salvatore Perri *achieved his Bachelor's degree in "Lingue e Culture Moderne" (Foreign Languages and Culture) at the University of Calabria, with a final dissertation titled Mascolinità vittoriana: la consunzione dell'archetipo tra repressione e ibridazioni col femminile (Victorian Masculinity: the erosion of the archetype between repression and hybridizations with femininity). He then continued his studies at Alma Mater Studiorum – University in bologna, at the Faculty of "Letterature moderne, comparate e postcoloniali" (Modern, Compared and Postcolonial Literatures), keep focusing his academic interest on identity – articulated on a gender and socio-geographical perspective – and he earned his Master's degree with a thesis titled «Seule maîtresse à bord de mon corps»: rivendicazione identitaria tra corporeità e scrittura nell'opera di Grisélidis Réal" ("Seule maîtresse à bord de mon corps": identity claim through corporeity and writing in the work of Grisélidis Réal).*

Sandip Mondal *is an Associate Professor at the Department of English, University of Calcutta. He has interest in pedagogy and the practice of theatre. Along with teaching canonical literature, he has also worked in the discipline of Film Studies. He has completed his research work on the film adaptations of Shakespeare. His publications and interest also include Cultural studies.*

Aditya Kant Ghising *is an Assistant Professor in the department of Political Science at City College, Kolkata. He is also a Doctoral Candidate at the department of International Relations at Jadavpur University, Kolkata. He has written several articles on North-East India, India's Southeast Asia Policy as well as the strategically located Siliguri Corridor, also known as the Chicken's Neck in strategic and military circles and is a keen observer of borders and borderland studies in the Himalayan region. He has completed his B.A. in Political Science as well as M.A. and M.Phil. in International Relations with a specialization in Southeast Asian economy and politics from Jadavpur University, Kolkata.*

Priya Menon, *Ph.D., is Associate Professor of English at Troy University, USA. This article was partially written when she was a Fulbright-Nehru Academic and Professional Excellence Fellow at The Centre for Development Studies, Thiruvananthapuram, Kerala in 2018.*

Nicoletta Policek *(PhD in Legal Studies, University of Edinburgh) is Associate Professor in Policing and Criminology and Head of the Graduate School at the University of Cumbria, UK. Nicoletta has been combining a career in academia with her passion for social justice and human rights, directing national and international NGOs. At present she sits on the Board of Trustees at HIV Scotland as the chairperson and she is a member of Community Justice Scotland's Academic Advisory Group. An enthusiastic social scientist, her scholarly interests are in the broad field of victimology, penology, gender and sexuality studies, migration and criminal and social justice. More specifically, she is concerned with the policing and the criminalization of migration and the criminalisation of statelessness. Currently she is engaged on the following research endeavours: ethics in policing; enforced mobility and abortion rights; victimisation of migrant women in prison settings; criminalisation of stateless children and women.*

Oriol J. Batalla *is a MA in Comparative Literature and Cultural Analysis graduate for the University of Amsterdam (2019) and an Independent Scholar from Barcelona. His research focuses on Environmental Humanities, Ethics and Justice, Political Ecology, Anti-Capitalist and Political Theory, Degrowth, Extinction Studies, Anthropocene Studies, Animal Studies, Contemporary Global Politics, Sociology, Media and Cultural Analysis and Critical Theory.*

Debapriya Paul, *Assistant Professor, Dept of English, University of Calcutta, has done his M A and MPhil from the University of Calcutta. Presently he is pursuing his PhD on the Mutiny Novels in English from Visva Bharati. Before joining the University of Calcutta he has worked as a Project Fellow in an UGC Project at the Dept of English, C U, and also as an Assistant Professor at Raiganj Surendranath Mahavidyalaya and University of GourBanga, Malda. He has contributed to journals like Victorian Periodicals Review, Journal of the Dept. of English, C U, and also in edited volumes like Tagore and Modernity. He currently specializes in 19th century literature, especially fiction, classical literature, Indian fiction in English and Literary Theory. He was the joint editor of the last issue of the Journal of the Department of English, University of Calcutta.*

Sharmistha Chatterjee, *is Associate Professor in English and Head of the Department, at Aliah University, Kolkata, West Bengal. Her areas of interest include, South Asian Literature, Translation studies, Postcolonialism, Partition, Eco-criticism, Gender Studies, Modern Linguistics and English Language Teaching. Dr Chatterjee has been the Trainer Associate from 2007-2013 in the UGC programme, Capacity Building for Women Managers in Higher education. Recipient of UGC Travel Grant, she has travelled to parts of Europe to present her papers. She has authored and edited books on Translations and Translation studies, Postcolonialism and Language studies. This apart, she has been published widely in National and International books and journals. Her latest book on English Communication has been published by Cambridge, U.K. Currently, she is Teacher Coordinator and Resource person in the People's Project on Partition, an Indo- Bangladesh endeavour under the aegis of Centre for Languages, Translation and Cultural Studies, Netaji- Subhas Open University, Kolkata.*

Sharmistha Das *was educated at the University of Burdwan where she obtained her Master Degree (Gold Medalist) and is pursuing her doctoral thesis on Doris Lessing. Serving under WBES, she had been a part of the English faculty of Barasat Govt. College and presently teaching in Hooghly Mohsin College. Her area of interest is Postmodern British Literature. She has extensively contributed to national and international journals and books.*

Rajarshi Bagchi *is an Assistant Professor in English at North Bengal St. Xavier's College. He is currently doing his PhD on French Feminism from Raiganj University. Rajarshi has presented seminar papers and published in scholarly journals like The Apollonian. His interests include Western and Eastern philosophies, feminism, post-structuralist theories and spiritual-mystical traditions in India.*

Emma Musty *teaches in Aberystwyth University, Wales, United Kingdom. She was awarded PhD in 2016 from Aberystwyth University. She has written and published extensively on borders and migration.*

Ratul Nandi *is an Assistant Professor of English in Siliguri College, West Bengal, India. He published research papers and articles in journals, edited volumes and newspapers. His research interests include Animal Studies, Anthropocene and Climate Change, Ecocriticism, Literary Theory and Continental Philosophy.*

Working as a Research Scholar at the Department of English, School of Languages and Literatures, Sikkim University, Gangtok, ***Priyanka Chatterjee*** *is trying to delve into the politics of gender and genre in detective fiction. While the politics and philosophy of gendered understandings in literature is her area of interest, she enjoys transcending disciplinary boundaries every now and then. She has had the opportunity to publish with Asian Journal for Women's Studies (Taylor and Francis), Feminist Review (Palgrave Macmillan), Asian Journal of Social Sciences (Brill), Journal for the Centre for Women Studies (Kalyani University), while also enjoying contributions to non-academic online forums like Feminism in India, Womens Web, Cafe Dissensus, among others. She can be reached at site.surferpc@gmail.com*

Nirjhar Sarkar *is an Associate Professor in the Department of English, Raiganj University. His publications include 'Existence as Self-making in Derek Walcott's The Sea at Dauphin' from Miami University Scholarly Repository. He has presented papers in the 2017 International Symposium on Culture, Arts, and Literature (Osaka, Japan) and Conference on Media and Culture (University of London).*

Goutam Buddha Sural, *professor, Department of English, Bankura University, has been in teaching since 1990. He joined Bankura Christian College in 1990 in the Dept. of English where he was Associate Professor and Head of the P G Dept of English. He went to Bristol University, U K, in 2006 as a visiting fellow. He joined the Dept. of English, Vidyasagar University, Midnapore, as a professor in 2008. A year later, in 2009, he came back to his old college and continued to teach there until July, 2015. He is the author of a book on Hopkins and Pre-Raphaelitism and has edited four books on Tribal Life. He has presented papers in various conferences and seminars and a number of his papers have been published in different national and international journals and books. His area of interest is Victorian Poetry, Indian English Literature and Tribal and Dalit Studies.*

Index

Abolitionist 296

Agency 25, 29, 32, 33, 34, 98, 110, 124, 127, 135, 185, 187, 194, 195, 208, 209, 215, 218, 223, 224, 227, 229, 232, 233, 234, 235, 246, 251, 258, 260, 262, 264, 343

Alienation 30, 32, 60, 130, 132, 133, 159, 161, 169, 210, 215, 268, 269, 299

Anthropocene 33, 40, 218, 241, 242, 243, 248, 249, 251, 254, 256, 372, 374

Anti-Humanism 253

Arab Spring 29, 122, 124, 125, 136

Area Studies 13, 14, 19, 35, 275

Asylum Seekers 9, 16, 69, 70, 227

Auto-Fiction 34, 258, 267, 272

Bahrain 121, 126, 129, 135, 138

Baptist War 297

Battala 342, 343, 346

Baul 7, 29, 141, 142, 143, 144, 148, 152, 154, 155, 156, 157

Becoming 313

Bengali 141, 143, 147, 148, 149, 150, 154, 155, 157, 209, 317, 321, 324, 326, 328, 338, 342, 344, 345, 348, 351, 352, 355, 356, 360, 366, 369

Benyamin 7, 29, 121, 124, 125, 127, 128, 129, 131, 132, 133, 134, 136, 137, 138, 139

Bhadramahila 328, 330, 336, 353

Bhakti 29

Bhils 293

Biocentrism 254

Biopolitics 90, 240

Black 7, 28, 31, 40, 53, 54, 73, 99, 100, 101, 102, 105, 106, 107, 113, 114, 117, 144, 169, 183, 185, 186, 187, 189, 190, 191, 192, 193, 195, 197, 198, 200, 201, 202, 204, 205, 220, 240, 242, 256, 298, 357

Body 16, 20, 25, 28, 48, 50, 54, 58, 60, 92, 93, 95, 96, 97, 98, 99, 100, 102, 104, 106, 107, 108, 112, 113, 114, 128, 135, 150, 173, 198, 201, 245, 277, 299, 309, 314, 318, 342

Border 7, 8, 9, 11, 13, 16, 17, 18, 19, 25, 42, 43, 55, 57, 58, 62, 63, 64, 65, 74, 77, 78, 79, 80, 83, 86, 87, 88, 89, 90, 91, 157, 163, 178, 179, 207, 215, 216, 217, 233, 241, 243, 253, 275, 353, 359

Bordering 11, 13, 17, 18, 19, 29, 74, 80, 85, 189, 207, 222, 227, 228, 229, 233, 235, 237, 245, 253

Border-Lands 35

Boundaries 10, 17, 19, 22, 30, 45, 49, 51, 78, 99, 127, 130, 159, 160, 161, 163, 164, 165, 167, 169, 171, 172, 174, 175, 178, 183, 244, 263, 276, 307, 309, 314, 320, 341, 344, 347, 351, 362, 363, 368, 374

Boundary 10, 17, 24, 54, 76, 99, 100, 102, 177, 178, 184, 193, 253, 257, 276, 359, 362

British Empire 291, 292, 294, 295, 300, 303

Buddhist 30, 149, 278

Cartography 46, 47

Caste 30, 145, 146, 147, 149, 321, 343, 344, 345, 359, 362, 363, 365, 368

Citizenship 28, 41, 59, 67, 80, 81, 82, 83, 84, 86, 88, 89, 171, 232, 267

Class 11, 25, 28, 30, 32, 34, 39, 41, 59, 78, 91, 134, 141, 143, 149, 159, 171, 175, 183, 184, 185, 186, 187, 190, 191, 194, 195, 196, 197, 198, 200, 202, 258, 261, 271, 282, 292, 315, 321, 330, 332, 337, 338, 340, 343, 344, 346, 347, 352, 353, 359, 360, 361, 362, 363, 364, 365, 366, 367, 368

Climate Change 33, 172, 220, 221, 223, 225, 228, 229, 232, 233, 240, 242, 243, 244, 250, 256, 374

Climate Refugees 8, 33, 217, 221, 227, 228, 231, 232, 235, 238, 242, 244

Colonial 32, 37, 41, 42, 49, 55, 56, 61, 72, 105, 141, 142, 145, 153, 210, 214, 222, 231, 259, 262, 267, 268, 271, 272, 275, 287, 291, 293, 297, 320, 322, 325, 326, 328, 332, 340, 341, 342, 344, 345, 346, 371

Colonialism 8, 41, 237, 260, 275, 284, 319, 323, 355, 373

Community 7, 27, 32, 39, 51, 54, 65, 67, 82, 83, 84, 86, 110, 112, 131, 133, 142, 144, 147, 152, 153, 161, 167, 169, 174, 210, 214, 221, 247, 252, 267, 277, 279, 305, 343, 357, 359, 365, 368, 372

Conceptual Frontiers 254

Connectivity 35, 173, 277, 281, 282, 285, 287

Consumerism 30, 159, 172, 173, 174, 178, 217, 248

Contact Zone 25, 26, 27

Contemporary Fiction 7, 27, 41, 42, 52

Corporeality 95, 105

Criminalised 66, 202

Cultural Analysis 372

Cultural Hybridity 34, 258, 259, 261, 263

Culture 27, 31, 32, 35, 37, 42, 51, 54, 55, 62, 100, 115, 128, 137, 145, 149, 154, 155, 156, 159, 167, 169, 175, 178, 179, 180, 183, 190, 192, 200, 202, 204, 207, 209, 219, 222, 230, 233, 236, 245, 251, 260, 261, 265, 275, 277, 279, 280, 281, 303, 304, 305, 309, 315, 316, 323, 324, 325, 326, 345, 365

Decolonizing 364

Degrowth 33, 222, 372

Deterritorialization 79

Development 21, 81, 87, 93, 121, 132, 193, 209, 211, 214, 217, 218, 220, 237, 238, 248, 253, 276, 278, 281, 283, 285, 286, 287, 300, 326, 339, 355, 365, 368, 372

Diaspora 35, 122, 260, 263, 289, 290, 299
Division 74, 80, 89, 160, 161, 164, 165, 167, 168, 169, 227, 260, 277, 340, 363
Dogma 147, 305
Dominican Republic 73
Donald Trump 160, 171, 219, 225, 241
Economic Corridors 282, 284
Elite 144, 146, 155, 157, 170, 178, 227, 236, 309, 340, 341, 347, 363, 365, 367
Environment 33, 87, 108, 159, 174, 184, 189, 193, 194, 202, 217, 218, 220, 221, 222, 225, 228, 229, 230, 231, 233, 234, 235, 237, 238, 244, 249, 250, 253, 256, 285, 309, 311
Environmental Humanities 33, 221, 241, 372
Epistemology 10, 187, 209, 263, 267
Eritrea 72
Essay 10, 13, 45, 62, 112, 147, 265, 268, 317, 318, 320, 322, 328, 330, 331, 333, 334, 335, 336, 338, 339, 341, 342, 351, 353, 359, 361, 363, 364, 365, 366, 368
Ethiopia 72
Eutopia 30, 155
Existence 20, 31, 34, 37, 47, 49, 56, 75, 76, 84, 91, 92, 99, 109, 111, 114, 115, 132, 137, 159, 219, 220, 225, 226, 234, 235, 245, 247, 254, 258, 269, 275, 283, 307, 309, 310, 313, 315, 319, 328, 329, 331, 336, 341, 347, 349, 353

Farmer 361, 364
Feudal 322, 361, 363
Fiction 11, 31, 43, 52, 63, 125, 134, 136, 159, 166, 189, 199, 214, 251, 265, 269, 342, 344, 346, 350, 373, 374
finis 17, 107
Fixity 110, 271, 304
Foreigner 19, 67, 77, 127, 135, 263
Former Soviet Union 72
French Feminism 120, 374
Gender 30, 31, 32, 34, 41, 59, 73, 88, 104, 112, 145, 146, 147, 186, 187, 190, 191, 196, 197, 198, 202, 220, 237, 258, 261, 266, 267, 268, 270, 321, 333, 334, 335, 341, 343, 344, 352, 371, 372, 374
Gender Discrimination 73, 191
Geo-Politics 280
girmit 291
Global Politics 229, 238, 275
Global Warming 33, 159, 172, 222, 225, 248, 250
Globalisation 88
Goyenda 345, 353, 356
Grisélidis Réal 7, 28, 91, 92, 93, 94, 95, 98, 108, 109, 110, 112, 117, 120, 371
Gulf Diaspora 121, 124
Harmony 29, 116, 135, 154, 167, 245
Hegemonic 11, 22, 32, 39, 100, 187, 191, 198, 202, 217, 253, 307, 359, 361, 363
Herrera, Yuri 27, 42, 56, 57, 58, 59, 60, 63

Hierarchy 142, 199, 258, 259, 303, 309
Hyperobjects 222, 223, 225, 240
Hyphen 34, 257, 258, 263, 264, 266, 272, 299
Identity 11, 27, 28, 36, 42, 53, 54, 58, 62, 66, 72, 73, 76, 80, 85, 91, 93, 98, 100, 110, 113, 116, 131, 132, 135, 142, 145, 194, 198, 202, 204, 207, 248, 258, 259, 260, 264, 266, 267, 268, 270, 272, 277, 278, 281, 290, 292, 304, 305, 309, 314, 315, 316, 324, 333, 337, 371
Im-Possibility 247
In-Between 34, 247, 254, 257, 262
indentured labour 36, 290, 291, 294
Indian 8, 29, 32, 35, 99, 130, 138, 141, 143, 148, 152, 153, 155, 157, 176, 179, 208, 275, 278, 285, 289, 290, 291, 292, 293, 295, 296, 297, 298, 299, 300, 301, 318, 323, 337, 345, 359, 363, 365, 368, 370, 373, 375
Indian 'Mutiny' 298
Individual and Group 183
Interdisciplinarity 18
Islam 29, 142, 149, 152, 279, 281
Isolation 30, 65, 146, 159, 164, 169
Jamaican Revolt 297
Juan Tomás Ávila 27, 42
Jus Sanguinis 65
Kerala 121, 138, 372
Kuwait 121
Lalon Shah 29, 144, 150, 157

Language 8, 33, 35, 44, 54, 55, 56, 57, 59, 62, 63, 73, 95, 124, 128, 129, 131, 134, 139, 147, 155, 169, 183, 209, 219, 233, 241, 260, 263, 264, 267, 271, 275, 277, 279, 280, 291, 317, 326, 333, 361, 371, 373
Liberia 73
Liminal Space 27, 34, 49, 61, 257, 258, 259, 265
Linear Time 311
Litchfield 184, 192, 194, 195, 196, 197, 198, 201
Logistics 286
Malayalam 125, 128, 129, 130, 131, 134, 138
Malet, H P 8, 35, 289, 292, 293, 294, 295, 296, 297, 298, 299, 300, 301
Maps 27, 41, 42, 43, 44, 45, 46, 47, 48, 53, 55, 57, 60, 61, 62, 63, 64
Marafati 7, 29, 141, 145, 148, 149, 151, 155, 156, 157
Margin 28, 37, 39, 67, 82, 85, 303, 304, 307, 359, 361, 367, 368
Marginalized 30, 152, 155, 169, 173, 266
Mauritania 73
Media 11, 31, 63, 98, 127, 160, 172, 173, 183, 185, 186, 187, 188, 189, 191, 192, 193, 197, 199, 204, 205, 217, 222, 225, 228, 234, 297, 321, 332, 371, 372, 374
Metaphysical Dualism 245
Mexico 15, 16, 18, 53, 55, 56, 58, 60, 170, 207, 277

Middle Class 31, 192, 195, 196, 321, 325, 326, 327, 328, 344, 345
Migrants 11, 15, 42, 78, 86, 160, 227, 229, 231
Migration Literature 27, 51, 52, 60, 61
Mobility Justice 41, 42, 61
Modernity 10, 19, 20, 22, 23, 26, 32, 38, 146, 208, 209, 210, 211, 212, 214, 215, 317, 319, 321, 324, 328, 333, 340, 341, 348, 353
More than Human 8, 245, 246, 253, 254
Mutuality 39, 359, 366, 368
Myanmar 73, 280, 282, 283, 287
Nationalism 9, 22, 89, 141, 145, 147, 156, 236, 281, 303, 304, 320, 325, 332, 336, 357, 359, 363, 368, 370
Nationality Rights 83
Native and Migrant 138
Necrocene 8, 33, 40, 217, 218, 219, 220, 222, 223, 224, 225, 226, 227, 228, 230, 232, 233, 235, 236, 238, 239, 242
Netflix 31, 183, 185, 187, 189, 192, 204, 205
New Woman 265, 266, 326
Oman 121
Onto-Ethical 34, 258
Ontology 13, 25, 76, 219, 226, 236, 264
Partition 7, 29, 141, 142, 149, 155, 157, 207, 280, 345, 373
Phallogocentric 34, 258, 264, 265
Political Theory 372

Politics 13, 16, 17, 18, 21, 25, 26, 32, 41, 64, 86, 90, 119, 124, 127, 135, 137, 141, 175, 190, 192, 204, 207, 218, 220, 222, 226, 229, 233, 234, 236, 238, 239, 240, 241, 242, 243, 247, 251, 256, 262, 264, 265, 267, 272, 273, 274, 289, 296, 297, 303, 319, 337, 360, 372, 374
Popular Culture 18, 30, 159, 161, 162, 164, 173, 175, 178, 180, 187, 205, 371
Postcolonial 22, 34, 52, 63, 190, 258, 259, 260, 261, 262, 263, 267, 271
Postcolonialism 373
Posthumanism 253
Private 37, 91, 103, 128, 132, 234, 260, 276, 318, 320, 323, 327, 328, 329, 332, 333, 335, 337, 340, 347, 349, 352, 353, 354
Prostitution 91, 98, 109, 111, 112, 114, 118, 119, 120
Psyche 343, 367
Public 37, 41, 50, 59, 84, 91, 124, 130, 131, 132, 142, 146, 162, 165, 175, 183, 186, 188, 189, 192, 200, 203, 209, 236, 260, 305, 318, 319, 321, 323, 327, 328, 329, 332, 333, 337, 338, 340, 349, 351, 352, 353, 354
Qatar 29, 121, 139
Race 32, 34, 41, 59, 101, 111, 185, 186, 187, 190, 191, 192, 196, 197, 200, 201, 202, 204, 219, 220, 237, 247, 254, 258, 263, 297, 304, 315, 316, 317, 325, 359, 363

Refugees 9, 63, 69, 70, 87, 88, 89, 222, 228, 229, 230, 231, 235, 243, 304

Religion 8, 29, 30, 35, 71, 73, 107, 108, 134, 141, 143, 145, 148, 156, 159, 192, 228, 275, 276, 277, 278, 279, 281, 317, 357

Resistance 7, 55, 62, 141, 170, 185, 186, 188, 197, 209, 262, 306, 307, 322, 353

Sahajiya 30, 146, 147, 149, 153, 154

Sameness 156, 252

Saudi Arabia 48, 121, 125, 138

Segmentarity 308, 314

Self-Identity 34, 258, 265, 269

Sex 28, 93, 104, 105, 107, 109, 110, 113, 198, 202, 204, 270, 294, 365

Sex work 28

Sierra Leone 73

Social Theory 10

Society 15, 31, 33, 37, 39, 49, 58, 88, 102, 103, 110, 114, 125, 130, 133, 136, 139, 142, 152, 159, 161, 167, 171, 173, 174, 176, 178, 191, 192, 194, 200, 210, 218, 233, 234, 235, 238, 242, 245, 261, 270, 277, 304, 307, 309, 310, 313, 315, 322, 331, 332, 333, 335, 338, 340, 344, 345, 348, 350, 351, 354, 359, 361, 362, 363, 364, 365, 366, 367, 368

Sociology 118, 183, 372

South Asia 8, 29, 35, 36, 124, 139, 275, 277, 279, 280, 281, 282, 284, 285, 286, 287, 290, 301, 373

Spain 53, 120, 267

Statelessness 7, 65, 66, 67, 68, 69, 70, 71, 72, 73, 74, 81, 82, 84, 85, 86, 87, 88, 89, 372

Subaltern 39, 144, 145, 152, 155, 217, 265, 272, 361, 362, 363, 365

Subcontinent 29, 141, 280, 291

Sudan 72, 88

Sufi 29, 143, 149, 151, 154, 156

Surveillance 16, 82, 160, 162, 165, 168, 170, 173, 187

Switzerland 102

Syria 48, 73

Systemic Oppression 203

Tantric 30, 147, 149

Terrorism 30, 48, 159, 164, 165, 166, 167, 168, 170, 175, 179

Threat 24, 25, 30, 159, 160, 165, 166, 167, 168, 175, 227, 281, 325, 326

Trace 22, 30, 34, 96, 135, 136, 142, 257, 258, 263, 322

Transnationality 34, 258

Trauma 155, 269

Unified Bengal 30, 155

United Arab Emirates 121

USA 48, 53, 57, 58, 61, 89, 180, 274, 277, 372

Vaishnavite 30, 149, 150

Viewership 31, 187, 189

Violence 9, 16, 29, 31, 46, 49, 50, 58, 59, 66, 83, 85, 88, 98, 104, 115, 117, 127, 132, 167, 170, 188, 189, 190, 220, 235, 243, 254, 268, 272, 306, 322, 343

Virus 161, 168, 175

Walls 9, 16, 18, 30, 154, 159, 160, 161, 162, 163, 164, 165, 166, 167, 168, 169, 170, 171, 173, 174, 175, 176, 177, 180, 270, 309, 315, 359, 368

War 9, 30, 47, 99, 113, 159, 164, 165, 166, 167, 168, 170, 175, 178, 180, 228, 229, 267, 270, 276, 282, 297

Woman Detective 342, 347, 348, 349, 350

ibidem.eu